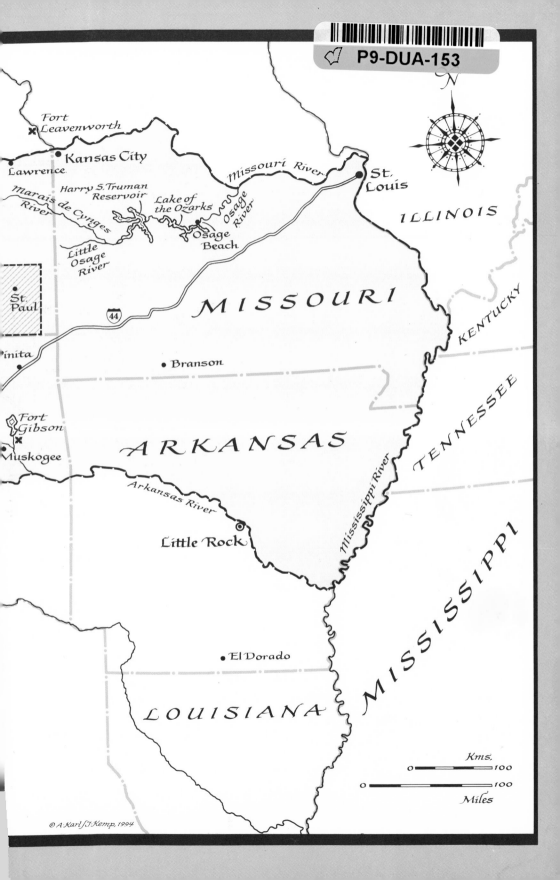

Fort
✕ Leavenworth
● Kansas City
Lawrence
Marais de Cygnes River
Harry S. Truman Reservoir
Lake of the Ozarks
Little Osage River
St. Paul
44
Vinita
Fort Gibson
✕ Muskogee
Missouri River
Osage River
● Osage Beach
St. Louis
ILLINOIS

MISSOURI

● Branson

KENTUCKY

ARKANSAS

Arkansas River

Little Rock

Mississippi River

TENNESSEE

● El Dorado

LOUISIANA

MISSISSIPPI

N

Kms.
0 ———— 100
0 ———— 100
Miles

© A.Karl/J.Kemp, 1994

The Deaths of Sybil Bolton

Dennis McAuliffe, Jr.

THE DEATHS OF
SYBIL BOLTON

An American History

TIMES BOOKS

RANDOM HOUSE

The photograph on the title page shows Sybil Bolton holding her infant daughter Kathleen and seated on the porch of her family's home in Pawhuska, Oklahoma, during the summer or fall of 1924. This is a computer-generated enhancement of the only extant photograph of Sybil, the original of which has been severely damaged over time. (Photo illustration by William Cone; original photograph courtesy of Kathleen Bolton McAuliffe.)

Grateful acknowledgment is made to the following for permission to reprint previously published material:

The Pawhuska Journal-Capital: Excerpt from article dated June 6, 1923, regarding the wedding of Sybil and Harry Bolton; excerpt from "Despondent Takes Life by Shooting: Death Came Quick" from November 8, 1925; excerpt from "Bolton Funeral Was Held Today; Large Body of Friends in Attendance" from November 12, 1925. Reprinted by permission of *The Pawhuska Journal-Capital.*

The Topeka Capital-Journal: Excerpts from "Barber, 91, Cutting Since He Was a Little Shaver." Reprinted by permission.

Library of Congress Cataloging-in-Publication Data

McAuliffe, Dennis
The deaths of Sybil Bolton : an American History / Dennis
McAuliffe Jr. — 1st ed.
p.   cm.
ISBN 0-8129-2150-X (acid-free paper)
1. Bolton, Sybil, d. 1925.   2. Osage Indians—Biography.   3. Osage
Indians—Government relations.   4. Osage Indians—Social conditions.
5. Petroleum industry and trade—Oklahoma—Pawhuska.   6. Murder—
Oklahoma—Pawhuska.   I. Title.
E99.O8B656   1994
976.6'004975—dc20   94-7157
                                                                    CIP

Manufactured in the United States of America
9 8 7 6 5 4 3 2
First Edition

To the real hero of this story,
My beautiful wife,
Fleur,
Who set me on this journey,
Then held us all together as it unfolded.

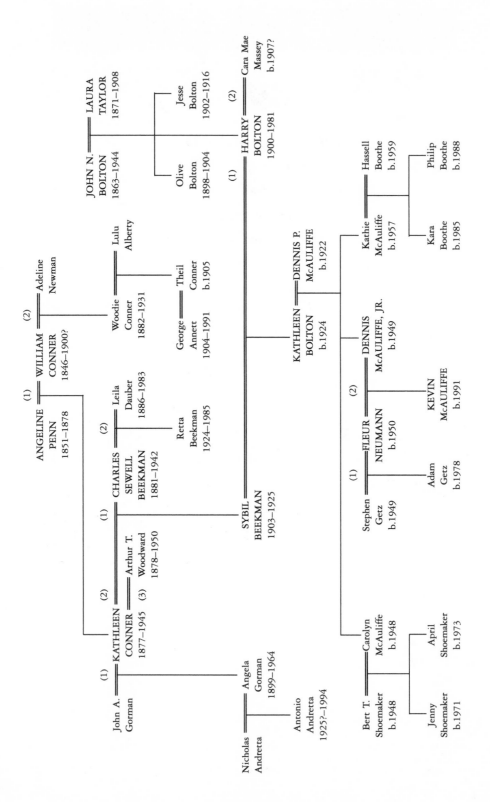

Contents

They plucked our fruit,
They cut our branches,
They burned our trunk,
But they could not kill our roots.

—MAYAN INDIAN SAYING

The Deaths of Sybil Bolton

ometimes when I look at my infant son, I see in him America in miniature. His tiny body holds an immense history, not only of the young, immigrant nation that grew to greatness but also of the ancient, indigenous people for whom the American Dream was a nightmare, and still is.

To the eyes of his father, he is a beautiful baby. But not all that long ago, the U.S. government would have referred to him in official documents—as it did to one of his great-grandfathers—as a half-breed, "breed" for short. Members of polite, even religious, society would have called him a savage. Now, in keeping with the socially correct sensitivity toward ethnic groups (foreigners, they used to be called)—in the same spirit that substituted the words "African-American" and "black" for "Negro," and other names—my son and I are considered mixed-blood Native Americans.

Names have changed, but not attitudes toward Indians. Like his father, my son will one day abruptly halt conversations by saying he is an Osage Indian. He will hear inherently racist remarks that his strawberry-blond hair and fair skin do not look Indian, but perhaps that accounts for his brown eyes. He will be asked what degree of Indian blood he has. I will teach him to answer the way I do now (I didn't always): Don't ask me how much Indian blood I have until you ask a black what his blood quantum is. My appearance may not be Indian, but my heart is—and it is what is in your heart, not what pumps through it, that makes you an Indian.

My son's heritage has placed upon small shoulders a burden so great that a mighty nation has been unable to carry it, or chooses not to. He must find a way to balance the two sides of himself, to find a place in his life for the Indian part of him, which continues to have no place, or part, in his society. That is his challenge, and his curse. That is my gift to him.

As much as a father can, I will see to it that my son does not shirk from his responsibility by ignoring his true identity—as I did. If he does, I fear, he will be doomed to repeat the upheaval that shook me, literally, to my roots. That was my grandmother's gift to me.

My life, and my mother's, are testament that you cannot ignore who you are, and that the shunned side of you will one day rise up to be recognized. The truth about oneself, I learned painfully, is like one of my son's new teeth cutting through his flesh as it pushes to the surface: It originates seemingly out of nothing, with which it crafts the material that makes it nearly indestructible; it proceeds to fill a space where, once, a void had been; the experience is excruciating, especially when—suddenly, unexpectedly, out of nowhere—it surfaces to correct a lifelong lie. Once it appears, you are never the same again, but you get used to it. While it may be ugly, it is not nearly as ugly as the lie it pierced.

Like all fathers, I will tell my son the history inside him one day. Unlike his father, and his grandmother, he will learn all of it, and sooner rather than later. I was forty-one when I heard the last chapter of what should have been my life's primer. My mother was sixty-seven when she heard the childhood story she was never told.

The stories I will tell my son will become the words that form his definition, the roots of his identity. In my case, and my mother's, they led to a redefining and an uprooting that were devastating at my age; at my mother's age, impossible to describe with merely a word.

. I will tell my son about his two grandfathers, who embody the Great American Success Story. He will hear of the courage of his maternal grandfather, Bruno Neumann, who fled the Nazis during World War II. He had committed a crime so heinous in Hitler's Germany that the SS pursued him all the way to England: He helped Jews escape, but he wasn't Jewish himself. In London, he read his first book in English, *The Forsyte Saga,* and decided he would name his first daughter after a character in the book, Fleur. He did so in 1950. By then, he was in America, an economics writer in his adopted language. No doubt swayed by her father's heroic acts to save Jews, Fleur became Jewish.

And my son will hear about his paternal grandfather, Dennis P. McAuliffe, who achieved the dreams of his Irish-immigrant parents by going to West Point and eventually becoming a three-star U.S. Army general. My father led part of the invasion of Cambodia in 1970. In the mid-seventies, he was commander in chief of the U.S. Southern Command in Panama during the negotiation and ratification of the treaties that will finally give to Panama ownership of its canal. He was administrator of the Panama Canal Commission when the United States invaded that country during Christmas of 1989.

I had always considered myself the "fortunate son" of my family, whose fortunes had been defined entirely by the success of my father. I even carry his name. And like most Americans, I had always faced east, toward Europe and my father's family origins—but away from my mother's. Now I have had to do an abrupt about-face, turning west to confront the conflicting reality of my mother's heritage.

She is part of the Great American Horror Story. She is the product— and, I learned, a narrow survivor—of the appalling destruction of American Indians in the death camps that were their reservations. This was a time far more devastating to them than the Indian-cavalry wars that have gotten so much movie play. It was a time far less capable of being rationalized by patriotic rhetoric than the military—and controversial—conflicts my father was involved in. Perhaps that is why this period in our history hardly dances with awareness.

It has been difficult for me, shaped and surrounded all my life by my parents' love, to accept the realization that, to a greater degree, my destiny was shaped by hatred manifested in the extreme; that the history I carry within me is colored by racial discrimination of the most violent kind—directed against one half of my ancestors by the other half.

It is the Great American Tragedy that I have to tell my son. It is my grandmother's story, and my mother's, and mine.

DANCES WITH AWARENESS

Chapter One

July 2, 1991, was a Tuesday. That evening, I was standing in the kitchen with Fleur, looking at new pictures of our two children— my twelve-year-old stepson, Adam, and Kevin, my only child, five months old.

One photo showed Kevin in a pose I had seen all my life. With his head held heavenward, his hands extended in exclamation, he was looking up at his brother, smiling with his whole body.

"Look," I said, "he looks like my mother."

This was a stunning observation for someone who had never been any good at recognizing resemblances in anyone. On the other hand, it was the first thing Fleur had said when she opened her eyes, delirious from delivery, and saw this red, wrinkled thing resting on her stomach like a rumpled rag: "He looks like your mother." These five months, I had often studied my son with the thought, He does?

We had come as close as any parents to naming a boy after his grandmother. We had picked the same initials, KBM: Kathleen Bolton Mc-Auliffe, Kevin Blair McAuliffe. This way, we joked, we could get all of her monogrammed towels. Over the months, we noticed that he acts like my mother as well—he enjoys expressing himself (in fact, he's a veritable tottering tower of burble) and is a pleasure to listen to. As for other likenesses, I had looked but saw only one: his joy.

But that night, staring startled at the photo, I could see my mother in his stance, profile, tilt of head, expression and smile.

Much later, after Fleur had gone to bed, I was sitting on the balcony, drinking beer, and couldn't shake a sadness growing over me. What if this happy baby lost his mother? How would that change him? I am his father, yes, but fathers of infants are like vice presidents—they take over the lesser functions and fill in when the boss can't make it. A baby's mother is his entire world. When Fleur is out of the room, he watches for her. When he's sick, it's not me he wants. When I'm holding him, he often stares at her. He turns this way and that, following her with his eyes as she goes about the room. When he sees her leaving the house without him, he cries—sometimes hysterically—until I can find a suitable diversion.

Suddenly, out of nowhere, it hit me—for the first time in my forty-one years—what a tragedy my mother had lived through. She was a baby when her mother died of kidney disease, alone in the house with her infant and only child, dropping dead suddenly, in front of the baby.

That was all I knew about my grandmother, other than that she was an Osage Indian and had attended a private, East Coast boarding school—and that she was buried in an ermine coat.

I knew about as much about the Osages. I knew how to pronounce "Osage" (OH-sage), which put me a leg up on those who say "oh-SAH-ga." My mother had told me our Osage ancestor was a chief, but over the years, as I noticed that all the Native Americans I met were descended from chiefs rather than from Indians, I had come to consider my mother's claim a cliché. I had read somewhere that for a time in France it was chic for aristocratic women, playing savage, to make love to Osages brought over from America for that purpose. (I was never sure, though, if sex was the way to play savage, or the goal of playing it.) When I lived in Germany and dressed in a turtleneck sweater and sports coat, I was often told I looked French. I would smile, wag a finger and say, "No, no, the French look like me."

I knew I looked just like a young Osage Indian warrior painted by George Catlin in 1832. I saw a reproduction of the portrait at a guest-house at Fort Leavenworth, Kansas, where I was having dinner with my parents one night in 1974. My father, who spotted it between bites, had the same reaction that I was to have looking at Kevin's picture. "Look," he said, in near shock, "he looks like Denny." It was like looking in the mirror: Although the hair and eye colors were different, and the flesh tone in the painting was slightly more bronze, the Indian and I had the same hairline, forehead, cheeks, mouth, chin, jawline, shape of eyes—and nose. "Big" is such a little word for the sun of my facial solar system. Many photos of me, especially those taken outdoors, show much of my face in shadow. I had always thought my nose was Irish, but according to this 142-year-old painting, it was Indian. Now I knew whom to thank.

I also knew the Osages had discovered oil on their reservation in Oklahoma. My mother gets quarterly oil-royalty checks from the U.S. government, because she has something called a "headright" from the Osage tribe. She inherited it from her mother, and the headright will be divided into thirds and passed to her children when she dies. She is on the Osage tribal roll, and she votes—absentee—in tribal elections. Although she had never visited the Osages, she cherishes the monthly Osage newspaper she receives in the mail, and I was to discover that she saved many issues, especially the ones with pictures of Osages who looked like her or members of her family.

I have an ID card from the Bureau of Indian Affairs—a Certificate of Degree of Indian Blood—identifying me as a member of the Osage Nation and giving my blood quantum and tribal roll number. I often joked that I was a card-carrying minority. A few years ago, after a particularly long and painful stretch of unemployment, I used the card to try to get a job. I showed it to a company personnel director, hoping it would help me hurdle the obstacle of being a white male competing with minorities and women for employment. I even called the Bureau of Indian Affairs' Osage Agency in Pawhuska, Oklahoma—the address was on the card—and asked someone if it would be too much of a stretch to say I was an American Indian when applying for a job.

"You're on the tribal roll," he said. "You're an Osage Indian, and you have every right to say you're an Osage Indian. We recognize you as a member of the tribe."

Then he added, much to my delight and delicious anticipation, "If you have any trouble with these people, have 'em call us. We'll be happy to set 'em straight." I loved it.

The personnel director loved it, too. He laughed when he took my card, laughed when he studied it, laughed when he said he had to hand it to me, an Indian with light brown hair, blue eyes, white complexion, a beard—and balls. And he laughed when he said I still wasn't getting the job.

I had never really thought of my mother's mother in terms of actually being my grandmother, for I had a perfectly good one who was still very much alive and lively, Cara Mae Bolton, my mother's stepmother. I had always called her Grandma, and thought of her only as that, because my mother had never considered her anyone other than her mother.

Like most children—even grown ones—I also never really thought of my mother or father in terms of actually being a child. But on the balcony that night, I began to think of my mother as a baby. Since I had just connected the physical similarities of Kevin and my mother in the photograph of Kevin, I pictured her as looking like my son, and loving her real mother the way Kevin loves his, watching her mother and watching for her, following her around the room with her eyes, smiling when she saw her.

But then to suddenly lose her mother, watching her one minute, seeing her fall, maybe falling with her in her arms, crying, *crawling over her*—my God, what a tragedy.

This baby was suddenly without the center of her universe. How much time—how many hours, days, weeks, months—did my mother spend looking around the room, over the shoulder of whoever was carrying her, looking down the hall, in every face that came into the room, for her mother, as Kevin might?

Then an equally strong feeling struck me: how remarkable it was that my mother turned out the way she did—so happy. A smile is the natural expression on my mother's face. Anything else is foreign. Laughter is her language. I found myself thinking that if Fleur or I should die while Kevin was still a baby, I could only hope that he would turn out as happy as my mother, that his joy would triumph over his tragedy.

My son, I hope, has inherited his joy from my mother, for hers is of the enduring kind. I see my mother's life as proof of the power of joy: Her joy not only survived tragedy but conquered it. Joy must be more power-ful than sorrow, I thought.

I went to bed thinking I had had too much to drink, but now I know: I was being prepared for what follows.

FIFTEEN HUNDRED MILES due west of my balcony, on the same day, July 2, but a few hours before my mental tour of the torture chamber of my mother's infancy, my sister is wandering around a cemetery in Alta Vista, Kansas, searching for the grave of a very old man.

Carolyn Shoemaker is on vacation, and making an overnight stop in Manhattan, Kansas. "The Little Apple," as this Manhattan calls itself, sits off Interstate 70 in east-central Kansas, a day's drive from Colorado Springs, Colorado, where Carolyn lives. It is midafternoon when she checks into a motel in Manhattan. After sitting in the car since sunup, Jenny, her teenage daughter, is bored. Carolyn suggests that, for fun, they visit Alta Vista, only twenty-six miles south, on a road called the Skyline–Mill Creek Scenic Drive.

Alta Vista is the boyhood home of our grandfather, Harry Ben Bolton. His parents and two sisters are buried in the Alta Vista cemetery. His father, my great-grandfather John Nelson Bolton, or J.N., as he called himself, got there by blowing himself up while lighting a gas stove in 1944. It wasn't so much the explosion that killed him as his run down the street afterward, on fire. No doubt he panicked when the stove blew up and he didn't know what he was doing when he took off down the street, feeding the flames that engulfed him. But in our family lore, J.N. decided to prove one last time to his disapproving neighbors—at age eighty-one he had just married a schoolteacher half his age—that he still had it in him, by damn, at least enough to wind-sprint through the Valley of the Shadow of Death.

The Alta Vista cemetery is the loudest place in an otherwise dead-still little town. Thirty flagpoles—fifteen on each side—line the driveway, and their rope-and-brass riggings all snap in the wind against the hollow metal flagpoles. The effect is similar to that of thirty Salvation Army workers standing outside the same supermarket at Christmas, all ringing their bells at the same time but each to his own tempo. It is probably the only cemetery in the world where visitors routinely sing "Jingle Bells" to themselves as they pay respects to their departed loved ones.

The search for J. N. Bolton & Family begins. It can be done by car. Tire tracks in the grass circumnavigate the cemetery, and bisect it, but Carolyn and Jenny choose to walk. The headstones face away from the entrance, so they have to hike to the opposite side of the cemetery, to a line of evergreens about one hundred yards away, and backtrack.

There are probably more headstones than people living in Alta Vista. Many of the markers are so old, or so obscured by a yellow residue (caused by protein deposits of an insect called a midge), that the writing on them is impossible to read. Marion Horten's tombstone has survived—so far—the ravages of years, wind and bugs. "Co. G, 1st Colorado Infantry, Spanish-American War," it says. William P. Drummond's tombstone is slightly less readable: "Missouri [illegible] U.S. Dragoons, Mexican War, July 5, 1908." Other markers did not need words to convey the sadness of their existence, such as that of Laurel Rachel Union Thomas, born October 10, 1897, died October 19, 1897. "For 9 d," her tombstone says. Nearby, a stone has broken into three parts, and is now held together by a rusted wire. Only the words "Rouse, died Dec. 9, 1889" are visible. Another broken stone, the remnants resting by the stump, says, "9y, 6m."

The Bolton family plot, Carolyn discovers, lies just a few paces from the car. The back of the family marker, about chest-high, is rough-hewn gray-black marble, the ripples on its surface like those of a pond that froze on a windy day. The other side is shiny and smooth, and says, "Bolton, Laura Taylor, wife of J. N. Bolton, May 10, 1871–July 20, 1908." Beneath that, "John Nelson Bolton, 1863–1944." Facing the stone, to the right, is "Olive, dau of J.N. and Laura Bolton. Died Feb. 22, 1904. Age 5y, 8m, 1d." Olive has two headstones. The newer is a light brown marble pillar supporting an orb the size of a cannonball. Leaves and stems of a plant are etched around her name. They are olive branches. The older stone, barely readable, says, "OB. Budded on Earth to bloom in heaven." To the left of Olive is "Mother," the next to die; then Jesse, the younger daughter. Her stone is a simple marker that says only "Jesse, 1902–1916." On the far left is "Father," and then an empty plot, intended for Harry, the last member of the family, just in case, like his sisters, he didn't make it out of Alta Vista alive.

After 1944, my grandfather was the only Bolton left, apart from my mother, so he must have been responsible for putting up Olive's newer pillar-and-olive headstone, which looked more recent than the mid-forties. That surprised me when I heard about it. I had never thought of my grandfather as being so sentimental, especially over someone he would have had only a vague memory of. Olive was Harry's older sister. He was four when she died, at age "5y, 8m, 1d" in 1904. I had never heard of her before, or don't remember hearing that my grandfather had another sister besides Jesse. She was his beloved younger sister. She died of whatever was killing Kansas kids in 1916—tuberculosis, diabetes, smallpox, typhoid, the all-encompassing consumption. Regardless, the end result was the same: life-altering grief for the survivors. Jesse's death made Harry long for a daughter, and for granddaughters. Perhaps he married my grand-mother because she looked like Jesse. Perhaps Carolyn reminded him of her, which would explain why he was so attached to my sister. Jesse died eight years after her mother, Laura, and a year before Harry graduated from high school and left Alta Vista for college, and for good. Even before he met and married my grandmother, he must have feared that every woman in his life was cursed to die young and that he was cursed to bury them. He must have been sick of burying them all—Olive, his mother, Jesse. The death of my grandmother, shortly after their marriage and at a young age, lengthened the list, and must have reinforced his fears about women and shovels. He must have feared terribly for my mother, his only child, a girl. Would she carry the Bolton female curse, and would he have to carry her to her grave, too?

Finding the grave sites of great-grandparents, whom you didn't know and know little about, is always anticlimactic. Once you have found them, there is not much to do but stand over them; perhaps squat by them; take pictures of the headstones; read them; do simple subtraction (1908 minus 1871); wonder what traits you may have inherited from them; make some profound, prophetic utterance like "Well, that's them, there they are"; place flowers on their graves, if the thought was afore (next time you should, you think, if there is a next time); wonder when the last time flowers graced these graves; observe that there are no flowers on any grave in this cemetery, plastic or real. Inevitably, your thoughts turn to returning to the real world, getting back to your life, the road to which lies through the town of Alta Vista, not much of an improvement over the cemetery, but a lot quieter.

Carolyn and Jenny walk the ten paces to the car and drive in silence past the jingling flagpoles. Black cows across the road watch them as they leave the cemetery and head toward town, a mile south. Wind blowing across a cornfield transforms the leaves and caps on the plants, for just a second until a blink washes the image away, into a lake reflecting a cloudy sky and showing the octopus path of invisible breezes.

Just past the field, a welcome sign stands almost as an amulet. "The Churches of Alta Vista Welcome You," it says, and lists them all, as if to turn back the unwelcomed—hell-raisers—from this particular heaven's gate: St. Paul's Lutheran, Baptist, Simpson United Methodist, Church of Christ.

"Maybe there's someone in Alta Vista who remembers Grandpa," Carolyn says.

One gear shift, and suddenly oaks, maples and elms—the few that survived the Dutch elm disease epidemic of three decades earlier—are shading the sidewalk and the front porches of small, two-story clapboard houses. The first Alta Vistan comes into view: a weighty woman wielding a weed-whacker, whittling away with it at waist-high plants growing wildly. An eye blink—shutting on a turquoise clapboard house, opening on a laundry line across the street on which big bras, bigger bloomers, flap like the flags in other yards for the Fourth of July celebration two days away. A pickup truck, hitched to a boat, is parked in the yard of a gray clapboard house. On a porch, a woman fans herself while her husband waves at a rare sight: a Japanese car with Colorado license plates.

An intersection of red-brick churches—three of the four—guards the entrance to Alta Vista's deserted, four-block main street, Main Street. Weed-grown lots, some filled with rusting farm equipment for sale, separate low, square granite buildings, whose brown facades give the street the look of a timeworn, fading photograph.

They pass a restaurant, Starvin' Harv's, park in front of the combined Alta Vista City Hall and Fire Station and go in. Carolyn asks a woman at the counter, the only person who appears to work there, if she knows anyone who knew the Boltons.

She doesn't, but "Bat Nelson probably does," she says. "He's ninety-one, and owns the barbershop two doors down. He knows everything about Alta Vista, and everybody who ever lived here." And in the same breath, not letting the chance slip away to raise twelve dollars for the town treasury, she asks, "Have you seen our centennial book on Alta Vista? It's full of old pictures. Maybe it has something on your family."

It does. The first page has a picture of a sign saying, "J. N. Bolton. For General Merchandise." It is part of a scoreboard at the ballpark showing the names of baseball sponsors who "chipped in" in 1920, as the caption says. According to the book, J.N. had a meat market in Alta Vista in the 1890s. In 1900, he moved into a one-story building, the south half occupied by the Alta Vista State Bank, and opened the Bolton Mercantile Grocery Story. A picture of it in 1907 shows "J. N. Bolton Dry Goods" painted on the window, and signs for "McCall Patterns 10 and 15 cents" and "Bradley and Metcalf Celebrated Boots and Shoes." Another picture, from 1909, shows J.N. standing in front of his store, one display window filled with shoes, the other with men's hats. It is now called the J. N. Bolton General Store. J.N. looks small in stature and is wearing a bow tie and dark suit. His face is hidden behind a bushy mustache and beneath a dark hat.

The photo is black and white, of course, so it doesn't show his one blue and one brown eye. J.N. apparently was quite a skirt-chaser, and gave new meaning to the act of giving a woman the eye. Perhaps he made his winks color-coordinated, one eye when he wore a blue suit, the other with brown. An old newspaper ad reproduced in the book says, "YOUR STORE: We call this YOUR STORE because we want you to realize that it IS in every way a store for you. YOUR interests demand you get full value for your money. And Style demands a certain smartness; and Service, a courteous tending to the many little things that make a store worth while. FULL VALUE—STYLE—SERVICE. You get all of these at BOLTON'S."

Carolyn and Jenny walk two doors down to Nelson's Barber & Beauty Shop. In the display window is a reprint of an article from a Topeka, Kansas, newspaper. The headline says, "Barber, 91, Cutting Since He Was Little Shaver." An accompanying color photo shows a sixty-something man, with a full head of brown hair, shaving a customer, a straight-edge to his throat. The photo is obviously an old one of a younger Bat Nelson. Who would trust a shaky ninety-one-year-old to run a razor across his face? The article says: "Seventy-six years ago . . . Alta Vista barber R. S. (Bat) Nelson had his first customer. Holly Johnson came in at 10:20 A.M. for a 10-cent shave. Nelson was just 15 years old then. He hasn't put away his straight-edge razor since. . . . At 91, Nelson's hands are rock-steady, and his schedule is just as firm. He still opens his shop at 8 A.M. six days a week. The cost for a haircut has risen with the years but is still a modest $3." Bat began in the business at age eleven, "as a shoeshine boy and janitor" at a barbershop in town. "Soon the barbers asked him to join them in their hair-cutting business. 'I started with $9.80 in tools. I borrowed $10 from my brother and I was to pay him back $2 a month, which I knew I could do since I kept the shoeshine business. . . . After three months, if I could get a man in my chair, he'd become a regular.' " The article also quoted Denny Buchman, owner of Buchman's Farm Supply across the street from the barbershop: "Bat's cut four generations of hair in my family, from my grandfathers down to my sons."

Bat Nelson is alone in the shop, sitting in one of two battered blue customers' chairs. The newspaper photo, to Carolyn's surprise, is recent. Bat doesn't look ninety-one, not that Carolyn has seen that many nonagenarians to judge, especially ones who jump up out of their chairs, energetically and enthusiastically—faster in fact than she is able to open and shut the squeaky shop door and approach him—and greet her in a loud, clear, steady, cheerful, businesslike young voice, "Well, what can I do for you today, young lady?"

Along the wall opposite him are two ornate barber chairs that he bought in 1923. ("You don't find them like that this day and age," he says later. "They weigh about three times as much as the chair you'd buy today.") In the center of the shop is a small, square counter. A red cash register, with a black dial phone attached to the back, occupies the countertop, rivaling the barber chairs in ornateness and age. The counter shelves display a collection of blue, red, yellow and green hair tonics—antiques, the article calls them. Three walls of the shop are mirrored to the ceiling. High on the mirror of one is a brown sketch of a buffalo. The mirrored wall next to the barber chairs holds the only other picture in the shop: a color drawing of a spaniel. ("That's my dog," Bat explains later. "I lost him in '37. Welsh spaniel. Oh, he was beautiful. Cocoa brown and white.") Like Mr. Bojangles in the song, Bat Nelson is still mourning the dog he lost more than a half-century ago.

"Whose granddaughter?" Bat replies, when Carolyn tells him that her grandfather grew up here and asks him if he knew him. She's beginning to think that this might be a waste of time. "Harry Bolton," she repeats.

"Harry Bolton?" Bat echoes. He's still shaking her hand with his two, squeezing it solidly and staring intently into her eyes, as if comparing. There is a momentary warble in his voice. Carolyn sees a slight squirt of water wet brown eyes set behind black-rimmed glasses.

"Harry Bolton's granddaughter," he repeats. "Oh, hell, how nice to see you." He smiles with delight, showing some gold in the back of his mouth. "He was perhaps my closest pal."

After a round of exclamations on both sides, he says solemnly, "I have always—I have always decorated the graves" of his family.

A momentary loss for words. Where to start?

It is Bat who breaks the silence, answering the question Carolyn is about to ask. "Harry was truly an all-American boy. He played basketball. He played tennis. He liked to play tennis. He was fair at it. Like I said, he was an all-American boy. Harry was talented."

"What did you do together, you and Grandpa?" Carolyn asks. The thought of growing up in Alta Vista and the full-time, unfulfilling quest for something to do makes her teenage daughter shift her weight. It was a mere eighty years ago, but Bat seems embarrassed by his inability to remember.

"Oh, I don't know," he says, fumbling. "Just like all kids, I guess."

He walks to a stack of scrapbooks in a corner of the shop and uncovers a thin, paperbound pamphlet. It is the 1917 Alta Vista High School yearbook. Harry Bolton was one of twenty-four graduates that year, twenty-three more than were in the school's first graduating class eight years earlier. The Harry pictured in the yearbook looks older than seventeen. Tragedies had chiseled their toll around his eyes and mouth. In photos of him taken ten, twenty, thirty, even forty years later, he would look younger. His hair is close-cropped on the sides; on top, long and slicked straight back, the way he wore it the rest of his life.

The caption under Harry's picture says, "Basketball, football, track, president of Shakespearians, debate, senior play." Then it quotes him as saying, "I always manage to maintain a very high standing with the faculty." (His father was chairman of the school board.) The debate subject in that year of America's entry into World War I was, "Resolved, that every able-bodied male citizen of the United States should have one year's military training before he is 25 years of age." Harry debated for the negative team, which lost unanimously to Harveyville High.

A humor section of the yearbook called "Senior Personalities" describes Harry as "Alias: Windy. Disposition: Grouchy. Future Occupation: Minister. Hobby: Going to church. Favorite expression: 'Rave on.' " A few pages later is another stab at humor, this one a fictional, futuristic account of coming back to Alta Vista in the spring of 1925, visiting for the first time since graduation: "I began to inquire after the Class of '17 by asking where Harry Bolton was. He was on Perry's Ranch, where he had the job of driving geese to water, was the answer. He was still waiting for Dora to finish her course in domestic science."

"Who's Dora?" Carolyn asks with a laugh.

Bat flips the pages to the *J*s and points to a picture of a mousy, dark-haired girl. "That was his girlfriend," he says. The caption identifies her as Dora Johnson, "modest, unpretentious one, merry though full of fun, winning friends from sun to sun." She was the daughter of the town jeweler, whose shop had been located across the street from Bat's barbershop. Harry and Dora dated all through high school, Bat explains, but after Harry went to the University of Kansas, "it was different. She went to Ottawa [Kansas], University of Ottawa. That broke that up." In fact, when Harry left Alta Vista for K.U., whose campus at Lawrence was only sixty miles east, "that was the last of him," Bat says, frowning abruptly. "I didn't get to see much of him after that."

"You know, I often wondered about how . . ." Bat lets the rest of the sentence drop. "It was just kind of an accident that I knew Harry passed away. I take the Alma [Kansas] paper, and I was reading it one day, and I saw his obituary." It was a simple death notice, short on details, such as cause of death. "And so I sat down and wrote his wife a letter. 'When the pain wears off, [and you] have a little time, write me and tell me [the details], won't you please.' But I never heard from her. Never heard from her."

In 1981, at age eighty-one, Harry was diagnosed with throat cancer. He spent his last three months in the hospital in Denver. He lost his vocal chords. Leukemia was discovered. Then he died of a stroke.

"Throat cancer," Bat repeats slowly.

"Stroke," Carolyn corrects.

Bat produces, seemingly out of nowhere, a black address book. His little black book. "This book here," he says exuberantly, "this book here is nothing but obituaries." Every page, every line of every page, is full. On each line, there is a name, a year and an age.

"These are all people that you knew?" Carolyn asks, at once impressed by the number of friends he had, and horrified at all the death, the number of friends he has outlived.

"Oh yes," Bat says, "yes, yes."

"Wow," Jenny chimes in.

"Here, you go down that list there," he says, pointing to a right-hand page and running his finger down the left side, looking for Harry's name.

"I'm sure, I'm sure . . . ," flipping the pages.

"Oh, there's Harry B. . . . ," Carolyn reads.

"Harry Bolton, there, in '81," Bat says. "He died in '81. And there, John N. Bolton, yes, '44, eighty-one years old."

"Oh, that's the same age as Grandpa when he died," Carolyn says. "He was eighty-one. Well, maybe I can count on making it to eighty-one."

"Eighty-one in '44," Bat says, still looking at J.N.'s entry. "You want to jot down some of those dates, or not?"

"Oh, I know them."

"Oh, you got 'em, huh?"

"Yeah, I made . . . it said that on his tombstone."

"Mrs. John Bolton died in 1908—his wife," he says, pointing to the entry for Laura Taylor Bolton, on the line above J.N., who occupied the line above Harry.

"Uh-huh," Carolyn says, "well, that was a long . . . oh, she was thirty-seven. How did she die?"

"She was only thirty-seven years old. She died in . . ."

". . . in 1908," Carolyn says, reading.

"I don't have the month. Do you?"

"No," Carolyn says. "Do you know how she died?"

"No, no."

"I understand J. N. Bolton remarried when—"

"You understand what?"

"That he remarried."

"No, no."

A silence. "The day before Grandpa died," Carolyn says, reaching to change the subject, to save a moment that had turned awkward, uncomfortable, "he got a haircut." His regular barber came over to the hospital to give it to him. The next day, the barber was in tears when he heard his favorite customer had died. Grandpa had beautiful hair. It turned gray, then white. He was always very proud of it, and kept it neatly combed and trimmed. "Did you use to cut his hair?"

"Oh yes, yes, yes, yes," Bat says ebulliently. Not just Harry's, but J.N.'s as well. "I started barbering when I was in eighth grade," Bat explains, and now, at age ninety-one, he is the oldest working and licensed barber in Kansas and most likely in the United States. "I can't vouch for that as yet," Bat says, referring to the latter distinction. "I have an affidavit here that I am the oldest licensed barber in the state of Kansas, and they think I might be nationally. There's a barber in Ohio, they wrote and told me, that is ninety-three years old, but in all probability he didn't start early in life like I did. So I'm sure I have the record."

"How much longer do you plan to work?"

"Oh, just as long as I can. If I drop dead over around the chair, that's okay."

Harry was one of Bat's first regular customers. He started cutting his hair when Harry was in high school. Harry was three grades ahead of Bat, but they were the same age. "I was born in the country north of here, eight miles north, and for some reason, my parents didn't start me in school until late, in the country school. So that put me back a little bit. In other words, Harry was a senior when I was a freshman. But he was perhaps my closest pal. His father had a general store. My folks traded with him when we were in the country. In 1900, when the bank building was built out here, he occupied the north half of it. I have an old cookie box [a display case] at home that was in his store."

The town thrived in those days. It was the golden age of Alta Vista, in fact. J. N. Bolton's was one of five grocery stores. "Five," Bat repeats for emphasis. "Five grocery stores." The town also had three hardware stores, two banks and two telephone exchanges. "Alta Vista had a trade territory of five hundred sixty families, families," Bat says, enunciating each syllable slowly, for stress, "fa-mi-lies, not people." Most lived on eighty-acre farms, "once in a while a hundred sixty," stretching fifteen miles toward the town of Eskridge. "Those little farms have all been absorbed, houses torn down, or fallen down. But I don't know of any little town that's held on as well as we have. Don't think that we're not suffering, because we are, see." Bat's barbershop is one of fifteen businesses left in Alta Vista. There used to be fifty.

J. N. Bolton rented the space for his shop from John Eberle, who had moved to Arizona on his doctor's advice. Like the Boltons, Eberle had lost a daughter, Nellie, to the Kansas kid-killers. The town doctor warned Eberle that if he wanted to save his remaining child, he had better leave Kansas. Eberle stayed in Arizona until the mid-twenties, when he returned to Alta Vista, wanting his building back. "There was nothing else available in town," Bat says, "and so Mr. Bolton sold out to him, went to Kansas City," where Harry lived. Harry had only recently graduated from K.U. J.N. "got a chair on the board of trade" in Kansas City, Bat says. "You knew that?"

Carolyn didn't but says yes. You have to draw the line somewhere on admitting to a stranger what you don't know about your family, especially a stranger who doesn't know everything about yours. What Bat didn't know about J.N.—apart from his remarriage—was that he also got a chair on Harry's front porch. Harry came home from work one day and there was J.N., in a rocking chair, just arrived from Alta Vista. Harry didn't even know he was coming. J.N. was rocking the chair back and forth, slowly, carefully, attentively, as if taking it for a test-drive, trying it out for a long haul. J.N. looked at his son and said, "Harry, I supported you all through high school and college, now it's your turn. You support me." Harry did, for the rest of J.N.'s life.

J.N. soon lost his chair on the board of trade, because—as my mother puts it—"he couldn't keep his mouth shut about politics." J.N. was a Republican. "Fervent" is too mild a word to describe his political beliefs; "fanatical" comes closer. To him, Democrats ranked right down there with . . . well, to J.N., you couldn't go lower than the "damn Democrats." He couldn't fathom being in the same room with one. There was little chance of that in his part of Kansas, but Kansas City, Missouri, was a Democratic ward city, in the pocket of Thomas Pendergast, one of the great "Big Daddies" of American political corruption. Pendergast

Democrats owned the town, and there was no room in it for them and a Republican—a Republican from Kansas, no less—holding down a cushy patronage job, who repeatedly told them with glee what fiery fate awaited them when they died, which he hoped was none too soon.

How intense were J.N.'s love of the GOP and hatred of the "damn Democrats"? One time in the thirties, J.N. went to Oklahoma City to visit Harry and his family. J.N. took an earlier train than planned and then a taxi to Harry's house. Cara Mae, Harry's second wife, and my mother had just left for the train station to pick him up, so there was no one at home but the yardman.

J.N. chewed the fat with him a while, then asked, "Son, are you a Democrat or a Republican?"

Now, this was the middle of the Depression, and the yardman wasn't mowing lawns because he had taken a degree in it. "Why, a Democrat, of course," he said, amused that J.N. should ask. "Isn't everyone?"

J.N. exploded.

"Get off my son's property!" he ordered, pointing to the street. *"I won't have any damn Democrat working for my son!"*

Harry was mortified, Cara Mae was furious, and both were without a yardman. J.N., of course, didn't do lawns.

J.N. once overheard my mother, then a young girl, coyly asking someone on the telephone, "Who's this?" at the start of a conversation. It was one of her school friends, and they talked a while. After she hung up the phone, J.N. said, "Katie, now, I don't want you talking to any stranger on the telephone."

My mother stood there silently, thinking she was about to hear another lecture on the dangers of strangers.

J.N. said simply, "It may be a Democrat."

"I remember," Bat says, "we had a clothing store here, moved in from Herington. Sold tailor-made suits. M. Born and Company. Most of the boys here got their suits from [M. Born], tailor-made. When they came in, Harry and I went down and he tried his on, and it was a nice fit for him. But he wanted to see it on someone else. We were about the same size, so he wanted me to put it on, see. And, God, that made me want one the worst kind, but I didn't have the money." Someone at the shop where Bat was barbering suggested he try getting a bank loan. He did, went back to M. Born's, "and I told him, I told him graduation was a few days off. I said, if you'll send a wire and tell them to duplicate that suit, and get it here before graduation, well, I'll buy it. And so he did." And so Harry and Bat, best of pals, wore the same tailor-made suit to graduation.

"Well," Carolyn says reluctantly, "I wish I could stay." She explains she has been driving all day, has to drive to Manhattan, has to get up early tomorrow for a full day's drive back to Colorado.

"Oh, I could . . . uh . . ."—sadness begins to shade Bat—"I could entertain you all day."

"Oh, I wish you could."

"See all those books over there," he says, glancing at his scrapbooks piled in the corner. Carolyn apologizes. She hates to be leaving. Jenny jots down their names, address and phone number in another little black book of Bat's, this one containing the names of the living.

"Left-handed," he says, "so was Harry. Harry was left-handed."

A round of thank-yous and other pleasantries—how wonderful it's been to meet a friend of Grandpa's, how special it's been to meet a granddaughter and great-granddaughter of Harry's, thank you for your time, thank you for coming in—and all the while Bat's mood seems to be changing. Perhaps it is an old man's sadness at saying goodbye to someone he'll probably never see again. He seems to be struggling with something, growing somewhat distant, even nervous. Poor old guy, Carolyn thinks.

"You know," Bat Nelson says, the old barber letting his hair down, "it really shocked a lot of people in this town when Harry married a squaw. But, oh"—shaking his head, and then looking away from Carolyn, gazing out the window onto Main Street, signaling that, after years of examining the evidence of the Great Scandal of Alta Vista, he has some inkling, some clue, some understanding as to why his closest pal, Harry Bolton, did it; signaling that he, Bat Nelson, is now ready to pronounce Sentence, long time coming, of the Great Unsaid—"I expect she was very pretty, or Harry wouldn't have—"

He abruptly jerks his head in Carolyn's direction, squinting suspiciously at her jet-black hair, suddenly realizing he may be talking to the wrong person. His expression relaxes when his eyes drop to her hazel eyes and very white skin.

"Now, tell me, I'm not clear," he says. "Was your mother the daughter of Harry's second wife, or of that Indian who committed suicide?"

Chapter Two

S uicide?" I asked, horrified.

It was July 8, a Monday and my day off. My mother was sitting on the couch in my apartment in Baltimore, telling the story.

Kathleen Bolton McAuliffe is slender and short—five feet two. She
has been the yardstick for all the other women in my life. I view her, even
now, at age sixty-seven, as a beautiful woman. She has stayed young in
both outlook and appearance. My mother looks like someone in her Indian
family, and I sometimes wondered if it was her Indian mother—or if this
was how my grandmother would have looked, and what she would have
been like, if she had lived to a grandmother's age.

My mother didn't always look Indian. Age's alterations have stitched
Indian features onto her face, like patches sewn on a military uniform to
denote distinction. Her cheekbones have pushed upward and outward,
like volcanic islands that appear abruptly and modify maps. The close
cropping of her hair has highlighted her ears like some schoolkid's yellow

marker, making them look longer, wider and more protruding. Gray is gradually conquering her hair, like weeds creeping haphazardly yet steadily through a lawn. Her brunet color is dulling in places, being driven out in others. Soon her original color will be anyone's guess, even the coarse blue-black that coats an Indian's head, at least to a white's mind's eye. Her once-auburn eyes are darker, browner, smaller than they were, and have set deeper, giving her brow a ridge that once was barely noticeable. Her nose, straight once, hooks now. A descriptive journey the length of her nose, from bridge to tip, would take longer. But her skin still holds the youth and whiteness it always had. Her father and stepmother used to purposefully keep her out of the sun, insist that she always be shaded, to keep her skin from bronzing beyond the limits of white, from trespassing upon the province of probing, and problems for them. Viewing the sun as an enemy was a habit she acquired long before its dangers were delineated. The lines that intersect her mouth did not form around a frown, so when her smile stretches in the opposite direction, an unnatural tautness takes over her face, muscles clench and bulge along her jawline, jutting her chin. This was the expression that greeted me when my father and I returned from playing golf, and its message moved across the room like a cloud shadow slowly shrinking a patch of sunlight.

"I have something to tell you," she said. "You better sit down."

I instinctively flinch and look for exits whenever I hear her say, "You better sit down." It is the same reaction I have when she calls me "Dennis," or worse, "Dennis Philip McAuliffe, Junior." I know bad news is about to follow, usually about me. As I approached the coffee table and kitty-corner love seat, I noticed that Fleur and my father had left the room, suddenly vanished, retreated to the safety of the back rooms, like cats at the report of a doorbell. I searched her face—and my mind—for any signs of a hint, at the speed of the computerlike scan of possibilities one's brain performs before answering a middle-of-the-night phone call. Me? Her health? My father?

"It's about my mother," she said.

"Oh," I frowned, relieved. Cara Mae. "What did Grandma do now?"

"My real mother."

My mother looked unusually calm for such turbulent words, "real mother." I sat.

She spread her arms open in a quick gesture, like the wave of a wand,

and, with a few magic storyteller's words, created Alta Vista in my living room, complete with cemetery, churches, Main Street, Bat Nelson's barbershop. After my interruption, she resumed the tale.

"Suicide?" my sister asks, horrified. Carolyn picks herself up off the floor (she didn't really fall, but my mother, when spinning a yarn, sometimes embroiders) and protests: "No, that's not true. She died of kidney disease."

"You didn't know?" Bat asks, mirroring the shock on Carolyn's face but with panic beginning to trace on his.

"No." Carolyn is still protesting rather than answering.

"This is the first time you've heard?"

"Yes." Carolyn is now responding.

"Your mother doesn't know?"

"No. She was always told she died of kidney disease."

"You mean I'm the one that leaked the story out?"

Carolyn nods.

Bat clasps a hand over his mouth and does an about-face toward the window. "Oh my God, what have I done?" He is on the verge of tears. "I'm so sorry. I'm so terribly sorry."

"No, that's all right," Carolyn says. Her immediate concern for the state and stability of this old man has transcended her shock over learning something that happened so long ago, about a woman she never knew, and never will. "Don't apologize. You've done a great service to our family."

"I feel awful bad about this. I'm afraid I've done the wrong thing."

"Oh no, no, no," she says consolingly. "I'm so grateful to you." She takes his hand in hers, and looks into his eyes with all the sincerity she can wring out of her face. "I'm so grateful to you for that information. Really."

End of story. Bat Nelson, the barbershop, Main Street, the churches, the cemetery, Alta Vista, all vanished. My living room was back to normal, or almost so. My mother was still on the couch. I was still on the love seat. But there was something present that hadn't been there before: a picture of a woman, whom neither of us had known, killing herself alone in the house with a baby, who happened to be this woman sitting on my sofa, my mother.

My mind raced back and forth, among proper phrases that I should say next, the horrible realization that my mother may have witnessed her mother killing herself, and the desire to kill my sister for telling her.

If ever there was a moral or ethical jawbreaker, this was it, and one for which there was no correct answer that I'm aware of. The subject never came up in any of the ethics or religious classes that I took in the Jesuit high school I attended in Washington, D.C., perhaps because the priests were too preoccupied with our souls and our sex lives: You have information that, at the very least, will force a sixty-seven-year-old woman to change the way she defines herself, and to realize that the way she had, that the whole foundation of her life, had been a lie. It also will color the way she remembers her deceased father, and introduce questions about his moral character, and into their relationship, that she had never before had cause to ask when he was alive and could answer. It will introduce new elements—tension and confrontation—into her relationship with her stepmother, whom she has known and loved as her real mother for most of the life that she can remember. The dilemma is complicated by the fact that this woman is your mother. She is not only the proudest and most sensitive person you know, but also sixty-seven. This news may age her. At worst, it will kill her.

Question: What do you do?

Answer:

In my case, the line is still blank, and I've had two-and-a-half years—as of this writing—to think about it. I'm still not sure.

At my noblest of times—or at least those rare times I think nobly of myself—I like to think I would have kept it to myself and said nothing, to anyone. It would be a lifelong secret. I would tell my mother in heaven. Perhaps that was Harry Bolton's intention. Other times, I think I would have called my father and let him wrestle with it, lose sleep, age, and decide whether, and how, to tell my mother. Every now and then, I think I would have called Cara Mae and asked her if it was true, and what should I do (no and nothing, she probably would have said). Ideally I would have independently investigated, gotten the death certificate, the police report, the coroner's report, the details, sorted out the story, and then approached my mother, raising the sheet from her infancy, like a body in a morgue.

Mostly I have thought, Thank God it was my sister. Better her than me.

But I would not have done what she did.

A wrestler's sweat was pouring off my sister as she drove back to

Colorado Springs on July 3, west from the Little Apple, first away from and then into the sun. She was tired from a sleepless night, upset. Thoughts and emotions bombarded her brain like bullets in a Nintendo game.

How dare these people who had nothing better to do with their lives than live in Alta Vista, Kansas, call my grandmother a squaw; look down on my grandfather's marriage to her, a woman educated at one of the finest schools on the East Coast; brand their baby, my mother, a "breed."

Should I, shouldn't I?

Carolyn spent another sleepless night at home. The next morning, July 4, she picked up the phone. It was 5:20 A.M., 7:20 in the Washington area where my parents live. The call woke my mother.

"Mom," Carolyn said. "Guess what?"

Independence Day.

My father—with perfect timing—returned to the living room as I was telling my mother that I should do some checking before she approached Cara Mae with the discovery, and the obvious question of why my mother was never told and had to learn this news via some stranger in the Middle of Nowhere, Kansas. Maybe the old man was wrong, I said. How did we know he wasn't senile, making all of this up, confusing us with someone else? The death certificate would show cause of death. I would get it.

It was natural, and no big deal, for me to volunteer. I had more experience in acquiring records and such things, and thus could do it faster and with less anxiety than either my mother or my father. I was an editor at *The Washington Post.* I'd make some calls in a day or two, when I had some down time at work, I promised.

I asked her when her mother had died. She said she didn't know but had the impression it happened when she was around eighteen months old. Her mother, therefore, must have died in either late 1925 or early 1926. I jotted down the dates.

Where? I asked. Kansas City? My mother was born there.

Pawhuska, Oklahoma.

You were in Pawhuska? I asked, startled.

She told me for the first time that her parents had separated. Like all young couples, she said, they had quarreled over money. They split up about six months before her mother's death. Her father stayed in Kansas City. Her mother took the baby and went home to the reservation.

ON WEDNESDAY, a lunchtime interview with Crown Prince Boevi Zankli of Togo fell through. I was the *Post*'s African affairs specialist; Prince Zankli, who was in self-imposed exile, had wanted to fill me in on the latest human rights outrages by the military government of his West African nation.

Now is a good time, I thought. Get it over with.

A woman in the Osage County clerk's office in Pawhuska answered the phone. I told her I was calling on behalf of my mother, and ran through the basics: a death from natural causes, now suicide. We would like a copy of her death certificate to confirm how she died. I gave her the range of dates. As I explained, I was thinking I really didn't have to go into all this detail. The woman probably would pass me along to someone else, to whom I'd have to tell the story again. She told me I'd have to call the Department of Health, Vital Statistics, in Oklahoma City—"All the records are sent there." That figures, I thought as I was about to say thank you and hang up.

Then she suggested I call Johnson's Funeral Home.

The mortician "might have a record of her," she said. His name was Mr. Dorsey McCartney. She spelled it. "He bought Johnson's Funeral Home from old Mr. Johnson," who had been the mortician for as long as anyone could remember. He had been the mortician "back then," when my grandmother died. It was, and still is, the only funeral home in town. She gave me the number.

I started dialing when it occurred to me I had overlooked one important detail.

I called my mother. I hemmed and hawed so much she probably thought I was asking to borrow money. I was embarrassed.

"What was her name?" I finally got it out. "My grandmother, what was my grandmother's name?"

"Sybil," she said. "Sybil F. Beekman Bolton."

"What was the F.?"

"Frances."

I asked her to spell Beekman.

A WOMAN ANSWERED with just a "Hello." They sure are casual for a funeral home, I thought. It turned out I had the wrong number, but without
even checking, the woman gave me the right one. Everyone must know
this place, I thought, or this must be one small town. When I dialed this
number, I was expecting another "Hello."

"Funeral home."

I asked for Mr. McCartney. After "Just a minute, he's right here," a
slow-talking, soft-voiced man came on the line. I could hear a trace of
drawl and of age in his voice. He sounded like an old Gary Cooper, back
from the dead.

I told my mother's story again. We would send for the death certificate in Oklahoma City, but, please, could you help us out in the meantime
by checking if Mr. Johnson had buried her and if he had noted the cause of
her death on the burial record? If not, do you know where I could find the
coroner's report on my grandmother?

He asked me when she died.

"Late 1925 or early 1926," I told him, reading from my notes.

"Well, the county attorney acted as coroner in those days." He didn't
know where those records might be kept. "But I can see if there's anything
in Mr. Johnson's old book."

I spelled her name. I said I'd be happy to call back if it was going to
take a while.

"No, shouldn't take more than five minutes."

I anticipated his return with a deep sense of dread. I was trying to
shake a chilling image that had been with me since my mother's visit two
days earlier—that of a child gazing up at her mother dangling from a rope.

My mother had recalled a phobia she has always had but that over
the years I had forgotten about. She becomes petrified, freezing in panic, if
anyone touches her neck, which then breaks out in a rash. She could never
wear necklaces, for instance. I can remember looking at a discolored, spotted patch on her neck, just to the right of her Adam's apple, through
much of my childhood. Her phobia is still there, only not so pronounced

now that she doesn't have children to carry around, within touching dis-tance of her neck. If her mother did commit suicide, then she must have hanged herself, my mother said she decided, and she either saw her do it, or got a glimpse of her suspended from a rope when someone discovered the body.

Mr. McCartney came back on the line in less than five minutes. Yes, he said, there was a funeral record for a Sybil Beekman Bolton.

"She died on November 7, 1925"—pause—"at eleven-thirty A.M."

"Does it list cause of death?" I asked.

"Well, yes." He paused again, more from reading—I got the impres-sion—than thinking about how to phrase what he would say.

I had the feeling I wouldn't be hearing the words "kidney disease."

I IMMEDIATELY CALLED my parents' home, wanting to talk to my fa-ther, not sure if I should—and not wanting to—tell my mother what I had learned. She answered. He had gone out.

My thoughts raced in panic. I sucked in my breath.

"Well, hell, Mom," I said, reaching for words. "They lied to you your whole life. You may as well finally hear the truth. You better sit down."

"What is it?" I could hear the alarm.

"She shot herself," I said. "Cause of death was 'gunshot wound, sui-cide.' "

"Oh my God." It was her first of many utterances of this phrase in the conversation, each time saying it differently, putting the stress on dif-ferent words.

I told her the date of death.

"How old was I?"

Her voice cracked. It would be the only time throughout all of this that my mother ever came close to crying.

We were both so upset we couldn't add the time between June 24, 1924, my mother's birthday, and November 7, 1925, her mother's death. After several attempts, we settled on sixteen months.

I told my mother about the rest of my conversation with Mr. McCartney, reading from notes that were barely legible.

Sybil's age was twenty-one.

She was given a requiem high mass at Pawhuska's Catholic church. This fact bothered even Mr. McCartney. "You know how Catholics are about suicide," he said. (I didn't know she was Catholic.)

Her body was placed in a temporary vault, then moved to a crypt in a mausoleum.

The certifying physician was Dr. Roscoe Walker. I asked if I could contact him. "No, he's been dead a long time."

The funeral record contained no reference to either an autopsy or a coroner's report. If there had been an autopsy or a coroner's inquest, I asked Mr. McCartney, would they be noted on the funeral record?

"Yes," he said. "Mr. Johnson kept very detailed records."

Then he said, "Now there's a name here . . ." His tone was changing to one of surprise. He even sounded impressed. "A. T. Woodward."

"A. T. Woodward?" I asked, writing it down.

"He was her guardian."

"Guardian? Why would she have a guardian?" I asked. "She had a husband."

"Now, A. T. Woodward was a very prominent, very well respected attorney in this town," he was saying. Mr. McCartney speculated that "as a favor to" Woodward, the authorities might have waived an autopsy or coroner's investigation. Woodward may have asked the police not to conduct an inquest "to spare the family any further pain," Mr. McCartney said.

"She was an Osage, one of the original allottees," he said with surprise. I said, yes, my mother is an Osage, we're all Osages, not sounding very convincing and making a point of not asking what an original allottee was. "Her allottee number was 933," he said.

"Body in perfect condition, face perfect," he read without comment.

Did she die on the reservation?

No. She died at 107 East 11th Street. "I know that area," he said. "It was then, and still is, what you'd call upper-crust."

I WALKED AROUND THE *Post* newsroom, then around the block, then around another block. I felt so unglued I asked to go home early.

She was so young, I thought, driving back to Baltimore. How many lives and lifetimes have I lived since I was twenty-one, and how much would I have missed had I died then? Having my only child, for example, my proudest achievement. I was haunted by a picture I could not erase of a girl with a gun. Did she point it for an instant at my mother in a planned murder-suicide, then quickly turn it on herself before she changed her mind?

I was angry. We should have known there was suicide in the family. That, rather than a family history of kidney disease, should have been in our medical records. We were done a great injustice. Perhaps this would have shed some light on periodic dark times. Knowing I carried violence within me of the sort that has no brakes might have driven me to seek a different cure than the one I chose. Instead, I suffered in solitude, like an Indian.

Later, at home, after another conversation with my mother and a round of phone calls to my sisters, my anger grew at their reaction. For them, as for me, the silt of this shock had not yet settled. My younger sister, Kathie, kept saying, "Poor Mom, what is this going to do to her?" My mother talked only about what a wonderful mother Cara Mae Bolton had been, that it was to her credit that my mother had turned out so happy. My sister Carolyn went on about what a saint Harry Bolton had been, how the suicide was the cross he bravely bore in life.

"One good thing has come out of this," Carolyn said. "At least we know Grandpa doesn't have to put up with her in heaven."

Their eulogies excluded someone, and the oversight upset me.

"No one is speaking for this poor woman," I told Fleur. "What about her?"

My wife had put the baby to bed while I was on the phone, and now was in the kitchen fixing his bottles for the night. I recounted my conversations. Something doesn't sound right, I kept saying.

"I don't believe it was suicide," Fleur said suddenly. I could tell by her tone that she was tired—and tired of my lamentations. "No woman would kill herself without first making arrangements for her children, especially an infant."

I thought about that for a moment.

"Well," I said hesitantly, "I always thought Grandpa killed her."

I felt instantly guilty for saying it. I had said it many times before, but never seriously—just socially. It made for a good story. It was one of the first things I had told Fleur about him. I'm not so sure I ever really believed it. The thought had taken shape more as a visceral reaction to him and his frequently brusque fashion than as an actual suspicion based on any kind of clue. Over time, it became my excuse for still harboring feelings that long ago should have been put out to sea. Saying it had always been an easy way to express my dislike for him and the complicated reasons why. It was a cheap shot, I admit, but I derived a certain satisfaction from taking it. But only hours before, I learned that a gunshot had killed my grandmother, and Fleur had just enunciated a thought whose syllables had been forming in my heart all day but had not yet reached my tongue for discharge. A gunshot requires a finger on the trigger, and it doesn't matter to the gun whose finger it is. We had just raised the possibility that it may not have been hers. Now saying that I always thought Harry had killed her made me actually look at the appalling picture I had been drawing of him all these years. The image nearly made my mouth jam, like a gun.

Fleur tightened the nipple on a baby bottle.

"Then prove it," she said, placing the bottle back on the counter with more force than she intended, the smack providing an exclamation point. She looked at me.

"Prove your grandfather murdered your grandmother."

She walked out while I was still in mid-gulp. I stood alone for a long time, counting the squares in the pattern of the kitchen linoleum—nineteen by twenty-four—as I sometimes catch myself doing when I'm drinking and lost in thought.

Prove my grandfather murdered my grandmother . . . how?

Abruptly I walked into the living room, without any clear notion of what I was doing or going to do. I went, as if guided, to the bookcase.

The answer is in history, I found myself thinking, except that the history of this woman's death is neither history nor dead. Her death was a time bomb set for sixty-six years that has just gone off, now, in the present, and the first shock wave just hit us, and it has not yet passed.

I got out a book on the Osages that my mother had given me ten years before. I had never read it. I had never opened it. It had been only a living-room bookcase showpiece.

I opened it and read the inscription for the first time—words that, like my grandmother, had lain in long-ignored repose:

"To Den—For a better understanding of your mother's heritage. With love, K.B.McA."

My mother's Indian heritage. That was what she also lost with her mother.

AND SO BEGAN MY JOURNEY.

In the 1970s, another writer of Osage ancestry, William Least Heat-Moon, traveled around the country on back roads. He called them "blue highways."

The road I took that night, leafing through the book, turned into one of America's darkest alleys.

The America he found was a land of decent, struggling people whose faces reflected the light of the ideals still radiating from the torch it held.

My Statue of Liberty held a gun.

Events of Osage history raced past my eyes like scenery along an interstate. As I scanned a page here, a paragraph further on, a sentence several pages later, an occasional fact, feature, an incident, an indignity caught my eye and stayed with me, like a memorable view from a car.

This was one:

For centuries, the Osages owned, occupied, and ruled over most of modern Missouri, the southern half of Kansas and the northern halves of Arkansas and Oklahoma. They had managed to hold this land since at least the Ice Age, through gruesomely brutal Indian wars and throughout a century and a quarter of French and Spanish colonial rule. But shortly after the 1803 Louisiana Purchase, which included the Osage domain, the Americans forced the Osages to embark on a "Trail of Treaties" that would confine them to a 50-by-100-mile, 12 million-acre reservation in southeastern Kansas. Over a seventeen-year period, the Osages ceded 98.6 million acres of their ancestral land for $166,300, mostly in livestock and merchandise—or one-sixth of a penny per acre. The United States paid less per acre for Osage land than the Dutch had paid two hundred years earlier for Manhattan Island.

There were several Osages in the pantheon of American Indians: the first Native American elected vice president of the United States, as well as to the House of Representatives and the Senate (Charles Curtis of Kansas, who served under Herbert Hoover); the first Indian to become a general (Clarence L. Tinker, of the Army Air Corps, shot down and killed in the World War II Battle of Midway, and commemorated by Tinker Air Force Base, Oklahoma); the most-decorated Indian in the Vietnam War (Andrew "Buddy" Redcorn, who now works at the Osage Agency in Pawhuska). The Osages also excelled in the arts: The first university-published book to be sold by the Book-of-the-Month Club was written by an Oxford-educated Osage, John Joseph Mathews (the 1932 *Wah'Kon-Tah: The Osage and the White Man's Road*), and two Osage sisters, Marjorie and Maria Tallchief, achieved international fame as ballerinas in the 1950s and '60s.

They were Sioux, spoke a Siouan derivative known as Osage, and were striking in their appearance. Washington Irving called the Osages "the finest looking Indians I have ever seen," and Thomas Jefferson described them as "the most gigantic men we have ever seen." (Their dignified demeanor impressed the president as well, for he added, "They are the finest men we have ever" encountered.) Typically, Osage men stood six feet five, and many were seven feet tall. The American painter George Catlin, who spent two months of 1832 trying to shrink them to his canvas, wrote, "The Osages may justly be said to be the tallest race of men in North America, either of red or white skins." Their "bulk" was equally "formidable," especially the numerous three-hundred-pounders he encountered. Despite their weight, he added, "they are at the same time well-proportioned in their limbs. . . . Their movement is graceful and quick."

The names by which many Indian tribes and geographical features are known today are the Osage names for them, some derogatory. Early French visitors, pointing to a map, would ask the Osages, "Who are these people over there?" and transliterate their responses. Kansas is the Osage name for a splinter tribe of the Osages, a clan that stormed out one night during a quarrel over buffalo sinew. In Osage, "Kansas" means "They

Desire to Run," or "Noisy People." The Omahas (another splinter tribe), the Quapaws (or Arkansas Indians), the Poncas, the Pawnees, the Wichitas, the Apaches, the Shawnee, the Neosho River—all are transliterations from the Osage. (An Osage name that didn't stick was for the Comanches, which is Ute for "Anyone Who Wants to Fight Me All the Time." The French and Spanish used the name the Osages gave them, the Padoucas, or "Wet Nose People.") Other Osage names the French translated. The Marais de Cygnes River was named after the Place of the Many Swans, the Osages' mythological birthplace and site of their main ancestral village in southwestern Missouri. A nearby river the Osages called "Snake with Mouth Open" became the Marmaton. Nebraska's Platte River derives from Osage for "Water Flat White." The river the Osages called Gray Green Bark Waters was translated to Verdigris.

They got their name "Osage" the same way "Indians" got theirs—through ignorance, but this time on the part of the natives themselves. The French priest Jacques Marquette and his traveling companion Louis Joliet were exploring the Mississippi River in 1673, looking for a shortcut to the Pacific. Stopping at the mouth of the Arkansas River, Marquette chummed up to some Indians he named the "Oumissouries" and asked them the names of their neighbors. They answered something that he scribbled down on his map as "Ouazhaghi." However, these Ouazhaghi had identified themselves to the Oumissouries only by their clan name, the Wah-sha-she, pronounced much the way Father Marquette spelled it. The English later Anglicized the name to "Osage." The Osages, who, as mentioned before, were sometimes seven feet tall, called themselves the Little Ones, Ni-u-ko'n-ska, or the Children of the Middle Waters, which came to be known as the Missouri River and its tributaries.

Throughout the period of French (1673–1766) and Spanish (1766–1803) colonial rule over the Lower Mississippi Valley, the Osages often accounted for more than 40 percent of Indian trade out of St. Louis—a town founded initially as an Osage trading post. In a typical year, they traded six hundred packs of luxury furs and dressed deer- and bearskins, weighing 22,200 pounds, for the European guns, bullets, powder, flints, knives, picks, clubs, and axes with which they killed unwanted whites and other Indians.

Before the Americans came, the Osages were the terror of the plains—Hell's Angels on horseback. They constantly warred on their Indian neighbors and beheaded hundreds of Europeans who ventured into their territory. Heads on stakes often served to inform travelers they had just entered the land of the Osages. "Those barbarians," responded a Spanish commander of a trading post in Arkansas when word reached him in 1772 that a Frenchman captured by the Osages had been "put on a spit and roasted alive," and then eaten. In 1777, the Spanish were particularly horrified when the Osages decapitated a French hunter in front of his young son, carried the boy and his father's head six hundred miles back to their main village in Missouri, and then made the youngster watch "those abominable dances which always accompany such trophies." Official European dispatches describing the Osages tended to be filled with such adjectives as "pernicious," "insolent," "despicable," "deceitful," "perverse." "It is a treacherous, cruel, audacious, robbing, wandering and very warlike nation," a priest wrote. When a Spanish officer learned that his outpost faced imminent attack from the Osages, he wrote what he feared would be his last letter: "There remains for us no other recourse than to die killing."

While other Indians lost ground to the Europeans, the Osages gained territory, overrunning tribes in decline from their growing dependence on the Europeans and from periods of deprivation, brought on in large part by Osage attacks. In 1793, for example, a Chickasaw chief told a Spanish officer that the Osages had stolen all the horses in his village, "which prevents us from going further to hunt." But that did not matter, he complained, because it was not safe to hunt anymore "without being killed or plundered by the Osages. You see the Arkansas [Indians], who cannot go hunting on the prairies without having their throats cut by the Osages. They as well as we are obliged to hunt roebuck on the Mississippi, while the Osages make themselves masters of all the hunting country. . . . I pray you . . . stop the white men of [St. Louis] from carrying goods to the Osages to kill us with."

In their first encounter with an official French delegation, the Osages demonstrated how they would continually confound European attempts to expand trade and dominion westward, and deprive other Indians of goods in the process. In 1719, they graciously received Charles Claude du Tisné, but when he did not offer to trade all the weapons he was transporting, saying he intended to barter with the Pawnees—a traditional enemy—the Osages grew surly and lightened du Tisné's load of all but three rifles. After the Frenchman set out for the Pawnee village, four days away, the Osages sent runners via a shortcut to warn the Pawnee chief that a white man was coming to enslave them. Du Tisné credited "the boldness with which I faced" the Pawnees' hostile reception for his luck in being able to write about his adventures.

In 1755, at the Battle of Fort Duquesne, the bloodiest British-American defeat of the French and Indian War, the Osages shot arrows at Colonel George Washington but missed him, killing his horse instead. Washington was wounded in the battle, but by whom is unknown.

IN THE MORNING, after a night of reading, I found a motive for murder.

The Osages were the Kuwaitis of the 1920s.

Oil had made the Osage Indians the richest people, per capita, in the world. There were more Pierce-Arrows—the Rolls-Royces of their day—on the Osage lands in Oklahoma than anywhere else in the country. The limousines often bore—etched in solid gold on the side panels—the initials of their owners, giant Osages, larger than life itself, sitting in the leather back seats while their chauffeurs navigated the pits and bumps of the dusty dirt roads. The Indians wrapped themselves regally in brightly colored blankets and sparkled majestically, head to toe, from the vivid array of beads that dotted their long, shiny black hair, their necks, wrists, dresses, broadcloth trousers, handbags and moccasins. Sometimes the glitter came from diamonds studded in the Osage women's patent-leather slippers, which showed the flash of silk stockings at the ankle. When a limo broke down, or just got a flat tire, the Osages did not bother with repairs—they simply bought another automobile, or several more. A visiting reporter noted: "It has been stated recently that every eleventh person in the United States owns a car. They do better at Osage, where nearly every Indian owns eleven cars, either at once or in due season."

They—their chauffeurs, rather—parked their cars outside the Osages' mansions, filled with the finest in furniture, paintings, sculpture, china, and other luxury items—but often no occupants. Many Osages preferred sleeping outside, on their lawns, or continued their nomadic tradition of frequent and seasonal traveling—but this time in style. They traveled the country and the world, often to visit their children at the exclusive private boarding schools they attended.

Tall, wooden, creaky, noisome oil derricks dominated the landscape of rolling hills of blackjack oak groves and tallgrass prairie. Photos from the 1920s show a forest of oil rigs, from the foreground to the distant horizon. The Osage oil-boom town of Whizbang, whose white workers "whizzed all day and banged all night," had sixty-nine derricks within camera range. In addition to the three main Osage towns—Pawhuska, Hominy and Fairfax, all built roughly where separate bands of Osages originally erected their villages in the 1870s—twenty-eight boomtowns weeded their way across the Osage countryside between 1906 and 1928. They housed tens of thousands of white oil-field workers, called roustabouts. During the mid-1920s, 45,000 roustabouts lived in company dormitories scattered across the 20,000-acre Burbank oil field, the Osages' largest pool, just twenty-five miles west of Pawhuska. The post office of Shidler, one boomtown, had 10,000 oil workers on its mailing list.

Their employers—white oil barons—leased 160-acre tracts of land from the Osages, paying cash bonuses per tract for the right to drill and then a royalty on each barrel extracted. In 1922, a bidding frenzy between two oil companies boosted the bonus of one tract to more than a million dollars. Seventeen other tracts also topped the million-dollar bonus mark in the 1920s, including one for which Midland Oil shelled out $1.9 million. Many of the oil barons who sat under Pawhuska's "Million Dollar Elm," where quarterly auctions for the tracts were held, made their first millions from Osage oil, and many of these have since had their names forever enshrined on gas-station signs: Frank Phillips, Harry Sinclair, George and Jean Paul Getty. Others became famous after they toiled among the Osages and their oil: Herbert Hoover, Alf Landon, Tom Mix, Clark Gable.

The Osages' oil-annuity payments were front-page news around the country—even *The New York Times* reported the amounts. Newspapers around the nation gobbled up stories about the Osages' spending sprees and their "Olympian indifference to money," feeding white readers accounts of the Indians' $1,000-a-month grocery bills—this at a time when steak sold for 25 cents a pound, and the nation was cutting back during the lean years of World War I. The country collectively gulped upon learning that one Osage man spent $100 a week to feed his dogs. Ten-year-old Osage schoolchildren routinely carried $50 and change in their pockets for lunch money. In one afternoon, an Osage woman spent $43,800 in cash for a fur coat, a car, a diamond ring, furniture, land in

Florida and a down payment on a house in California, plus $600 to ship her new furniture there.

"Lo, the Rich Indian!" newspaper headlines and magazine-article titles declared. A visiting reporter, who had expected Pawhuska to be a "small, dreary one-horse town," instead "found marble office buildings, smart Fifth-Avenue-looking shops, and magnificent custom-built cars rushing by. . . . I was never more surprised in my life."

Surprise was a common reaction of observers of the Osages. They did not fit the stereotype of "Poor Lo," a cliché for the penurious and pitiful condition of reservation, "blanket" Indians. Stories about the Osages, written by whites, for whites, tended to echo a commonly shared belief (among whites) that the Osages' riches were undeserved—"this joke," one writer put it; this "queer turn of fate" that had made the Osages "the richest nation, clan or social group of any race on earth, including the whites, man for man."

THE OSAGES WERE RICH even before the term "rich Osages" became redundant.

They had lived on their Kansas reservation during the "Bleeding Kansas" rebellion, the Civil War, and the start of the Indian Wars, and had watched other tribes marched off their land and resettled in Indian Territory—now Oklahoma—much of it part of the ancestral Osage domain. The Osages knew that any day they, too, would be moving south.

Disease from encroaching whites and warfare with neighboring Indians had reduced the Osages' number from 17,000 in the late seventeenth century, to 12,000 by 1815, to 3,000 in their last days in Kansas. This little tribe of Indians could no longer do much to alter the sweep of history, as they had been able to do during the French and Spanish years. But in 1870, the Osages became the lucky benefactors of a sudden and short-lived policy shift in Washington—generosity toward Indians. The U.S. government offered to buy the Osage reservation for $1.25 an acre; Washington's previous offer—two years earlier—had been 19 cents an acre. Motivated by a desire to influence their own destiny, the Osages agreed to sell.

So while "all them other Indians got [was] their ass and a hat," as an

Osage chief later put it, "the Osage got money," lots of it—nearly $9 million. This staggering sum in 1870 dollars they deposited in the U.S. Treasury to draw 5 percent annual interest.

When they signed the Kansas removal treaty on September 10, 1870, the Osages became the richest Indians in America. But they achieved a more significant uniqueness by what they did with their money. They bought a new reservation in northeastern Indian Territory, paying 74 cents an acre to the Cherokees for 1.47 million acres of former Osage land. The generosity of the Cherokees, once a bitter Osage enemy, was forced on them by the U.S. government in punishment for fighting on the Confederate side during the Civil War.

Since the Osages owned outright the land they lived on—rather than it being their "gift" from the American people—the United States, at least in its dealings with the Osage Nation, was not able to display the trait that already had become a cliché in the English language—an "Indian giver."

The purchase and ownership of the land also enabled the Osages to be exempted from many of the Indian laws whose professed good intentions all too often paved a road to hell for all other Indians. Congress had to tailor specific laws to the Osages, usually after rounds of negotiations.

One such law was the Dawes Act of 1887, or the General Allotment Law, which struck at the centuries-old Indian practice of community ownership of land. The bill's authors—philanthropic, religious types ("do-gooders," their political opponents might call them today)—genuinely believed that the "communism" of tribal land ownership was the root cause of Indians' evil "savagism" and the last roadblock to Christian civilization. "Common property and civilization cannot co-exist," a commissioner of Indian affairs declared. Declaimed one member of Congress in the debate on the bill: "What shall be [the Indian's] future status? Shall he remain a pauper savage, blocking the pathway of civilization, an increasing burden upon the people? Or shall he be converted into a civilized taxpayer, contributing toward the support of the Government and adding to the material prosperity of the country?"

Henceforth, the law decreed, all reservations in Indian Territory would be subdivided into 160-acre plots and a tract deeded to each member of the tribes. Whites could settle on any tribal land in excess of the allotment.

Of the dates of infamy in U.S. history, the Dawes Act was the Pearl Harbor of Native Americans, for it sank any chance of the Indian way of life surviving the white world. The law, hailed by proponents as the "Indian Emancipation Act," disbanded the reservations of the more than sixty tribes in Indian Territory, except those of the Osages and the Five Civilized Tribes—the Cherokees, Chickasaws, Choctaws, Creeks and Seminoles—all located in what is now eastern Oklahoma. Thus was created the Territory of Oklahoma—a Choctaw word meaning "red people"—which was opened to white people on April 22, 1889. More than 50,000 whites staked claims to 2 million acres of former Indian land from noon to nightfall in this first of Oklahoma's five land rushes. The new Oklahomans soon clamored for statehood, but Congress, pitying the Indians who had been left out of all the civilizing by their exemption from the Dawes Act, would not grant Oklahoma statehood until the last reservation in Indian Territory had gone the way of the buffalo.

The Osages hemmed and hawed with Congress for the next fifteen years over whether they would accept allotment. By this time, they saw not only the disastrous effects of allotment on now-landless Indians, but also the same inevitability that had precipitated their move from Kansas. Congress was seriously threatening to impose allotment on the Osages, even though they had legally purchased their reservation with their own money. As whites demanded more Indian land, Congress had nullified the Dawes Act exemptions for the Five Civilized Tribes and disbanded their reservations. Only the Osages remained, holding up Oklahoma statehood.

The tribe's ranks, meanwhile, were growing with mixed-bloods, as white men discovered the beauty of wealthy Osage women, described by a white observer only decades before as being either "horrible—more horrible—[or] most horrible . . . the squaws are hideous to behold." By Osage custom, the "half-breeds," as the U.S. government and other Americans called mixed-blood Indians, were full members of the tribe, and many were pushing for allotment. They were attracted to the law's provision of U.S. citizenship in reward for allotting their lands, and they saw a golden opportunity in privately owning some of the Osages' land.

By the turn of the century, there were nearly as many pro-allotment mixed-bloods as anti-allotment full-bloods. With luck, if the allotment opponents acted before they became the minority, they might be able to conform to the will of the white man on beneficial terms—as they had done in Kansas.

And, as in Kansas, they made a decision that would have an overwhelming economic impact on them, and their descendants.

They negotiated their own allotment act with Congress in 1906. The Osages would accept individual allotment of the 160-acre tracts, but, unlike under the Dawes Act, surplus land would not be made available to whites. After all, it already had been bought and paid for by the Osages. After the 160-acre tracts had been parceled out, any excess land on the reservation would also be divided equally, and given to each member of the tribe.

Each Osage was deeded 657 acres of land, more than four times the amount of land that other tribal members in Indian Territory had received. But this largesse paled in significance to the next concession the Osages extracted from Congress.

Individual ownership applied only to the surface land. It did not extend to what was underneath it. Any mineral riches would be held in common by all members of the tribe.

Congress agreed. Who cared about these 2,000 Indians anyway, except that they were preventing the whites of Oklahoma from joining the Union?

Did the Osages forget to tell Washington that they were sitting on top of one of the biggest oil fields in the United States?

THE OSAGE TRIBAL ROLL WAS CLOSED on July 1, 1907. It listed all 2,229 members of the tribe. Each of the Osages, regardless of age or blood quantum, received one allotment, called a "headright." Each headright was worth 657 acres of land in what was soon to become Osage County, State of Oklahoma, and one annuity share, or 1/2,229 of the total, of the tribe's yearly bonuses and royalties from the production of oil and natural gas beneath the reservation, regardless of who owned the land above.

The number of headrights would remain at 2,229 in perpetuity. When the holder of a headright died, it would pass to his or her heirs— even if they were not Osages, even if they were white—and could be divided among the heirs. A headright holder could also inherit a benefactor's share, meaning that some Osages ended up with more than one headright.

One of the names on the final tribal roll and one of the initial recipients of a headright—called "original allottees"—was Sybil Frances Beekman, headright number 933. Three-year-old Sybil Beekman was now the owner of 657 acres of oil-logged land and the recipient of a yearly income to be disbursed in quarterly cash payments, for life.

Picture a toddler at the payment window on the west side of the Tribal Council House in Pawhuska, straining on tiptoes, her small, outstretched hand growing heavy with cash as it is counted out and stacked high—that was what I pictured my grandmother doing four times during each of her childhood years.

In 1925, the year she died, the Osages received their highest payment for the oil on their reservation. That year, each member of the tribe, including Sybil, was paid an annuity, in cash, that today would have the buying power of more than a million dollars.

Chapter Four

Family storytime.

I hadn't always been an Indian.

For half of my life—well, one-third of it now—I was just an ordinary, run-of-the-mill white kid like everyone else I knew, with nothing ethnically extra that met the eye, no footnotes to the Great American Success Story that my father embodied.

My view of myself changed one late-summer night in Arlington, Virginia, when I was fifteen. It was 1965. My father, then a lieutenant colonel, was in South Korea. My mother had invited to dinner her closest friend, Frances Johnson. Her husband, Charles S. Johnson, Jr.—or Colonel Johnson, as I still call him—a West Point classmate of my father's, was in Vietnam. Their son, Charles, was and still is my best friend.

We were having steak, and I was the designated cook. In those days, we grilled steaks Eisenhower-style. My mother had read a recipe in *The Washington Post* from Mamie Eisenhower that said, Forget the sissy grill, be like Ike: Throw the steaks directly on the charcoal. We did for years. I'm probably the only kid in America, home of the barbecue, land of the backyard grill, who grew up thinking that steaks were roughage, ashy instead of juicy, and that they built character (and probably cysts—I think we stopped around the time President Eisenhower died of heart failure complicated by an intestinal blockage).

After dinner and dessert, my mother became ill. Mrs. Johnson put her to bed. She stayed, in fact, through much of the night to take care of my mother. Later, Mrs. Johnson came downstairs and said to me, "Your mother wants to see you."

I don't think the mere sight of my mother will ever cause me so much pain until, God forbid, I have to look at her for the last time.

She was in bed, crying as I've never seen anyone cry. "Crying" is not the word for what she was doing, nor is any other word I can think of to convey this act. "Grief" is woefully inadequate as a description.

Between gulps and convulsions of sobs, she told me that Grandma (Cara Mae Bolton) was not her real mother, that her real mother had died, that she was just a baby when her mother died and she had no memory of her, that she was an Osage Indian. It was the first I had heard of any of this.

"You're an Indian, Denny. I'm so sorry."

This admission opened floodgates to the breaking point. My fifteen-year-old brain, torn between the shock of seeing and that of hearing, zoomed back and forth between these two focuses like some berserk camera, resulting in a confusion of facts that has lasted to this day.

For one, I thought all these years that my grandmother died of diabetes, that she had some sort of diabetic episode that caused her to drop dead in front of my mother. Kidney disease, when I overheard my mother telling Fleur the story a couple of years ago, was news to me. All my medical records show a history of diabetes in my family. I even asked for, and received, a diabetes test in the Army.

And I became convinced that my grandfather killed her.

That a fifteen-year-old boy with a vivid imagination got his facts mixed up in a moment of shock is understandable. I do not apologize for leaving my mother's room that night saying to my shaken self that Grandpa did it and, for the next twenty-six years, suspecting him of murder because of what I thought I heard that night.

This was the story as it ended up in my mind: When my grandmother and grandfather got married, she kept from him that she was an Indian and a Catholic. But he found out. When he confronted her, they got into a huge fight. He stormed out. She was then found dead, alone in the house with the baby. Any self-respecting, television-addicted American kid who did not find that suspicious would be brain-dead.

My mother later told me that she had been so food-poisoned by the combination of my charcoaling and Mrs. Johnson's lemon pie that she seriously thought she was dying, and wanted to use her last moment with her only son to set the record straight. That was why she was so upset, she said, and chose that moment to redefine my life. In the scope of things, this wasn't much, I must admit—one kid's trauma over his momma tearfully telling him that some essential information about the way he viewed his then-fifteen-year-old life was in need of amending. But such is the stuff of shock. Whenever I think about this one night, I usually am one inhalation away from tears, one lumpy swallow, every now and then making the transition.

I never discussed my suspicion about my grandfather with my mother or any member of my family, so I never got the story straight. I just shoved that image of my mother down into my subconscious, from which it would bob to the surface every now and then, usually late at night when my defenses were down. But any mention of my Indian grandmother, or of the Osages, would turn on the projector of that movie of my mother's *Trail of Tears,* if only for a second.

Since I called Pawhuska, it was screening again, and I couldn't stop the projector. That old film of my mother and that night was playing and replaying in an eternal loop. It was not easy for me to make those phone calls, and I damned myself the instant I volunteered to do so. I anticipated inquiring about my grandmother's death with deep foreboding. *Trail of Tears, Part II.* Here I was, treading blindfolded into the emotional minefield I had been successful thus far in detouring—my mother's Indian past.

It had to be me, didn't it, who had to confirm the cause of death, and tell my mother. But I couldn't let it end there, could I. I couldn't say to myself, Okay, my grandmother committed suicide, lots of people do, that's life, don't be judgmental, try not to do it yourself. I couldn't let it rest in peace. I had to decide to dig deeper, to try to kill the memory of my grandfather as well.

I had to suddenly start believing in my grandmother, this woman I had refused to think about for twenty-six years.

What if Harry really did do it?

Would I have the nerve, or the heart, to tell my mother that?

Hi, Mom, your beloved father, whom you worshiped, murdered your mother, in front of you.

Could I do that?

Yes. I wanted to.

RACISTS USUALLY START YOUNG, so I assume that by 1917, when he left Alta Vista, Kansas, at age seventeen, my grandfather had fully developed the prejudices that would last him a lifetime. They were against the religious and ethnic groups to which he did not belong. Throughout the sixties, he and Cara Mae visited us at Christmas, and we could always count on hearing from him something derogatory about Catholics, Jews and "niggers," as he rarely ceased calling them, even in public. It was his refrain.

Out of deference to my mother, I guess, he dropped Indians from his list, at least from the one he vocalized in our presence. Until she married a laconic one, the "loudmouthed Irish" were on his list, along with such "foreigners" as "Wops," "Spics," "Polacks," "Frogs" and "Krauts." I always marked it up as a miracle, direct from God, that my parents survived the wedding my grandfather hosted for them in Houston in 1946. They were married at his home, with an Irish priest presiding. My grandfather spiked the priest's punch with Irish whiskey, a fifth full of appropriateness. The poor priest got plowed, nearly passed out, and had to be stuffed into the back of a cab, to the glee of Grandpa and his pals, but to the horror of my devoutly religious Irish grandmother, Mary Kate Ryan McAuliffe.

My mother would explain to us children that her father's prejudices were unfortunate but not unusual for a man his age who lived in places in the Midwest where prejudice grew like the weeds and wildflowers coloring Kansas.

The people my grandfather was most intensely prejudiced against were the ones least in evidence in the place where he grew up, based on my sister's observations. The indigenous Kaw Indians, whose tribal land Alta

Vista occupied, had been driven out in the last century. That was probably when the last black ventured into town. There are none in Alta Vista today. There used to be churches of Christ, United Brethren, Quakers, Southern Methodists, Baptists, Presbyterians, and Lutherans, but never a synagogue. There had been a couple of Catholics. The Alta Vista centennial book, which Carolyn sent me, devotes seven full pages to its churches, but cryptically remarks that "a Catholic Church also existed in Alta Vista at one time, but no information concerning it [is] available." They were probably ridden out on the rails laid at the edge of town in 1887. My mother remembers her grandfather, J. N. Bolton, telling her that he moved to Alta Vista because too many Catholics were moving in at his nearby hometown of Paxico.

Despite my mother's valiant attempts to rationalize—but never to minimize—my grandfather's prejudices, I always was deeply offended by them. I also was deeply frustrated that I wasn't able to confront him, with my objections and beliefs, to try to correct his, to stand up to him, to take just one shot at trying to put him in his place. I was restrained by my parents, by the respect for elders that they instilled in me, by fear of his quick-draw acerbic tongue.

Finally, happily, however, I got back at him.

All of my grandfather's descendants are Indians. I am Catholic. My wife is Jewish. Our son, Kevin, is all three (if that is technically possible). My wife and I had a *brit* (pronounced "briss") for Kevin. It is the Jewish rite of circumcision and the ceremonial naming of a Jewish boy, conducted on the eighth day of his life. For it, we had to pick a Hebrew name for Kevin. The rabbi advised that it be the name of one of Kevin's relatives. Without hesitation, I insisted on my grandfather's name. During the *brit,* when the rabbi named my son, pronouncing "Harsh Benyamin" as his Hebrew name, I swear I heard a rumble of earth as Harry Ben Bolton rolled over in his grave. It was the sweet, satisfying sound of social justice digging in.

Harry was eighty-one when he got throat cancer. He spent three months in a hospital in Denver on sheepskin sheets, to keep him from chapping. His vocal chords were removed, which offended his very great dignity. It embarrassed him to use an electronic device to be heard. He wrote notes rather than talk. One day he jotted a note to Cara Mae saying she should beware of a certain doctor. Harry, still in love with her and romantically jealous after all those years, said the doctor was flirting with her. My mother, who was then living in Panama, sat at her father's bedside nearly every day for the months he was in the hospital. She flew back to Panama on October 26, 1981, the day Harry was told there was no more trace of throat cancer but that he had leukemia. She returned to Denver on the next flight.

I was living in Darmstadt, Germany. On October 27, I woke up around 2 A.M. and couldn't go back to sleep. I went for a walk. Suddenly I found myself thinking, "Show 'em what you're made of."

The thought almost took on a voice of its own, one I hadn't heard in years. It startled me. It was one of my grandfather's favorite expressions. He had said it often to me, and would have said it had I asked his advice on whatever career, financial, social or personal dilemma I was wrestling with then. But I hadn't talked to him since 1977, four years earlier. I hadn't thought about him in years, or at least thought of him in nice terms. I was still smarting over the last time I heard his voice. I had ignored repeated pleadings from my mother to write him a letter, even a short get-well note, while he was in the hospital. I went home, resolved to do so. The phone rang a few hours later. It was the Red Cross, saying he had died of a stroke. I was on my walk when it happened.

All of Harry's grandchildren lived on a different continent then. Carolyn was in Panama with her husband, Bert T. Shoemaker, an Air Force officer. Their house was only about a mile from my parents'. My younger sister, Kathie, was in college in Virginia. Each of us got a similar visit, one last word of advice from the family patriarch—"Show 'em what you're made of"—a final goodbye from Grandpa, see you later, at the moment of his death.

Harry, like his father, J.N., was a lifelong Republican, too, but at the much milder "fervent" level. When he visited us in Arlington at Christmas 1963, a month after the assassination of President John F. Kennedy, a Democrat, and a Catholic, and a "loudmouthed Irishman," my grandfather announced that he would like to be taken to Arlington National Cemetery, not far from our house. He did not want to pay his respects. His Republican cronies had offered him five hundred dollars to put out the eternal flame.

My biggest mistake with my grandfather, I realized only in retrospect, was teasing him that I was a Democrat. I didn't care one way or the other, but I couldn't pass up the chance to graze in the delicious grass that could get my grandfather's goat. In 1977, I was unemployed and looking for a job in New York. I called my grandfather one afternoon. We talked pleasantly about the job hunt and that particular year's recession. I told him in jest that I had gotten so desperate I had applied for a job at the Jimmy Carter White House.

A few weeks later, I called again. This time I really was desperate. My mother was visiting him, and I needed to borrow money from her. I was broke, so I called collect.

"No, operator," I heard my grandfather say, "I won't accept the charges."

That was the last time I ever heard his voice.

If the measure of a grandfather's success is getting your grandchildren to think about you during their lifetime, and long after your own, then Harry Bolton was a great grandfather. I have struggled much of my life—I struggle even now—with why I couldn't get along with him. The feelings were often mutual.

I'm not sure he gave much thought to our relationship, but I sure have. Many of the simplest accoutrements of life can still flash an image of him in my mind. Handkerchiefs, for example, hold him in their folds. Each Christmas, he would gather my sisters and me around him, pull out his handkerchief and say, "See this. I put this in my pants' pocket twenty years ago, and haven't used it once." Money has his face on it. He would pull a money clip from his pocket and quiz us on the bills, who and what were on them, front and back. In my grandfather's fingers, I saw my first hundred-dollar bill, my first fifty. I sometimes got the impression—or at least I enjoy imagining I got the impression—that he used these bills as often as his handkerchief.

The battlefield that is my memory of him does not hold hallowed ground, but he is not forgot. The many times I blow my nose (I have allergies), I think about him. The few times I've seen a Grant and a Franklin, I think about him. When I look at my hands, I think about him. I have his hands, right down to the wrinkles, sunspots, veins, and moons on my fingernails. I used to fear that I have his personality, and to speculate that maybe that was why we couldn't get along—two of a kind. But now I know.

Only my hands are like him. The rest of me, I have learned, is a clone of the one person in his life he genuinely hated: his Indian wife, my grandmother, Sybil Bolton.

It wasn't fair on his part to hold that against me.

And I confess now that it wasn't fair on my part to keep secret my belief that he killed her, to hold it so closely that I never gave him the opportunity to defend himself, to prove otherwise.

And now that I was trying to prove it, now that Sybil Bolton was no longer the unmentioned member of the family (indeed, she was the only conversation), now that I was thinking about her and the Osages, and learning something about my hidden heritage, I came to realize the significance of what I saw that night in 1965 on my mother's bed.

I had come face-to-face with the Stigma, the mental cruelty and torture inflicted upon one young mixed-blood Indian by her white father, white stepmother, and white friends in a white world that hated Indians more than the Catholics, "niggers," and Jews who populated the bottom of their caste system of untouchables. The Stigma did not live on hatred alone, though. It also fed on fear. It flourished in their foreboding of the consequences, to career and status, of any news leaking out that there was an Indian skeleton in Harry's closet.

My mother was the key, the difference between the lockout of scandal and the openings of social acceptance by the right people. The figure who lay on her bed that night, crying for shame and apologizing for being an Indian, was the measure of their success in trying to suppress all trace of her Indian heritage, her mother's existence, to ensure no shortage of rungs on her father's career ladder, no whisperings or raised eyebrows, no cessation of cocktail-party invitations, no blackballs of applications for country-club memberships.

And I found that the Stigma was contagious. The sight of her, the sound of her pain, the touch of comfort I tried to give her that night, all of these imparted the Stigma to me, passed it to me like some virus, some demon not yet exorcised.

So I never made any attempt to learn anything about either my grandmother or the Osages—even when I came upon the Catlin painting of my Osage lookalike; even when my mother, for Christmas 1981, two months after my grandfather died, gave me a history book on the Osages, signifying that it was all right now to be an Indian, to be open about it.

I never opened the book. I kept it through years of moving. The cover is worn now from packing and unpacking. I always displayed it in my living room. But I never opened it.

ALL THAT MY MOTHER POSSESSES of her mother are an eye-sized diamond ring, and one photo that she found in her father's basement closet: a three-by-three-inch brown-and-white snapshot, whole sections of which are disappearing with age.

It pictures my mother as a baby, wearing a dark dress with a white collar, looking into the camera, as is a mixed-breed dog sitting beside her and her mother on a stoop. Sybil Bolton is holding her daughter on her lap, showing a large hand with long, elegant fingers. She is looking away, to the left, away from the baby and the dog.

The eye of the beholder focuses on an aquiline nose, and dark hair in the bobbed style of a 1920s flapper.

The cropping of the photo cuts off the top half of her head.

Sybil Bolton, a young Osage Indian from Oklahoma, had studied at Notre Dame Academy, a girls' school in Philadelphia, and then attended the University of Kansas, where she met Harry Ben Bolton. They married, and lived in Kansas City. Sometime after my mother's birth on June 24, 1924, Sybil left her husband and moved to Pawhuska, where she lived at 107 East 11th Street.

That, sadly, was the extent of my knowledge about my grandmother in life—apart from knowing that she owned an ermine coat, which she was buried in.

Of my mother's early life, I also knew little. After Sybil's death, Harry took her to Oklahoma City to be raised by her maternal grandfather, Sewell Beekman, and her step-grandmother, Leila Dauber Beekman—Sybil's parents had divorced many years earlier and her father had remarried. My mother stayed with them until she was nearly seven. Harry remarried then, and took her to Kansas City to live with him and her new mother, Cara Mae Bolton. About a year later, they returned to Oklahoma City. They stayed there until my mother's high school years, when they moved to Houston. She went to college at the University of Texas in Austin.

In her senior year, she met my father, an Army lieutenant back from combat in the European theater of World War II. When she graduated, they married. Their first communal home was in Korea, where my sister Carolyn was born in 1948. I followed a year later in Philadelphia, where my father was taking a master's degree at the University of Pennsylvania. I turned out to be the only boy, and the only one of my parents' three children born in the United States. My sister Kathie completed the family in Okinawa in 1957, one of the three years we lived there. My mother never returned to Pawhuska, even when we lived in the early 1950s at Fort Sill, Oklahoma, 240 miles to the southwest, and in the late 1950s and early 1970s at Fort Leavenworth, Kansas, 210 miles to the northeast.

I told my mother that I had decided to investigate her mother's death, to see if I could prove she was murdered. I did not mention, however, that I was trying to prove that Grandpa murdered her. We agreed that, henceforth, since there were so many names and family relationships involved, we would use only first names. Now that her real mother had come roaring, stormlike, into our lives, my mother was beginning to confuse—and annoy—me whenever she referred to her stepmother as Mother or Mom: I couldn't help but notice her tendency not to call her real mother that. Her real mother became Sybil, her stepmother Cara Mae, her father Harry, her grandfather Mr. Beekman. She had always called her step-grandmother Mrs. Beekman, so that was no problem.

When I mentioned how much money the Osages, including Sybil, were receiving at the time of her death, my mother gasped with wonderment, and asked with innocence: "Do you think she was murdered for her money?"

"If that were the case," I said, "you have to ask who profited from her death."

"Well, Pop and me," she said quickly.

An abrupt silence took hold as the implications came into focus at both ends of the telephone line. At my end, a reality check was taking place. It was one thing to plot, over late-night beer, how Harry murdered Sybil, but quite another to have him kill her in front of my mother, in sobering daylight. Do I really want to do this?

I would let my mother halt the investigation before it started. Breaking the stillness finally, I said, "Look, I'll stop this anytime, if you get too uncomfortable. . ."

"No," she said, "keep going."

Then she embarked on a story of hearing something as a child about Sybil. I asked her to start writing down these childhood stories, as they pertained to learning things about Sybil, of whom my mother has no actual memory. I wanted them to come to the reader through her pen, not mine, to avoid any temptation or tendency on my part to color them, especially any incidents involving her father.

What Kathleen Bolton McAuliffe wrote comprises the rest of this chapter.

MY EARLIEST MEMORY was of a time when I was about two and a half years old. I was lying in my crib and watching Mrs. Beekman tie my hands to the rails. She was determined to force me to stop sucking my thumb. As soon as she left the room and closed the door, I started sucking happily on my toe. Already by that young age, I had learned to adapt. Soon, my father came in and untied my hands. Once again, my beloved Pop had rescued me.

I was told of my arrival at the Beekmans by their cook, Stella. She was standing in the front hall, lined up with the rest of the family and servants to view the newest addition to the household. Pop carried me in. Solemnly, he made a slow procession past them, then stopped at the end of the line, where Mrs. Beekman stood. Solemnly, she took me slowly out of his arms—and I spit in her face.

That was the first shot in a hate war whose battles lasted until I was almost seven—when my father remarried and I finally left the Beekmans' house—but whose memories have never ended. I thought of her often during my child-rearing years, each time I saw *The Wizard of Oz*. Leila Beekman looked and acted like Margaret Hamilton, or at least the way Margaret Hamilton looked and acted as the Wicked Witch of the West. Except for a regional accent, she sounded like her, too. Mrs. Beekman was mean, manipulative, and menacing—and prone to rages. She had a broomstick figure and wore no makeup, except for a chalking of Cody's, a drugstore face powder, that coated a layer of Pond's cold cream. A bun of dark hair that she wound tightly atop her head each morning seemed to stretch her face upward, past a bump of a chin, a narrow mouth, thin lips, a sharp nose, and nearly black eyes. Only sleep relieved her of an apparent need to wear navy—either in a crepe shirtwaist dress or a plain tailored suit—and black old-lady, lace-up shoes. Two diamond pins, which she wore each day, and a two-to-three-carat solitaire ring provided the only glimmer to this dim star, whose light finally darkened in 1983, when she was ninety-seven.

I called my father Pop, because my half-aunt Retta, only two months older than I, already had claimed the more endearing name, Daddy, for her father, my grandfather Charles Sewell Beekman. My father hardly resembled a Pop. He often was mistaken for Clark Gable. Pop showed the imprint of his English and Scottish ancestry in his tall, slender figure, his very white skin and fine, raven-black hair. He had hazel eyes and thick, perfect eyebrows. His hands were long and tapering, and I loved watching his graceful gestures. During most of the years I lived with the Beekmans in Oklahoma City, he lived and worked in Kansas City but visited every weekend.

I called my grandfather Daddy Beekman. He looked like Jackie Gleason, but without the humor, or the ebullience, or the sound. He rarely talked at home. Others may have found him dour, gruff, aloof, even frightening, but children often see qualities in their grandparents that others overlook. To me, he was kind and generous, and I loved him dearly. He was a contractor, and also a crook. Like crooked contractors everywhere, he had made many powerful friends in the state capital. His funeral in 1942 would have been well attended by all the living luminaries of Oklahoma state politics—past and present—had he not been shrouded in scandal when he died.

I loved my grandfather's room. It had four windows from which I viewed the world, and was by far the prettiest room in the house. The furniture was French style and painted in pastels decorated with roses and vines. I loved to trace the flowers with my fingers. Mrs. Beekman's room and Retta's, by contrast, were serviceable oak and very plain. My room in the back of the house had maple twin beds—one for me, one for Pop—a maple chest of drawers and matching dresser. When my father was away, I slept in Daddy Beekman's room in a crib, and later a daybed, put there for me. He didn't use the room at night. He left the house each evening after dinner, and was driven away by his chauffeur, Arthur. I always tried to glimpse Daddy Beekman when he came downstairs to leave each night, dressed in his gray spats, gray fedora, pearl-handled cane, diamond stick pin and huge diamond ring. Each morning, he'd come home for breakfast, shower and redress for work—leaving the house this time in a conservative business suit.

One day when I was three, I found a small stool, which I carried into Daddy Beekman's room. I wanted to play with the silver comb, brush and hand mirror on his dresser. Instead, I found a number of snapshots under the glass top of the dresser. They showed a tall, somber girl with black hair, worn in bangs and a bob to the top of her neck. In one picture, she was wearing a dark, pleated skirt and a white middy blouse. I could see high cheekbones and sad dark eyes. In none of the photos was she smiling. Mrs. Beekman walked in then, and I asked her who the girl was. It was my first introduction to my mother. I had been aware there was no mother in the house for me—and no talk of her, either.

I heard for the first time my mother's name. It was the same as my middle name.

Where is she now? I asked.

She's in heaven, Mrs. Beekman said, and she then explained in simple terms that my mother had had a terrible time having me and never got well after I was born.

So now I knew the hideous truth: I didn't have a mommy, because I had killed her.

Your mother died of kidney disease, Mrs. Beekman said. Remember when you had kidney stones? she asked. She died of something like that.

I remembered my kidney stones, and they were terrible indeed. It must have hurt very much to die of them.

Soon I checked the tops of all the dressers upstairs. Except for a blue jar of Pond's and an orange box of Cody's, Mrs. Beekman's was as plain and bare as she was. I climbed up on my father's bed, leaned against the dresser, stretched on tiptoes to peer over the top—and there she was again, framed this time, looking at me with her dark, deep-set eyes. My mother's expression in this photo also was very somber. I remember her with a wide mouth and what seemed a long face. Her cheekbones were high. Her nose was straight and long. She was wearing a dark, sleeveless dress, and the finger of her left hand hooked over a long pearl necklace. Her hand looked as long as my Pop's. I was to spend many hours propped against the dresser, studying the face of my mother and comparing it to mine. I'd feel the end of my rounded nose, and decide that mine was like Pop's. But I had her cheekbones. She did not strike me as especially pretty, but I guessed she was elegant and handsome. I would wonder what she was like, and what it would be like to have a mother of my own, to have her as my mother. But I never asked Pop about her, and I don't know exactly why. He had never said anything about her, not even her name (and for as long as he lived, he never did, referring to her only on the rarest of occasions as "she" or "her"), and I must have known instinctively that death had made my mother an unbroached subject for him, had destroyed even his memory of her, had buried her very existence. Perhaps I was afraid to bring her up. Perhaps I just had come to treasure my childish fantasies about her and did not want adult reality to intrude.

But one day I finally asked. What was she like, Mrs. Beekman?

Your mother was much too tall for a woman, she said, conveying the impression that I was doomed to the same fate. She continued: Your mother had gorgeous white, straight teeth. She had bought an ermine coat, and she was buried wrapped in the fur coat. She was very generous. If you complimented her on something she owned, she would give it to you as a gift, regardless of its value. But she was very moody, and no one could tell what she was thinking. I was too young then to realize that Mrs. Beekman always tempered a positive with a negative. She would not allow anyone, including her then-three-year-old step-grandchild, to walk away feeling good about anything.

Another name went nearly as unspoken as my mother's—Osage. The first time I heard the word—and learned that I was one—was right before my Indian grandmother's visit when I was four. I didn't know I had a grandmother, in fact, until Mrs. Beekman told me she was coming for a thirty-minute layover at the Oklahoma City train station and wanted to see me. Her visit occasioned a nearly frantic preparation for me to meet her. I suspect Pop and the Beekmans were making up for past neglect of what I began to gather was a very sore subject. Pop, of course, said not a word about my Indian heritage, leaving it to Mrs. Beekman, who delighted in torture. The subject became a crate-size Pandora's box of pain she could now open and afflict me with. She would make me sit for session upon session, drilling me—dentistlike—on things she had told me about my grandmother and the Osages. She probably would not have subjected me so intensely to this torment had I not initially reacted to the news that I was an Indian with stone silence—ironically, an Indian trait.

She would look menacingly at me and say, Your grandmother is an Osage Indian, so was your mother. As I recall, she couldn't bring herself to utter the next clause in the sentence—"and so are you." But before those words had a chance to form in my own mind, she would demand, Now, what tribe of Indians are they? and I would answer dutifully, Osage.

Then she would continue, Your grandmother and mother are descended from the greatest chief the Osages ever had, and she would say his multisyllabic name, and, on demand, I would repeat it—but promptly forget it.

You were named after your grandmother, Mrs. Beekman would say, and your middle name is your mother's, she would remind. These, however, she would not ask me to repeat, assuming, I guess, that I knew my name by that age.

Your grandmother has been married three times, she would say, and her two children, including your mother, were each by different fathers. By this time, she was spitting out the words like seeds of a sour fruit. I didn't know at my young age that being married three times went beyond avant-garde in those days, especially in the moral Midwest. It was sinful and scandalous and must have driven this rigidly religious woman to her knees to be reminded that her husband—her first and only—had been number two in a threesome, of an Indian woman, no less. To this day I don't understand why she would want me to know about my grandmother's marriages. Surely she did not expect a four-year-old girl to discuss them in her first, or any, conversation with her grandmother. All I can assume is that, in her mind, she was preparing me for the next revelation, and trying to convince me—or herself—that, despite her wealth, my Indian grandmother surely was a godless savage. If her marriages were not proof enough, then her religion was confirmation. My grandmother was Catholic. The entire family was Catholic, my mother included, and I gathered by the expression on Mrs. Beekman's face that this was worse than being married three times, but perhaps not as bad as being Indian. To Mrs. Beekman, as to so many other people in Baptist-dominated Oklahoma in the 1920s, Catholicism was as close to hellfire and damnation as one could get without actually dying. For years, Oklahoma City had but one Catholic church that I was aware of, St. Joseph's.

These conversations whetted in me a thirst to know more about Indians. I had seen Indians before, rocking on the front porch of the Broadmoor Hotel in Colorado Springs, where I had spent two summers with Mrs. Beekman and her daughter, Retta. In all likelihood, the Indians I saw there were Osages, since Colorado Springs, I learned later, was a favorite vacation spot of theirs in their heyday oil years. Why didn't anyone mention them in the house? With growing years, I realize that an adult's silence or expression can convey to a child something far more meaningful, powerful and impressionable than any amount of verbal explanation. So I knew without being told that Indians were nonentities and never to be mentioned. I assumed then that Mrs. Beekman was protecting Daddy Beekman, shielding him from anything that might resurrect his grief over losing his first daughter, my mother, and that must have been the reason her name was never spoken, or why the Osages were never discussed. I learned later that my mother's death tormented Daddy Beekman till his own—because she had called him the day before she died, asking him for help, and he did nothing. My grandfather J. N. Bolton told me this when I was seven, and I heard about it again when I was fifty-seven. One day in 1981, I was walking out of the hospital in Denver with my stepmother, Cara Mae Bolton, after visiting my father there, and she just abruptly started talking about the phone call as if the subject was near at hand and something we commonly discussed. She repeated, nearly word for word, what my grandfather had told me fifty years earlier. This is what each of them told me was said:

Daddy, you've got to come, my mother begged. She was very upset.

I need you, she said, frantically.

Bring the car, she said.

Come *now,* she insisted.

He dismissed her urgency.

Oh, Sybil, he said, I can't pick up and leave my business. Next time I'm in Pawhuska, I'll come see you.

He was in Pawhuska a few days later—for her funeral. He never forgave himself for his inaction, and was always haunted by the thought that if he had come to my mother's aid when she asked, then maybe he could have done something to save her. As J.N. told the story, he implied that she had wanted her father to take her to the hospital.

Daddy Beekman talked to me just once about my mother. He swore that he had actually died once, and come back to life, when he and Pop were driving through Kansas in a blizzard and their car got stuck. He wanted Retta and me to understand about death and not to be afraid of it. He told us about the white light and plummeting down a tunnel. Retta soon lost interest and wandered off—she always had a short attention span. After she had left the room, Daddy Beekman put his arms around me and spoke to me about not being afraid of my mother dying and accepting that she was in peace.

Around noon on a cold but sunny day, my father drove me to the train depot to meet my grandmother and her husband, Mr. A. T. Woodward. Mrs. Beekman had assured Pop that I was well prepared, although he did not personally see for himself. He could see, however, that I was well dressed. I wore my navy-blue sailor coat and hat. My hair—jet-black and worn in bangs—had been cut to perfection the day before at my father's barbershop, where he took me each weekend he was home. I also had gotten a manicure for the occasion. I wore white stockings and patent-leather shoes. These I studied intently after we got out of his car and, hand in hand, approached the train and then walked down the line of cars until he found the one in which my grandmother was waiting.

Outside the door, Pop leaned down and said, You are to go in alone. I'll wait out here. Your grandmother and Mr. Woodward are the only ones in the car. You can't miss them.

I quickly stifled a whimper, knowing it would do me no good at that point, and not wanting my grandmother to see me with tears in my eyes. Why wouldn't he go in with me? Alone, I walked the length of the car, looking in empty compartment after empty compartment. Maybe she isn't here, I thought, and instantly my hopes began to rise. I was nearing the far end of the car, and approaching two large, dark spots covering the aisle rug. One of the spots moved and I realized, crestfallen, that they were shadows. About two gulps later, I was face-to-face with the figures the shadows were attached to.

They were seated at a table. Mr. Woodward, a rather heavyset man, with light, thinning hair, rimless glasses, and a red face, rose when he saw me, and smiled, but my eyes immediately swept past him to my grandmother. The look on her obviously Indian face was severe, and did not brighten when she saw me. My smile quickly faded. Her deep-set, dark eyes reflected neither kindness nor sweetness, warmth nor any hint of love.

She just stared at me, saying not a word, even when Mr. Woodward introduced me, saying, Kathleen, this is your grandmother, Kathleen, and—with a chuckle—Kathleen, this is your granddaughter, Kathleen.

She was actually a smaller version of Mrs. Beekman. My grandmother's dark hair was pulled back in a bun, and she wore a black suit and a small black hat. Around her shoulders was a silver fox boa. (When I saw the fur in later years, my mind immediately matched it with the garment I had stored in memory.) After Mr. Woodward introduced us, he immediately fell silent, and except for a throat-clearing and a cough or two, a creepy silence filled the compartment. My grandmother never opened her mouth, and after my initial hellos, neither did I. Her eyes mesmerized me. I stood in front of her, and we stared at each other. I doubt that I changed the expression on my face, either. I leaned my left arm on the table to anchor myself, and we continued to look into each other's eyes. She did not kiss me or touch my hand or hug me. My name did not cross her lips. She did not say hello or tell me goodbye. When my father opened the compartment door to tell me to come, failing to address either of them, I politely told Mr. Woodward goodbye and gave my grandmother one more probing stare. I turned around and walked out to join my father. I never heard her voice.

We stood outside the train car to watch it leave. Neither of them came to the window for a last look or wave. As the train pulled slowly out of the station, for a startling moment I thought I heard my grandmother wail over the train's mournful sound—at first slowly, *G-o-o-d-b-y-e K-a-t-i-e, g-o-o-d-b-y-e K-a-t-i-e;* then a little faster, *Good-bye Ka-tie, good-bye Ka-tie;* and faster: *Goodbye Katie, goodbye Katie;* and faster: *Goodbyekatie, goodbyekatie,* until the words grew faint as the train took this silent, stoic woman out of my life forever—I thought.

That moment on the train platform has haunted me to this day, and in all the years since, whenever I've seen a train, I've heard my grandmother calling after me. I'll never forget her, or any moment of my time with her. For more than sixty years, I have tried in vain to figure out what she was thinking, and what she saw in me. Was she rejecting me? Did she think that I looked too much like my father? Was I not Indian enough for her? I'll never know—but now that I am a grandmother myself, I do know what she was doing. She was imprinting her will and power into my very soul. My grandmother made certain that I would never, as long as I lived, forget her. Her eyes are impressed until eternity upon my mind's eye. I didn't then, but now I know that her way was the Indian way. Of course, I had no way of knowing then that my returning gaze was as Indian as hers.

The frustrations of my visit continued. My father had no comment, driving me back to the Beekmans in silence. No one there—not even my pals, Stella and Arthur—asked me about it. Daddy Beekman, who had been married to my grandmother, didn't say a word. I sat on his footstool for what seemed like hours that afternoon, staring at the back of his newspaper and hoping for a question and a chance to talk about my visit. Occasionally he would lower the paper and look down at me over the top of it, but soon return, without a word, to his reading. For the life of me, I could not fathom why my father did not take me into the train car for my visit, and I was dying for someone to tell me. Why didn't they speak to each other? My grandmother had been his mother-in-law. But I just didn't dare ask anyone. Or possibly I was too proud to ask. I thought about this puzzle months later, when Christmas arrived and in a great box I unwrapped a beautiful white fur coat, matching hat and muff. I had never seen anything so beautiful, and I threw my arms around my father, thanking him. He told me quietly, and with a frown, that it was not from him but from my grandmother.

Oh, I exclaimed, she must have liked me after all! No one said a word or questioned my remark.

As I approached five, Retta began to exhibit signs of following in her mother's footsteps. By then, I had learned ways to avoid much of Mrs. Beekman's wrath. I had inherited an important survival tool from my Indian ancestors—very light, quiet feet. I could enter and exit a room without anyone noticing. This was my number-one method of protection from Mrs. Beekman. By wandering in and out of rooms undetected, I was able to keep constantly abreast of Mrs. Beekman's violently swinging moods—without her ever seeing me. Most days I hid in the basement with Stella, who did the laundry when she was not cooking. Whenever I heard Mrs. Beekman coming downstairs, I hid under a pile of blankets positioned under the laundry chute. Stella always kept some there for me—not just for hiding, but for when I came flying down the chute from the second-floor linen closet in an emergency. The first time I slid down the laundry chute from two floors above, trying to get away from Mrs. Beekman, and landed with a splat on the concrete basement floor in front of Stella, I scared the poor woman to death. She decided it would be best to soften my landing. She didn't want me to hurt myself in my flight to avoid getting hurt by Mrs. Beekman. Stella protected me. No, ma'am, I haven't seen Miss Katie, she would say to my raging step-grandmother. Arthur often hid me under the lap robe in my grandfather's car. I had great friends in those two wonderful people—but my success in hiding made an enemy out of Retta. With me so often out of harm's way, she bore the brunt of her mother's outbursts, and Retta in turn took her frustration out on me. She, as I, had detected that in the Beekman house my Indian heritage was a source of shame, and it did not take her long to discover that it could be a pretty effective tool of torture, too. She began to taunt me with my middle name.

Sybil, Sybil, Sybil, you little Indian! she would scream.

You are an Indian! You are an Indian! she would chant in a bitter singsong.

I'm going to tell everyone I know you're an Indian! she would threaten.

She knew I hated the name Sybil with an uncontrollable fury. I hated it because Sybil died and left me with the Beekmans. I hated it because she had made me an Indian, and there was something obviously wrong with being one. I hated it because I sensed she had made my beloved Pop grieve for many years.

When the taunts first started, I didn't know anyone for Retta to tell, outside of my piano teacher, who looked as Indian as my grandmother. I didn't go to school yet. I had no playmates or friends. Retta regularly went to birthday parties, but I was never allowed to go. This shocked Cara Mae Massey, the beautiful woman who would become the wonderful and loving mother I had always prayed for when she married my father when I was almost seven. She asked me to tell her about all the parties I had had or gone to, but I didn't have the vaguest idea what a party was. As the years went by, however, I made many friends. Retta's threats to expose me were continual, and the thought that I might lose my friends, so long in coming, just because I was Indian, scared me.

And so began our cowboy-and-Indian wars. Whenever Retta called me Sybil, or reminded me that I was Indian, I fought like one. Unfortunately, our battles usually went the way of those of history, and for the same reason—Retta was better equipped. She was much larger than I in girth as well as height. For some reason, that Osage size that Mrs. Beekman had implied would be my fate was painfully slow in arriving. I remember once Retta knocked me to the floor and started stomping on my neck. Fortunately, Arthur was there to pull her off. When I got to my feet and recovered my breath, I shouted: Just you wait till I grow up. I'm going to be as tall as my mother, and then you'll be sorry. Over the years, Retta grew to be five feet eight, my mother's height, and I stopped at five feet two. My mother had failed me again.

Our last big fight took place in 1942, over Daddy Beekman's grave, as his coffin was being lowered into it. He had dropped dead on his office desk with a heart attack one day that spring, and Arthur put his body in the limousine, drove it home, carried it into the house and up the stairs, and put it on the bed in which Daddy Beekman had never slept. Mrs. Beekman found thousands of dollars in cash stuffed in his pants' pockets. He was to have been indicted the next day, and I imagine the cash was from some last-minute office cleanup he was doing when the heart attack struck. As I recall, one Oklahoma City newspaper reported his death under the headline "Beekman Beats Embezzlement Rap." After the funeral service at the First Presbyterian Church in Oklahoma City, all the cars lined up behind the hearse to form the cortege for the drive to his burial 130 miles north in Arkansas City, Kansas, on the Oklahoma state line. It was Daddy Beekman's birthplace and site of the family plot. Mrs. Beekman got in the first car, as did Daddy Beekman's gorgeous mistress. I had met her several times over the years, and on each occasion was smothered in hugs and kisses. I was twelve when I figured out where Daddy Beekman was sleeping each night. The woman invited me to her house for a meeting of a social club. She whisked me off to her bedroom, where, amid embraces and uttered endearments, I spied a picture of Daddy Beekman on her bedside table. I took in the room as well. It contained none of the serviceable oak that filled Mrs. Beekman's room. White satin covered her bed, headboard, her two windows and the dressing table, which held all the accoutrements of a beautiful and skilled seductress.

That gloomy spring day, riding three cars behind Daddy Beekman's wife and mistress, I saw a look of apoplexy grow over the face of my father, who was sitting in front of me. He was always such a prim and prudish man, and had such expressive chords in his neck, which bulged when he was upset. I am not sure what troubled Pop more: the death of his friend, former father-in-law and grandfather of his only child; the indictment that

Daddy Beekman had escaped but which was being played out in the newspaper articles about him; the appearance of his mistress at his funeral; or her cheek in climbing in the same car with Mrs. Beekman. Oh, to be a fly in that car . . .

Retta also was troubled that day, as I discovered at graveside. As my grandfather was being lowered into the grave—in those days, family was still allowed to watch—Retta suddenly shouted out: Now I don't have to put up with you ever again. I thought she was referring to Daddy Beekman, until I felt her hand on my back giving me a shove. I shoved her back, and kicked her. She kicked me and shoved me harder, which sent me teetering over the open grave. Things happened so fast that my brain had not yet registered my danger of falling. As I found myself hovering nearly directly over the coffin, all I could think was, Oh look, Daddy Beekman's almost all the way down. Rescue—yet again—came in the shape of Pop's hand on the back of my coat. Luckily it was buttoned fast. He grabbed Retta with his other hand, and held the two of us apart like the tussling children we had suddenly become. We were both eighteen then. I never had much to do with Retta again. Rest in peace, Daddy Beekman. You earned it.

My last close encounter with Mrs. Beekman came the day my father finally granted my fervent wish for a home and a mother of my own. This momentous day was May 28, 1931, when he and Cara Mae got married in the Beekmans' house. No sooner had Pop said "I do" than Mrs. Beekman clutched me to her bosom and sobbed, Oh, my precious baby, I'm losing you.

Mistakenly believing I was out of Pop's earshot, I retorted, Come on, who do you think you're fooling? It's me, Katie.

Suddenly I was over Pop's knee, and in front of my new mother and all the guests, he gave me a paddling. My father was furious with me for being so rude to Mrs. Beekman—but also apparently fearful of what she might do to me when he and Cara Mae left for their honeymoon. Pack a bag, he ordered, you're coming with us! So I got to go on the honeymoon. It was great—I thought so, at least.

Before he remarried, my father had sat me down in our room and asked me to promise him two things: As long as I lived, he made me swear, I would never admit to anyone that I had Indian blood—and I would never tell anyone that Cara Mae was not my *real* mother.

She did not exist for you, he said, using his name for my real mother. *She* never happened. Cara Mae and I brought you into this world. Promise!

These were easy promises to make, and to keep. I would never again have to mention the thing I had come to be ashamed of, and I was to have a mother all my own. And such a mother. She was, and still is, absolutely beautiful. She was tall, but not too tall, and blessed with a spectacular figure. She had long blond hair, gorgeous creamy skin, and almond-shaped, turquoise eyes. Everything about her was perfect. The night before the wedding, I said a prayer of thanksgiving for a mother all my own and a home of our own. And thank you, Lord, for not letting me stay one more day at the Beekmans! What paradise! I would have a dog to love as well. And as for the Osages, it would be easy to deny their existence. My only living link to the Osages, my only grandmother, ignored me—and my Indian heritage had brought me nothing but endless fights with Retta.

My Aunt Angela, my real mother's half-sister, once came to see us on a train layover in Kansas City. Mrs. Beekman had told me that she was the daughter of my Indian grandmother and her first husband. She was very attractive, not quite as tall as Cara Mae, very slim and brunette. She had the high cheekbones and deep-set brown eyes of my grandmother. Unlike my grandmother, Aunt Angela talked to me, letting me sit on her lap. I was seven. She told me that my mother went to a private, Catholic boarding school—Notre Dame Academy—in Philadelphia. My mother had been a talented harpist, and her harp still sat in my grandmother's living room. My mother loved the theater, Angela said, and their mother took both her daughters to New York many times for the theater and opera season. One year, my mother left Notre Dame to join Angela in studying music at a school in Italy. They lived in a convent. Angela told me that my mother had a beautiful collection of dolls from all over the world. Angela had the dolls now. She also had my mother's diamond-and-emerald bracelet. It was never made clear to me why Angela had these things and not my father or I. The bracelet, I assume, complemented a diamond-and-sapphire ring that had been my mother's and that I would inherit. I hadn't seen it yet—only heard about it from Mrs. Beekman and Retta, both of whom talked of it as an object of envy. I finally saw the ring for the first time when I was dressing to go to a high school formal at the Houston Country Club. My father got the ring out of the vault and let me wear it. I wouldn't see it again for nearly twenty years. I was thirty-five and visiting my parents in Denver from our home at Fort Leavenworth, Kansas. Pop tossed this magnificent ring on my bed one evening with no explanation or comment, except to warn me to insure "the damn thing."

Cara Mae drove Angela back to the train station, where my aunt bought me a Patsy doll. I hated Patsy dolls, but I didn't tell her that. Over the years, it served as a reminder of my mother's doll collection—I didn't care about the bracelet then. Whenever I looked at the Patsy doll, I wondered what kind of dolls my mother had collected, and why I didn't have them.

I finally took the question to my other grandfather, J. N. Bolton, who shared neither Daddy Beekman's reticence nor reluctance to talk about my mother. Grandpa Bolton, after my new mom and my father, was my nearest and dearest. I loved his merrily twinkling, mischievous eyes, especially the brown one.

Well, honey, Grandpa explained, when your father got the phone call that your mother had died, he got in his car and raced from Kansas City to Pawhuska. He stayed there a few days, until after the funeral. Your grandmother, meanwhile, called your Aunt Angela to stop by Kansas City on the way to the funeral and clean out your father's house. She stole anything of value—of your mother's. The silver, china, ornaments, that bracelet—all were taken. The only thing she missed was a ring your mother owned. So I guess the dolls went as well.

How awful, I thought, thinking only of the dolls.

That started him talking. When your father got to Pawhuska, he said, "those people" wouldn't let him in their house. Your father was left standing outside in the yard, worried sick. He didn't know where you were, or if anything had happened to you.

This time a very real hatred started up in me. "Those people" had been cruel to my Pop. It was a good thing I didn't know this before Angela's visit.

Is that why he wouldn't talk to my grandmother?

Oh, they just never got along, he said, even from the very beginning. I think your grandmother wanted your mother to marry someone else. All that money your grandmother spent to keep your mother on the East Coast and in Europe all that time, she goes off and marries a poor Kansan. Your grandmother tried to get some of your mother's money to pay for a second home in Arkansas. But your father stood in her way. Your grandmother stole you away from your father. That's why she wouldn't let him in the house. She didn't want him near you. But your Grandfather Beekman used some of his political influence to get a judge to say that you belonged to your father, not to your grandmother. It's a good thing your Grandfather Beekman has a lot of powerful friends, or you might be a little squaw right now, living with the Indians.

The thought terrified me. Grandpa Bolton then gave me two snapshots of my mother that I could keep for my very own. (I didn't keep them very long. They soon disappeared.) In one, my mother looked as I had never seen her in other photos: She was smiling. She was pushing me in a large baby carriage. Children being what they are, I remember more details about myself than about my mother. I was sitting up, with one hand holding the side of the carriage. I had black bangs showing under a bonnet. My face was very round, and my expression suggested that I was barely tolerating the ride. We were followed by a small dog. The other photo, Grandpa told me proudly as he handed it to me, was taken right before I was born. My mother was enormously pregnant, and looked very uncomfortable sitting on a porch. Absent was her smile.

She's so big, I exclaimed, looking at her protruding belly.

So were you, little girl, my Grandpa replied with a chuckle.

Is that why she died? I asked suddenly.

Grandpa grew grave. Something like that, he said. Your mother got very heavy when she was carrying you, and her body filled up with water and that killed her. She was very swollen before she died.

Again, I was pronounced guilty of matricide.

When I was eleven—we had moved back to Oklahoma City by then—the state conducted a census of Indian schoolchildren. One day in class, Mrs. Morgan, my sixth-grade teacher, announced suddenly, All those with Indian blood, no matter what amount, raise your hand.

I was at once embarrassed, ashamed and scared. I could see at least ten or more children put their hands up.

All right, Katie, what are you hiding? Get your hand up. I know you're an Indian.

Now I was mortified. She handed me and the other Indians a piece of paper. We were to take it home to be signed.

All the way home, I was almost sick from fear and shame. I walked with Regna Lee Simpson, who became a lifelong friend. She kept saying,

I'm so mad I'm not Indian! I'm so jealous of you, Katie. Why can't I be Indian?

Here, you take it home, Regna, I said, offering her the paper.

Ironically, this girl who had wanted so badly to be an Indian has the same Indian blood quantum that I have. But she didn't learn she was Cherokee until her father's death at age seventy-one. Her uncle told her then that her father had been so ashamed of his Indian heritage—and so worried about its impact on his career—that he swore his brother to secrecy.

I took the paper home. Not a word was said, to my relief. The next day, I dutifully returned the signed form. The day after, however, Mrs. Morgan told me in front of the class that my father had called her. If there ever was another such request, he informed her, she was to call him at his office—and never again give such a paper to me, or include me in any activity with other Indians.

What are you hiding in the woodpile, Miss Katie? she asked.

The same year, I looked up from my school desk one day, and saw Cara Mae walking in. After a few words with her, Mrs. Morgan told me to leave with my mother. She rushed me home and instructed me to bathe quickly and put on my very best church and party dress. She combed and fussed over my hair, then drove me downtown. It was not until she pulled into the parking lot outside the Oklahoma Club that she informed me my grandmother and Mr. Woodward were in town, and we were to see them at the club.

This time, there were other people at the table to carry on the conversation while, once again, my grandmother and I locked eyes. Once again, no kiss, no hug, no questions, no stories about my mother, not a word. We just sat and stared at each other. She looked more Indian than she had before—I thought she had to be a full-blood. She seemed shorter now, with more roundness. Her eyes were further set back in her head. There was a little gray on it. She wore the same type of unrelieved black suit as before. Mr. Woodward was talkative, and he and Cara Mae seemed to enjoy the occasion. He gave her a box of candy. My grandmother and I again didn't say goodbye to each other when we were ready to leave. I was simply immobilized and speechless in front of her. Before leaving, we gave one last, penetrating look, and Cara Mae and I left.

She said that when we got back to the car, I exclaimed, Good heavens, my grandmother is a squaw. But I don't remember that. I remember only my disappointment, and my sense of rejection again. For my birthday that year, my grandmother sent me a beautiful Italian vase. It had a rose entwined on the base of gold-flecked glass. It was very beautiful, but like other things connected to my Indian family, it, too, disappeared. I really suffered over writing the thank-you note to my grandmother. She must not have liked it, because I never heard from her again.

Sometime during my first three years of college, Arthur drove Mrs. Beekman to Houston to visit my parents. Lo and behold, with her was my grandmother! The first and the second wife were now friends. I knew nothing of this trip until Cara Mae told me nearly fifty years later. She also said that my grandmother was very charming. I also never saw or heard from Aunt Angela again. She and her charming husband, Nick Andretta, became friends with my parents, visiting them many times, but never when I was home. Nick, who had a traveling job, visited several times a year, without Angela. In the mid-1960s, Cara Mae told me that Angela had said on one of her visits that my mother had been deeply depressed before she died, and that my grandmother's dying words had been, "It was all my fault, all my fault. I caused Sybil's death."

My grandmother died when I was twenty-one years old. I was a senior in college but home one Sunday afternoon in early October 1945 when the phone rang. My father answered. I was standing nearby but—as was so often the case—unobserved. I heard him say, à la the actor he was so often told he looked like, "Frankly, Angela, I don't give a damn what you do with her body." "Her" was my mother, of course. Then he said he wasn't going to sue Mr. Woodward: "Kathleen doesn't need their damn money."

He hung up and said disgustedly to Cara Mae, "Those damn people never change." My grandmother, he explained, bequeathed to her husband her Osage headright, which entitled the holder to a share of the Osages' oil money. Angela wanted to sue to block Mr. Woodward from inheriting the headright and, instead, to keep it among my grandmother's Osage heirs—Angela, her son Tony, and me. Angela asked my father to join her in a lawsuit so I could share in the headright. We must do it for our children, she told him. But my father was having none of it. "She claims the money belongs to the Osages," he told Cara Mae. "I say he had to live with her, he earned it." As for my mother, he explained, Angela wants to bury her mother next to "her," but to do so she had to move "her" body and needed his permission. He didn't want any part of it.

Pop, unaware that I was eavesdropping, said not a word to me about the conversation—or the event of my grandmother's death. I've since wondered when they might have gotten around to telling me, if ever. It would not have been impossible for me to go to her funeral, six hundred miles to the north of Houston. But of course, that would have been out of the question.

On July 1, 1981, my father entered the hospital with throat cancer. The day before his voice box was removed, I brought his mail to him there, and included was the quarterly Osage oil royalty check. Pop had been awarded half of my mother's headright, and I the other half. He removed the check from the envelope, studied it a minute and looked at me. "You know, Kathleen," he said, "this money from her"—he started turning the check over, rolling it around end-to-end in his fingers—"has really come in handy at times." He endorsed it and asked me to deposit it in his bank. Then he looked at me with those unfathomable hazel eyes and said, "Your grandmother hated me and"—he paused—"with good reason." He said no more. The subject was closed. His eyes warned me not to inquire further.

Bodies of

Evidence

Chapter Five

From the notebook of a library sleuth:

JULY 15

A copy of my grandmother's funeral record arrived in the mail from Mr. McCartney, the Pawhuska mortician. To accommodate the size of "Mr. Johnson's old book," Mr. McCartney had made two 8½-by-14-inch copies, which had to be overlapped to be read.

The "Record of Funeral" was a form, with headings in print and entries in handwriting. Some of the ink had smeared. The left side of the ledger contained the kind of information Mr. McCartney had read to me over the phone: date, place and cause of death, certifying physician, funeral services, clergyman. The first item listed was the lifeblood of morticians: "Charge to," it said.

Sybil Bolton got to pay for her own funeral. The bill went to

"Estate." "Mr. & Mrs. A. T. Woodward and Harry Bolton" were added as responsible parties, in case her estate couldn't cover all the costs.

She was buried on November 12, 1925, five days after her death, and her funeral, based on the "Yearly No." notation at the top of the page, was the 112th in Pawhuska that year.

Next to "Name of Deceased" was a category for "What Race": "Osage Indian (#933)," it said. She was born in Pawhuska, which I hadn't known. Only her age—twenty-one—was listed, not her birthday, which I didn't know, nor did my mother.

On the right-hand side of the page were the funeral costs, which totaled $1,742.25. That struck me as a lot of money for a funeral of an American Indian in the West, but my grandmother did not get—or at least did not pay for—the kind of pine box so often shown in cowboy-and-Indian movies. Her casket was "Pershing Bronze," and its price was $1,500. The rest of the expenses included $150 for a "Grave Vault"; $50 for embalming; $15 for the hearse, $5 for a limousine to the cemetery, $5 for a "flower car" and $1.50 for putting the flowers in it and transporting them to the cemetery; $5.25 for a basket of roses; $1 each for four hand bouquets, and 50 cents for "empty boxes."

The bill was sent to the Citizens Trust Company "administrator," presumably of her estate, on December 12, 1925. It was paid February 20, 1926, by a Citizens Trust Company check from "E. E. Grinstead, Pres."

The entry for "Interment at" read "Temporary Vault." Just under that, filling a rectangle intended for a "Diagram of Lot or Vault," were these seven lines:

> May 12, 1926
> Removed from vault
> to Cript no.
> in Mausoleum.
> Body in perfect condition.
> No mold. Face perfect
> as when interred. No change whatever.

Now I understood what Mr. McCartney had meant when he told me, "Body in perfect condition, face perfect." He had considerately left out the "No mold" part. Old Mr. Johnson had reopened Sybil's Pershing bronze casket and sneaked a peek at her when he moved her body on . . . I did a quick double take at the date. It was exactly six months from the day of her funeral.

That was very odd, I thought. Why did it take six months, exactly to the day, to move her to the mausoleum? Had there been an investigation into her death, contrary to the impression Mr. McCartney had gotten from Mr. Johnson's "very detailed records." Had some kind of legal hold been put on her body?

I called Fleur to the balcony to see what I had uncovered. But before she got there, I found something even odder. The funeral form had been filled out in what appeared to be two different penmanships. Half of the handwriting appeared almost Jeffersonian in its large, sweeping strokes, some of the letters showing a hint of a tremor and bordering on the illegible. The other entries—especially those pertaining to price—were neatly printed, in smaller script, and much easier to read. The capital F in "Floral," for example, appeared as if printed, but in "Father Van Durme," the priest who said Sybil's funeral mass, it was written in fancy handwriting, with a looped wave forming the top of the letter and the F crossed all the way through, as Europeans do their sevens. In many words, e was lowercase, but in others, a small capital letter. The S in "C. S. Beekman" was written as if it were an ampersand, but in "Sybil" and "Suicide," it was a printed capital S.

I stared at the word "Suicide" on the line for "Cause of Death." Then I compared the u in it with the same letter in the two words that had been written just in front of it: "gunshot" and "wound." Next I examined the d's.

When Fleur got to the balcony, I asked, "Am I crazy, or is the handwriting of 'gunshot wound' different from 'Suicide'?"

She studied the words a long time, as I pointed out the common letters.

Finally she said, " 'Suicide' was written by a different person."

JULY 16

Among the puzzle pieces that Mr. McCartney, the Pawhuska mortician, had laid out for me was one I pursued immediately. He had called A. T. Woodward Sybil's guardian. Woodward was her stepfather, I learned from my mother, but why guardian? Sybil was twenty-one, and married. Why would she need a guardian when she had so many direct relatives: her husband, Harry Bolton, or her father, Sewell Beekman, or mother, Kathleen Woodward? The only thing I could guess was that, for whatever reason, Sybil had required a special legal status, and Woodward's guardianship was connected to his profession. Woodward was "a very prominent, very well-respected attorney in this town," Mr. McCartney had said. But Harry was a lawyer, too, albeit non-practicing.

The Osage history book at home was no help. It started at the Ice Age and proceeded through time in a slow melt, evaporating in the 1920s. (I read later that the Osage author John Joseph Mathews had been too pained by the tribal transformation that took place during the big-money oil years to write about them.) But at the Baltimore County library down the street, I found another book on the Osages. It had been written recently for young students, part of a scholastic series on Indians of North America. There seemed to be nearly as many pictures as words, but some of the latter gave a definition of the Osages' guardians.

Guardians, I read, were "local lawyers and business owners appointed to handle the business affairs of Osage who were declared incompetent"—and they had swindled their rich wards out of millions of dollars. In 1924, two dozen guardians were brought up on corruption charges by the federal Department of the Interior, but all wiggled out of punishment by settling out of court.

A subsequent paragraph stated that there had been a murder spree against the rich Indians called the "Osage Reign of Terror" that brought in the Federal Bureau of Investigation. The murders began in 1921 when an Osage woman "was found at the bottom of a canyon" with "a bullet lodged in her head." Her mother died "two months later . . . from poisoned liquor"; a relative was "shot to death in his car. Finally and most spectacularly, Rita Smith, her husband, . . ." The next page—the last of the chapter—was ripped out.

The Reign of Terror sounded like a good yarn but did not concern me. That was 1921. I wanted to know about 1924, a date closer to my grandmother's death. If Sybil had a guardian, did that mean she was mentally incompetent? And was Woodward one of the guardians charged with swindling? Could she have found out, and Woodward killed her?

Their names were not in the book—my first setback.

I called the National Archives in Washington and spoke to one of the keepers of Indian records deposited there. What could I find and how? He said many—but not all—of the Osage records were in the Washington archives, "but if you want to get a picture of Joe Indian on the hill, you have to go to Fort Worth." Most Indian material was stored at the Southwest regional archives there.

Okay, I decided, I'll spend my next vacation in Fort Worth. Fleur will love it, taking care of the baby in a motel room all day while I roam the archives in search of Joe Indian on the hill, or in this case, Josephine under the hill. But still I wouldn't be guaranteed of finding the guardians' names. More like it, after leafing through a zillion pages of bad handwriting, I'd learn that Woodward's name was not on the list.

The slope of my optimism was beginning to tilt downhill already.

After a couple of beers on the balcony, I thought of a shortcut to Fort Worth.

JULY 18

I called the author of the library book, Terry P. Wilson, a professor of ethnography at the University of California in Berkeley.

I told him about my grandmother's two deaths—kidney disease and suicide—and that I hoped to make it three. I was trying to find out why she had a guardian, I said. Was his book's definition of guardians all-inclusive: Were there any other reasons besides incompetency that an Osage might have a guardian?

No, or at least he didn't know of any. What year was I inquiring about, because the law on guardians was changed.

1925.

He let out an "Oh" that bordered on condolence. Then definitely no, based on what he was aware of. At that time, the Osage Agency took "applications from those interested" in becoming guardians, and there was only one reason anyone wanted to be a guardian—the easy swindle. "By far the majority" of them were corrupt.

So if an Osage was twenty-one or older, and if she had a legal guardian, then she would have been declared mentally incompetent?

Yes.

What about Osages under twenty-one?

Those under twenty-one—in other words, minors—were not allowed to manage their financial affairs.

Their money went to their families?

To accounts, but the accounts were controlled by their families, or by guardians, until they turned twenty-one. By the way, did the suicide take place on Sunday?

I don't know. I know the date but not the day of the week. Why?

Because many suicides of Indians occur on Sundays. It was odd that her death had taken place in the morning, but he was not surprised that she had not received an autopsy. He would have been surprised, in fact, if she had. It was all part of a "pattern of exploitation" of the Osages. As a matter of course, authorities did not do autopsies, coroner reports or police investigations on dead Osages—to make it easier for whites to murder them. It was "extremely likely" she was murdered. Any original allottee who died of a gunshot wound in Osage County in the 1920s was probably murdered. The preferred mode of murder in those days was poison, because it could be blamed on bad bootleg whiskey. And the murders are still going on. People in Oklahoma assume all Osages are still rich. He got interested in the Osages because he had been married to one. A couple of years before, two Osage relatives, the Cheshewallas, were found tied up and shot to death in their car after a robbery.

Where can I find a list of the two dozen corrupt guardians in 1924?

Their names might be in his other book, maybe in footnotes, or at least the source of the information would be footnoted in that book. Unlike the book I had, his other one was for adult readers, a scholarly work, researched and attributed. He apologized for not having a copy handy. Students had borrowed all the copies he had.

Does the name A. T. Woodward ring a bell from your investigations of the 1920s?

Yes. He had heard it before but couldn't place it.

JULY 21

I'm not sure what made a greater impression on me at the Johns Hopkins University Library in Baltimore—the cemeterylike rows of perfectly aligned, untouched Indian books that cracked with newness when opened, or the condom machine in the men's room.

If the police had dusted the books for fingerprints, they would have found none—or, after I left, only mine. In a sense, as I picked up books and my fingers tracked dust from covers to pages, here again were the footprints of an American pioneer, taking his first step of a long trek to a new life in a new frontier. And as with the first American settlers, others might follow. Already the trail back is crowded.

The 1990 census detected a nearly 38 percent increase since 1980 in the population of American Indians, which now stands at 1,878,285. Indian babies alone do not explain the population growth. What I was doing at Johns Hopkins comes closer. Something was afoot.

I wasn't the only mixed-breed Indian taking this trip. Tens of thousands of Americans had changed their ethnic identification over the past ten years. For example, more than 308,000 Americans declared themselves Cherokees—163,000 more than the tribe's official enrollment. Alabama experienced a 118 percent rise in its Indian population. Newspapers quote some Indians as being skeptical of the government's numbers—"the feds always get things wrong," said a Navajo tribal spokesman. But other Indians accept the figures as "a legitimate increase," in the words of a Cherokee tribal official, who attributed it "to general awareness and pride"—and to *Dances with Wolves,* the Kevin Costner film about the Sioux that turned many moviegoers into "wannabes."

But not one Indian tribal leader saw the population phenomenon, this westward expansion of the mind, as a possible solution to their considerable social and economic problems. If every American with any Indian blood were to declare himself or herself an Indian, and demand fair treatment and justice for other Indians, the U.S. government suddenly would find itself surrounded by tens of millions of voting, taxpaying, angry Indians whom it couldn't ignore, rather than the paltry number it disregards.

An Osage chief, Fred Lookout, suggested in the 1930s that the solution for Indians lay in mixed-bloods: "If you let your white man tongues say what is in your Indian hearts, you will do great things for your people."

Professor Wilson's "adult" book was one of the "untouchables" on the shelf. I quickly scanned the index for Woodward's name, then checked the *B*'s for Bolton.

If my grandmother was murdered, I found myself thinking, and the authorities had made it an easy killing by not requiring an autopsy or a coroner's inquest, how many other Indians had met the same fate? How many coffins hold slugs of lead or traces of poison in the remains of Indians officially dead of natural causes?

The pristine condition of the library books made me realize that the killers of Indians got away with murder because nobody cared, or wanted to know, just as they don't really care or want to know about the condition of Indians today. The condom machine in the stacks served as a reminder that we as a people are always able to find ways to insulate ourselves from exposure to the unwanted, the often tragic and horrific results of what we have wrought.

Sybil Bolton's name was not in the book, nor Woodward's, nor the names of the guardians brought up on corruption charges in 1924. On the three pages devoted to the Reign of Terror, I read this: "FBI agents began an undercover investigation of the murders months before a grand jury was convened."

I left the library and got a beer, and entertained myself with the thought of Eliot Ness, played by Robert Stack, posing as an Indian.

JULY 22

I'm doodling on my map.

First, with a light green marker, I highlight Pawhuska, twenty-five miles south of the Kansas line, a hundred miles west into Oklahoma from Missouri. Then I trace the lines of Osage County. It is the largest of Oklahoma's seventy-seven counties, 2,265 square miles, bigger than the state of Delaware. County population was 41,645 in 1990. No town in Osage County is included on an almanac list of U.S. places of 5,000 or more people. The county's northern and eastern borders are straight lines. The top edge is the Kansas boundary, then the line drops down, straight south, skirting the cities of Bartlesville and Tulsa, which forms Osage County's lower right-hand corner. The boundary then meanders northwestward along the Arkansas River, juts back sharply eastward around Ponca City—in Kay County, the former Kaw reservation—then shoots straight north again to Kansas.

Next I turn to Missouri and Arkansas, and let my marker flow eastward with the Missouri River as it bisects the state of Missouri—from

Kansas City to St. Louis. I do the same with the Arkansas River as it cuts diagonally across Arkansas from Fort Smith to Little Rock and then south-eastward to the Mississippi River. Then I follow the Mississippi as it courses south from St. Louis to the Arkansas River, forming the eastern state lines of Missouri and Arkansas. My marker lines highlight the northern, southern and eastern boundaries of former Osage territory in those two states. Everything in the states west of the Mississippi, south of the Missouri and north of the Arkansas belonged to the Osages. Their domain also extended west, encompassing the southern half of Kansas and the northern half of Oklahoma.

Then I backtrack from St. Louis, following the Missouri to Jefferson City, about a hundred miles to the west. From there, I track southwestward, tracing the Osage River. Much of the river is now underwater—a concept hard to fathom—covered by a reservoir named for Harry S Truman, born on former Osage land. So was George Washington Carver. So was Jesse James. So were thousands of Ozark hillbillies. The Osage River is one of the few places in the former Osage domain named for the original occupants of the land. There's an Osage Beach and Osage County, Missouri; Osage City, in Osage County, Kansas; an Osage, Arkansas. But that's it for the land the Osages occupied from the Ice Age to the early 1800s, when the Americans gave them this choice: Leave "or be declared enemies of the United States."

When the Osages heard in a dispatch to their resident French trader that the Americans were now their colonial "masters"—Napoleon Bonaparte unloaded the Osage domain and other Indian land on President Thomas Jefferson for $15 million—they burned the letter. They didn't think much of Americans.

Jefferson thought a lot about them, though, not as a people, but rather as a crucial piece of a jigsaw puzzle of ideas that fitted into an ideal. He thought more of Indians than of blacks. Jefferson, a black slaveholder, called the early Spanish habit of enslaving Indians "an inhuman practice." Unlike America's black slaves, including Jefferson's own, Indians were "equal to the white man . . . in the same uncultivated state," such as those found in the "North of Europe" (Germans, presumably).

Jefferson spent several pages of his 1787 book, *Notes on the State of Virginia,* defending Indians against a popular belief, expressed by a French naturalist, Count de Buffon, that all Indian traits, from mannerisms to morals, derived from having small penises. Jefferson, citing personal knowledge from having "seen some thousands myself," found male Indians "masculine" and "neither more defective in ardor, nor more impotent with his female, than the white reduced to the same diet and exercise." Indian women do "multiply less than we do," Jefferson noted, but argued that this was the result not of men's shortcomings but of Indians' unhealthy environment, including sudden, violent death in their constant warfare.

"Indian women, when married to white traders, who feed them and their children plentifully and regularly, who exempt them from excessive drudgery, who keep them stationary and unexposed to accident, produce and raise as many children as the white women," Jefferson said. "Instances are known, under these circumstances, of their rearing a dozen children." And therein lay Jefferson's hope for them.

Indians could do something that blacks never could—they could become white. With enough interbreeding, all trace of their traits—character and physical—would pale. But Indians didn't do agriculture like the slaves he and fellow southerners owned, so this made them "a useless, expensive, ungovernable ally." Besides, they didn't vote, whites did and whites didn't want them anywhere near them.

Jefferson saw his Louisiana Purchase as the enlightened solution to this problem. Indians would go on the western side of the Mississippi, whites would stay east, and they would live happily ever apart— at least until whites moved west onto Indian land. Jefferson saw the inevitability—and desirability—"for us to procure gratifications to our citizens, from time to time, by new acquisitions of [Indian] land." Jefferson reasoned that Indians eventually "will perceive how useless to them are their extensive forests, and will be willing to pare them off from time to time in exchange for necessaries for their . . . families." To ensure that this happens, he said, "we shall push our trading uses, and be glad to see the good and influential individuals among them run in debt, because we observe that when these debts get beyond what the individuals can pay, they become willing to lop them off by a cession of lands."

Eventually, Indians would run out of land. Unable to hunt freely and widely in the manner to which they were accustomed, and unable thus to feed themselves or support their communal, tribal lifestyles, they would turn to the one option left them for subsistence: private farming, like whites.

As silly as all this sounds, U.S. policy toward Indians as formulated by Thomas Jefferson remained essentially unchanged until well into the twentieth century—after it had destroyed the Indian way of life, not to mention tens of thousands of their lives.

Five tribes living in the Southeast—the Chickasaws, Choctaws, Creeks, Seminoles and, by far the largest, the Cherokees—gave Jefferson hope that his Indian dream was achievable. They lived in houses. They owned land. They owned black slaves. Thus they were called the Five Civilized Tribes. Their progress was Jefferson's hope for all Indians. The men had learned to raise cattle, fence farms, do arithmetic, and write, and "the women to spin and weave." Jefferson said, like a proud father, "To read *Aesop's Fables* and *Robinson Crusoe* are their first delight."

Still, civilized or not, slave-owners or not, they were Indians, and had to go. Their white neighbors in Georgia, Tennessee, and North and South Carolina, many of whom couldn't read, much less delight in, *Aesop's Fables* and *Robinson Crusoe,* wanted their land. In White House meetings, Jefferson informed the chiefs of the Five Civilized Tribes that he had decided to resettle them west of the Mississippi—Phase One of his "I have a dream" for Indians. Unwilling to coerce them, however ("It is essential to cultivate their love," he wrote), he made their resettlement voluntary. He promised them free land and freedom from whites if they freely moved west, but continued harassment and encroachment if they stayed east.

Jefferson said nothing about the likelihood of their being beheaded by the Osages, to whose land he intended to move them.

Jefferson worried about how the Osages might interfere with his plans for their land. "The truth is, they are the great nation South of the Missouri . . . as the Sioux are great North of that river," he said. "With these two powerful nations we must stand well, because in their quarter we are miserably weak." On July 16, 1804, only four months after the United States took control of its new territory, Jefferson met with a delegation of Osage chiefs in his White House office. He, of course, failed to mention what he had in mind for them. Rather, he sweet-talked and played the generous host, inviting them to tour "our country and towns toward the sea coast." He would spare no expense "for your comfort." The Osages would be treated to a show of force cloaked in hospitality.

"My children," he addressed them in general, and then specifically: "White Hairs, chiefs, and warriors of the Osage Nation. . . .

"The Great Spirit has given you strength, and has given us strength; not that we might hurt one another, but to do each other all the good in our power. . . . No wrong will ever be done you by our nation, and we trust that yours will do none to us. . . . We have no views upon [your people] but to carry on a commerce useful to them and us; to keep them in peace with their neighbors, that their children may multiply, may grow up and live to a good old age, and their women no more fear the tomahawk of any enemy. . . .

"May the Great Spirit look down upon us and cover us with the mantle of his love."

The man Jefferson incorrectly called "White Hairs" was principal chief of the Osages. The Spanish called him by a French name, Les Cheveux Blancs. To the Osages, he was Paw-hiu-skah, or Pawhuska, which translates as White Hair, as the Americans later came to call him, correcting Jefferson's pluralization of "Hair."

The Indian was born Gra-to-moh-se, or Iron Hawk, but earned the nickname White Hair at St. Clair's Defeat, also known as the Battle of the Wabash, on November 4, 1791. General Arthur St. Clair led 3,000 American troops to squelch an Indian uprising in the Northwest Territory. Never ones to pass up a good fight, especially against their least-favorite people, the Americans, the Osages joined the warring Indians—mostly Miamis, as well as Shawnees, Delawares, Ottawas, Iroquois, Chippewas, and Potawatomis.

St. Clair, who had the distinction of having surrendered Fort Ticonderoga to the British during the Revolutionary War, failed to post adequate guards the night of November 3 when his army camped on the Wabash near present-day Fort Recovery in western Ohio, a few miles from Indiana. While the Americans slept, the Indians crept into camp but waited till sunrise to start the killing. More than 600 perished. Another 300 were wounded. It was one of the biggest defeats that Indians ever inflicted on an American army.

One of the casualties was an American officer cut down by young Iron Hawk. The Osage leaned over the prostrate man, grabbed his hair to scalp him—and the officer's white wig came off in his hand. The Indian screamed, startled at how easily the American's hair detached from his head. At his scream, the officer suddenly resuscitated, and screamed, too, seeing he was about to be scalped by a giant Indian. The Osage screamed again, this time at the sight of what he thought was a man returning from the dead. His shock gave the wounded American the chance to run away, leaving the Indian holding his wig. For the rest of his life, Iron Hawk, now called White Hair, wore the white wig, thinking it an amulet against death.

Eventually it didn't work: White Hair was buried in it, along with a Bible he was given in New York, which he and the other Osages visited after their meeting with Jefferson. (The president had presented the Osage chief with a general's uniform, a stovepipe hat and an American flag.) An 1826 book quoted White Hair on the subject of his life's defining moment: "I felt a fire within me, and it drove me to the fight of St. Clair. When his army was scattered, I returned my steps to my country. . . . The fire still burns, but I must . . . die in obscurity among the forests of the Osage."

But not before he helped ruin Jefferson's dream of an easy exodus of eastern Indians west, and was forced to walk the Osages' Trail of Treaties.

Hundreds of the first wave of volunteer Cherokee immigrants to "the forests of the Osage" ended up on stakes. Scared survivors repatriated east, and soon word spread among the Civilized Indians about "those barbarians" out west. The eastern tribes refused to budge.

With a few tomahawk strokes, the Osages had brought Jefferson's policy of voluntary Indian removal to a standstill. By 1808, Jefferson realized that his Indian policy was a failure, all because of this "Nation of Bad Indians." He decided to use the one weapon on the Osages that in the end would fell all Indians—he gave them his word that if they abandoned some of their land, they could live in their remaining territory for "as long as the grass grows and the waters flow." Indians are suckers for someone's word—or were.

The U.S.-Osage treaty of 1808 marked the beginning of a long tradition of Americans swindling the Osages. The U.S. side refused to allow the tribes' longtime and trusted interpreter, Noel Mongrain, to be present at the negotiating session, which consisted of the Americans telling the Osages what they had already decided for them— they were to abandon their Place of the Many Swans and move seventy-five miles north, within monitoring distance of an Army outpost, later named Fort Osage, outside present-day Kansas City. Mongrain was half-Osage, half-French, had grown up and lived with the Osages, and was White Hair's son-in-law. His loyalties were to the Osages, not to the Americans, and he was fluent in Osage—qualities that disqualified him to the Americans. They insisted that the Osages' U.S. agent, Pierre Chouteau, who spoke little Osage, do the interpreting.

George C. Sibley, later founder of Lindenwood College in Missouri, observed the treaty-signing at Fort Osage on September 12, 1808, and offered this account of the Americans' negotiating technique with the Osage delegation of seventy-five chiefs and warriors: "Having briefly explained to them the purport of the treaty, [Chouteau] addressed them to this effect, in my hearing, and very nearly in the following words: 'You have heard this treaty explained to you. Those who now come forward and sign it, shall be considered friends of the United States, and treated accordingly. Those who refuse to come forward and sign it shall be considered enemies of the United States, and treated accordingly.' "

Chief White Hair, Sibley continued, "replied in substance: that if their great American father wanted a part of their land he must have it, that he was strong and powerful, they were poor and pitiful, what could they do? He had demanded their land and had thought proper to offer them something in return for it. They had no choice, they must either sign the treaty or be declared enemies of the United States."

They thumb-marked, thus ceding to the United States most of Missouri and Arkansas for $317 worth of bullets, gunpowder, knives, tobacco, blankets and paint. White Hair was given a gun and a copy of the treaty. When Noel Mongrain later translated the treaty properly for White Hair, the horrified old man informed the Americans that neither he nor other Osages would honor a fraudulent treaty. White Hair had had no idea he was giving away so much land, and accused the Osages' U.S. interpreter, Chouteau, of leaving that detail out of his translation of the treaty.

Unwilling to impose the treaty provisions on the Osages militarily, the Americans declared the treaty void and renegotiated—and brought Mongrain into the process. The U.S. government was even a little more forthcoming with compensation, although not much more. The new treaty was signed November 10, 1808, and went into effect nine months later. White Hair decided he wasn't going to move to Fort Osage. After the signing, he returned to his village at the Place of the Many Swans and died.

In this treaty, designed to make Missouri and Arkansas the Cherokees' home on the range, the Osages ceded to the U.S. government 52.5 million acres—seven-eighths of Missouri (all but the western sliver) and the northern half of Arkansas (excluding the northwest corner)—for $1,200 in cash, an annuity of $1,500 in merchandise, a guarantee to pay $5,000 in claims against the tribe for stolen or destroyed property, and American promises that the Osages could live in their remaining territory forever.

Forever lasted only nine years. In 1817, President James Monroe was drumming his fingers on the negotiating table. Missouri was a mess. American settlers had taken over the designated Cherokee homeland and were pushing the eastern Indians farther west, onto the remaining Osage land. A large band of Osages had settled along the Arkansas River near present-day Muskogee, Oklahoma (Fort Gibson was erected to keep an eye on them); these Arkansas Osages, as they were called, were launching devastating raids against the immigrant Cherokees. As a result, the voluntary western migration of eastern Indians remained stalled. Furthermore, the Osages had flown British flags over their villages during the War of 1812, and had traded with America's enemy. Something had to be done about these ingrates. Something was.

In 1817, while the Arkansas Osages were on their autumn buffalo hunt, a 600-man eastern Indian war party, comprised mostly of Cherokees, attacked their village, deserted but for 200 women, children, elderly and infirm. The warriors killed nearly all of the Osage women and elderly and many children—83 in all—and took 103 children captive, to be sold as slaves. The United States, its eye on yet another Cherokee homeland carved out of Osage land, pounced on the opportunity to declare the Osages a defeated nation, and to reward the Cherokees for their great military victory, dubbed the Battle of Claremore's Mound, after the Arkansas Osage chief.

The U.S. government forced the Osages to sign another treaty, using the promise of securing the return of their captured children as a lever. This one ceded a 1.8-million-acre triangle of land: their remaining sliver of Arkansas and a slice of east-central Oklahoma. But this time there was no compensation, only a guarantee to pay $4,000 in claims against them, and another promise about grass and waters. The government immediately sold the ceded Osage land, for which it had paid nothing, to the Cherokees for $2 million.

The Arkansas Osages, perhaps taking their cue from American promises, ignored this treaty. They stayed put and stepped up their attacks because the Civilized Tribes refused to return the Osage children, still slated for slavery. Meanwhile, a growing number of American settlers, having filled up Missouri and drifted onto Osage-now-Cherokee land, were getting caught in the middle, and tens of thousands of eastern Indians still were ruining the neighborhoods of southern states by their continued presence. The U.S. government decided on a solution, and Osage grass and waters suddenly ceased growing and flowing.

Half of the remaining Osage land, now northern Oklahoma, would go to the immigrant Cherokees and become the foundation of a designated Indian Territory; the other half, southern Kansas, would go to whites; the ousted Osages would be confined to a small reservation in the middle. Under threat of military subjugation, the Osages thumb-marked yet another treaty in 1825. In this one, they ceded more than 45 million acres—one-fourth of modern Kansas, one-fourth of Oklahoma, and their remainder of Missouri—for $7,000 annually for twenty years, without interest; $10,000 worth of worthless (to the Osages) cows, chickens and farming equipment; horses valued at $2,600; $6,000 in merchandise; and, of course, the usual grass-and-waters promise.

The Arkansas Osages refused to join the main body of the tribe on the Kansas reservation until 1839, but by then, continued warfare and a smallpox epidemic had drastically reduced their numbers and effectiveness—and by then, the United States no longer cared about the damage the Osages could continue to cause to its eastern Indian policy. In 1830, President Andrew Jackson had ordered the forced removal of these Indians, including some of his neighbors in Tennessee. The Five Civilized Tribes were marched under armed guard west of the Mississippi. Thousands died along this "Trail of Tears."

The Osages' "Trail of Treaties" had led to a fifty-by-one-hundred-mile swath of southeastern Kansas, about 12 million acres. Their reservation ran along the boundary with Indian Territory, now Oklahoma, from Kansas's eastern border with Missouri to about Wichita. They were free to hunt buffalo to the west twice yearly as was their custom, but the hunt was bringing back less food each year. There were complaints of starvation among them, and whites were encroaching on what little land they had left.

In an 1870 report on the Osages, their U.S. government agent, Isaac T. Gibson, delivered such an elegant, impassioned and insightful overview of their place in history that it took on the tones of a eulogy. In a sense, it was. But America wasn't through with them yet.

> This tribe of Indians are richly endowed by nature, physically and morally. A finer-looking body of men, with more grace and dignity, or better intellectual development, could hardly be found on this globe. In judging of their moral character, some facts in their history must be remembered. They were once the most numerous and warlike nation on this continent, with a domain extending from the Gulf to the Missouri River, and from the Mississippi to the Rocky Mountains; but they have been shorn of their territory, piece by piece. . . . Their numbers have been wasted by war and famine. This little remnant [numbering then about 3,000] is all that remains of a heroic race that once held undisputed ownership over all this region.
>
> *It is almost without precedent, yet strictly true, one great cause of their decline has been fidelity to their pledges.* More than sixty years [ago] they pledged themselves by treaty to perpetuate peace with the white man. That promise has been nobly kept—kept in spite of great and continual provocation. Individual white men have committed upon them almost every form of outrage and wrong, unchecked by the Government, and unpunished. Every aggressive movement of the whites tending to the absorption of their territory has ultimately been legalized. Thus, a kind of premium has been offered by the Government to enterprising scoundrels to ply their vocation at the expense of the Osages. The Government itself has been careless of its obligations, indifferent, it would seem, alike to its own honor and the security of the Indians. It has failed or neglected to afford them protection, and yet has allowed [the Osages'] persistent

fidelity to truth to tie their arms and render them powerless to protect themselves. . . .

Thus it will be seen that an exercise of the highest virtue, such as can hardly be paralleled in history, has placed this people between the upper and lower millstone. The process of grinding them to powder might almost be inferred a meritorious work from the indifference and apathy of many, and the exultation of some, who think themselves living in the light of Christian civilization.

JULY 25

"Pawhuska Woman Suicide" was the headline of a short article by the Associated Press on page 2 of the Sunday, November 8, 1925, edition of the *Muskogee Daily Phoenix*. The two other Oklahoma newspapers of that period archived in the Library of Congress in Washington, D.C.—the *Tulsa World* and the *Daily Oklahoman* (Oklahoma City), the newspaper that Sybil's father, Sewell Beekman, would have read—did not carry the story.

Although I had never regarded suicide in terms of days of the week, I was relieved to read that Sybil's death did not take place on a Sunday, about which Professor Wilson had wondered.

"Mrs. Sybil Bolton," the article began, "known to Pawhuskans as Sybil Woodward, committed suicide about noon [Saturday]. No cause for the act is known other than she was separated from her husband."

JULY 27

Saturday afternoon, at work, I was poking around *The Washington Post*'s news research library and came across *The New York Times Index* for the 1920s. I looked in the October–December 1925 quarterly volume to see if the *Times* reported Sybil's death, and had to chuckle that every boy thinks his grandma rates a *New York Times* story. There was nothing even on the Osages.

Despite my self-amusement at how ludicrous it was to think that the mighty *New York Times* would pay attention to some dead Indian in Oklahoma, I turned to the January–March 1926 volume to see if, instead, the newspaper of record belatedly reported her death. Since her final inter-ment took place exactly six months after her funeral, maybe there was some legal reason she had been placed in a temporary vault. Maybe a "hold" had been put on her body while an investigation was being com-pleted, and the news came out later.

I read this entry for the January 8, 1926, issue: "First wit-nesses heard in Federal Grand Jury investigation of murders of Osage Indians. . . . Federal Govt investigation reveals reign of terror."

The *Post* library's microfilm collection of *New York Times* issues did not go back as far as its set of *The New York Times Index,* so I checked Washington newspapers of that month. The January 2, 1926, *Evening Star* carried this front-page story by the Associated Press:

> PAWHUSKA, Okla., January 2—One hundred and forty sub-poenas have been issued in the past three days in Osage County in connection with the Federal investigation of the Osage In-dian murder cases, it was learned here today. . . . The arrest of several men, some of them prominent, was expected within 48 hours.

The AP reported on subsequent days that "the Osage murder mys-tery [was] as dramatic as any created by a novelist's pen" and that "the United States Government's investigation of an alleged death ring in the Osage country of Oklahoma has revealed a condition that will astound the Nation when the details are known. . . . It was indicated officially that the grand jury's activities have been so successful thus far that the Government expects the Osages to be protected forever from the cupidity of white men, which, it is charged, revealed itself progressively through many devious methods to defraud and finally cropped out in a sinister conspiracy of death that levied on the lives of the Indians, known as the world's richest people."

Although the deaths had taken place in the early 1920s, it was not until a year before the convening of the federal grand jury in January 1926 that the FBI began "a definite effort to run the mystery to earth." Profes-sor Wilson had said in his "adult" book that the FBI launched an under-cover investigation "months" before the grand jury.

My mother recalled being told that Sybil had separated from Harry

Bolton and moved to Pawhuska with the baby about six months before her death on November 7, 1925.

This meant that Sybil's return to Pawhuska had coincided with the FBI investigation, and her last days with the undercover operation.

This put my grandmother, and my mother, in the midst of the Reign of Terror.

Chapter Six

AUGUST 2

A month after all of this started for me. Today is my last day of work before a two-week vacation at the beach in Nags Head, North Carolina, with my family and parents. I have promised to bring my notes and books and go through them with my mother. She will tell me her childhood stories that I never had ears for, and I will try to mine her memory for more details.

A curious thing has been happening to me. As my interest in, and knowledge of, Sybil and the Osages grow stronger, I grow weaker. I've been getting weepy on my hour-long drives to work in downtown Washington, after a few bars of a song, or a few songs at a bar.

I've traced this leak of emotion to fatigue: too many beery late- or all-nighters under my balcony lightbulb, poring over books, government reports, copies of old magazine articles, newspaper stories, my own notes, searching for clues, Sybil's fingerprints. I have become a Sherlock Holmes whose magnifying glass is a green bottle of imported beer. In my single-minded pursuit of Sybil's death, the things I am ignoring in my life have begun to multiply, press and finally breach through the tear ducts. I am beginning to feel that I am pursuing more than "my project," as lately I have come to call my investigation.

At first, I thought it was my mother I was reacting to, the violence and tragedy that had engulfed and shaped her, defined her destiny—and by extension, us, me. All the history of hatred and discrimination against a people—until now viewed from the safe, impersonal distance of books, television and movies—was suddenly in my face, and it was personal and threatening, and present, like an intruder bent on harm.

But soon my sadness shifted to my grandmother. Was it possible, I'd ask myself driving down the Baltimore–Washington Parkway, to simulta-neously fall in love with and grieve for a woman from across the chasm separating life from death, the present from the past—whom I had never met, never seen, never known anything about, and never until now thought or cared about?

Yes, it was, yes, I had already, as down would drip another tear, and I'd wipe my eyes and hope that passing drivers wouldn't see me. After the first couple of times of this, I grew annoyed at my gushiness. It was sixty-six years ago, for crying out loud, enough already, knock it off, and I'd silently run through a host of holy names and curse words.

What is happening to me?

This couldn't be just my grandmother, I finally decided. Something else, beyond her, is stirring inside me. I began to ask myself how my life might have differed had she been in it. As an Army brat, I grew up in Philadelphia; Fort Bragg, North Carolina; Fort Sill, Oklahoma; Fort Leav-enworth, Kansas; El Paso; Okinawa; Arlington, Virginia. As a student, I lived in Nashville; as a soldier, Fort Jackson, South Carolina; Monterey, California; San Angelo, Texas; and Berlin, Germany; and since the Army, with my parents in Fort Leavenworth again and in the Panama Canal Zone; then New York; Berlin again; Mannheim and Darmstadt, Germany; Alexandria, Virginia; Arlington again; and finally Baltimore. Despite liv-ing in forty-seven different residences—the longest time in one house, only about three years—I've been homeless, in a sense, rootless. I've never felt I was from anywhere. My grandmother, I was sure, would have filled that one empty place in my very full life. She would have brought with her a sense of place and belonging. She would have brought me to the Osages. She would have brought me home.

Was she doing so now? I wondered with a spinal chill. Were these tears the watering of ancestral Osage seeds, now shooting into life, taking root, sprouting to the light? I found myself often repeating a quote from an Osage principal chief, Joseph Paw-ne-no-pashe, Not Afraid of Pawnees, also called Governor Joe and Big Hill Joe. Referring to the head of a Jesuit mission school for the Osages on their Kansas reservation, Governor Joe said: "It took Father Schoenmakers 15 years to make a white man out of me, and it will take just 15 minutes to make an Osage out of myself."

This mental wrestling I was doing—was it my body trying to expel something newly introduced, like a transplanted organ? Was the white American world that constituted my being again trying to drive out, as it did historically, the Indians in its midst? Had I become a battlefield for a new war between the Indians and the cavalry in my head?

AUGUST 4

Beach reading.

Like all American kids, I'm a sucker for Custer stories. My reason, though, is different from our national, morbid fascination with Custer's Last Stand (my favorite gory detail: there were so many arrows sticking out of the bodies that the soldiers who discovered them thought, from a distance, that they were riding toward thickets of cactus).

I lived in Custer's house.

And it was haunted.

By Phil Sheridan's wife.

This story is not as juicy as it sounds. Lieutenant Colonel George Armstrong Custer and General Philip H. Sheridan lived in the same house, at different times, at Fort Leavenworth, Kansas. A plaque by the front door of the Old Sutler's House, as the place is now called, lists all of its occupants, including my father. Custer lived in the house in 1867, and Sheridan from 1868 to 1869, when he was the southwestern U.S. Army commander. The house is a grand wooden structure, painted white. Its wraparound porch accommodates several swings. The interior has not cramped even the largest of generals' families who have lived in it, or the regiment of Army servants who have worked in it. Its parklike front yard, with a gazebo-style, cottage-size bandstand at the far end, is often filled with hardened convicts from the military prison, tending the lawn and gardens.

Mrs. Sheridan was supposed to have died in a small bedroom at the top of the stairs, across a long hallway from the master bedroom. General Sheridan appeared to be as sensitive toward his wife as he was toward Indians. He once encouraged buffalo hunters to empty "the Indians' commissary": "Let them kill, skin and sell until the buffalo are exterminated. Then your prairies can be covered with speckled cattle and the festive cowboy." Mrs. Sheridan was dying, and her death imminent, so the story goes. Rather than stay at her bedside, the general went to Chicago to play poker with his cronies; she died while he was away, and has been haunting the house since.

For more than 120 years, the rumor of her ghostly presence in the Old Sutler's House has passed from each departing resident to each new arrival, who, soon enough, has confirmed the story. Doors slam in empty bedrooms. Empty rocking chairs rock. Household pets refuse to enter the little bedroom. When my parents lived in the house in the early 1970s, the closed bathroom door would swing open on my mother when she was taking a shower—alone in the house. One time, my parents returned from a trip, unpacked their suitcases, but left them in a corner of the bedroom to be put away the next day. The empty bags started rocking back and forth, and our dog just sat there in front of them, mesmerized, cocking his head back and forth, almost to the sway of the suitcases. My niece April, Carolyn's younger daughter, slept in Mrs. Sheridan's room on visits. April was a baby then, and she would play all night in that room, laughing, giggling, burbling with delight.

So when I came across a Custer-Sheridan-Osage story that took place when Sheridan lived in the house, it drew me like a magnet. I was astounded to learn that the Osages rescued Custer's career from ruin by helping him win his first major victory over Indians, thus saving him for "the last really good time [Indians] ever had," his massacre at the Little Big Horn eight years later. Custer's "It Doesn't Take a Hero" memoir, *My Life on the Plains,* tells the story, and offers one of the only looks in popular American literature at the Osages in action. Even Custer's egocentricity, ethnocentrism, anti-Indian bias and use of popular racist language were not able to conceal the strength, dignity, grace, superior intelligence and courage of the Osage Indians.

In the winter of 1868, General Sheridan ordered a military campaign on the Plains against warring Cheyennes, Comanches, Arapahos and Kiowas. Cavalry detachments, one commanded by Custer, set out to "fight the devil with fire," as he put it, but could not locate their winter villages.

Custer had been recently ruined by a court-martial, but Sheridan decided to give his Civil War buddy a second, and last, chance with this campaign. Sheridan also decided to ask Osages to act as guides to save his troops the hardship—and himself the failure—of roaming around the snow-covered plains all winter without finding the Cheyennes; higher-ups had already criticized Sheridan's decision to launch an Indian war in the dead of winter.

Custer described the Osages as "reduced in power" and confined to a "well-chosen" reservation in Kansas after "engaging in long and devastating wars with the whites and with other hostile bands." These "reservation Indians," now "living peaceably and contentedly," he added, "were most generally the objects of hatred in the eyes of their more powerful and independent neighbors of the Plains . . . [who] did not hesitate to visit their wrath" upon them. The Cheyennes "had been particularly cruel and relentless in their wanton attacks upon the Osages." Thirteen Osages, including a chief, Little Beaver, and a tribal "wise man," Hard Rope, signed on with Custer and his eight hundred troopers of the Seventh Cavalry. They did so not out of love for Custer and the Army but out for revenge. The wife of one of the Osages recently had been dismembered by raiding Cheyenne warriors.

They tracked their horses through deep, blowing snow for days, south from Dodge City, Kansas, across the Oklahoma panhandle, then making a fishhook swing into Texas and following the Washita River twenty miles back into Indian Territory. Walking three hundred to four hundred yards in front were two Osages, who "seemed to glide rather than walk over the snow-clad surface." When the Osages told Custer that "our enemy's village was probably not far away, and most likely was in the valley in which we then were," Custer ordered a night pursuit. A freeze followed nightfall, so the main body of troopers, whose horses were noisily breaking through the crusted surface of the snow, dropped a half-mile behind the advance party of Osages and white scouts.

Custer rode with the point men. "We rode mile after mile," he wrote. Suddenly the two Osages stopped, and "we were furnished an example of the wonderful and peculiar powers of the Indian."

"What's the matter?" Custer whispered after a tiptoe to them.

"Me don't know," one Osage said, "but me smell fire."

Custer and some of his officers started "sniffing the air" but smelled nothing. They decided "that our guide was mistaken . . . probably frightened, but we were unable to shake the confidence of the Osage warrior in his first opinion." Custer ordered the crawl continued.

A half-mile or more later, the scene was repeated. The Osages stopped, and Custer crept up to them.

"Me told you so," said the Osage with the good nose and command of English. He was pointing to a stand of timber about seventy-five to a hundred yards to his left, where, "sure enough," the embers of "a wasted fire" smoldered. Custer gulped at the thought that he had just ridden to within pistol range of sleeping Indians whom the U.S. Army had pursued for weeks.

"We were too near already to attempt to withdraw undiscovered," he said. "Our only course was to determine the facts at once, and be prepared for the worst."

He called for volunteers for a suicide mission: Scout out the woods, see if you trip over any sleeping Indians. "All the Osages and a few of the [white] scouts quickly dismounted, and with rifles in readiness and fingers on the triggers silently made their way to the nearest point of the timber, Little Beaver and Hard Rope leading the way." The Osages soon emerged from the woods and waved to Custer to approach.

Studying the fire and numerous pony tracks in the snow around it, the Osages decided it had been built by Indian boys watching a herd of ponies, which meant that the main body of Indians would be two or three miles away.

"Again we set out," Custer wrote, "this time more cautiously, if possible, than before." By now, the Osages had won Custer's complete confidence, at the expense of that he had had in his white scouts. These he ordered to drop back, and the main body and the scouts to proceed "at a greater distance in rear." Only Custer and the Osages remained in front, and he accompanied the two Osages at point, "I mounted, they on foot, keeping at the head of my horse. Upon nearing the crest of each hill, as is invariably the Indian custom, one of the guides would hasten a few steps in advance and peer cautiously over the hill."

Custer suddenly noticed the Osage who had smelled the fire "place his hand above his eyes as if looking intently at some object, then crouch down and some creeping back to where I waited for him."

"What is it?" Custer asked.

"Heaps Injuns down there."

Custer crept to the crest, squinted into "the valley beyond," and saw only the blackness of night. "Turning to the Osage, I inquired in a low tone why he thought there were Indians there."

"Me heard dog bark."

This time Custer strained his ears. "I waited quietly to be convinced; I was assured, but wanted to be doubly so. I was rewarded in a moment by hearing the barking of a dog in the heavy timber off to the right . . . and soon after I heard the tinkling of a small bell" that lead ponies of a herd wear around their necks. When his eyes had adjusted to the darkness of the distance below him, he spotted the animals.

"I turned to retrace my steps when another sound was borne to my ear through the cold, clear atmosphere of the valley—it was the distant cry of an infant; and savages though they were and justly outlawed by the number and atrocity of their recent murders and depredations on the help-less settlers of the frontier, I could not but regret that in a war such as we were forced to engage in, the mode and circumstances of battle would pos-sibly prevent discrimination."

Custer left the Osages "to keep a careful lookout" at the crest, but sent one back to the main body with word that the commander wanted his officers to join him up front. He had each officer take off his saber, creep to the crest with him and peer over the edge "in order that they might indi-vidually learn as much as possible of the character of the ground and the location of the village." Then he gathered them in a circle around him and told them his plan of attack. He wanted the command split equally into four detachments, each numbering two hundred troopers. They would surround the village "to attack the Indians from all sides."

One aspect of his battle plan was curiously similar to advice that Lit-tle Beaver, the Osage chief, had given him a few hours earlier at the outset of the night march. Little Beaver had "strongly advised that we delay fur-ther pursuit until daylight," Custer wrote. "When asked for his reasons for favoring such a course, he could give none of a satisfactory nature. I then concluded that his disinclination . . . arose from the natural reluctance, shared by all Indians, to attack an unseen foe, whether concealed by darkness or other natural or artificial means of shelter. Indians rarely attack between the hours of dark and daylight, although their stealthy movements through the country either in search of an enemy or when attempting to elude them are often executed under cover of night."

Although his comments appeared to disparage Little Beaver's "disinclination" for a nighttime assault, a strategy that gained favor in Custer's hero days of the Civil War, he ordered his officers to attack . . . at daybreak, hours away. It was by then after midnight. The waiting was to commence immediately.

After taking a nap, Custer spotted the Osages sitting under a tree "a little distance from the ground occupied by the troops. . . . They were wrapped up in their blankets, sitting in a circle, and had evidently made no effort to sleep during the night." Custer joined his new "friends." They were talking in Osage, and scarcely acknowledged his presence. He asked what they were talking about and got no answer. Unaccustomed to being ignored, he walked away. "It was plain to be seen that they regarded the occasion as a momentous one and that the coming battle had been the sole subject of their conference."

Custer's assumption was not entirely correct. They talked about the battle, yes, but also about how little they trusted Custer, his good faith and fighting ability. After the battle, he again asked one of the English-speaking Osages what they had discussed that night, and this was his answer, as related by Custer: "With the suspicion so natural and peculiar to the Indian nature, they had . . . concluded that we would be outnumbered by the occupants of the village. Disaster seemed certain in the minds of the Osages to follow us. . . . To prevent a complete defeat of our forces . . . [and] to save ourselves," Custer would offer to turn the Osages over to the Cheyennes. "The question with them was to secure such a position in the attack as to be able promptly to detect any move disadvantageous to them . . . [and thus] take advantage of circumstances and save themselves as best they might."

So, on the assumption that the front row offers the best view, the Osages decided to help lead the attack, going into battle behind the standard-bearer. This way, they reasoned, if the charge took the course they feared, they could just keep right on going, past the village and over hill and horizon, or at least die killing, far faster and less painful than the alternative, to die captive.

By the time "faint signs of approaching day were visible," the Osages had transformed themselves into warriors, dressing "in their war costume" and "painting their faces in all imaginable colors." The lines formed for the attack, with the Osages taking up position with the forward platoons, behind the standard-bearer; behind Custer rode the regimental band, with instructions to play "the rollicking notes" of "Garry Owen" at the sound of the first shot.

The detachment eased over the edge of the hill. Gradually they came near enough to the village "to plainly catch a view here and there of the tall white lodges as they stood in irregular order among the trees." Custer turned in his saddle to order the bandleader, "his cornet to his lips," to sound the charge, "when a single rifle shot rang sharp and clear on the far side of the village from where we were." The band launched into "Garry Owen" as the cavalrymen launched the charge, and the air at once filled with the sound of music, gunfire, "the loud and continuous cheers" of the soldiers, and soon "the defiant war-whoop of the [enemy] warriors."

His men quickly took "actual possession of the village and its lodges." But the killing of their occupants took several hours. At the sound of the charge, many Indians "seized their rifles, bows and arrows, and sprang behind the nearest trees, while some leaped into the stream, nearly waist deep, and using the bank as a rifle-pit began a vigorous and determined defense . . . pouring in a rapid and well-directed fire from their stations . . . [and fighting] with a desperation and courage which no race of men could surpass."

Around 10 A.M., Custer saw one of the Osages, a "tall, fine-looking warrior," riding furiously toward him, "waving wildly overhead something I could not distinguish." When the Indian stopped beside Custer, he saw what it was: "an entire scalp, fresh and bleeding." This was the Osage whose wife had been killed by Cheyennes, and for whom the other Osages had joined Custer. By tribal custom, the Osage had not been allowed to don war paint or "war costume" until his wife's murder was avenged by scalping a member of the guilty tribe. So done, the next time Custer saw the Osage "on the field, his face was completely hidden under the stripes of yellow, black, and vermilion, the colors being so arranged, apparently, as to give him the most hideous visage imaginable."

Custer's men killed 103 warriors, 16 women and a "few" children—as well as 875 Cheyenne horses—in and around the fifty-one lodges of the village, including the Cheyenne chief, Black Kettle. Custer said only one woman was purposefully killed, "a squaw endeavoring to make her escape, leading by the hand a little white boy, a prisoner." When she saw that escape was impossible, "with savage malignity . . . she drew from beneath her blanket a huge knife and plunged it into the almost naked body of her captive." A trooper's carbine delivered "retributive justice." Among the 21 of Custer's men killed was Captain Louis Hamilton, a grandson of Alexander Hamilton, shot out of his saddle and dead before he hit the ground.

The Battle of the Washita would be Custer's career salvation, his first major military victory over Indians and touted as a devastating defeat to the warring tribes. Most of the Osages left Custer and returned home after Sheridan declared his winter campaign a victory and called it off. According to the Kansas State Historical Society, "some of these Osages" remained with Custer until his, and their, bitter end at the Little Bighorn in 1876.

The battle that saved Custer's career—and him for the ages—also spawned one of America's best-known, but most unfortunate, sayings.

After the Battle of the Washita and the subsequent surrender of the warring tribes, a Comanche chief, Toch-a-way, or Turtle Dove, was taken to General Sheridan.

Professing his loyalty, the chief said, "Me Toch-a-way, me good Indian."

Sheridan looked at him with scorn and, within hearing distance of a reporter, said, "The only good Indians I ever saw were dead."

A U G U S T   8

A few days before leaving for Nags Head, I had called the Pawhuska Public Library and asked one of the librarians, A. Yvonne Rose, to check if back copies of the local newspaper were on file there and if the newspapers had reported Sybil's death.

Call back in about a week, she said. The library staff was down to just a couple of ladies, and it would take them that long to hunt down the articles and type them. Our copy machine isn't working, she said. Yvonne made clear, her drawling voice taking on a firm tone, that this was not a free service. The charges would be about four dollars, including postage, she said.

I called from the kitchen phone at the beach house. My mother and father sat at the kitchen table with me, and Fleur stood at the entrance to the dining room, keeping an eye on the baby.

"Denny, I've got some news for you here," Yvonne said. The Pawhuska newspaper, the *Daily Journal-Capital,* had reported Sybil's death on page 1 on Sunday, November 8, 1925, under the headline "Despondent Takes Life by Shooting; Death Came Quick," and the sub-headline "Member of Well-Known Family Destroys Self in Parent's Home."

Yvonne began reading.

"Mrs. Harry Bolton shot herself to death at her home at 11:30 Saturday morning, death resulting almost instantly. The act was in a moment of despondency, presumably over ill health—"

"Over ill health?" I asked, surprised. I had been expecting to hear something about her separation from her husband, as the Associated Press had reported.

"Over ill health, 'presumably over ill health,' it says." Yvonne resumed reading: ". . . and carried out shortly after reaching home, and making preparations for rest.

"From the evidence of preparations for the act, it appears that self-destruction had been carefully planned. The maid was sent from the room and had been urged to go for some time. A call at the door made the opportunity which the victim no doubt had been seeking. Although dead almost instantly, in distinct tones Mrs. Bolton called to her maid and said, 'Eleanor, I have shot myself.' "

Sybil "had spent most of her life" in Pawhuska, the article said. An Osage, she "was one of the most beautiful girls ever reared in the city. She was popular in the younger social set before her marriage, a girl of charm and winning ways."

The article also stated that funeral arrangements would be announced later, "upon the arrival of Mr. and Mrs. Woodward from El Dorado, [Arkansas]."

Then Yvonne read an article dated November 12, 1925. Under the headline "Bolton Funeral Was Held Today; Large Body of Friends in Attendance," the article said: "The funeral of the late Mrs. Harry Bolton, held in the Catholic church this morning, was largely attended. Father Van Durme conducted the requiem mass and the chants by the choir completed the service. The mounds of beautiful flowers in a measure expressed the friendship of the deceased.

"Many friends formed the cortege to the cemetery, where the body was placed in a temporary vault awaiting the completion of the mausoleum, when it will then occupy one of the crypts." The next paragraph listed the pallbearers.

Sybil's survivors included "a little daughter Kathleen."

Sixty-six years later, after a stunned silence, Kathleen's reaction to hearing the details of her mother's death for the first time was to say, "Well, at least we know she didn't blow her head off."

AUGUST 10

More beach reading.

The tens of millions of adoring fans of Laura Ingalls Wilder's books, and of the television series based on them, should be grateful that the Osages didn't dismember her when they had the chance. One day, I was staring at a map of the Osages' rectangle of reservation in Kansas, and my eyes stuck on a red dot in the middle of it, signifying a "Point of Interest." The words "Little House on the Prairie" came into focus.

Little Laura Ingalls, her sisters and their beloved Ma and Pa were illegal squatters on Osage land. She left that detail out of her 1935 children's book, *Little House on the Prairie,* as well as any mention of ongoing outrages—including killings, burnings, beatings, horse thefts and grave robberies—committed by white settlers, such as Charles Ingalls, against Osages living in villages not more than a mile or two away from the Ingallses' little house.

Mrs. Wilder's unwitting association with the Osages would last a lifetime. She started writing the "Little House" children's books—there were nine—in the 1930s, in her sixties, while living in a big house located on former Osage land in the Missouri Ozarks. The "Little House" books—especially the one that took place "on the Prairie" of the Osage reservation in Kansas—would be much read, broadcast and beloved. Shortly after

World War II, the State Department ordered Mrs. Wilder's books translated into German and Japanese, the languages of the United States' most recently defeated enemies, who had just joined the list of America's other Vanquished, including American Indians. The "Little House" books were "positive representations of America," the U.S. government decreed, a good way to show other peoples of the world the American Way. Obviously someone in government forgot to consult the Osages.

After the Civil War, caravans of white settlers started overrunning the Osage reservation, and the Ingalls family joined them in 1869. They were drawn there by the U.S. government's giveaway of 160-acre plots of free land to each adult settler under the Homestead Act of 1862, signed by Abraham Lincoln early in the Civil War as a way to keep the hearts and minds of poor northern people planted firmly in the Union, and maybe win some from the South. The subliminal message of the law was "Stick with us, and we'll reward you—if you win this war. Trade in your slums for the wide-open spaces of the West, where you can be your own boss, on your own land. All you have to do is kill a couple of Confederates." Railroads passed the good news to Europe—or at least to northern Europeans such as the hard-working Swedes, Norwegians and Germans. The railroads' flyers, however, never made it to the Italians or Slavs. A song was even written to give settlers something to sing while traveling west, either to America or to their new homesteads west of the Mississippi:

> Oh, come to this country
> And don't you feel alarm
> For Uncle Sam is rich enough
> To give us all a farm!

Osage writer John Joseph Mathews could have been staring at a family portrait of the Ingallses when he described the covered wagons filling up Osage land as being full of "dirty-faced children peering out from the curtains, and weary, hard-faced women lolling in the seat beside evil-eyed, bearded men." The actor Michael Landon was horribly miscast as Pa in the television series "Little House on the Prairie." Landon was too sweet-faced, clean-shaven—and focused. The real Charles Ingalls wore a two-foot-long vinery of beard. His dark, narrow, hard, glassy, chilly, creepy eyes would, a century later, stare out of photos of Charles Manson, the Hollywood murderer. Pa's résumé reads like that of a surfer bum in search of the perfect amber wave of grain. He couldn't stay in one place or hold down a homestead. He moved from Wisconsin, professing overcrowdedness, to the Osage reservation, back to Wisconsin a year later, then to Minnesota, where he was eaten out by grasshoppers, then to Iowa, where he worked in a hotel, then to South Dakota, where he finally settled in De Smet.

In *Little House on the Prairie,* Mrs. Wilder described one encounter with an Indian she identified as Osage by his scalp lock and leather leggings. A tall Indian, she said, suddenly materialized in the doorway, without anyone hearing him, then walked in the house and squatted by the fireplace, without saying a word. Pa joined him, and Ma served them dinner. They ate in silence. They smoked pipes in silence, using Pa's tobacco. That done, the Osage spoke.

Pa, shook his head to signal that he did not understand the Indian's language.

The Osage got up and walked out—in silence.

Pa may not have understood what the Osage was saying, but he did recognize the language—French.

Sitting on the beach and reading *Little House on the Prairie* for the first time—I did not do so as a boy because it was a *girl's* book—I find myself growing dismayed at its popularity. It took several trips to my local library to find a copy (about a half-dozen were listed in the card catalog—all checked out—and I could not bring myself, at age forty-one, to tell the librarian I wanted to reserve one).

Why are children still reading a book so unsuitable for children? I keep asking myself.

If Pa Ingalls had built his little house on the periphery of an antebellum southern mansion and Mrs. Wilder had described its black slaves in the same terms she depicted the Osage Indians, her book long ago would have been barred from children's eyes, or at least sanitized like some editions of Mark Twain's *The Adventures of Huckleberry Finn.* Mrs. Wilder's books even contains the popular variation of General Sheridan's racist remark about what constitutes a good Indian. I find to my amazement that I take personally her denigration of the Osages, and it bothers me that no one has ever noticed her portrayal of Indians, or objected to it. What commentary does it make on the status of Native Americans in our society that in 1991 you can't find a library copy of a fifty-six-year-old book replete with anti-Indian ethnic slurs, not because it is out of print or circulation, as it should be, but because it is in such demand by impressionable children?

I would not want my child to read *Little House on the Prarie.* I would shield him from the slights she slings upon his ancestors. They appear in her book only as beggars and thieves, and she adds injury to insult by comparing the Osages—who turned Thomas Jefferson's head with their dignity and grace—to reptiles, to garbage or scum (depending on the definition of the word she actually uses). Mrs. Wilder assigns them descriptive adjectives that connote barbarism, brutality, and bloodthirstiness, and makes much ado about their odor. But she makes light of their obvious plight: In one passage, she describes almost mockingly the skeletal figures of two Osages who are fed cornbread by Ma, the eating noises they make and the pitiful sight of them stooping to eat specks of food they spot on the floor.

The Osages were hungry because white men such as her father were burning their fields, forcing them at gunpoint from their homes and threatening them with death if they returned, stealing their food and horses, even robbing their graves—all to force them to abandon their land. There is no proof, of course, that Charles Ingalls took part in these crimes, but I assume that he did, since he was sleazy enough to willfully steal their land, their most valuable possession. He did disappear for four days— according to the book, it took that long to get to Independence and back, all of ten miles away—and returned with food and other supplies. He unabashedly told little Laura, trying to explain why he had moved the family to the Osage reservation, that because they and other whites were there, the Army would drive the Indians away.

In the words of the Osages' U.S. agent in 1870, even being "kind and generous to the Indians . . . [does] not relieve these men from the reproach of being trespassers, intruders, and violators of the nation's law."

The annual reports of the Osages' U.S. agent to his superiors in Washington, the commissioners of Indian affairs, provide the chapter of *Little House on the Prairie* that Laura Ingalls Wilder failed to write:

The Ingallses moved onto Osage land in 1869, about ten miles southwest of Independence, and only about five miles from the Kansas border with Indian Territory. The Ingallses were not alone. That year, more than 500 families trespassed on the reservation and "built their cab-

ins near the [main] Indian camps"—in the Ingallses' case, only a mile or
so away. The 1870 U.S. census listed the Little House—and the Ingallses
as its occupants—as "the 89th residence of Rutland Township," although
"a claim was not filed because the land was part of the Osage . . . Reserve."

Squatters had "taken possession of [the Osages'] cornfields, and forbidden them cutting firewood on 'their claims,' " wrote agent G. C. Snow.
"Their horses are constantly being driven off by the white men," he said.
The Osages "have had, to my certain knowledge, over 100 of their best
horses stolen [in the past month]. I learn that scarcely a day passes that
they do not lose from five to twenty horses. . . . Not one of [the horse
thieves has] as yet been brought to justice, or one in a hundred of the Indians' horses returned to them."

The settlers "threaten me with Crawford's militia, and say they will
hang me if I interfere with them," the Indian agent complained, referring
to the Kansas governor. Samuel J. Crawford was so opposed to Indians in
general and Osages in particular that he once told a white constituent,
Theodore Reynolds, complaining about problems over filing a claim because of a mixed-blood Osage, Augustus Captain: "Shoot the half-breed
renegade and I will pardon you before the smoke gets away from your
gun."

U.S. agent Isaac T. Gibson wrote in his annual report for 1870 that
settlers had grown bolder, forming vigilante groups "pledged to defend
each other in the occupation of claims, without regard to the improve-
ments, possession, or rights of the Indians. Many of the latter were turned
out of their homes, and threatened with death if they persisted in claiming
them. Others were made homeless by cunning and fraud.

"While absent on their winter hunt, [the Osages'] cribs of corn, and
other provisions, so hardly earned by their women's toil, were robbed.
Their principal village was pillaged of a large amount of [casks], and
wagon-loads of matting hauled away and used by the settlers in building
and finishing houses for themselves. Even new-made graves were plundered, with the view of finding treasures, which the Indians often bury
with their dead. . . .

"The question will suggest itself, which of these peoples are the savages?"

The outrages of 1870 were a turning point for the Osages. At that spring's payment in provisions of promised treaty annuities, the government again pressed the Osages to sell their Kansas lands. In 1865, the Osages ceded under pressure nearly 4 million acres on the northern and eastern perimeters of their reservation, and in 1868 were forced to agree to sell their 8-million-acre "diminished reserve," as the government called the remainder of their land, to a railroad corporation for 19 cents an acre. But President Ulysses S. Grant withdrew the treaty in 1870 when it became obvious that the Senate would not ratify it amid an explosion of outrage from settlers that the sale would put the Osage lands in the hands of the railroads and not in theirs. Gibson noted the weariness of the Osages at the 1870 spring annuity payment, quoting "one of their head-men" as complaining, "Why is it that our Great Father can never even send us our annuities, without asking us to sell and move once more?" The Indian added, "We are tired of all this." Gibson described the Osage as having "the look and tone of a man without hope."

It was in this spirit that the Osages agreed to sell, and luckily for them, their decision to wave the white flag coincided with a radical change in the government's Indian policy. President Grant had just relieved the Army from administrative responsibility for Indian affairs, and turned the whole problem over to Quakers, such as Gibson. They saw in the Osages the chance to inject a missing ingredient—fairness, or at least their conception of it—into official treatment of Indians. The Quaker commissioners of Indian affairs—"true friends of the Indians," they regarded themselves—persuaded Grant to up the ante: $1.25 per acre, and the opportunity for the Osages to use their money to purchase a new reservation in Indian Territory. Grant had no choice but to agree. The president had announced his "peace policy" with much flourish and fanfare in his inaugural address on March 4, 1869, and would have suffered a humiliating political embarrassment if he had rejected his new Quaker commissioners' counsel.

When the Osages signed the treaty on September 10, 1870, they became the richest Indians in America with nearly $9 million in the U.S. Treasury—although their signatures on the Kansas removal treaty actually put them between reservations, having given up one and having only the historically questionable word of the U.S. government that they would get another.

The Quaker commissioners hailed their treaty as "so just that in itself it marks an era in the history of our government in its legislation on Indian affairs," and as proof "of the overruling goodness of God." But the Osages did not share the Quakers' joy. The morning after they signed the treaty, "the air was filled with the cries of the old people, especially the women, who lamented over the graves of their children, which they were about to leave forever," a Kansas newspaper reported.

Most of the Osages left Kansas in late fall for their annual winter buffalo hunt on the plains, and did not return, staying instead in Indian Territory. Laura Ingalls—and her readers—did not know it, but she witnessed a watershed moment in the history of the Osages—their removal from Kansas—when one morning she looked out the window of the little house and saw a traffic jam of Indians riding past. They came from the creek bottoms to the east and rode west, past the house, on an old Indian trail that later was paved and became U.S. Route 75.

One of the Osage warriors who rode past the little house that day was my great-great-grandfather, and one of the Osage women Laura saw was my great-great-grandmother.

The Ingalls family left Kansas a few weeks later. Mrs. Wilder claimed that a cavalry troop rode in one day and warned Pa to vacate or be evicted, since the house was located just inside the Osages' diminished reservation. But that could not have been the reason the Ingallses left Kansas and moved back to Wisconsin. The U.S. Army had not moved one squatter off the Osages' land when it was their reservation, so why would that happen when there no longer was an Osage reservation in Kansas?

The Ingallses' neighbors were not through with the Osages yet. Nearly twenty mixed-blood Osages had decided to remain on farms they had developed and improved over the years, and to formally enter the white man's world by becoming U.S. citizens. They secured a special treaty with the good citizens of Independence to allow them to stay. But in the weeks after the main body of Osages left Kansas, the mixed-bloods' farmhouses, one after another, were burned down.

One night, the white neighbors of Joseph Mosher broke into his house—a mile or two from the Little House on the Prairie—dragged him, his wife and children out of their beds and into the yard, where they beat them and torched the house.

Then they took the Osage man to the nearby woods, and pistol-whipped him to death.

AUGUST 12

It took weeks of urging to get my mother to call Mrs. Theil Annett, Sybil's cousin. My mother had always prided herself on being able to talk to anyone, anywhere, anytime, about anything, and often did. But suddenly she developed a case of shyness, claiming that she did not like to talk to strangers and was not any good at it.

Theil Annett had written my mother five years earlier, and had enclosed a picture of herself and her husband. My mother never answered the letter but saved it, and kept the photo displayed on her desk. "It was a very sad, hurtful experience for me," the letter had said, referring to the death of her cousin Sybil, whom Theil said she had worshiped: "No one was more wonderful than my cousin." Sybil was her idol, she said. Theil's father, Woodie Conner, was the half-brother of Sybil's mother, Kate Conner Woodward. Theil was a couple of years younger than Sybil, which meant she was well into her eighties now.

My mother remembered the unusual spelling of her name, her husband's name, George, and the town where they lived, Cleveland, Oklahoma, just across the Arkansas River border of southern Osage County near Tulsa. The operator gave me their number, which was listed under George Annett. That meant at least one of them was still alive.

I was determined to get my mother to talk to Theil, as a courtesy, if nothing else, before I quizzed her about Sybil's death. Theil was, after all, close to Sybil; my mother was Sybil's only child; and Theil probably knew my mother as a baby. It would not be right for my mother not to talk to her first.

On this rainy afternoon at the beach, after another round of protests from my mother, I simply dialed Theil's number and handed my mother the phone, ringing.

Her frown quickly gave way to a wide-eyed expression.

"Mrs. Annett?" my mother asked, speaking slowly, loudly but with a slight quiver. "Oh, I'm so glad you're there. I think you better sit down.

"I'm, uh, Sybil Bol—Beekman Bolton's daughter, Kathleen, and I received your letter when we lived in Panama, and the reason I never answered is very complicated. But we, I wanted you to know something." She couldn't get it out. "I still have your letter and I carry it around almost wherever I go, and your picture is on my desk, with your husband"—she tried it again—"and I wanted you to know that—"

"He died just the other day," Theil said.

"Your husband died just the other day?" my mother asked incredulously.

"Yeah, well, it seems like just the other day," Theil said, "but it was January the twenty-second—"

"Oh, I'm so sorry."

"—and I've been kind of put out since then."

"I would imagine. Are you still living at the same house?"

"I don't want to go where my kids are. You know how that is," Theil said. "I like to be my own boss."

"Yes, my children boss me around a lot," my mother said, giving me a slight smile.

"Well, my children, they've never had the chance because I've never been near them for so many years, you know. But, anyway, I think your kids are happier when they don't have a mother around to take care of, and think of, and everything like that. Although I'm eighty-six, I'm in good health. The doctor said—he just examined me thoroughly, ran me through all of those tests and everything—and he said it's unbelievable but I can't find a damn thing wrong with you."

Theil laughed, my mother laughed and relaxed. The ice had melted. They talked for more than an hour.

Theil told my mother she could call her by her first name, and how to pronounce it—like Theel, rhyming with "wheel."

My mother told Theil about her children and grandchildren, their names and where they lived. And then she said as smoothly as if they were next-door neighbors and she was inviting her to lunch: "But I called to tell you something that probably will surprise you. I now am sixty-seven years old, and on the Fourth of July of this year was the first time in my life that I ever knew that my mother, Sybil, committed suicide."

"Didn't you know that all this time?"

"I was never told. My father never mentioned her name to me."

"She shot herself."

"Isn't that terrible?"

"Well, it is, but you know, Sybil couldn't keep things straight," Theil said. There was a slight tremble in her voice. "She was just thinking that she was going to have to lose you."

"Why would she have to lose me?" There was alarm in my mother's voice.

"Her husband was going to take you away from her."

"Oh my heavens." There was a look of panic on my mother's face.

"Well, I don't know very much about it," Theil said, "but I know that that happened to be, because we just talked about it a long time." Theil explained that she was away at school, the University of Oklahoma at Norman, at the time of Sybil's return to Pawhuska and her death. Theil and her mother went to the funeral and stayed at the Woodwards' house. "I'll tell you who told us. They had an old colored woman—"

"Eleanor."

"Yeah, she had been there for, oh, I don't know how long," Theil said. After the funeral, the Woodwards were off in another part of the house and Eleanor told some of the story to Theil and her mother. "She told us about how Sybil was in bed, and she just was having a time all the time."

The newspaper said Sybil had been in ill health, my mother said, "and I had always been told she died of kidney disease." Was that the problem?

"Well, now," Theil paused, mulling her words. "She just drank herself to death, I think. She was awfully bad to drink. That was part of it, anyway. I think that caused the trouble really between your daddy and her.

"The whole family," Theil said, "they were all drinkers mostly."

"Those were the days," my mother said.

"But Sybil, I don't think she would sober up and keep off of it, and of course the baby was there." Theil explained that after Sybil met Harry Bolton, "a fella at school she was just crazy about," she stopped drinking. But after they were married, "she had the baby and everything, and then just started drinking again awful bad after that. And he was going to get a divorce—"

"*He* was getting the divorce?" my mother interrupted.

"He was going to take the child away from her. And she was afraid he would go on through with it."

"He's lied all these years," my mother said, "because he told my [step]mother that [Sybil] called him at work and said, 'Harry, *I* want a divorce.' "

"Oh, I don't think Sybil did that."

"Well, you knew her and of course I didn't."

"Well, that's the problem there. We lived far apart here"—Theil's father, Woodie Conner, had a ranch in Vinita, in Craig County, fifty miles east of Pawhuska—"and we just never did visit very much," Theil said. "I'm just telling you what is hearsay. You just don't know how much of it is true, but a lot of it sounded like it would be true."

Theil described Sybil. "She was as tall as I am"—five feet seven—"and she was big-boned. She was a husky gal. I mean kind of a, well, she wasn't fat at all, but she was a big girl. She wore her hair, any time that I ever saw her, straight bob."

"Straight bob," my mother repeated. Then she asked, point-blank, "Did she shoot herself in the head?"

"No, I think in the chest. I think that's what Eleanor said."

"Did she leave a suicide note?"

"No, she never did mention a note. But Sybil went downtown and bought the pistol," Theil said. "That's what I heard all my life. She went down there and she bought—I think it was just a little one—a little pistol. Of course, she would have to shoot herself almost in the heart to die with that."

"The newspaper said she called out in a distinct voice, 'Eleanor'—"

" 'Look what I've done.' Uh-huh, that's what I heard," Theil said.

"It didn't say that," my mother said. "She said in the newspaper, 'Eleanor, I have shot myself.' That of course bothered us because if you've shot yourself, you don't use perfect grammar. But how did she have a requiem mass having killed herself ? You know that's against the church law."

"Well, nobody saw her, I guess."

"Well, there was no coroner's report. . . . Why did they [the Woodwards] go off and leave her when she was in this state? You know they were in Arkansas. They left her in the house with Eleanor and me. . . . The doorbell rang, according to the newspaper, and Eleanor went to get the door, and I want to know"—my mother was beginning to sound forceful at this point; an edge was forming in her tone—"we were wondering, what happened to the people at the door? Would they have heard the gunshot?"

This was the first Theil had heard about anyone being at the door, but she said: "Well, they could have. Now, I think [Sybil] was upstairs. I think she was upstairs in her room. Now, I don't know that. That's just the idea I got out of it."

"Do you have any idea"—the bitterness had finally broken through—"why I never saw, I saw my grandmother twice in my whole life?"

"No, I don't know," Theil said, consoling. "But Aunt Kathleen was kind of hard to get along with.

"I saw you one time," Theil went on. "You were out in the kitchen, in your high chair, and Eleanor was feeding you oatmeal, and you got enough of it. Eleanor would try to feed you, and you kept on going until you got enough, and she wouldn't leave you alone. So you just whacked that spoon, and the oatmeal"—Theil started laughing—"went in every direction. I never will forget that.

"You were just a very cute baby, all dressed up, so nice you know. We were there for . . . well, I'll tell you what it was for.

"It was for the funeral."

AUGUST 28

My mother called me. We were home from the beach, and I was at work. My mother sounded upset and angry. She couldn't sleep the night before, she said.

"If this was so well planned," she said, if Sybil had bought the gun and wanted to send Eleanor home so she could shoot herself, "what would happen to baby Kathleen," whom she loved so much she would rather kill herself than lose?

My mother had had many maids as a general's wife in Panama, and her experience with them was that it did not take much urging for them to fly out the door for a day off. But the Pawhuska newspaper article would have us believe that Eleanor "had been urged to go for some time," but refused to take the rest of the day off, a Saturday no less. One wonders who is the maid and who the matron in this scenario. When Sybil gives Eleanor an order—Go home—does the maid say no?

But what if Eleanor had taken the day off? my mother asked. The maid would have left that Saturday morning. Sunday is a holiday. Eleanor wouldn't return until Monday.

That's nearly forty-eight hours for a baby to go without food, liquids, diaper changes, to crawl around the house, to fall down the stairs, to climb over her mother's bloody body, to play with the gun, to chew on it.

"I can't believe she'd let a sixteen-month-old baby loose alone in the house," my mother said. "I just had cold shivers all night thinking of this.

"Denny, I think she was murdered."

SEPTEMBER 3

The FBI FOIA Reading Room at the headquarters of the Federal Bureau of Investigation in Washington, D.C., is the repository of all FBI files released to the public under the Freedom of Information Act.

The room is about seventy-five paces past the Pennsylvania Avenue entrance to the J. Edgar Hoover Building. Its glass doors are barricaded by a metal-detecting machine, manned by guards wearing blue windbreakers and matching blue-steel pistols, who rifle through my briefcase. The walk, under escort, takes me past a bust of J. Edgar Hoover as well as his oil portrait. His painting catches the light from the entrance; the portraits of his lesser-known successors do not, and so they seem shadowed by the man, as they were in reality. Once inside the reading room, the escort transforms into a watcher, who sits by the door and waits. When I ask where the men's room is, the watcher again becomes an escort. Fortunately, she waits outside.

The reading room is about the size of an average public rest room. Where the sinks would be, against one wall, are four Formica-top tables, with folding metal chairs tucked underneath. The rest of the room is taken up by a wall of two-sided, sliding, wood-veneer bookcases that move, toward the entrance to the room or away from it, with the turn of a metal crank.

Here are the most heralded deaths of modern America, or at least the bodies the FBI is willing to put on display. While I was there, a Spike Lee look-alike was studying Malcolm X; an aging beach boy—peroxide-blond (black roots), open-front Hawaiian shirt—was examining Elvis; a tall, heavy, sixtyish black man wearing a three-piece suit and thick bifocals was mesmerized by Martin Luther King.

On a bookshelf opposite JFK, down the aisle from the Lindbergh kidnapping, on the shelf below the Rosenbergs, was the 3,274-page file entitled "Osage Indian Murders."

I had come to see if my grandmother was buried there.

Since her return to Pawhuska coincided with the FBI's undercover investigation, I thought that maybe there was a chance she might have talked to one of the agents, or that her death was recorded in the files, or that the FBI had put a "hold" on her burial while it investigated her death, or that the records might contain just one clue that cast the shadow of murder over it.

After decades of being sensitized to the rights and plights of American minorities, such as Indians—and after a day of being numbed by page after page of gruesome killings of them—it was difficult for this white American, with rising Osage blood, to decide what to be more cynical about:

That up to sixty wealthy Osages—nearly 3 percent of the tribe—were murdered for their money in the early 1920s before law-enforcement officials stepped in.

Or that the FBI did not enter the case until a white man was killed.

Or that the Osages had to pay the FBI to come in and investigate their murders.

I grew sickened at the thought that my mother, my grandmother or any other relative of mine may have been touched by the hatred, harm and horror held in the pages of the FBI reports.

An Osage woman is chopped into tiny pieces, not by her killer, but by doctors performing her autopsy—to try to make it impossible to determine that she had been shot to death.

Another Osage woman's grave is blown up.

An Osage family's house is blown up, with so much nitroglycerine that traces of the maid, sleeping inside, were not immediately evident.

A white lawyer working for the U.S. government's Osage Agency is stripped, beaten to a pulp and thrown off a train.

A white rancher takes out a $25,000 insurance policy on an Osage man, boasts to insurance officials that he is going to have the Indian killed, then sues when the insurance company does not pay up for the murder.

A Catholic parish priest is an FBI informant, and apologizes one week that he has nothing new on a particular suspect, because the man's wife is no longer coming to confession.

The going rate to hire a poor white to kill a rich Osage is $500 and a used Roadster.

It is apparently not against the law to kill an Osage Indian. The bodies of "one after another of the heads of rich [Osage] families," in a newspaper's words, start showing up in fields, ravines, on roadsides, whiskey bottle in hand, sometimes bleeding profusely from wounds to their heads or bodies. But the (white) county attorney has ruled all of these deaths—the suspicions of the Osages notwithstanding—as accidental poisoning by tainted bootleg whiskey. The victims' wounds were caused by their drunken falls to the ground. That traces of strychnine were found inside the bottles does not seem to sway authorities in their verdict. The poison is just another reason to call it rotgut.

As the bodies piled up, so, too, did the headrights—the Osages' oil shares—in the hands of white men, entitling them to the same quarterly royalty payments as Osage headright holders. The headrights of deceased Osages would pass to their immediate survivors, even if they had no Osage blood and were not members of the tribe. Local newspapers were calling the string of murders "the Osage Reign of Terror," and the Osages viewed the fact that none of the murders had been solved as proof of a wide-ranging, organized plot against them by whites: White lawyers would steal their money; white husbands would inherit their oil lands upon the deaths of their Osage wives; white law-enforcement officials would ensure that none of their murders was solved. The Osages had become so terrified they would all be killed that they had strung the perimeters of their houses with bright lights that burned all night.

The theory on which the FBI operated did not bode well for my grandfather, Harry Bolton. The FBI suspected that many of the murders—those of Osage women—had been committed or ordered by their white husbands. In fact, the rapidly diminishing Osage population automatically assumed that, regardless of the official cause of death of any Osage woman, her white husband had killed her.

But there was another aspect of the Reign of Terror that unfolded in the FBI files and seemed to let Harry off the hook. In some cases, all the headright-holding Osage relatives of a white man's wife had been murdered: her mother, father, grandparents, brothers, sisters, nephews, nieces, aunts, uncles, cousins. Some Osage women, with just a few bottles of whiskey or pulls of a trigger, suddenly found themselves worth multiples of millions—and yet their lives weren't worth a plugged nickel. If my grandfather had followed this pattern, first he would have killed Sybil's cousin, Theil Annett, and her mother and father; then Angela Andretta, Sybil's half-sister, and her husband; then Mr. Woodward, to make sure he wouldn't inherit Mrs. Woodward's headright when she went; then Mrs. Woodward; then, in case he might inherit from Sybil, her father Sewell Beekman; and finally Sybil—after she was holding at least six headrights. But why stop there? If Harry had gone to all that trouble—but taken little risk—to do all that killing to gain all those headrights from Sybil's Osage family, why share them with his Osage daughter?

I found what I had come for about halfway through the files.

The FBI began making arrangements to convene a federal grand jury on September 7, 1925. Agents in the field complained that they needed more time, so the date was postponed to November 1.

For the November 1 grand jury, a list of 140 witnesses to be subpoenaed was drawn up. A long, meticulously typed document called an "abstract"—comprising all of Volume Seven of thirteen "folios" of the FBI reports—listed the names of witnesses, what they were expected to testify (if they previously had given sworn statements, those were transcribed verbatim), and occasional comments about them (one would-be witness was described as being so "yellow" he could be expected to change his story under any degree of questioning).

Witness number 97 in one of the cases was A. T. Woodward. The abstract said that "this witness was Osage Tribal Attorney at the time" of the murders and "it is believed that he can give detailed information material to this investigation."

Two other key witnesses to be called were brothers, whose last name was Bolton.

Sybil Bolton died November 7, six days after the scheduled start of the grand jury, and only days after a copy of the abstract was mailed to Washington. The copy was stamped "Received" at FBI headquarters on November 12.

The grand jury was postponed to January 7, 1926. No reason for the delay was given in the FBI files. There is no mention in the files of my grandmother's death, and no report specifically mentions her by name.

However, one of the FBI reports in the late 1920s contains a curious comment from a white man convicted in one of the killings. He was by then serving time in a Leavenworth, Kansas, prison cell, awaiting retrial. He told his cell mate—an FBI stoolie, naturally—that he had learned a valuable lesson from a 1923 murder he had ordered, and for which he was convicted.

He had "made a great mistake," he said, in not making sure "the job" was done "right." The Osage was shot in the back of the head, and of course his death could have been only one thing—murder.

"Shoot [someone] in front," though, the convict said, and you can make "it appear that [he] had committed suicide."

SEPTEMBER 12

Claribel Shaw's voice on the telephone sounded so young and vibrant I almost asked her if her mother were home.

A few years before, Claribel had jotted a note atop a campaign position paper of her husband, John Shaw, who was running in an Osage Tribal Council election (as a headright holder, my mother votes in Osage elections). The note said, "I was your mother's best friend and, after she died, became your grandmother's best friend."

Like Theil Annett's letter, my mother saved Claribel Shaw's note, memorized her name but, as with Theil, made no attempt to get in touch with her.

And as with Theil, my mother was suddenly struck with shyness at the prospect of calling Claribel.

This time I called. I had asked Yvonne Rose, the Pawhuska librarian, to check if Sybil's pallbearers, listed in the article she read me, were still alive, as well as Claribel. She was the only "yes" of the bunch, but I began having anxiety attacks over the possibility that she would be a "no" by the time my mother worked up the courage to call her. Yvonne had said Claribel and John Shaw lived in Burbank, a small Osage County community twenty miles west of Pawhuska.

I told Claribel my name. "You don't know me, but you knew my grandmother, Sybil Beekman Bolton. Do you remember her?"

"Why, yes, of course," she said briskly but brightly. "She was my best friend."

"I'm Sybil's only grandson."

"Kathleen's son?"

After a round of exclamations, she said she always felt a special attachment to my mother, because they shared the same birthday, June 24.

"Well, you may find this hard to believe," I said, "but Sybil, whom you knew only as a young girl, now has three grandchildren and five great-grandchildren, the youngest of whom is my seven-month-old son."

She was delighted at the call. I told her about my family—Sybil's family—how Kathleen was, where she and her children lived.

Then I told her why I called. I apologized for my mother not calling, saying she was uncomfortable talking about her mother's death.

"Well, that's a sad fact," Claribel said about Sybil's suicide. "It's real strange she didn't know. But Harry would have seen to that," referring to my grandfather but not elaborating.

Sybil's death had left her "dumbfounded," she said. She was living in Kansas City when it happened.

They had grown up together. Claribel had attended one of the most exclusive boarding schools in the country, the Chevy Chase School for girls in Maryland, just outside Washington, D.C. Sybil's half-sister, Angela, had gone to Italy to study music, and Sybil decided to study there with her sister rather than go to Chevy Chase. When they came back, Sybil attended, and graduated from, Notre Dame Academy in Philadelphia. But after high school, Sybil and Claribel decided to go to college together, at the University of Kansas.

What she said next left *me* dumbfounded.

"It happened on the lawn," Claribel said. "The way I heard it she and the baby were out on the lawn when she killed herself . . .

"I can still see it," she said, describing the house and lawn as situated on a hillside overlooking Pawhuska. "This house sits on the hill. . . . They were out on the lawn and . . ."

And now, sixty-six years later, her voice wavered with emotion and she left the rest of the sentence back there on the Woodward property that Saturday morning in 1925.

Part Three

MANIFOLD
DESTINY

OVERLEAF: A gasoline motor rail car at the Pawhuska
train station, circa 1920. (Western History Collections,
University of Oklahoma Library.)

G reat expectations. A leave of absence from work, and the summer on the Osage reservation.

May 31, 1992. 6:45 A.M. I begin my trip backwards, in a driving rain. The car rolls in reverse. Fleur is waving frantically from the front door, but it is not a goodbye wave—and not a good sign. I stop. She points over her head. Through the sheets of rain, I can see two syllables sprout from her mouth. *Cof-fee.* I have left the thermos on top of the car. I get wet again, finally pull away, put the car through its five-gear paces on the quarter-mile warm-up run to the Baltimore Beltway, and a raven swoops down low over the hood and flies in front of me, eye-level, all the way to the ramp.

A raven is my copilot.

In many Native American legends, a raven is responsible for the origin of mankind and is a guardian spirit, especially for hunters. I should be comforted by my companion, but I feel spooked by this Indian symbol that, in real life, has suddenly flown into my life, at the birth of my hunt for my Indian origins.

This damn bird has been following me around for two weeks, or so it seems. Maybe ravens have always been just over my shoulder, shadowing, shielding, shepherding me, and I've only just now begun to notice, and to question what it means. I'm an Indian, but I'm not a real Indian. I don't know the things that Indians are supposed to know, but maybe on this trip, to this place that has pulled at me like undertow, I will learn. I want to learn. It has become important to me.

We've moved again. Two weeks ago. Our townhouse, situated in a new housing development cut out of the north side of a large hill, faces a construction site, now being filled in with truckloads of dusty red clay, soon to be filled out with cul-de-sacs of costly colonials. About a hundred yards to the west of our sodded front lawn is a thick grove of tall trees. Its setting in the middle of a denuded construction site is incongruous but welcome, blocking our view to the main street, about a quarter-mile away, and to the ugliness of the plank-by-plank growth of our neighborhood. It was thoughtful of the builder to leave the trees there, unusual for one to do so, and I said as much to his foreman a few days after we moved in.

"It wasn't him, it was the fucking Indians," he said.

That got my attention, Indians not being known for their presence or political pull in Maryland.

He explained that when workers were preparing the site for construction—a euphemism for cutting down trees—they discovered an old rock structure at the base of the hill where the trees are. "Some son of a bitch"—his euphemism for a culturally curious citizen—called the Maryland Historical Society, which decreed the ruins to be an ancient Indian mill and declared it a historic site. The architects had to erase a couple of rows of townhouses from their plat.

The foreman, I detected, did not share my enthusiasm for this small victory over progress—"a bunch of old rocks," he called the mill. Fleur and I call him the Nigger Farmer. His job is to count the number of trucks that drive by our house and dump dirt on the construction site. He said he owns a farm across the Chesapeake Bay and grows collard greens, turnips, black-eyed peas and other fruits and vegetables "that only niggers buy"—hence, our nickname for him. Selling to what I gather are his un-wanted neighbors saves him from driving to farmers' markets "all over the fucking state." Instead, he drives a couple of hours each way to count dirt trucks. The ethnic gardening business must be in the off-season, I de-cided—or maybe his clientele has stopped buying from him. Perhaps they can taste the prejudice in his produce, much as one can taste fear in meat that is not kosher, of an animal that has been killed harshly.

Harsh Benyamin. When I look at this man, I think of my grandfather.

"What kind of Indians?" I asked him.

He squinted at me, perplexed.

"What tribe of Indians were they?" I clarified.

"Shit, I don't know. Just Indians, I guess."

Ah, the largest tribe of Native Americans in the United States: the Just Indians.

Another dump truck passed. The Nigger Farmer ended our conver-sation with a spit and some advice, designed to dampen my moment of marvel. My mind was racing faster than the dust rising from the tracks of the dump truck. The presence of a mill signified that this spot, now cut of trees and slit with rows of suburban dwellings, once housed an ancient Indian band's permanent village, not just a campground for nomads. I thought of the Osages' Place of the Many Swans and wondered how many centuries Indians had lived here, where I live now, in this Place of the Many Suburbanites. Would the builder have had to erase one pencil mark from his blueprints if live Indians had been occupying this spot? I doubted it. Only by being dead, it seems, are Indians able to stop the march of white civilization.

I have seen plenty of historical markers on the East Coast that say "Ancient Indian Site," but they all give the impression that the original occupants' absence was an accident of nature, that they had somehow melted at the end of the Ice Age. Maybe I will get civically involved and lobby to have a historical marker put up here. But will there be enough space to say truthfully how these Indians were "removed"? Did they leave on their feet or on their backs, "removed" to just below the surface of soil that now supports the structures of a new people? I can see the site of the Indian mill from my front yard, and I drive past it each day—I have driven past it again to begin my trip to the state of "red people," Oklahoma. I am grateful for my proximity to the mill, and for the humbling reminder it brings to my daily life: just a hundred yards from our newly constructed house is irrefutable proof that it, too, like so much else of American society, is built literally on the bones of historical injustices, indeed outrages.

"I wouldn't go down there if I were you," the foreman advised. "The place is crawling with yellow jackets."

They let me pass. So did the stickers and poison ivy that also guard the ruins' thick-foliaged approach. A shin-high strand of yellow tape—the kind used to cordon off police crime scenes—marks the mill's upper ledge, to warn unsuspecting walkers that their next step is twenty feet straight down. The mill looks like a cross section of a well. Moss-covered stones, each about the size of a football, are imbedded in the hillside to form a curved wall, about ten feet in diameter. Only a few stones are missing from the mill, from its top ledge—located at street level, and just twenty feet from it—to its base—about thirty feet uphill from a creek. A few moss-gathered stones have rolled creekward, giving lie to the adage. The floor of the mill also is inlaid with stones, as is a trough leading to the creek and covered with what looks like a small stone bridge, most of it intact. The millstone is missing. Even centuries of time and humid weather have been unable to obscure the mill's intricate construction, or the sophistication of its design. Where is any trace of the log cabins whose inhabitants thought themselves more civilized and more deserving of this spot than the builders and operators of the mill? It is older than the nation, older still than its monuments. Yet, like most Indians and things Indian in the United States, this memorial is hidden from view—and marked as if a crime took place here.

One did.

I began climbing the hill to go home, running the gantlet again of poison ivy, bees and brambles, when a shriek shot across the tree shade, shattering the churchly silence. Something large streaked above my head and the upper reaches of the mill. I both jumped and ducked, and slipped a few feet downhill, my feet scraping a path through the dead leaves on the ground. Stickers ripped into my legs. To my left came a shriek of laughter. When I stood up, I saw it.

The damn raven.

INTERSTATE 68, West Virginia.

The Washington Post sent an intern reporter to some hick hollow in West Virginia one summer to do a story about a woman arrested for selling babies. The reporter was British. A little kid, upon hearing his accent, asked him if he was a "red man." Unfamiliar with the West Virginia twang and thinking the boy may have meant "redcoat," the reporter asked a nearby adult what the boy said.

"He thinks you're an Injun, 'cause you talk funny."

"Wild and Wonderful," the blue welcome sign at the West Virginia state line says.

Interstate 68 is newly opened and is not shown on my map. Uncharted territory. The highway runs out in Morgantown, on the Monongahela River. One hundred and fifty years ago, the Monongahela unleashed a tidal wave of whites across the West. Settlers boarded steamboats on the Monongahela from Morgantown and other places south of Pittsburgh; boated to the Ohio, to the Mississippi, to the Missouri; then, from Independence, St. Joseph or Council Bluffs, sailed across the Great Plains on prairie schooners, hoping the coast was clear of any "red man," who might shoot first and "talk funny" later.

On the first day of my drive, I would cross the Ohio four times—at Wheeling, West Virginia; Cincinnati; Louisville and Henderson, Kentucky. Henderson, across the Ohio from Evansville, Indiana, gave the world John James Audubon. After failing at a milling business on the banks of the Ohio in Henderson, Audubon rivered west, where he shot birds, stuffed them, stretched them into poses, painted them and ultimately lent his name to a conservation society that combats bird-killers like John James Audubon.

Outside Henderson is the farm of my childhood friend, Charles S. Johnson III. I would spend a day or two on the farm with Charles, then drive to Pawhuska, where I would meet, at different times, my sister Carolyn and her daughters, my mother and father, Fleur and Kevin, and finally my sister Kathie. A family reunion among the Osages. Every member of the family would go there, in fact, except Cara Mae.

Cara Mae Bolton is having none of this murder business, and she is none too pleased about her stepdaughter's sudden interest in her real mother.

My mother has a picture of her stepmother as a young woman, perhaps Sybil's age at the time it was taken. This photo my mother keeps in a prominent place in her living room. The browning, disappearing snapshot of her real mother she keeps in her bedroom closet.

In the portrait, Cara Mae is striking what we call her Jean Harlow pose. Blond hair, hand on hip, the elbow of her other arm resting atop a waist-high Greek pillar. Her dress is dark, shoulderless, strapless, low-cut, amply filled, a shining sheath. Slinky is how Fleur describes it.

Sybil, Cara Mae explained to my mother, was too sophisticated for Harry, whatever that meant to this woman whose picture even now, six decades after it was taken, stops men and seduces them to ask, in almost a whistle, "Who is that woman?"

Cara Mae was differently attired five months ago when she sat in my living room. She was wearing a suit that Fleur said First Lady Nancy Reagan often wore, sporting an Adolfo signature and costing at least $2,000. It was the day after Christmas 1991. She was spending the holidays with my mother and father, but on this day, she was visiting me and my family in Baltimore.

It was Sybil's birthday. I had recently received her "Marriage Card" in the mail from the Osage Agency, and it listed the birth date. December 26, 1903. December 26 is also my due date, the day I was expected to be born. As usual, I was late.

Sybil would have been eighty-eight on this day.

Cara Mae didn't know it was Sybil's birthday, of course, or if she did, she was not saying. I didn't bring it up. Cara Mae is now eighty-something, the low eighties, or just turned eighty. One of the reasons she likes me so much, apart from being what she calls her "favorite grandson" (she has no other), is because I don't know when her birthday is. I've never remembered it, never wished her a happy one. For her, there's been no such thing for years, indeed decades.

Had a bullet not ended her life, Sybil, not Cara Mae, could have been sitting in my living room on this day after Christmas, and the conversation could have been about something other than death.

"She committed suicide," Cara Mae said. "That's a fact."

"Harry had nothing to do with it," she said.

"You should be ashamed of yourself, Denny," she said, "digging up things about the Boltons. I can't understand why you'd want to do such a thing, Denny. Your grandfather was such a wonderful man, he truly was."

All of this, of course, took much longer for her to say than for me to write. Cara Mae stammers. The trait developed a few years ago, and is highly contagious. It takes only a few minutes with her for my speech, and that of anyone else in the room, to degenerate into syllables, which sputter past the tongue, over the teeth and out of the mouth, the words finally coming to life but only after a very difficult birth.

My mother had decided that her mother's death was not a telephone topic, so she waited until Cara Mae's planned Christmas visit to discuss it with her in person. I was not present at these sometimes emotional confrontations—nor did I want to be—but got daily progress reports over the phone from my often exasperated mother.

Over the course of the holidays, Cara Mae at first denied that my mother had never heard about Sybil's suicide.

"Well, of course you knew, Kathleen," she said repeatedly.

"Mother, I never knew," my mother said repeatedly.

But my mother kept pressing her. She asked her again and again why at age sixty-seven she had to find out via a ninety-one-year-old stranger in Alta Vista, Kansas.

"How do you think I felt? Everyone knew this but me," my mother said with outrage. Why, she kept asking, did her father and Cara Mae never say anything all these years?

Finally Cara Mae gave her the answer.

Harry and Cara Mae just assumed Kathleen knew.

They assumed my mother had picked it up at the Beekmans when she was a child, and hadn't wanted to talk about it. One time, Cara Mae said, she asked Harry if he thought Kathleen knew the truth, and he said, "Of course she knows."

Harry Bolton and the Beekmans had decided that, for Kathleen's consumption, kidney disease would be the cause of Sybil's death, and Harry had barred all mention of Sybil's name in his presence. He wouldn't permit it for two reasons. He initially didn't want Kathleen to pry, and he just didn't want to talk about it, to be reminded of it.

But other people talked about it, out of Harry's presence, and out of

Kathleen's, too. Why, Cara Mae said, Mrs. Beekman and she had talked about it for years. Surely Kathleen must have overheard it.

No, never, my mother said. I never knew.

My goodness, Cara Mae asserted, for years Mrs. Beekman and I talked about how Sybil had gone to a party that Friday night, got drunk, came home and—that Friday night—blew her brains out.

Harry had told that story to Cara Mae on their second date, and that was what Mr. Beekman had told Mrs. Beekman when he came home from the funeral, when he got the details of his daughter's suicide from the Woodwards. (The Oklahoma City newspapers did not carry the Associated Press report of her death.)

If Harry had had any doubts about the cause of death, Cara Mae said, they were dispelled by Sybil's college roommate and best friend, Claribel Shaw, when Harry stayed with her for the funeral. The Woodwards wouldn't let him in their house.

"Claribel," Harry had asked her, "was it really suicide? Could she really do such a thing?"

"Yes," Claribel had answered.

"And Sybil left a suicide note," Cara Mae said. Before Sybil shot herself, she wrote Harry a suicide note, and mailed it.

After days of pressing by my mother, Cara Mae adjusted the story.

"Well, it wasn't a suicide note exactly," she said. "It was more like a letter." And Sybil hadn't mailed it. It was there in the house, in her room, found after her death, and the Woodwards wouldn't give it to Harry at first, or even show him.

"He just had a terrible time trying to see it," she said. Finally, after the funeral, he sent Mr. Beekman into the Woodward house to retrieve it. Harry waited outside in the car.

But Cara Mae didn't know what was in it.

More pressing from my mother.

"Well," Cara Mae said, "Sybil apologized for leaving Harry and for asking for a divorce. She said it was all her fault."

Even more pressing.

There was nothing more to read, Cara Mae insisted.

Finally she said why: The rest of the letter had been torn off from that point. And what Harry did receive—the start of the letter—had been crumpled up.

But Cara Mae still wasn't buying murder.

"Harry didn't do it," she kept saying. "He had nothing to do with it."

During Cara Mae's visit with us, we talked about the time she took Kathleen to visit her Osage grandmother at the Oklahoma Club. Cara Mae remembered Mrs. Woodward well. "Her eyes were so hard," Cara Mae exclaimed. "And she was dressed just like . . . like an Indian." Cara Mae's eyes widened, and her disgust came out like a sneeze. "I just don't understand why she would dress like that, having all that money and everything. . . ."

I showed her an Osage book that contained several pictures from the 1920s, including group photos of unnamed white Osage Agency officials, all wearing suits and hats. I asked her to look through it to see if she could spot A. T. Woodward, whom Cara Mae had met on the visit with Mrs. Woodward.

"Oh, I don't remember what A. T. Woodward looked like," Cara Mae said, recoiling from the book with a jolt. She wouldn't even take it in her hands. "It was so long ago," she said dismissively.

I realize now what I was witnessing.

Cara Mae, welcome to the Stigma.

It is the same Stigma that she and Harry imparted to my mother when they tried to suppress all trace of her Indian background, including her own mother.

I saw one of the Stigma's faces on my mother the night she tearfully told me that she was an Osage Indian and so was I, and that Cara Mae was not her real mother.

And I saw another face of the Stigma on Sybil's birthday, the day after Christmas 1991, when Cara Mae fidgeted so in my living room and refused to even touch a book with pictures of Osage Indians.

And Cara Mae is seeing another face of the Stigma. It is not the prospect of the Bolton name being linked to a suicide scandal, or even of Harry's involvement in it being questioned. It is Cara Mae's fear that her friends in Denver might learn about her Indian connection, might find out there was an Indian skeleton in Harry's closet.

But there is another side to the Stigma that now possesses Cara Mae.

Her insistence that I not resurrect Sybil in the family is out of a desire to keep her hidden on the reservation to which Cara Mae and Harry had assigned her—this one being mental—and to which we as a nation have assigned all Indians, and for the same motives. If we finally release Indians from their reservations, as I am doing now with my Indian grandmother, if we finally bring them back into the land we took from them, then we would have to confront them, come face-to-face with them. That is a discomfiting, even horrifying prospect, as Cara Mae's recoil at seeing Indian pictures demonstrated. Coming face-to-face with Indians requires doing what I have done—coming face-to-face with our history, and our personal links to it, and the very real pain that even one small injustice such as the possible murder of one Indian, an insignificant act in the sweep of events, can cause generations later—in our case, sixty-six years after the gunshot. Coming face-to-face with our history requires coming face-to-face with our history's victims.

Looking close-up into the eyes of our victims would show not just their pain and suffering but reflect back a true picture of ourselves, show us as they see us, show up the blood on our hands that we are blind to.

"Harry didn't do it," Cara Mae said again, this time as she headed out the door after a round of goodbyes and kisses. "He didn't have anything to do with it."

Cara Mae Bolton never ceases to amaze me. I've been married three times, and each of my wives has wanted to steal her clothes. She's the only person I know who subscribes to *Barron's Business and Financial Weekly*. She bought a Mercedes because it came with free weekly washes. When I was between marriages, she gave me tips on the best places to meet women. (Church, if you must know.) She kept saying over and over that Harry didn't kill Sybil.

How did she know I had suspected?

I hadn't told anyone but Fleur.

Had Cara Mae suspected Harry as well?

DRIVING ACROSS OHIO, Kentucky and Indiana, I made lists.

Things I don't believe:

1. I don't believe Sybil and Harry had separated and were on the brink of divorce.

She was in Pawhuska on a temporary visit. Either she was visiting family and friends on pleasure or personal business, or she was cooling down from a fight with Harry that ended with the classic, and dramatic, "I'm going home to mother." In either case, Sybil planned to return to her life with Harry in Kansas City.

When a woman goes somewhere, what is the one thing she never fails to take with her?

Her jewelry.

It is often the first thing she packs, and if she goes somewhere for good, she doesn't leave any of it behind. Yet Angela Gorman Andretta, en route to Sybil's funeral in Pawhuska, stopped off at Harry's house in Kansas City to collect her half-sister's jewelry.

Sybil also had left behind with Harry the china, silver, ornaments and doll collection—all purchased with her Osage oil money and all associated, especially in those sexist days, with women's ware: possessions that a female would be expected to lay claim to in a permanent separation and relocation.

Assume for a moment that Sybil and Harry had separated and were in the process of getting a divorce. It does not fit my image of him, but Harry, in an attack of vindictiveness that marital warfare sometimes launches, might have insisted on keeping the good silver and china—but the dolls?

I just can't picture this young Clark Gable look-alike, as my mother remembers him, exercising his new right to date, going out with some woman, dining, wining and wooing her, wrapping his arm around her waist and whispering, "Wanna see my doll collection?"

2. I don't believe it was to discuss her personal problems and state of mind that Sybil phoned her father, Sewell Beekman, and begged him to visit her in Pawhuska the next day.

Daughters tell their love, relationship and psychological problems to their mothers or girlfriends, not to their fathers—and fat, tough, humorless, laconic and crooked Sewell Beekman was a man to be feared, not to confide in.

There is also no reason to believe that Sybil was even close to her father, since she had dropped Beekman as her surname and was known as Sybil Woodward before her marriage. (In contrast, her sister Angela Gorman kept her father's name until she married.)

There was only one reason to seek the company of a father as gruff and ill-humored as Sewell Beekman: Sybil was afraid of something.

Something must have happened that Friday—a confrontation, a caustic remark, a threat?—that scared Sybil so badly she called the one man she knew could protect her.

But her father failed her, and the next day she was dead.

3. I don't believe Sybil said, with a bullet in her chest, "Eleanor, I have shot myself," as the Pawhuska newspaper reported (or even "Eleanor, look what I've done," as Theil Annett remembers Sybil saying).

Not only were Sybil's last words in perfect grammar, but they also provided a legally usable—but all-too-convenient—deathbed confession. Had there been a suicide note, the article no doubt would have recorded every word, given the unusual detail of the report. Since there apparently was none, what better way to provide proof of suicide than to have it coming out of the mouth of the victim, her dying words, "in distinct tones" no less, not to mention in perfect English?

4. I don't believe Sybil spoke at all after she was shot.

Had the bullet hit her heart, she would have died before she hit the ground, or even had a chance to open her mouth to speak. Had it missed her heart, it would have entered her lung and given her a sucking chest wound.

I learned about sucking chest wounds in the Army. They are like blowing a tire—the wound sucks all the air out, and quickly. To save a soldier with a sucking chest wound, the Army teaches you to cut off a piece of plastic poncho raincoat, cram it into the bullet hole to make the lung airtight, and hurry. You have about a half-minute before the victim literally runs out of air and dies.

Sybil would have been in no shape to say anything while life was sucking out of her, and she certainly would have died before Eleanor the maid—answering the front door, according to the newspaper—arrived on the scene to hear her last gurgles.

5. I don't believe Sybil would have gotten a Catholic funeral had she committed suicide.

Today she would have. The church makes an exception to its rules if there was "some mental disturbance" and it was not "a deliberate and malicious suicide," as a priest put it—in other words, if the person was not aware of what he was doing.

But in the 1920s, the American Catholic Church still maintained strict adherence to the Vatican canon, and one of its strictest rules pertained to suicide. Catholics were simply not permitted to commit suicide, and there were no exceptions. At the instant of suicide, a Catholic ceased being a Catholic. The committer of this mortal sin was automatically excommunicated, which precluded any right to a funeral mass and burial in consecrated soil.

I called the Immaculate Conception Catholic Church in Pawhuska and asked the pastor, the Reverend Joseph Mazaika, whether Father Van Durme—the priest who said Sybil's funeral mass on November 12, 1925—had left behind any sort of diary or journal of his duty in Pawhuska. I was looking for confirmation of a suspicion that Father Van Durme permitted Catholic rites for Sybil because Mrs. Woodward had confided in him, told him the truth, that her daughter had not committed suicide.

No, Father Mazaika said, after checking, no such record. However, Father Mazaika's recollection of Father Van Durme reinforced my suspicion.

Father Mazaika explained that Father Van Durme's predecessor had been the Pawhuska parish priest for many decades and had grown lax over the years—marrying non-Catholics, for example, even failing to maintain parish records of the baptisms, marriages and funerals that took place in the church. Father Van Durme, a young, tough, no-nonsense, strict-constructionist Belgian priest, was given the Pawhuska parish with specific orders to turn it into a Catholic church again—and he took over not long before Sybil's funeral.

To me, it was doubtful that since Father Van Durme was new to the job—and his orders were to go strictly by the book—he would have said Sybil's requiem mass if he knew she had committed suicide. Her death was front-page news in Pawhuska, so he must have been aware of the reported cause of death. But he must have received—probably from Mrs. Woodward—some sort of proof or assurance that Sybil did not kill herself, and an explanation of why her death was ruled a suicide.

Mrs. Woodward must have convinced Father Van Durme that someone else, besides Sybil, had put the bullet in her heart.

6. *I don't believe Sybil shot herself by accident.*

This theory was suggested early on by my sister Carolyn. She conjectured that Sybil, out in the yard with the baby, started cleaning her pistol—which, according to Theil, she had recently purchased—or pulled it out of her purse for some reason, maybe to double-check the setting of the safety. The gun went off, shot Sybil in the chest, and was found next to her body—ergo, suicide.

I was skeptical. This theory assumes that Sybil was not off her rocker, and I doubted that any sane mother would be handling a pistol while playing with her child. As for cleaning a gun in a toddler's presence, if baby Kathleen were anything like my son Kevin, she would have walked off with some crucial part and thrown it somewhere, never to be seen again by human eyes. How about the baby chewing and swallowing one of the bullets?

But the main reason I don't buy the theory is that you just cannot shoot yourself accidentally in the chest—it is as close to a sure-shot certainty as you can get. I checked this with my father—an expert marksman and possessor of an Army-issue general's pistol for a decade. He concurred. In an accidental pistol discharge, you can blow your head off, you can put a bullet in any of your extremities, you can shoot your baby, but you cannot hit your chest, especially your heart.

7. *I don't believe Sybil bought the pistol that killed her.*

Are we to accept that in 1920s Osage County, Oklahoma, a violent place in the grip of a Reign of Terror, in which sixty Osages had already been murdered, there was not one gun for Sybil to shoot herself with in the house of A. T. Woodward, a white man married to an Osage? There was probably a gun in every room.

The logic of Sybil's pistol purchase assumes that she committed suicide, and rules out even the chance of another possibility. As best as I can track it, the train of thought goes something like this: The pistol found near Sybil's body was not one of Woodward's, so it must have belonged to Sybil, so she must have bought it herself, so she must have intended to end her life with it. As the newspaper said, "From the evidence of preparations for the act, it appears that self-destruction had been carefully planned."

No one seems to have considered the possibility that the gun belonged to someone else, who left it there after using it on Sybil.

If there was no suicide note—and assuming her confession to Eleanor that "I have shot myself" was made up—how could anyone be certain that Sybil committed suicide, or even have gotten that idea?

The pistol must have been found in her hand.

We've seen it in detective movies and trashy TV shows a thousand times: gunshot, running footsteps, door opens; light floods into room and onto woman's body on floor, and reveals wrinkle-free dress hiked up to respectable length on leg, knees always together, not a hair out of place and, of course, pistol in hand.

Ah, the viewer decides, she shot herself.

Ah, the real-life homicide detective decides, someone shot her and is trying to make it look like suicide.

When you shoot yourself, the gun always ends up across the room.

That is the result of the simultaneous effect of the weapon's recoil and, literally, a death throw. When a bullet rips into a vital organ, a suicide's body spasms, his arms jerk and his hands open, at the same instant that the gun he is holding kicks. Pistols of suicide shooters have been found a good twenty-five to thirty feet from the body.

8. I don't believe Sybil was depressed enough to shoot herself in front of her baby.

This is probably the real reason I embarked upon this journey to solve the mystery of Sybil Bolton's death. At some point along the way, it became more important to me to disprove her suicide than to prove her murder by Harry Bolton. I simply did not want to have a grandmother who would shoot herself in front of her baby. I did not want to be related to anyone who could do such a thing. I did not want to carry within me, and pass to my children, the genes of such horror.

Generalities breed exceptions, of course, and in suicide the exceptions are shocking. An expert in suicide and murder—a state's attorney—said that when people get the suicide bug, they can kill themselves any time, anyplace and in front of anyone. But suicide tends to be a personal, not a social, act. It happens in isolation—born in the isolation of a depressed mind and carried out in the isolation of a basement, a locked room, a lonely spot outdoors, often at night.

The site of Sybil's alleged suicide was not exactly isolated or lonely: the lawn in a busy neighborhood, in front of an inquiring toddler and most probably neighbors, at nearly noon on a mild, sunny Saturday. According to the local weather report for November 7, 1925, the temperature was around fifty degrees, dropping in the afternoon, and it was the first sunny day after a week of rain.

Although her spot was not, her choice of method was consistent with the pattern of female suicides. Sexism exists even in self-destruction, a coroner explained. Men and women choose different ways to end their lives.

Men tend to shoot themselves in the head, a reflection perhaps of their desire to kill the source of their pain and not to prolong their dying. In doing so, they show a disregard for the reaction of others to the sickening sight. (An exception I heard about was a man who left a note apologizing for any cleanup he might necessitate and shot himself with his head in the basement sink to avoid spilling any blood on the floor.) But women, the coroner said, are too vain to blow their heads off. They kill themselves with a view to how they will look in their coffins (these are the coroner's words, not mine), so they tend not to mar their faces. They also tend to be more thoughtful than men about the mess their deaths might create. They use pills in bed or a razor in the tub. In the rare instances they use a gun, they are the heart shooters.

My mother tells the story of a close friend's in-law who was eating dinner with his family, suddenly pulled out a .45 and blew himself all over the kids and food.

That is one of the horrifying exceptions, as Sybil's death might be.

People who kill themselves in front of family members are extremely depressed, more depressed than "ordinary" suicides, so depressed that they are unaware of what they are doing, apart from relieving their pain.

Was Sybil?

The view I get of her in her last two days does not indicate a depressed person. It points, instead, to someone very active and aware.

Sybil was active and aware enough to become frightened, even terrified, of something on Friday, November 6. A depressed person probably would not have had such a reaction.

She was active and aware enough to go to the considerable length of calling her father long-distance that day, and to care enough about her welfare and future to ask him to visit. There was no easy push-button, direct dial in those days; long distance meant long waiting and much hassle. Would a deeply depressed person have gone through all that trouble, have even tried, or cared?

Sybil was active and aware enough to go shopping that Saturday morning, as the newspaper reported. Her death was "carried out shortly after reaching home," it said. A depressed person probably would not have gone out, especially on a crowded Saturday morning when he or she didn't have to.

And Sybil was active and aware enough to do something that the maid in the house easily could have done for her—take her baby outside and play on the lawn with her, the last thing Sybil did in her life, except die.

Things I do believe:

1. *I believe A. T. Woodward was "dirty."*

Osages were being terrorized by killers and robbed of millions of dollars by their corrupt lawyer-guardians. To the Indians, the Reign of Terror encompassed not only the murders but also the swindling. Both were parts of a wide-ranging plot to deprive them of their wealth and oil lands. All white men were suspect, especially those who were married to Osages and those who were lawyers.

Woodward was both.

The year before Sybil's death, the Interior Department had charged two dozen Osage County lawyer-guardians with corruption. Not only were the murders under investigation by the FBI—outsiders who couldn't be bought like the local law-enforcement officials—but the feds were now scrutinizing guardians' accounts. Numbered were the days of easy pickings for the eighty lawyers practicing in the Osage County seat of 8,000 people—alleged to be almost as many lawyers as in the Oklahoma state capital, which then had a population of 140,000. And some of these guardians of the law might end up in jail. Pawhuska was not a happy place in 1925, among either the whites or their Indian victims.

One would assume by Woodward's job that he was on the side of the Osages. According to the FBI files, he was the Osage tribal attorney, responsible for counseling and representing the Osages legally.

However, if Woodward had been a "good guy," Sybil's death by gunshot would have made him an immediate target of all of Osage County's "bad guys"—lawyers, law-enforcement officials and killers alike—looking for a way to take the federal heat off and get the FBI off their trail. Sybil's shooting death, in fact, would have been cause for rejoicing, and Woodward may have wound up the scapegoat for all the county's crimes.

If Woodward had been "clean," any one of the "dirty" dozens of lawyers and authorities in Osage County certainly would have tried to implicate the Osage tribal attorney in the Reign of Terror killings. For Sybil's death mirrored the Osage murders: a headright holder ends up dead by violence, and the financial benefactor is the white head of household. That Woodward was a federal official working for the legal protection of the Osages would have made the possibility of pinning the Indian murders on him irresistible. It might even have derailed the feds' investigation, if one of their own was ruled to have dunnit.

But only if Woodward had been "clean."

If he had been "dirty," involved in the plot against the Osages, his partners in crime would have rushed to Woodward's defense. They would have shielded his stepdaughter's death from notice by the FBI—if for no other reason than to protect themselves from the possibility that the feds might pry some incriminating details out of him, might use him to crack the case.

So what happened to Woodward?

Was he "framed" for the Osage murders—or was he able to sweep Sybil's death silently under the carpet and dodge a police investigation, an autopsy and a coroner's report?

What amazes me is how quickly Sybil's death was declared a suicide.

The Sunday morning newspaper of Muskogee, Oklahoma, eighty-five miles southeast of Pawhuska, carried the AP report of her death. I don't know the *Muskogee Daily Phoenix*'s deadline for Sunday's paper in 1925, but I imagine it was pretty early in the afternoon. Today, in the age of computer communications, satellite transmission of newspaper pages to presses, high-speed printing and a distribution system that takes advantage of interstate highways, the deadline for stories for the Sunday first edition of *The Washington Post* is 5 P.M. (*The New York Times*'s is even earlier.) Stories, of course, can be added to later editions throughout the press run, but there has to be a pretty important reason to do so. I can't imagine the *Muskogee Daily Phoenix* tearing up the Sunday paper to report the suicide of one unknown Indian woman whose tribe is located far outside its circulation area.

The body was probably still warm when the Pawhuska police authorities gave the AP reporter the story that Sybil Bolton had committed suicide "around noon" and told him that "no cause for the act is known other than she was separated from her husband."

They forgot to mention that Sybil was an Osage headright holder, saying only that she was the daughter of "Mrs. A. M. Woodward."

2. I believe the extraordinarily high price of Sybil's funeral—$1,742.25, including a stiff $1,500 for her coffin—was payment to Mr. Johnson for no-questions-asked services.

Osages often were charged higher rates than whites for goods and services in Osage County, but Mr. Johnson's bill was unusually high, even for the shameless rip-off artists of Pawhuska.

In 1926, a newspaper report that bereaved Osage parents had been charged $1,000 for their young son's coffin caused such a stir in Washington that the Interior Department stepped in to regulate Osage County morticians, ruling that the funeral bills of Osages would not be paid until the Osage Agency reviewed them and approved the prices.

But the boy's coffin that caused the controversy cost one-third less than Sybil's.

What were the Woodwards trying to hide in Sybil's $1,500 coffin?

The bullet being in the wrong place for a suicide, perhaps?

More than one wound?

3. I believe that days before Sybil's death, she sat down at her childhood desk in her bedroom and started writing Harry a normal I-miss-you, I'm-thinking-of-you letter.

She began by saying, with all the feeling she could wring out, how terribly unhappy, lonely and frustrated she was, away from her husband and shouldering alone all of the responsibilities of caring for a baby. Perhaps it included an apology for a spat, saying it was all her fault and she was sorry.

After the first sentence or so, she changed her mind, maybe dissatisfied with how it read, perhaps spotting a spelling or grammatical error that embarrassed this educated young woman. Or maybe she was interrupted and found herself no longer in the mood when she returned to the letter.

In a mechanical motion, she ripped the paper in half, wadded it up and tossed it in the trash basket in her room, just as she had done with countless sheets of botched homework assignments since she was a young girl, growing up in this room.

After Sybil died, Mrs. Woodward found the aborted, crumpled and discarded letter and read it as a suicide note, desperate either to understand why her daughter had taken her life—or desperate to find anything to make it appear as if she had done so.

4. *I believe that the three substantially different versions of Sybil's suicide point to only one thing—suicide's alternative.*

Somebody lied.

The suicide accounts from the Pawhuska newspaper and Theil Annett, from Claribel Shaw and from Cara Mae Bolton can all be traced to one source: the Woodwards.

Theil Annett told my mother that everything she knew about the suicide came from the Woodwards.

Harry Bolton lived in Kansas City, so his version of the death had to come from the only people left in Pawhuska whom he knew—the Woodwards.

The Beekmans heard the same story. Since they lived in Oklahoma City and Sybil's death was not reported there, their source of information had to be Mr. Beekman's ex-wife, Mrs. Woodward. If there had been any discrepancies between what the Boltons and Beekmans knew, these would have come out in the conversations between Cara Mae and Mrs. Beekman about Sybil's suicide.

Claribel Shaw indicated that her version—about the lawn—was just something that was known among the circle of Kate Woodward's close friends. After Sybil's death, Claribel Shaw and Mrs. Woodward became best friends, as she said in her note to my mother. Mrs. Woodward must have confided in Claribel and her other friends, telling the truth about where the death took place.

Claribel's account—along with her emotional reaction sixty-six years later when she recounted the story—has the ring of truth to it, but as a suicide scenario, it is the most improbable version.

But why would the Woodwards lie about suicide?

Of the four different ways that a person can die—natural causes, accident, murder and suicide—suicide is by far the most difficult to admit to others, and to publicize.

Once you have done the hard part—admitting that the death of a loved one was a suicide and not by natural causes or by accident—why then would you lie about the method, time and place? What difference does it make that the suicide took place on a Friday night or a Saturday morning, by rope, razor, pills, plunge or pistol?

And why lie about it more than once? Why tell your son-in-law and ex-husband one thing, your immediate family and the newspapers another, and your best friend yet another?

There is only one reason to lie about suicide: murder.

If I were a police detective investigating Sybil's death, the Woodwards' lies alone would persuade me to discount suicide as the cause of death, and to start hunting for suspects. But I wouldn't suspect the Woodwards of the murder.

The Woodwards didn't do it. If either of them had killed Sybil, they would have stuck to one story.

The Woodwards' lies also prove one other thing.

They were desperate to try to convince others that Sybil committed suicide and that they were not Reign of Terror killers. But if they could have pinned the murder on someone else, found an easy fall guy, they probably would have.

That means that my grandfather, Harry Bolton, did not kill my grandmother. Because if he had, or if there were even the slightest hint that he had, if there had been any possible way to suggest that he had, the Woodwards would have nailed him for murder.

INTERSTATE 44 IN MISSOURI offers a fast-forward cue of stolen Osage land. These days, interstates are delineated on maps in blue, perhaps out of some up-yours reaction by Rand McNally to *Blue Highways,* which is, among other things, the back-roads, anti-interstate book by William Least Heat-Moon, an Osage.

Buried beneath the asphalt, concrete, gravel and graded ground of Interstate 44 is an old Osage foot trail. Ancient Osage paths also lie beneath many of the roads that exit from the superhighway. Some of these former Osage trails are now filled with Cherokees, Navahos, Dakotas, Apaches and Winnebagos, their drivers—mostly white and retired—headed for Branson, Missouri, near the Arkansas border in the southwest corner of Missouri.

Branson, located in what was once the heart of Osage territory, entertains the notion of dethroning Nashville, Tennessee, as the country-music capital of the world. Once in Branson, country-music fans, after driving "65 smiles per hour" (as one show promises to deliver), can catch the Soghi Tabuchi Show (he plays the fiddle and is "the talk of Branson," perhaps because he is Oriental); they can "see Americana live" at the Moe Bandy Show, "a rodeo of hit songs and hilarious surprises" that will "keep you coming back for Moe!"; or they can visit the late Ray Stevens's "beautiful all new" 2,000-seat theater on Shepherd of the Hills Expressway, where "you'll have more fun than if you were at a Mississippi squirrel revival or a Shriners' convention." Even country singer Johnny Cash, part Cherokee, originally from former Osage land in Arkansas, has set up shop in Branson. For tickets to his theater, call 335-CASH.

Interstate 44 starts at St. Louis and courses southwest, its billboard signs illustrating why the Show Me State is called that: Missourians can't seem to get from here to there, and back again, without a sign showing them the way. Drivers are invited to visit the "tour-r-ri-fic" Jesse James Wax Museum; house-hunt at Mobile Home in the Sky, so named because a rusty blue trailer is perched on poles twenty feet above the ground; head for Fantastic Caverns—"America's only ride-thru cave"—or its competitor, Meramec Caves ("caves are cool: 60 degrees all year round"); wash their vehicles at XVIII Wheelers Truck Wash; go bass-fishing on Tracker Boats, Landau Boats, Boats by Lowe, and Appleby's Boats & Motors ("we don't sell retail, we sell shirt-tail"); be buried by Holman Funeral Homes ("caring service when you need it most") or part with their pets at Friends of the Family Memorial Gardens; see live animals at Exotic Animal Paradise ("cats, cats and more cats," "largest herd of African cattle in America"); buy Indian and western jewelry at the Mule Trading Post, Totem Pole Trading Post, Old Time Antiques, Shaw's, "the Midwest's gem center" ("low country prices"), and Ozarkland ("famous bargain center," "worth waiting for"); be fitted for teeth at the Springfield Dental Center ("quality dentures in a day"); get fireworks at Red Rocket ("best bang in the Ozarks"); sleep, or whatever, at the Du Kum Inn; and get a "free 72 oz. steak if eaten in 1 meal" at the Big Texan.

No sign of the Osages, though.

In making this observation, I chose to ignore Osage Beach, about halfway between St. Louis and Branson. Osage Beach is a Branson clone.

Just as Branson is trying to become the next Nashville, Osage Beach is trying to become the next Branson. The Osage in its name refers not to the Indians but to the Osage River, which, like the old Osage path beneath Interstate 44, lies buried under the Lake of the Ozarks and its extension, the Harry S Truman Reservoir.

Missouri seems to have a knack for burying its Indian past. For all I know, my entire ancestral Osage family—grandfathers, grandmothers, aunts, uncles, cousins and in-laws—is underwater, floating around southwest Missouri, just because people there wanted cheaper electricity and closer water sports. If you fish in the reservoir and on the lake, and cook what you catch, you may have eaten some of my relatives.

In addition to fishing at Osage Beach, you can camp at Der Vater's Edge RV Park (if that doesn't have space, Hava Space RV Park promises to). If you're looking for a motel, there's Gorilla Villa. Hungry and tired of fish (and my family)? Try Frog's. For entertainment, "no other show offers . . . more class" than the Main Street Opry, presented by Gabby Gumm and recommended by the governor of Missouri, John Ashcroft. ("The music of the Main Street Opry is the music of America," he says.) At Osage Beach, you also can go boating—including excursion boat tours and dinner cruises—horseback riding, and antique shopping. You can mall-linger, play miniature and regular golf, take trolley and go-cart rides, do country crafts.

You can do just about anything, in fact, but find an Osage.

This is not unique to Osage Beach. Try finding one Delaware in Delaware, an Arkansas in Arkansas, a Missouri in Missouri, a Kansas in Kansas, any Indian in Indiana. When I am asked about Indians' objections to sports team names such as the Washington Redskins and the Atlanta Braves and their "Tomahawk Chop," I think about all the states, counties, cities, towns, rivers, creeks, lakes, resorts and children's camps named after Indians where none are in evidence, much less in residence, and from where they were driven out by beatings, burnings, killings or cavalry, and I wonder which is the greater insult.

I had never driven through the Osage part of Missouri before. Looking at it for the first time, through the eyes of the Osage part of me, I felt at once attached to this land and alienated from it.

Stripped of the cultural schlock of the last two hundred years, the scenery I was seeing was the landscape of my ancestors' lives. This was where they lived, left descendants who ultimately led to me, and died, sometimes gruesomely. These were the types of trees they saw, that shaded and sheltered them; these the forests, hills and plateaus; this the view of the sky; this river, this creek they crossed, perhaps here; this was their land, and the lay of the land they gazed upon, that confined their lives, provided them with food and shaped their religion, and from where they would find out—like all of us, someday—if their belief in God and Spirit-land were true, or a facet of their fears of dying. Yet this is the land from which they were driven—discarded and disregarded, without any sign of them left now, after living here for so many thousands of years—by new-comers who moved in not quite two hundred years ago, and reshaped the land and rewrote its history, to mirror their own image and intellect, or lack of it.

After the umpteenth sign showing a hillbilly in yellow tatteralls toking lazily on a corncob pipe, I started thinking how nice it might be to see just one trace of the Osages on this, their old trace. Would it be too much to ask, I asked, for just one historical marker acknowledging the Osages' former presence and—yes, hard to fathom by people who regarded them as subhuman savages, who now choose to ignore them and, for the most part, who have never heard of them—these Indians' important con-tributions to the shaping of the United States? A simple sign in the Show Me State, just to show politeness, if nothing else, on the part of these im-migrants to Osage Country, now Ozarkland. Perhaps on Interstate 44 in Springfield, where the traffic backup for Branson begins in the right lane.

The sign could say, "The Osage Indians lived here since the Ice Age and were the dominant power of this area until the United States govern-ment drove them out in 1808, to make the Ozarks safe for hillbillies and country music."

Too subtle, perhaps. Too hard to read at "65 smiles per hour."

It was to live as near as possible to the Missouri burial grounds of their ancestors that was the Osages' prime concern in shopping for a new reservation after leaving Kansas in 1870. The Osages also hoped to find land that could not be farmed and thus would not cultivate an interest by whites.

The Osages chose an area to the south, across the state line, which once had been part of their territory, an ancestral hunting ground. In fact, the area was a microcosm of their former domain. The eastern part mirrored the hilly, wooded Missouri and Arkansas Ozarks, flattening gradually on the western side into tallgrass plains, such as those in Kansas and beyond. Most of the terrain was forbidding—rugged, steep hills and ravines, embedded with limestone boulders, baked red in the scorching sun of summer and coated with thick stands of blackjack oak. It was perfect.

Before leaving Kansas, part of the tribe had wanted to move west, rather than south to Indian Territory, and throw in their lot with the Plains Indians chasing the dwindling herds of buffalo. Certainly if the Osages had done that, the tragedy that later befell them—and my family—would not have happened. But, who knows, the Osages instead may have ended up like the Oglala Sioux now living on the Pine Ridge reservation, which, according to the 1990 census, encompasses the poorest county in the United States—Shannon County, South Dakota, with 63.1 percent of the population below poverty level, a per capita income of just $3,417 and an unemployment rate of more than 70 percent; or in Ziebach County, South Dakota, on the Cheyenne River Sioux reservation, the seventh-poorest U.S. county, with 51.1 percent living below poverty level; or in Todd County, South Dakota, on the Rosebud Sioux reservation, the tenth-poorest, with 50 percent living below poverty level and 90 percent without jobs.

At least in this regard, the Osages were lucky to have heeded the counsel of Wah-ti-an-kah, a tribal leader with a reputation for persuasive oratory. He won the debate over the Osages' relocation by pointing out the new reservation's proximity to the Place of the Many Swans, and why whites wouldn't want it:

"White man cannot put iron thing in ground here. White man will not come to this land. There are many hills here. . . . White man does not like country where there are hills, and he will not come, I believe. This country is not good for things which white man puts in ground. . . . If my people go west where land is like floor of lodge, white man will come to our lodges and say, 'We want your land.' Government will come to our lodges and say, 'We will buy this land for white man; white man wants this land; he will plant things there.' Soon land will end and Osages will have no home; they will be far from place where their grandfather is; from graves of their grandfather. . . . It good for my people to go to this land in south."

The Osages purchased their new reservation in Indian Territory on the mistaken assumption that ownership of the land would give them the legal right to keep out whites. That right, they also believed, somehow would be strengthened by the fact that the money to pay for their land came from the proceeds of a commercial transaction—a real estate sale— rather than from an appropriation or grant by the U.S. government.

How naive these Osages were. Perhaps in the euphoria of sensing a solution to their problems, they momentarily forgot with whom they were dealing. To the "Indian givers" of Washington, Indians had only one right—the right of giving way to whites. It was appropriate, I think, that the Osages' main town, the capital of the Osage Nation, was named after their great chief, Paw-hiu-skah, White Hair, whose name derived from his unsuccessful attempt to scalp an American. The story of White Hair provides a powerful symbol that the Osages' fate in history, and fortune in life, were determined, even defined, by the Americans, whom the Osages never could quite grasp.

As Wah-ti-an-kah had predicted, whites bypassed the new reservation—but for only a couple of years. One day in 1872, my great-great-grandfather, William Conner—he was listed as the father of my great-grandmother, Kathleen Woodward, on one of her three "Marriage Cards" kept at the Osage Agency—sat on a rock atop a barren hill, where the Osage Agency is now situated. He stared down into the valley that would become the town of Pawhuska.

"It'll be a long time before white men occupy this land," Conner said.

I found the quote in a memoir of an Osage Agency cook, Laban S. Records, whom Conner had befriended. Conner was complaining to Records about "how things have changed here," just two years later.

"Now look at these buildings and the business that's being done here" by whites, Conner groused.

Records described my great-great-grandfather as "an educated half-breed Osage," but Conner also must have been clever, even wily, buddying up to a cook, whose kitchen had an unlimited supply of food, during a time of starvation.

Although they were then the richest Indians in America with nearly $9 million in the bank after they bought their reservation, the U.S. government was starving them out. (The government did not actually pay Indians their treaty-provided money in cash, but rather its equivalent in supplies, known as annuity provisions.) It was nothing personal—all Indians' rations were being drastically reduced. In 1874, when Conner fed Records the cook with tall tales of hunting adventures, the United States was in the second year of a five-year depression, triggered by the Panic of '73, a period of hard times that rivaled the Great Depression of the 1930s in severity.

The politicians of Washington, determined to strip the budget of even the slightest appearance of lavishness for fear of angering hard-luck voters, spared no cutback on the population that couldn't strike back on Election Day. Indians didn't vote. The shapers of Indian policy rationalized that hunger would finally force Indians to turn to farming.

On the uncultivable Osage reservation, the only thing that grew was hunger. Congress had made no appropriation for Osage provisions for the second half of 1874, so Osage agent Isaac T. Gibson urged the tribe to spend the summer months buffalo-hunting on the plains—this in addition to their semiannual hunts in spring and late fall. "It was necessary for them to obtain a few [extra] weeks' subsistence on the plains, or starve," Gibson wrote.

The tribe set out in early June and, once on the plains, split up into bands. "Finding but few" buffalo, smaller parties broke off from the bands. By August, one of the hunting parties—consisting of eighteen men, ten women, two of whom were pregnant, and two boys—had wandered into south-central Kansas, on the trail of a small buffalo herd. They killed some, camped, chased and killed some more, camped—and stayed at this campsite three days "killing buffalo and curing meat." The Osages were located outside the town of Medicine Lodge, seventy-five miles southwest of Wichita. On the morning of the fourth day—August 7, 1874—they were packing to head back to the reservation, when about forty armed white men rode up to them.

The Indians thought the whites were soldiers of the Kansas militia—a few wore uniforms—but they noticed that some rode plow horses. According to a sworn statement to U.S. Indian commissioners by three Osages—Ah-kah-ka-he-kah, Che-hah-ka-she and Ne-hah—the white riders surrounded eight Osage warriors, who rode out in separate groups of two or three to greet the whites peacefully, and disarmed the Indians. Suddenly "one of the white men fired, [and] they all broke and run [on their horses], some toward camp, and some in other directions; and at the same time those [Osages still] in camp also ran [on horseback]. They chased us about three miles, firing at us all the way. . . . The chase ended about sundown, and the white troops [left], and soon after we also returned to look after our missing men.

"We soon found one of them with two shots near one eye, one near the other, one in the cheek, one in the neck, two in the breast, one in his bowels, and he was scalped, and his horse shot near him. Another was found dead near where we were first taken prisoners, with two shots in his breast, one in his leg, breaking it; he also was scalped. Near our own camp was found [a] third man, shot through the small of the back, the ball coming out through his breast; he was not scalped; he had on, when killed, a finely-worked belt, which was taken off. It was now dark, and we were unable to find our other missing man, who, we suppose, was killed, as we saw him shot through the body, still running, and afterward saw him fall from his horse. We did not again return to the place of the fight, but started directly for home, traveling slowly, as two of our women were about to be confined, and others were sick."

The whites had stolen fifty-four of their horses, all of their cured buffalo meat "and all their other property," agent Gibson reported. The journey back to Pawhuska took five days, "without food, several of [the Osages] on foot, and most of them nearly naked," he said.

The Osages denied the allegation of the whites' leader, Kansas militia captain Cyrus M. Ricker, that the Osages had fired first, were in fact on the warpath and had attacked his men. "War-parties never take their women and children," the Osages scoffed.

The commissioners found in favor of the Indians, not that it got them anything, including what the militiamen stole—or rather, alleged militiamen. At the time of the attack, which the Osages came to call the Medicine Lodge Massacre, the instigators were just Medicine Lodge townies. To make it appear that their "act of murder [was] an act of war," the commissioners said in their report, Kansas Governor Crawford had named them to the militia ten days after the attack, backdating their appointments.

The United States government, its commissioners' finding in hand, moved swiftly to mete out justice in the case: The Osages, and all other Indians in Indian Territory, were confined to their reservations, and forbidden to hunt buffalo on the plains that autumn and winter. What crops their women had planted in small plots were eaten by swarms of grasshoppers that swept the West that year. Famine followed the first frost.

Congress authorized the government to spend some of the Osages' money in the U.S. Treasury to buy provisions for them, but stipulated that only those Indians who performed manual labor—either farming for themselves or odd jobs for the tribe, such as splitting rails—would receive food as payment-in-kind. The Osages were furious, telling Gibson, as he later wrote, that the stipulation was "odious. . . . They insisted that it was great injustice to require them to work for their food, which was purchased with their own money, thus paying twice for their subsistence, and that they did not authorize the Government to expend their money for supplies, nor would they permit it, demanding their money in hand."

The Osages kept "demanding their money in hand" for five more years. The Osages' millions—derived not only from the sale of their Kansas reservation but also from land cessions under previous treaties—earned $55,000 in interest annually in the U.S. Treasury. This was the money they received each year—but only $15,000 in cash, paid semiannually. For the year 1878, for example, each of the 2,203 Osages listed on the annuity roll—including my great-grandmother, Kate Conner, or To-wam-pah, then five months old; her father, William Conner, age thirty-two; and her mother, Angeline Penn or Hum-pa-to-kah, age twenty-six—received $3.40 in cash for the first half-year and $3.50 for the second. Another $5,500 in interest was set aside for educational purposes, and the rest was paid in rations, doled out weekly—which the Osages likened to being "fed like dogs," and small dogs at that.

In 1879, the Osages sent a delegation to Washington, to lobby the commissioner of Indian affairs to stop the rations, pay them in cash instead, and pay them more. As with their decision to move to Indian Territory, Wah-ti-an-kah played a decisive role. He went to the meeting wearing a red blanket wrapped so high on him that it covered most of his face. The Osages were seated around a conference room.

The commissioner entered the room, abruptly pulled out his watch and said he had another appointment. "I am sorry," he said to their interpreter, "I had forgotten about it until just now. Tell them to make themselves comfortable, and that I shall not be gone any longer than necessary."

Wah-ti-an-kah suddenly sprang to his feet and, just as swiftly, placed his tremendous Osage height and bulk between the commissioner and the door—and flung off his blanket. In the account of this encounter, one can almost hear the gasps around the room and the commish's heart pound. The Osage wore only a breechcloth. His chest was lined with tattoos, and his face with red, yellow and black paint.

Wah-ti-an-kah was dressed for war.

"Tell this man to sit down," the scowling Osage told the interpreter.

The commissioner leaped for a chair. Sitting made the glowering figure above him even more towering.

Sitting, the commissioner tried to belittle the giant Indian by tsk-tsking that the Great White Father "was almost ready to believe that these people were ready to be paid in money instead of having rations given to them, but here is a man who has come to Washington with his war paint on. If the White Father saw him this way he would think that all Osages were savages yet and would not know how to use money. He would say that the rations ought to be continued until these people became civilized. Surely this man who doesn't know how to act—who comes to my office almost naked, with war paint on his face, is not civilized enough to know how to use money."

But Wah-ti-an-kah stood his ground. He sucked in his stomach and touched his expanding chest. God "has made me as I am. I am glad, I am not ashamed of my body. I do not wear clothes to hide body that [God] gave me; clothes that reach up to neck. If these things make white man civilized, I believe it is good that this man wears them. Tell this man we have come long way to talk about rations. Tell him we did not come to talk about white man's" ways.

The commissioner inhaled, about to say something, but only silence came out with the exhale. He put on a visible display of thinking, glancing at the floor, at the ceiling, at Wah-ti-an-kah, into space. Then he said, looking past Wah-ti-an-kah to the Osages around the table, "I think that we can assure you gentlemen that there will be no more rations."

Wah-ti-an-kah walked to his seat and sat down. But he quickly rose and said to the interpreter, "Tell this man it is all right now—he can go now."

The Osages thus became the first American Indians to receive all of their annuities, including rations, in cash. In July 1879, each member of the tribe, including my year-and-a-half-old great-grandmother, received a quarterly cash payment of $40—$160 a year. By 1897, their per capita income had risen to $214 a year.

The first cash payment of 1879 was a watershed event of Osage history—and started the clock ticking on the Reign of Terror forty years later. The Osages now possessed—and received on a regular basis—the one commodity in short supply in the cash-strapped West, only one year out of the nation's harshest depression to date. It has been the Osages' curse to always possess what whites did not, and would go to any length to acquire: in Missouri, furs and access to the west; in Kansas, land suited for farming. Once again, in their new home in Indian Territory, the Osages had something that whites wanted.

The Osages were no longer being "fed like dogs"—instead, they were fed on by wolves.

Historians have described the white men who now descended upon the Osages variously as "riff-raff," "rowdies," "vagabonds, gamblers, whiskey peddlers, criminals," "sharpers, thieves, bandits," "lawbreakers, fugitives," "outcasts," "human predators, confidence men," "swearing illiterate men," "uneducated rough men," "unscrupulous white men," "low-down, sneaking pillaging dogs," "horse racers," "buzzards," "dishonest scamps," "schemers, crooks, floaters," "backwash," "convicts, bad men, card-sharps, former cow-punchers," "renegades, grafters," "petty thieves, barbarians, cutpurses, murderers, rapists, human rats," "half-savage frontiersmen," "ruthless men who would cut a baby's throat just to see if their blade was keen," "the vile and the wicked from everywhere."

By 1888, violent crime, bootlegging and illegal squatting had become so rampant on the reservation that the Osage Agency asked the federal district court in Wichita to recruit a white marshal to head and train a twenty-five-man, all-Osage police force, formed a decade before but engaged mostly in rounding up truants from the reservation school. There was only one taker for the $8-a-month position, a nineteen-year-old U.S. deputy marshal.

The Osages' new police chief was Bob Dalton. He spent his time on the Osage reservation—at least a year and a half—honing his murder, graft and robbery skills for his future fame as head of the notorious Dalton Gang of outlaws.

He hired his brother, Emmett, for the $5-a-month police sergeant's job, and later his brother, Grat. To supplement their meager salaries from the Bureau of Indian Affairs, the brothers formed what became known as the "most-efficient horse-stealing ring" in Indian Territory. They stole Indians' horses and sold them to whites in Kansas and Missouri border towns. They also did some bootlegging and bribe taking on the side. In his spare time, Bob Dalton paid Pawhuska boys a quarter to toss tin cans in the air so he could practice shooting at moving targets. He put the skill to use on a weekend visit to his ex-girlfriend, a distant cousin, outside Coffeyville, Kansas, located on former Osage land on the Indian Territory border. Dalton killed her new boyfriend, shooting him in the neck with a Winchester rifle.

Accounts vary on how the Daltons' employment with the Osages was terminated in June or July 1890—they were caught engaging in one of their illegal pastimes and were either fired, quit or galloped away just out of range of a posse's six-shooters. There is no dispute, though, about the end of the Dalton Gang in 1892.

Angry citizens of Coffeyville cornered them in an alley and riddled them with bullets right after the gang had robbed two of the town's banks. Bob and Grat Dalton and two other members of the gang were killed. Townspeople took turns posing for photographs with the dead Daltons, and pumping the corpses' arms up and down to watch the blood spurt out.

Emmett Dalton took twenty-one slugs but survived. He was imprisoned in the Kansas State Penitentiary until 1907, at which time he moved to Bartlesville—twenty-five miles from Pawhuska—and lived down the street from Frank Phillips, Harry Sinclair, George and Jean Paul Getty and other oil barons taking more wealth out of the Osage reservation than in the Daltons' wildest fantasies. In the 1920s, Emmett—now an anti-crime and prison-reform advocate—moved to Hollywood, where he wrote and got some bit parts in Westerns.

The Daltons started a decades-long tradition of outlaws taking up residence on the Osage reservation. Among them were Jesse and Frank James, the Younger Brothers, Bill Doolin and the Wild Bunch, Belle and Henry Starr, Henry Wells, Al Spencer and Frank Nash. Most lived halfway between Bartlesville and Pawhuska in a small town named Okesa—an Osage religious word meaning "halfway" to the Happy Hunting Ground. Okesa's grounds were inaccessible by lawmen, since it was situated atop steep hills that offered long-distance views and good ambush sites of all approaches to town. In 1911, an outlaw named Elmer McCurdy robbed a train at Okesa. He was killed a few days later, but death wasn't the end of Elmer McCurdy. It was the start of a whole new career for him.

His body was brought to Johnson's Funeral Home in Pawhuska. Mr. Johnson embalmed Elmer, stood the body against a wall—and there it remained for years. Perhaps this was an indication of Mr. Johnson's sense of humor or of interior design, or maybe he was just waiting for someone to come by and pay the bill before he planted Elmer.

Someone finally did—a California couple—saying they'd been looking all over for their long-lost cousin. Elmer's body soon started popping up in exhibits and House of Horror shows in Texas carnivals and county fairs. Finally, like Emmett Dalton, Elmer, too, ended up in Hollywood, used as a prop in movies. One day, the loudest "Oh my God" ever to emit from a living human mouth was heard in a Hollywood studio when Elmer's arm fell off during a shoot and it was discovered the dummy was for real. That was in 1977, sixty-six years after he was carried into Mr. Johnson's funeral parlor. The story is a testament, if nothing else, to Mr. Johnson's embalming skills. It also makes me wonder about the origin of the brand name, Elmer's Glue.

Contrary to popular belief, even in the 1920s, the Wild West was not yet ancient history, the stuff only of novels and of radio and movie dramas. It had merely moved to Osage County, Oklahoma, and the protagonists had acquired more accurate and lethal weapons. Proof of that is the following compilation of Osage County crimes in 1923—all committed by whites—reported in the *Pawhuska Daily Capital.*

In January of that year, a man was shot at his home and two banks were robbed in Pawhuska.

In February, a store in Shidler, twenty miles northwest of Pawhuska, was "held up and robbed"; but the freezing weather must have made white Osage County residents meaner than usual, because three people were shot: two men in a gun battle in Pawhuska, and an "out-of-town salesman" killed by a Pawhuska woman.

March also was a murderous month, with two women and a man killed in a shootout in Webb City, near Shidler, and a bank bandit blown to pieces by a posse, whose overzealousness may have been compensation for an embarrassing jailbreak thirteen days earlier by Buck Collingsworth, caught robbing the bank in Burbank, twenty miles west of Pawhuska.

April, and headline writers were just warming up, to say nothing of the shooters and robbers: "Three Bandits Captured in Wild and Thrilling Gun Battle," "Terrific Gun Battle Near Webb City" (an opinion probably not shared by the three men shot in it, one fatally). Police also raided the White Swan Dance Hall and arrested five gamblers.

April showers of bullets flowered into mayhem in May: car hijackers beat a Webb City man to death; a Pawhuska man was killed in a "fierce gun battle" in Wynona, eight miles to the south; and a Kaw City man lost his life in a "street duel" in Pawhuska.

In June, two safes were "blown" in Pawhuska, and two Pawhuska men were killed: one in a Webb City fight, the other thrown off a train and found, "dead and naked," on the Midland Valley Railroad right-of-way near Hominy, twenty miles south of Pawhuska.

In July, three Osage County banks were bumped off: the Barnsdall Bank, the First State Bank of DeNoya and the Fairfax Bank, whose "robbers made good their escape."

On August 3, the day after Warren Harding died and Calvin Coolidge took over as president of the United States, a Hominy man was shot to death in a "drinking brawl"; later in the month, "Lone Hijacker Kills Oil Worker on Santa Fe Right-of-Way," "Grainola Bank Robbed, and Southbound Train Held Up Near Okesa," "Man Shot and Killed for Hitching Horses to a Post," and a worker at the Carter Nine oil-drilling site was shot to death.

In September, a Pershing man resisted arrest and the sheriff shot him, and on the sixteenth, "Famed Outlaw Leader" Al Spencer, who for years had made his hideout in Okesa, was shot and killed.

In October, a Burbank doctor was murdered, and a man was shot in a Pawhuska dance hall.

November: "Webb City Bank Cashier Shot," "Pawhuskan Stabbed," police raided a tent near Avant and arrested twenty-three gamblers, and an "Audit on Accounts of City of Barnsdall Turns Up $16,000 Shortage."

In December, the Grainola Bank was robbed "For Second Time," and a Pawhuska woman was shot to death.

"Phantom Bandits" stuck up the Shidler Bank to kick off 1924, the year Harry and Sybil Bolton had their first and only child, my mother.

On November 6 of that year, the bodies of Lee and May Worthington were found in their Pawhuska home. Mrs. Worthington had been riddled with so many bullets that pieces of her dress were sticking out of the walls and floor. Lee Worthington had two .45-caliber bullet wounds on each side of his heart. A coroner's jury—the Worthingtons were white, so therefore entitled to the county coroner's services—ruled that Mr. Worthington had shot his wife and, in a murder-suicide, turned his .45 on himself and fired but missed his heart. Despite the probability that being shot point-blank with a .45 would have knocked him through the front window, over the front yard and into the street—and propelled the pistol into the back yard—the jury decided that, somehow, Mr. Worthington gathered himself up, located his gun, put it to his chest and fired a second time, missing his heart again but dying anyway.

The famous Dodge City, located on former Osage land in Kansas, got its reputation for lawlessness in the late 1870s because fifteen murders were committed there over a three-to-five-year period. Osage County morticians like Mr. Johnson were burying that many bodies every couple of months.

OKLAHOMA.

Just past the state line, the terrain abruptly changes personality, from the onerousness of the Ozarks' rocks, ridges, woodlands, plateaus and monuments to bad taste, to the peacefulness of prairie. Its sleepy pace is set, like a hypnotist's watch, by a gentle wind slowly swaying the tops of trees that crouch over creeks of barely moving green water, the breeze singing softly through tall, browning grass that waves across an ocean of hills. It is a landscape where a blink of the mind's eye reveals ghosts—or at least ghostlike images from old cowboy-and-Indian movies that all look as if they could have been filmed on the horizon just in front of you, that screen on a newcomer's memory of things that are dead, that lived only in the time of once upon a time.

A few miles inside Oklahoma, I passed a sign erected along a rancher's fence that paralleled the highway. "Abortion Stops a Beating Heart," it said.

Oklahomans know more than one way to stop a beating heart, I thought.

I drove into a thunderstorm, or it drove into me. The rain was so thick, I stopped behind a convoy of empty school buses that had pulled to the side of the road, the lead bus sheltered under a bridge.

What did Indians do when they were caught in the open in a storm like this? I thought.

When it stopped, I started again. Vinita, where I got off the Will Rogers Turnpike to begin the final, seventy-five-mile, two-lane lap to Pawhuska, was washed out, a river of rainwater coursing down Main Street. Nowata also was underwater. Bartlesville, home of the Phillips 66 oil company, was merely wet, punctuated by puddles, gray with clouds.

I drove down Frank Phillips Boulevard, past the Jane Phillips Episcopal-Memorial Hospital Center, the Phillips Petroleum Company Headquarters Plaza, the 66 Federal Credit Union, the Bartlesville Munici-pal Airport—Frank Phillips Field—site of one of the town's big annual events, the Biplane Expo. Along the way, signs pointed to the Frank Phillips Mansion, the Hotel Phillips, Phillips's Woolaroc Museum, and plugged the yearly classical music festival, OK Mozart, the other big event of the year in Bartlesville. The spaces between all of these places were seemingly filled with the town's ten Phillips 66 gas stations.

On the west side of town, I stopped at a red light. Across from me, to my left, was the Phillips 66 Research and Development Center, a giant complex laced with gray steel girders, pipes and poles. "You Are the Key to Safety," said a sign announcing that the site had had 1,469,434 "Safe Man Hours."

"Last Accident: 11-21-91," it said. "This Year: 0. Safety Pays."

To my right sat a tall hill whose brown sides were denuded of growth and darkened with oil stains. It looked like a giant dirt mound. Atop were perched two battleship-gray oil-storage tanks. They were visi-ble from much of Bartlesville, and seemed to lord over the city, to stand taller than even the town's two other sky-scratching structures, a red-brick Phillips office building that resembled a clock tower and rose above the center of the company's headquarters plaza and, near it, the nineteen-story, glass-and-copper Price Tower, the tallest building ever built by Frank Lloyd Wright.

On my side of the street was a Phillips 66 car wash and a dilapidated wooden shack, whose peeling white-and-red sign showed an Indian in a war bonnet and advertised the "Cherokee Smoke Shop."

Just as the light changed and I accelerated, the sun burst through the overcast sky. A brilliant light hit a puddle directly in front of me with a blinding, almost explosive flash, and the rays ricocheted right into my eyes.

I grabbed for my sunglasses, put them on—and found myself staring at the faded green letters on a small, smudged white sign.

"Enter Osage County," it said.

As I drove into the land of my people, a chill shot up my spine. A voice on the radio was singing:

>*Have you come here for forgiveness?*
>*Have you come to raise the dead?*

Chapter Eight

C old feet on a hot afternoon.

       I drove all of a half-mile into Osage County and pulled off at a yellow roadside fireworks stand. "Buy 1, Get 2 Free," a sign said, but no one was buying. A shadowy figure behind the counter inflated to attention as I drove into the parking area, but shrank back to a slump when I started turning around.

If ever there was an obvious metaphor for the futility of human endeavor, this was it: trying to make a living off a Fourth of July celebration on an Indian reservation.

I drove back to Bartlesville. My reasons outraced my odometer clicking off tenths of a mile. I was tired. Dusk was falling. I wanted to cross the finish line in Pawhuska in the light. There was no place to stay there, or so Father Mazaika, the Pawhuska priest, had told me. The one hotel in town—the Duncan—burned down in the fifties and never was replaced.

And it was Miller time. I wasn't sure if I could buy beer in Pawhuska. I assumed that the "civilian" parts of Osage County surrounding the reservation were dry. I didn't know Oklahoma liquor laws, but I knew about Indians and drinking, and that alcohol was illegal on reservations. The forced temperance would make it easier to honor the promise I had made to Fleur not to drink in Pawhuska. This was work and I never drink on the job, I had assured her to ease her worries that I'd be spending all my evenings and money in Pawhuska bars.

But I wasn't there yet. Tonight, I was going to stock up for a dry spell—and drown out the voices feuding in my head.

Over the months of my "project," the more I thought about my Osage grandmother, the more I thought of myself as an Osage. An Osage identity took root and grew greedily, perhaps in overcompensation for the many years of neglect. The Osage branch of my family tree, bursting with the vitality of newness, grew beyond the bounds apportioned it by its percentage of the whole, the degree of its actual ethnic makeup, my "blood." I assigned it a much larger percentage, a new blood quantum based on the degree of its actual influence on my life.

I came to realize that my mother's Indian "blood"—including her father's cold-blooded determination to squash all trace of it, and the loss of her Indian mother and Indian home—had instilled in her the behavior and character traits that affected my life. "Osage," I found, became the answer to all the questions of my childhood and youth—the good and the not so good, the happy and the painful—that I still puzzled over, that became the engine of my adult life's unwitting drive to the Indian condition of personal dysfunction: three marriages (I have something in common with my great-grandmother), a penchant for exploiting emotional weaknesses in women, a tendency to torpedo relationships, an inclination to confuse drinking with socialization, and my isolation stemming from an inability to fit in, to belong, to be at home, to feel a part of American society. Why was she like this, I'd ask, why did she do that?—and by extension, why am I like this, why did I do that? The answer was always "Osage."

As my "project" progressed, in other words, it came to have as much to do with my life as with my grandmother's death, and began to transform my family tree from a European import into something resembling a native species, such as the Osage orange, a type of mulberry that coated the tribe's ancestral domain and produced the strongest and deadliest bows.

But as my Osage branch grew and crowded out the other boughs, as the leaves of my new identity began to spread across the whole tree, the other, incompatible foliage of my heritage fought back, and a little guerrilla war erupted in my head. Ever since crossing into Oklahoma, formerly Indian Territory, the hit-and-run skirmishes had exploded into full-fledged combat. Attacks of doubt over what I was doing and what I was intent on doing grew in frequency and fury as I neared my destination. It seemed as if my white, Irish side was determined to prevent me from arriving in Pawhuska—or so I decided moments after turning back and touring, in search of a motel, this chunk of former Indian land now known as Bartlesville, driving past streets named Cheyenne, Chickasaw, Choctaw, Comanche, Kaw, Nebraska, Quapaw, Seminole, Seneca, Wyandotte.

If I actually made it to the land of the Osages, to the capital of the Osage Nation, only twenty-five miles to go, I would repair the accident of history that had befallen my Osage family, and set its train back on the track of the Indian way of life from which it had derailed—or so my Osage, Indian side intended, but not if my Irish, white side could help it.

My Irish and Indian War, my Battle of Wounded Need.

It was always the same. The first shot—while walking, waking, in my car, at a bar—sounded like this:

Who are you kidding?

No sooner would that question shoot across my bow unanswered than other rounds of critical thoughts would walk in, mortarlike, each exploding a few feet closer than its predecessor to the target—my self, my will, my confidence.

You're not fooling anyone. They won't accept you. You're not a "real" Indian. You don't have enough Indian blood. They'll laugh at you. They'll look at your blue eyes, your sandy hair, your pale face, and laugh you off the reservation. You're an Indian joke: You remember everything you've read the past year about Osages; don't forget what you've also read about whites such as you. You're the typical white who claims Indian ancestry to mitigate his guilt. You're even more stereotypical than that—you claim Indian descent from your grandmother. Nearly every white who tells a "real" Indian that he, too, is of Indian heritage claims to have some unknown, unnamed Indian ancestor on his grandmother's side. It's a joke.

Finding a white who claims Indian ancestry through his grandfather—the war-rior side, the side that killed, scalped, beheaded and dismembered whites—is like trying to find a German who fought, or whose parents or grandparents fought, against the Americans in World War II; they were all on the Russian front. Indi-ans say that if all whites' claims of having Indian grandmothers were true, then every tribe would have to have been entirely female. And of course, your In-dian grandmother had to be a "princess," daughter or granddaughter or great-granddaughter of a "chief." That's another Indian joke: whites' claim to instant royalty, all chiefs and no Indians in their bloodlines.

You'll insult them by claiming to be one of them. You ignored them for forty-two years. You had no interest in them or curiosity about them. You had nothing to do with them. The only time you ever contacted them was to use them to get a job. But now you've tripped over your Indian roots, read a couple of books about the Osages, shed a couple of tears in your beer over the Indian body buried in the family basement, and now you call yourself an Indian.

YOU DIDN'T EVEN KNOW HER NAME!

But now she's your guiding light.

Your family walked away from the Osage Tribe nearly seven decades ago. You were too good for them then. You don't have the right to come back now.

YOU HAVEN'T EVEN SEEN A REAL INDIAN YET!

AT THE BAR of the Bartlesville Holiday Inn, located next to a be-draggled motel with a replica of an old-time wooden oil derrick in front and a sign saying "Okie Owned and Operated," I saw my first Native American. In Panama, I had seen Cuna Indians, makers of molas, but I had never seen (at least not in person) an American Indian of the United States, a real one, I mean, one who—unlike myself—looked like one.

I tried not to stare. He was a big man, with bronze skin and black, shiny, long, ponytailed hair. His slow walk across the room exuded dignity.

Who are you kidding? my inner voice asked. I cut short the ensuing argument by ordering another beer, and watched the Indian in the bar mirror. He was sitting at a table behind me. His clothes defied every pic-ture—real or imagined—ever presented of an American Indian: He wore a three-piece, banker's-gray suit. He and his two white companions, also in suits, were probably with Phillips, having a few drinks after work, getting tanked talking oil.

Was he an alcoholic?

Drunken Indians. Firewater. Even that term is derived from whites' habit of cheating Indians. Before buying whiskey from traders, Indians used to splash a shot on the fire to check the alcohol content: If the fire flared, it was fine; if the whiskey doused the flames, it had been watered down. Indians and drinking. "Like giving whiskey to an Indian." Someone warned me once that, on an Indian reservation, you should always check for legs sticking out from under your car before pulling away from a curb—some poor schmuck might be fixing himself a Prestone sandwich. Indians crawl under your car, I was told, unplug your radiator, drain the antifreeze through a loaf of bread and then drink what filters through—alcohol, for the most part.

A white sitting at a bar is having a good time. An Indian doing the same thing is having a problem.

I caught my reflection in the bar mirror, and felt suddenly awkward and self-conscious on my barstool, the one place where I've always felt comfortable and at home: Here I was, an Indian in the former Indian Territory—a self-defined Indian, at any rate—sitting at a bar drinking firewater and wondering if the other Indian across the room—a "real" Indian—was an alcoholic. I was disappointed in myself. I had just fallen prey to a cliché.

Our perceptions of Indians are papered in prejudice, and even the most discerning among us seem blind to it. Native Americans have somehow escaped the scrutiny that has scoured our other racial prejudices and softened them with ethnic sensitivity. The reason could be as innocent as benign neglect, but Indians seem to be exempt from all the don'ts that apply to other ethnic groups. I guess we have to have someone to kick around, since even dogs and cats are no longer fair game. But Indians seem to be.

Americans are not a cruel people; we're just thoughtless sometimes. Why else would a group of highly educated and successful men and women, at my going-away party before leaving Baltimore, give me the Indian name of "Two Dogs Fucking," the punch line of a joke—told to much laughter—about how Indians get their names (after the first thing a father sees upon leaving the tepee after seeing his newborn baby).

Thoughtlessness.

Habit.

At the same party, I heard lots of sentences with the word "me" as the subject, with verbs ending in "um," and with "heaps" of such words or phrases as arrow (broken or usable), blue coats, bows, braves (or Braves), buffalo, buffalo chips, canoe, chief, the cliché "all chiefs and no Indians," the cliché "bury the hatchet," the cliché "on the warpath," firewater, forked tongue, Geronimo!, ghost-dancing, how, Indian giver (a misconception of the term's origin has given Indians the bum rap that they take back their presents), Injuns, peace pipe, powwow, Redskins, scalp, the simile "like giving whiskey to an Indian," smoke signals, squaw, tepee, tomahawk, Tomahawk Chop, tom-toms, totem pole, ugh, wickiup, wigwam, wampum, war bonnet, war drums and war party.

At a similar going-away party a few months before for a friend leaving to visit his ancestral homeland in Africa, I heard not one disparaging word. Nothing but respect, admiration and good wishes emitted from the mouths of the same people who attended the party for me. No one made up a name for him. Neither were there any references to the lifestyles or customs of his ancestors in terms of what they might have eaten, drunk, worn, thrown, fought with, killed, constructed, slept in, slept with, said, smoked or otherwise done.

Why are Indians so special?

A recent *Washington Post* report about a truce in Somalia quoted an unidentified U.S. diplomat in the capital, Mogadishu, as saying, "There's still a danger of something happening, someone getting off the reservation." The cliché "off the reservation" is a disparaging racial epithet rooted in a tragic and shameful period of American history when starving Indians were forced to violate their treaties with the U.S. government to feed themselves, were thus considered to have gone "on the warpath" and then brutalized accordingly. But did anyone object to the diplomat's undiplomatic remark? Was he summarily dismissed, or forced to issue a public apology, as would have happened had he made a racial slur disparaging the American ethnic group whose ancestral homeland is the continent the diplomat was talking from? Did his comment even raise an eyebrow?

In the void of thinking, old habits hardly die. Why else is it still illegal to sell or consume alcohol on Indian reservations, while the same federal government that sets and enforces that rule subsidizes the price of liquor—and provides plush places to consume it—at the greatest alcoholic mills in our country: military reservations?

Why else would the nation's capital, a city containing some of the best and brightest minds in the country, support a professional football team whose name is a slang word for an ethnic group's skin color—and be in a genuine fog over what the fuss is all about? But imagine, if you will, the international outcry of horror that would arise if the professional soccer team of Germany's capital were named after the people it tried to exterminate, and the name were a slang word for a stereotypical physical feature of that group?

I believe Redskins owner Jack Kent Cooke when he says he sees nothing offensive about his team's name. He doesn't—just as people don't see how racist it is to ask the Indian Question.

"What percentage of Indian are you?"

It's innocuous enough, and posed with the most virtuous of intentions. Some stranger or acquaintance we've never had the slightest curiosity about says he's Indian, and suddenly we're tripping over ourselves to know not just his ethnic background—nothing wrong with that—but the exact percentage or fraction of a certain portion of his racial makeup, commonly referred to as "blood."

We've all popped the question: "How much Indian blood do you have?"

I've asked. I've never asked a black. I've never asked an Asian. I've never asked a Hispanic. I've never asked a European. I've never asked any hyphenated American. But I've sure asked an Indian, and I've sure been asked.

Why are we so special?

There are two problems with the Indian Question, apart from its selectivity and rudeness. When the Question is directed at mixed-bloods such as me—half-breeds, if you will—too often it is couched not in curiosity but in disbelief, and we are forced to answer as if our honesty, not our ethnic backgrounds, are under scrutiny.

This can sometimes lead to hairy situations. In Baltimore one evening, I was talking to a woman sitting at the adjoining barstool whose leathery tan, taut face-lift and peach-painted hair gave me the impression she was visiting from a Florida retirement community. I mentioned my Oklahoma travel plans and Osage descent, and as predictable as the ending of a cowboy-and-Indian movie, she asked me how much Indian "blood" I had. When I politely explained to her that I don't do percentages because of the inherent racism of the Question, she flat refused to believe I was an Indian—and loudly.

"You're putting me on," she kept responding to my continued insistence. "You're not an Indian. You're making it up. There's no way you're an Indian."

Finally she put down her drink, stretched her face-lift into a tight frown, and said coolly, "There's only one way to find out for sure if you're an Indian."

She reached across to me with a liver-spotted hand, whose daggered fingernails matched her hair color. Then she quickly grabbed my collar, plunged her hand down my shirt and felt around my chest. After a few laps, she withdrew, returned to her drink, took a sip, and said, "Well . . . part."

The main problem with the Question, though, is its historical intent. It may be just a bad habit now, but quantifying an Indian's "blood" used to be the way the U.S. government planned to finally exterminate Indians, this time with math. By asking an Indian the percentage of his "blood," the questioner is speaking the discredited language of assimilation, and continuing the now-halted dirty work of the U.S. Bureau of Indian Affairs (BIA), helping it meet its historical goal of getting out of the Indian business.

For more than 150 years, the government bus marked "For Indians Only" was driven by Thomas Jefferson, and its destination sign above the front windshield said, "White Plains, U.S.A." The ultimate task of the federal Indian Affairs bureaucracy was to bring about Jefferson's dream to assimilate Indians into white society. The method was Jefferson's, too: whitewashing Indians' racial appearance, diluting their "blood" by interbreeding with whites and numerically quantifying the process. Each new generation reduced the "fraction" or "degree" of an Indian's "blood." Below an arbitrary "percentage"—25 was the BIA's benchmark—an Indian was no longer Indian. He was white, which made him ineligible for what the government regarded as a generous federal benefits program.

Each year, the Indian population shrank, at least by the government's count. If a "one-quarter" Indian, for example, did not marry at least a "one-quarter" Indian, their offspring was not an Indian, by the BIA's standards. Each year, fewer and fewer Indians were added to the BIA's list of wards, whose affairs it oversaw because officially designated "uncivilized savages" were not allowed to personally manage their own lives. With its list growing shorter, the BIA was approaching the day the names would run out. Upon the death of some future "Last of the Mohicans," the chief of the BIA, the Bureau of Indian Assimilation, could stand up from his desk, dust off his hands of eraser bits, and say, "Well, no more Indians."

And the dream of Indian-fighters and -killers and -haters all throughout our history would be realized—Indians finally would have been exterminated.

Mission accomplished.

The government, however, got impatient and couldn't wait for that day. In 1947, the BIA decided to speed up the process and start striking whole tribes from the list. It compiled a new list, this one of victims of its new policy, called termination. Included on the BIA's initial list of tribes whose federal recognition—and thus federal services—would be yanked immediately were the Osages. They managed to wriggle off the chopping block by employing a successful lobby on Capitol Hill. But not so lucky were the Menominees of Wisconsin; the Alabama-Coushattas of Texas; the Catawbas of South Carolina; the Poncas of Nebraska; the California Rancherías; the Wyandottes, Peorias and Ottawas of Oklahoma; mixed-blood Utes and Southern Paiutes of Utah; and the Klamaths and sixty-one other tribes and bands of Oregon. The Paiutes were too poor to travel to Washington to protest their termination, and did not even speak English yet when they were dropped from federal care and soon sank from sight. Congress, though, was thoughtful enough to include funds for English classes in the Paiutes' termination act.

The terminations were enacted between 1954 and 1962 and effectively took place from 1955 to 1970, removing 13,263 Indians and nearly 1.4 million acres of their land from federal protection. Most of the terminated tribes, not coincidentally, occupied richly timbered reservations. The forests did not stay empty of occupants for long, however; they soon came alive with the deadly drone of buzz saws. Their former Indian owners, who had been so thoughtful of American timber companies to leave their woods untouched for centuries, were compensated with millions of dollars, for which their local auto dealers, clothing retailers, liquor stores and bars were thankful but eventually their state welfare agencies were not.

Harsh denunciation of the "anti-Indian activities of the Bureau of Indian Affairs" made Congress ax-shy about terminating any more tribes, but it continued to consider—"cold-bloodedly," as one Indian writer put it—abandoning the ships of other Indian nations while simultaneously launching the lifeboats of the War on Poverty to rescue America's more visible sinking ethnic groups. President Richard Nixon, perhaps stirred by his religious identification with the nineteenth-century Quakers who had considered themselves "true Friends of the Indian," denounced termination as contrary to the "immense moral and legal force" of U.S. treaties with Indians, and asked Congress to "renounce, repudiate and repeal" the House Concurrent Resolution 108 of 1953, which had authorized the terminations. It never did. Instead, the Nixon and Ford administrations effectively terminated the policy—along with its parent, assimilation—by restoring federal recognition to the Menominees and some smaller tribes and winning passage of the Indian Self-Determination and Education Assistance Act, which became law on January 4, 1975.

The new policy—self-determination—allows the Indians themselves to determine who is one of them. Each tribe is now free to set its own criteria for membership, and for many, blood quantum is not one of them. But white Americans apparently failed to read the papers the day it was reported that the government's policy of assimilation had gone the way of covered wagons.

Most Americans still appear to believe that you have to be a full-blood to be an Indian, although you could probably put all the full-blood Indians in the continental United States on a 747 and still have some empty seats. Even people who should know better—Washington policymakers, notably—continue to make public shows of their ignorance about Indians. A few days after the 1992 election, for example, Republicans were whispering to the Washington media that the newly elected Democratic senator from Colorado, Ben Nighthorse Campbell—the third Native American to win a U.S. Senate seat and the first male senator in the modern era to wear a ponytail—was not "really" an Indian, as he represented himself, because he was only three-eighths Northern Cheyenne. Thus they ridiculed his publicized plan to ride a horse and wear his tribe's traditional clothing and eagle-feather headdress in the Clinton inaugural parade. A Campbell spokeswoman angrily attacked the insinuations: "Each Indian tribe decides who is an Indian—not the Republican Party. If the Republicans want another war with the Cheyenne, they can have it."

Assimilation may no longer be taking place officially, but it doesn't have to. Its ever-subtracting mathematical equations still are computing on the social and personal level, like some doomsday machine that has started its irreversible countdown. It is a virus that has invaded the national psyche and ultimately produces the disease of insensitivity toward Indians.

On the notion of personal assimilation, I speak from experience. One reason I did not consider myself an Indian until now—apart from lack of interest—was lack of knowledge. I didn't know I could be one. I assumed I didn't measure up to the government's blood-quantum standards and thus wasn't officially a "real" Indian. Not once, for example, did I ever identify myself as an Indian (or later, Native American) on school, medical, Army, bank or tax records, or on any document or application form asking for racial or ethnic identification. The 1990 census count of 1,878,285 American Indians was one shy.

When my mother was growing up—through childhood, adolescence and into early adulthood—whites regarded one drop of Indian blood as too much, and people suffered who shouldn't have, by inclusion in their cruelty. During the same phases of my life, one drop was too little, and Indians suffered who shouldn't have, by exclusion from whites' compassion.

Now it's the way it should be: It's none of their business.

Probably the only place in the United States where an Indian won't be asked his blood quantum anymore is in the Bureau of Indian Affairs. The BIA now regards as a "real" Indian anyone listed on the membership roll of one of the 318 federally recognized tribes in the forty-eight contiguous states, and 226 in Alaska. In many tribes, including the Osages and the Cherokees, blood quantum is not among the requirements for tribal membership. Other tribes have "fairly stringent blood-quantum requirements, half-blood or greater," a BIA official said. Still others have adhered to the BIA's old 25 percent benchmark.

The BIA's new role is to serve as a sort of pusher to the tribes, providing them with the drug of federal money and entitlement programs from a $1.8 billion budget each year but leaving it up to the tribes to determine individual members' eligibility for the assistance. The BIA also stands as watchdog over the 85,468 square miles of land held in trust for Indians by the federal government. The land is owned either tribally or by individual Indians, on or off 278 Indian reservations in thirty-four of the forty-eight contiguous states, comprising a total area slightly larger than Minnesota. On reservations, the BIA "does every doggone thing," as a BIA spokesman put it, that city, county, state and federal governments do. Its money goes for building the roads, collecting the garbage, hooking up the water, sewage and electricity, as well as for programs to manage and conserve tribes' forests, oil, gas, grazing or other natural resources, and for economic-development programs.

The BIA no longer plays the percentages, at least to the degree it used to, but it still requires a blood quantum of one-quarter or more for an Indian's eligibility for the big-ticket item: government-funded scholarships. (Technically, it requires tribes to require the restriction: The BIA does not deal with individual Indians, except those applying for jobs at the agency.) Many tribes, including the Osages, have their own scholarship funds to help out Indians of less than a quarter "blood" degree who, contrary to the government's assumptions, don't have the cash to get a college degree. Indians with a Certificate of Degree of Indian Blood (known in official parlance as a CDIB)—the Indian ID card, as I call it—can use the free Indian Health Service, a division of the U.S. Public Health Service, and thus separate from the BIA. Regardless of blood quantum, Indians with a CDIB get first preference for jobs at the BIA. The agency employs about 11,700 Native Americans out of a total workforce of 13,000.

But the kindly old Dr. Jekyll conducting the government's newest (and so far most successful) experiment with Indians occasionally shows flashes of a vicious, vindictive Mr. Hyde. Self-determination, it seems, applies only to those tribes that determine to do what the BIA wants. About 5,000 Navajos lived without electricity or running water for twenty-six years until 1992—the BIA had cut their utilities in 1966 to try to force a settlement of a land dispute between the Navajos and the Hopi Indians. When another tribal council was unable to comply with an agency bookkeeping request, the BIA punished that tribe's 10,000 adult members by making them the only Indians of all the nation's 544 federally recognized tribes to need a 50 percent blood quantum to be eligible for BIA scholarships and jobs. This was especially cruel punishment because this tribe's tragic history had made it one of the most "assimilated" and "diluted" in the United States.

The Osages.

A lawsuit brought by some members of the tribe in March 1990 has prevented the Osage Tribal Council from submitting to the BIA a current membership roll. The lawsuit involved tribal voting rights, but the issue was central to the question of tribal membership, assuming tribal members should have the right to vote in tribal elections.

The sole governing document of the Osages has been the 1906 Osage Allotment Act, which set up the headright system for the division of reservation land and disbursement of oil and other monies to members of the tribal roll. The act required the closing of the tribal roll on July 1, 1907, creating, in perpetuity, 2,229 headrights, one for each Osage alive on that date, including one born that day. As of March 1994, only 56 of those "original allottees" were alive, the youngest being at least eighty-six years old. Following a strict interpretation of the Osages' sole government authority—the 1906 allotment act—those are the only Osages on the tribal roll, or the membership list that the BIA seeks.

Osage government has revolved around the central feature of Osage life created by that law—headrights. The instrument that determined an Osage's right to riches also was interpreted to determine his right to vote. The final tribal roll of 2,229 Osages created, in effect, 2,229 "votes"—and like the number of headrights, the number of votes remained unchanged. When an original allottee died, his headright passed to his heirs, and so too did the vote entitled by that headright. If the headright was split among multiple heirs, each would get a fraction, along with a fraction of a vote. When my mother dies, each of her three children will inherit one-third of her headright (her mother's headright, number 933, is one of relatively few of the 2,229 that have not yet been fractioned—meaning that my mother is one of relatively few Osages who actually have a whole vote in a tribal election). My one-third of a headright would entitle me to cast a third of one vote in a tribal election. When I die, my portion of the headright will pass to my natural children. Let's say Fleur and I have two more. That means Kevin and his siblings would each inherit a ninth of a headright, and a ninth of a vote. If Kevin has six children, each of his heirs would get—I can't do the math. Needless to say, it takes days to compute the 2,229 final votes in an Osage election—and the Osage County school system must teach a pretty advanced fractions course.

The Osage Tribal Council, then, regards the voting list as the effective tribal membership since the names on it are the voters who could put them out of a job. However, for all other, nonpolitical aspects of Osage tribal life—the issuance of the all-important CDIB that gains access to free health care and other assistance programs—the Osage government considers the census list, which includes nonvoters, as the operative document.

For decades, thousands of nonvoting Osages—typically the children of headright holders—have been trying to gain access to Osage political life by getting the right to vote. As their numbers increased, so too did the obduracy of officeholders, who spread fear among voters that nonvoters— their own children—were just after their headrights. Resentments and rhetoric roiled, as reflected in the letters and council-meeting minutes published by the tribal monthly newspaper, *Inside Osage.* Finally somebody sued and a federal judge in Tulsa intervened.

The legal dispute was resolved by a tribal referendum in February 1994 that ratified a constitution granting the right to vote to all Osages— with or without a headright. Eligible voters in the referendum were Osages eighteen years of age and older who either were on the tribal census roll or could prove Osage descent. The constitutional principles had been decided in a similar referendum in July 1993—the first time that I, and thousands of Osages like me, were allowed to take part in a tribal vote.

The Osages—all Osages—elected a new government in June 1994 under the new constitution, which finally codifies tribal membership requirements. The original allottees or their direct descendants are now undeniably official members of the Osage Tribe, regardless of blood quantum. The constitution also separates management of the Osage Mineral Estate from the jurisdiction of the tribal government. All Osages can vote for their government, while only headright holders can select the managers of the Mineral Estate. In effect, headright holders have become shareholders of an oil and gas corporation. The new tribal government will submit a current membership roll to the BIA, and hopefully the federal agency will accept it and allow the Osages to return to the new era in U.S.–Indian relations.

In the meantime, however, Osages were being deprived of government scholarships and jobs because of their blood quantum. Minutes of a recent Osage Tribal Council meeting reminded readers of *Inside Osage* of that outrage by reporting the story of Gregory Kidder, who appealed to the council members for help.

Kidder had applied for a job at Haskell Indian Junior College in Lawrence, Kansas, "but his application as an Osage was denied because he was only three-eighths Osage. The job is a federal job and as the Osages have no federally recognized roll, any Osage applying for a federal position must be one-half Osage to qualify."

How could this happen? Kidder asked. He did not understand why even the Bureau of Indian Affairs discriminated against Indians.

"Kidder's only options," the minutes read, "were to file a discrimination suit or to apply using his other [Indian] blood (Pueblo). If he uses his other blood, this means a trip out of state for him and many hours of dealing with another tribe." A council member recommended that Mr. Kidder "consult a lawyer."

Can you imagine a federal bureaucracy turning down a black for a job because he wasn't black enough?

Come to think of it, can you imagine a Bureau of Black Affairs?

Not in America. That would be South Africa, but not the United States.

The United States was the loudest voice in the international chorus of outcry over pariah South Africa's heinous system of racial separation known as apartheid. Under apartheid, blacks were denied basic human rights and most were removed from their homes in white-ruled South Africa proper to artificially created, generally undesirable and mostly isolated tribal homelands that were declared self-governing, nominally independent nations. South African Prime Minister Hendrik F. Verwoerd instituted apartheid between 1958 and 1966, but devised it while minister of native affairs in the early 1950s. Searching for a historically proven model to imitate, he studied how other countries had segregated and suppressed their unwanted racial groups, and sent delegations of white South African intellectuals abroad on fact-finding missions. In the United States, they found the answer, the inspiration and model for apartheid, not in the South, where racial discrimination was an art form in the Fifties, but in the West, touring the Indian reservations.

The greatest danger facing Indians as they approach the twenty-first century is that whites' perceptions of their reservations are changing—from the flip side of the American Dream, places born of the same evil that spawned apartheid, places of pitiable poverty, to places of enviable wealth, where Americans' wildest dreams of getting rich quick come true.

The story of the Osages should serve as a cautionary tale of what happens when Indian wealth attracts whites' notice, and envy.

Self-determination has given Indian tribes the right to make their own decisions about ways to improve their economic well-being, to make the best of a system that was not designed for their benefit. Perhaps the only beneficial result of the nineteenth-century treaties that put Indians on reservations was recognition of their sovereignty as nations, albeit defeated ones. Their power to rule themselves in their own nations, now reservations, was highly limited; their treaties, in fact, acknowledged their dependence on the federal government. The result was a special legal status known as dependent sovereignty. The practical application of that concept meant basically that reservations were outside the jurisdiction of states in which they are located. In other words, state law didn't apply.

In the 1980s, some Indian lawyers and MBA types—the new warriors in their ongoing battle with the U.S. government—figured out a way to cash in on tribal sovereignty. Reservations, in keeping with their founding principles to remove Indians from the sight and scene of American society, tend to be in out-of-the-way places, and state governments have reinforced this isolation by simply not building any roads—or no more than one—to reservations, ensuring that America's economic benefits bypass them. In a twist to a major theme of American history, this time Indians wanted what whites possessed—the contents of their wallets.

The only way to entice whites to reservations and to part with some of their cash on them would be to offer them something that would make it worth their while to go out of their way (and on lousy roads), something that wasn't otherwise available to them—in other words, something illegal. Whites wouldn't go to reservations, but they would fly thousands of miles, and spend thousands of dollars, to go to Las Vegas or Atlantic City. In the forty-eight states where these two meccas of money were not located, public gambling was illegal. But—reservations weren't states.

The Indian Gaming Regulatory Act of 1988 legalized the concept, permitting casino gambling on reservations—sometimes just a building and parking lot that Indians have bought and gotten the BIA to declare a federal Indian reserve. Now more than fifty tribes and bands operate more than a hundred bingo halls and casinos in nineteen states, and take in $6 billion a year.

Of course, white gambling interests not in on the Indian action (Donald Trump of Atlantic City, for example) are challenging the constitutionality of the 1988 law as an unfair advantage "to a very limited class of citizens" (Trump's words)—"so offensive to the basic tenets of democracy," as Colorado Governor Roy Romer put it, because Indian tribes, invoking the sovereignty of their reservations as Indian nations, have forced casinos on some states that do not permit gambling and diverted a lot of cash away from state tax coffers.

Of the huge amounts of money that reservation gambling generates, individual Indians actually receive usually no more than an hourly wage for working the tables, the cafeteria line, the cash register or security. The tribes also receive very little after all the whites who manage and operate the gaming resorts take their cuts. But it's still something. It's dramatically improving the lives and livelihoods of Native Americans, who otherwise would have nothing. And it's offering something that Indians have not had since the arrival of Americans—hope for a better future.

But if you think about it, it's pretty shameful. The Indians' new buffalo—even if it survives the threat of extinction from the hunting rifles of Buffalo Bills like Donald Trump—is just buffalo chips anyway, compared to all the other facets of the American Dream that Indians are still denied.

We should be proud. White American fathers tell their sons and daughters that if they play their cards right, they can become president of the United States.

Indian fathers can now tell theirs that if they play their cards right, they can play cards.

I MET MY FIRST INDIAN a few beers into the evening when I returned from the men's room. She was sitting at my place at the bar, and drinking my beer. (I would learn this was almost an area tradition, part of the local flavor.)

"I should have known it wasn't mine," she said, after a round of apologies and nodding at my beer. "I never drink imported."

I ordered another round.

She was Cherokee. My first question, of course, was how much (old habits, etc.). Half, she said. I told her my Osage percentage.

Tonight was her first night out after her longtime boyfriend's slow and painful death by heart disease, many agonizing details of which I sat through. Streaks of gray in her hair highlighted a sickly pallor to her face. Her hands were skeletal, and shook as she poured the remainder of my former beer into a glass and lifted it to her lips. She said she didn't feel comfortable going out so close to the funeral, many months ago, but her girlfriend, the bartender, had insisted.

"What's a Harvey Wallbanger?" she asked, cheerfulness abruptly appearing. She ordered one after her bartender friend listed the ingredients.

"Wanna see pictures of my granddaughter?"

Soon I was matching hers, snapshot for snapshot, with photos of Kevin, and there at the bar, flipping through our wallets, a new generation of Indians unfolded before us—children with strawberry-blond hair.

Then came the inevitable wherefores, wherefroms and wheretos.

"Pawhuska? God, I feel sorry for you." Then she yelled across the bar to a friend, "Hey, this guy's going to live in Pawhuska." She added a string of condolences that startled me in their sincerity. When the bartender joined in with such words as "run-down," "god-awful," "hellhole," "deserted" and "dump," I grew disconcerted. This wasn't your ordinary bar razzing I was being subjected to.

What was I getting myself into?

"My first husband was an Osage," the Cherokee woman said, "and we lived in Pawhuska when we first got married. We finally had to move, because he was an alcoholic. He couldn't stay out of the bars there."

"There are bars there?" I asked. My spirits strangely revived.

"Oh, there were bars there, all right. He knew where each and every one of them was, what time they opened . . ."

"Any good places to go?"

"None," she said with authority. Then she smiled knowingly.

"You'll be back in here in no time."

I WOKE UP LATE, achy and angry at myself for closing down the bar. The next hour was a mad, disoriented dash to shower (I skipped the shaving), dress, pack, load the car, check out, stop at the restaurant for a large coffee to go and to drink on the drive to Pawhuska, where I was to meet my sister Carolyn at the public library on Sixth Street at eleven.

There are two things guaranteed to ruin a morning for me—doing anything in the morning, because I'm always late, and being late. When I got in the car, I saw by the dashboard clock that I already was. In a pique of frustration, I made a reflexive action that startled me. I shaped my right hand like a pistol, pressed it against my chest above my heart and pulled an imaginary trigger.

I was surprised not so much by what I did but by where I did it, and when: out in the open, in the plain-daylight sobriety of morning. Shooting myself with an imaginary pistol was something I had caught myself doing of late, but only late at night—in those solitary, idle, beery, blankheaded moments when I used to practice my golf swing.

This was tricky terrain, I knew. I hadn't told Fleur about it, or she'd have marched me off to a shrink and wouldn't have let me make this trip alone. I also had kept to myself recurring dreams about opening Sybil's coffin, or about visiting her in death and waking up crying because I didn't want to come back. I had tried not to think about the darker implications. There were none, I had been telling myself. I was not getting weird or suicidal. It was normal and natural to walk around the house—or now, to sit in the car in the parking lot of a Holiday Inn—and shoot myself in the chest with an imaginary pistol, or dream about a girl who died sixty-six years ago. My brain at night was merely uncoiling its tight daytime focus on the things I had learned and, like the index finger aimed at my heart, on the things they pointed to.

I also hadn't told Fleur that I intended to see a real estate agent in Pawhuska. The dust hadn't settled yet on our move to my forty-eighth house, when I began talking about number forty-nine. Don't bother with these, I'd tell Fleur, motioning to all the boxes stacked up in room after room. If we leave everything in boxes, it'll be easier when we move to

Pawhuska. She'd laugh, but hesitantly. She knows that, with me, the serious stuff sometimes is shrouded in humor.

Fleur would be horrified to move again, of course. She's one of those people an Army brat like me has never understood and always envied—a civilian. She's from somewhere, has always had a "home," has only moved five or six times in her life—half of her moves in the three years we've been married.

I wasn't sure what she would find more appalling: moving again, or moving to Pawhuska to live among the Osages. She had been telling me that "my project" has become an obsession. Granted, I had been way out in front of her on this one. "My project" was not something we were doing together. I knew she missed me, worried about me, wondered what happened to me and when I'd be coming back to present-day Baltimore after mentally living in 1920s Pawhuska for almost a year now. I knew Fleur hoped that when I did come back at the end of the summer, I would leave Sybil behind, finally bury her, this stranger who had entered my life and intruded on Fleur's.

I had been telling her that she doesn't understand, that I don't really have anything to do with this. My grandmother is doing it all, acting through me. All I'm doing is bringing Sybil home, bringing her into the family she was denied, and in return she's bringing me home, too, to the place that I was denied. Sybil is giving me a sense of being from somewhere.

I've finally become a part of something. Now all I have to do is join it.

THE ROAD TO PAWHUSKA was covered with the carcasses of flattened box turtles. It was apparently mating season (why did the turtle cross the road?) and, like me, they were going home, returning to the place of their origin, pulled by the undertow of nature, genetics and something even more mysterious that they didn't understand any better than I. On the road to my place of origin, they were taking some heavy hits.

Would I?

A pickup truck trailed me as I wove my way around shattered and gooey turtle shells, over thickly forested hills of gnarly, dark green oak trees, past pastures of rusty brown barbed wire, yellowing tallgrass, red-baked boulders. Fields blushed with lilac-colored wildflowers. In one, a crowd of cows cooled off in the shadow of an oil pump.

The pickup suddenly veered into the oncoming lane. In my rearview mirror, I could see a cowboy hat shading the steering wheel and a rifle glaring from a rack against the back window. But the driver did not pass me. Instead, he lined up on a live turtle. After he hit it, he swerved back in behind me again. Just before impact, the turtle had stretched its neck straight out, as if straining against its nature for a burst of speed. Its shell shot sideways across the road and into a brush-filled ditch.

Past Okesa, a tarantula was walking down the middle of the road, a sitting duck to join the road kill. I steered to avoid it. I didn't look behind me. For such a rarity, the cowboy probably would have stopped, backed up and tried again if he missed it the first time.

Death was in the driver's seat of this place that drove the life out of my grandmother.

Erase pictures in your mind of great, flat plains. It is almost as if God had slept here and made his bed like Adam, my now-teenage stepson, smoothing out a few places but, in doing so, merely spreading around the folds, creases and lumps. This part of Oklahoma is situated in an ecosystem of tallgrass prairie that once extended for 220,000 square miles from Canada to Texas and across Nebraska, Iowa and Illinois. Ninety percent of it has disappeared in the three hundred years of white settlement. About all that is left of the tallgrass prairie now is a swath through eastern Kansas, whose southern tip is Osage County, Oklahoma. The area is called the Flint Hills, but it should have been named the Flat Hills. The tops of these hills are so high and flat that often the horizon and countryside suddenly zoom out, like a camera lens, to give a wide-angle view of miles ahead. Then your lens, and vision, abruptly zoom back to myopic view as the flat ground heads downhill. Driving this country is like walking down steps. One descends upon a broad, flat plain, then descends again onto another, only to do so again, and again—and each step takes you deeper down the hillside of history, into a time that elsewhere is long dead and buried, but that here plays at the edge of your pool of vision, romps in the earthbound shadows of clouds skipping in the sky. Surely the frustration born of nature must have spawned some of the violence that shaped the history of this area, shaped in turn by an enveloping, unsettling contradiction: hilly flatness.

As I took in the scenery, it occurred to me I had not yet seen any of the mansions or other accoutrements of wealth that dotted the landscape of my Osage reading. After the fireworks stand and a couple of suburban ranch-style houses that had spilled over the county line from Bartlesville, only one dwelling was visible from the road: the charred shell of a burned-out mobile home.

My mind wandered as I drove the last of the 1,500 miles that separated my life in Baltimore from . . . from what? I soon would find out. The 1,500 miles that separated my life from Sybil's death? That separated the life I have from the life I might have had?

No, that wasn't right and I knew it: maybe the life I wanted, yes, but not the life I might have had. I knew I was alive only because she was dead. I would not have been born if Sybil had lived. If my mother's life had been any different—if she had been raised as an Osage, here on the Osage reservation—she would not have met my father, and I would not have gotten this chance to redefine my life as an Osage, and to relive my grandmother's death.

Who killed Sybil Bolton?

Maybe I did—out of some across-the-ages determination to live, like these turtles' across-the-road determination to give life.

I did it.

I killed my grandmother.

A sign over a small bridge snapped me back to the present—reality—but at the same time pulled me deeper into the past. "Salt Creek," it said. That was where my great-grandmother, Kate Conner Woodward, was born and spent her childhood—in an Osage wigwam on Salt Creek.

By the time I turned my head to look for it, it was gone. History.

THE "OH MY GODS" STARTED when I saw the first buildings, a mile and a half past the "Welcome to Pawhuska" sign.

Heading west, Pawhuska begins with a pawnshop, just after a

maroon-and-white sign saying "NBC Bank: Positively Pawhuska," and an oil well just a spit from the side of the road, black steel glistening greasy in the baking, near-noon sun.

Pawhuska Pawn sets the tone of the town—not so much by its window signs saying it specializes in firearms and jewelry, or by any sign of disrepair (on the contrary, its appearance looks as if business is good), but by the statement its presence makes. A town that begins with a pawnshop also ends with a pawnshop—for those going back, leaving town, leaving period. No need to make a special trip, you can sell out on the way out.

As I drove down Main Street (what else?), past streets named Lynn, Rogers, Revard, Prudom, Leahy, Palmer, Mathews, Trumbly, Tinker—all names of Osages that I recognized from my research—I strained to see the Pawhuska of my reading: the "marble office buildings, smart Fifth-Avenue-looking shops, and magnificent custom-built cars rushing by." But rather than springing into life from the pages of my history books, the Pawhuska that unfolded before me was receding into them. Buildings were abandoned, some falling down. Doors were boarded up. Windows were broken, some held together by yellowing tape. Peeling paint hung like spiderwebs. Roofs sagged. The only things that went "rushing by" were my expectations, dashing desperately down the street to find something to match them, past dozens of dusty, dented, decade-old pickups and passenger cars parked along sidewalks, where a few hatted cowboys poked along in the shadow of decay.

I have to spend three months here?

Pawhuska looked like the face of a frail and frightful old woman, baring her teeth (the few that remain) in defiance of death. The buildings lining its streets were the wrinkles rippling her face, unsightly scars of survival. They at once showed the beauty of her youth and the ugliness of her age. Her dire condition suggested that her attributes were not the objects of cherishing and care but rather the keys to the door of decadence that was opened too many times. If Pawhuska's walls could speak, they probably wouldn't, out of deference to proprieties that would be offended by vocalizing the ghostlike fragments of memory that haunt its sleep.

Only a few buildings and businesses seemed to have ducked the tornado of time that had gutted Pawhuska. Modernity had established a tiny beachhead on the eastern edge of town: a glassy Homeland supermarket, a Pizza Hut of cookie-cutter structure, a Circle K convenience store with gas pumps in its parking lot and its windows curtained with movie posters of videos for rent inside. A liquor store had set up shop in a mobile home with chalky white-and-green aluminum siding. (Its wheels were still attached, I noticed. It, too, wasn't sure it was going to stay.) But a Texaco station still clung to the age when self-service meant stealing: retirement-age attendants worked the gas pumps, checked under the hood, cleaned the windshields.

At the center of town, only six blocks from its perimeter, loomed the Pawhuska Sphinx—Agency Hill. More than a century ago, the U.S. government grabbed the high ground, choosing the steepest, highest hill, visible from the Indian camps at its base, to build the symbol of its power, the Osage Agency. The government's massively cut sandstone headquarters was an architectural show of force, and its purpose is not lost, even today. Osages had to look up to the government. They still have to, for everything but jobs. Most Osages don't have the 50 percent blood quantum to work at their own agency; Indians of other tribes administer their affairs. The Osage Agency building rivaled everything in town until white private enterprise, flush with Osage cash, erected bigger buildings along Kihekah—"Chief"—Avenue, which runs north-south along the base of the hill. Then white lawyers decided they liked the view from up there—looking down on Indians—so they had the Osage County Courthouse and Jail constructed next to the agency building, dwarfing it in size and outclassing it in structure and grandness—granite, with Greek columns.

But now Authorities' Row was sending a new message to the denizens below—government was bust, too poor even to hire a couple of Indians to take down the Christmas decorations. A house-size metal frame of a star was attached to the courthouse roof, rising a good story and a half above it, and Christmas lights dangled from the poles, acting as a weather vane when the wind kicked up.

I turned onto Kihekah—Pawhuska's main thoroughfare, focus of many old-time pictures of bumper-to-bumper traffic and sidewalks crowded with commerce. Forming a large, triangular traffic island at Kihekah's entrance from Main Street was the Triangle Building, also the star of many long-ago pictures. Then (it was built in 1914), it was Pawhuska's landmark, a five-story, four-sided, wedge-shaped brick building, filled with lawyers' offices. The building was testament to Pawhuska's growing prosperity and promising future, and its unusual design reflected those of its occupants: they intended to drive a wedge between the Osages and their wealth.

Now the Triangle Building was empty—not just of people and offices but most of its windowpanes—a bust of Pawhuska's past, testament to the thoroughness with which the whites fulfilled their dreams, to their success at enriching themselves at the Osages' expense, and when nothing was left, leaving—a monument, in short, to the American Dream. Orange-and-white-striped police barricades surrounded the building to keep passersby from joining it in death from something falling from its upper reaches. From a second-floor window, the name SHOEMAKE was visible through a film of dirt; two down from it, SHO MAKE. Venetian blinds were askew behind broken glass. At the street level, display windows were decorated with snow-painted Christmas trees, twinkling stars, gliding birds—scenes frozen in time by abandonment. Joy was not their message now.

I noticed a building whose wooden facade was painted Rustoleum red and bore the words OB RT P K LLY. Across the street, a large copper box hung from the marble wall of the former Citizens National Bank. The box had a white-stained glass front that used to flash, in urgent red letters, ROBBERY ALARM, when one was in progress, back when there was something inside worth stealing. Next door, each of eight windows on the second floor of a brick building showed a yellowed shade, each pulled down to the same three-quarter length, a sort of half-mast salute to its memory. Tatters of a wind-ripped, pink-and-white-striped awning flapped across the top of its storefront windows. In one was the sign "Sorry We're Closed."

In the glass door of another closed building, a poster hung. "Year of the Indian," it said.

You have to spend three months here! My *who-are-you-kidding* voice was gloating. *You wanted to be an Indian when you thought Pawhuska was all mansions and Mercedes. Do you want to be one now?*

CAROLYN WAS WAITING for me outside the library when I pulled up. After hugs, kisses, a round of "Howzit goin's" and an apology for my lateness, she gushed, "What a neat place!"

I looked at her for any sign of teasing, a specialty of hers, but she appeared to be serious. "You're kidding," I said.

Carolyn wasn't. She also wasn't planning to spend the summer in Pawhuska, and was staying at the first-class Hotel Phillips in Bartlesville. Her cup runneth over with enthusiasm.

"I can hardly wait to show you around," she said. She and her daughters, Jenny and April, had anticipated my lateness, in fact had counted on it, and arrived the day before to sightsee on their own without being slowed by Uncle Denny.

Carolyn was anxious to show me a picture of Kate Conner Woodward, our great-grandmother. They had found it at the Osage County Historical Society Museum, and Carolyn was excited about it. "You won't believe it," she said. "It's Mom wearing an Indian dress."

But I persuaded her to stop first at the house at 107 East 11th Street. I was anxious to see it. On my drives between Baltimore and Washington, I sometimes rehearsed talking my way into the house: "Excuse me, ma'am, do you have a dark spot in your hardwood floor upstairs that won't come out? Is there a place in your yard where the grass won't grow?" I hoped the presence of Carolyn, Jenny and April would make less threatening to the owners the prospect of letting in a stranger to tour the house.

Carolyn drove. East 11th Street was five blocks north, the last two steeply uphill. While we drove, Carolyn talked about her trip. They had visited Alta Vista before coming to Pawhuska, 155 miles due south. April had wanted to see it, and Carolyn wanted to see how Bat Nelson, the barber, was getting along—and pry him for details.

Harry hadn't told him much, Bat had said reluctantly. All Bat knew was that Sybil was in the back yard with the baby, and was "sitting on some kind of pump platform when she did herself in."

"A pump?" I asked.

"That's what I asked," Carolyn said. "And Bat just shrugged and pumped his arm up and down"—like Carolyn was doing now.

So it did take place outside, on the lawn, in front of the baby, and Harry knew. But why did he lie to Cara Mae, telling her that Sybil had killed herself on a Friday night after getting drunk at a party? Maybe he suspected she wouldn't have believed that a mother would shoot herself while playing with her baby in the back yard on a Saturday morning, and wanted to keep her from prying. But why?

The house was a huge, square, two-story, stucco structure, with a flat roof and a deep, covered front porch supported by two thick, rectangular columns. It was located in a neighborhood of houses of similar age and size. Some were "uppercrust"—as the mortician, Mr. McCartney, had said—others just cruddy. The house was situated halfway up a steep hill that rose northward—Agency Hill jutted from it to the southwest—and was only two doors east of Kihekah Avenue. Adjoining Kihekah at almost a forty-five-degree angle at the intersection was Grandview, which runs past the Osage Agency. A. T. Woodward, when he lived in the house, had only about a five-hundred-yard walk to his office at the agency. Although the house sat high above Pawhuska, the view was blocked by thick, tall trees and houses across the street.

The house's design probably was considered gauchely modern when it was erected but now would evoke nostalgia for the pre–World War I architectural era. The house shows influences from the turn-of-the-century Prairie School, Craftsman, and Arts and Crafts movements whose architects, rebelling against the Victorian vogue, favored function over frills and, in effect, created house styles that were Indian in their concept: simple, basic, natural, in harmony with their surroundings.

This house once had been all of those—but now was Indian only in its reality: abandoned. It showed all the neglect that my family had accorded Sybil Bolton in our lifetimes.

The stucco was cracked and graying. The white paint on its wood trim and window frames had come down in chunks, and the exposed wood was rotting. A wrought-iron love seat rusted on the porch. Boards were falling from the porch ceiling. Someone had smudged "Meet me at" in the dirt of a glass-and-aluminum storm door; the time or place had been erased by the elements. On the flat porch roof, a tall aluminum ladder had toppled over. Next to its uplifted legs, an air conditioner protruded from a yellow-shaded window, probably of the master bedroom. A plank of wood trim along the edge of the roof had broken off at a downspout, showing a strip of black hollowness.

At the street curb, the roots of a large tree had uprooted a square of sidewalk. On the left edge of the property, weeds grew in cement cracks of the driveway and, as it ran past that side of the house, halfway up three ground-floor windows. The driveway led to a two-door garage built at the back corner of the quarter-acre lot. The garage had had an addition built onto its right side that looked like a lean-to. It was mostly rickety roof and rent screen, but visible through weeds growing inside was a small room. Perhaps that was where the Woodwards' chauffeur had lived. Stucco had crumbled off most of the garage, leaving dark wood planks exposed. One of the garage doors had been pried one-quarter open. A rust-brown chain-link fence, some of it partially collapsed under the weight of greenery, enclosed the yard. Along the back, it ran parallel to an alley.

On the other side of the house, tree branches pushed against windows and the overhang of the roof. Screens hung haphazardly off their frames. In the back, windows were open, and shreds of draperies trembled in the breeze like the hand of an old woman.

We found the pump three or four feet to the left of the stoop of a rotting wood-and-screen porch leading to the back door. Even the ivy growing thickly on the ground around the base of the porch didn't dare climb the structure. What Bat had understood to be a "platform" was a raised cover, about three feet square, now rusted brown. The pump was underground. All of us took turns squatting by it and touching the cover.

"So this is where it happened," somebody said somberly.

After almost a year in which even a wisp of a thought about my grandmother evoked a wave of emotions, I felt oddly cold touching the sunbaked cover of the pump, the wellspring of my family history's watershed event. It didn't happen here, I kept thinking.

Why would Sybil sit on the pump to do herself in? Though sunny that day, it was forty to fifty degrees outside and the ground was saturated from five days of rain. The pump cover may still have been wet.

If she sat while keeping an eye on the baby in the fenced back yard, why wouldn't she have picked the porch stoop, only a few feet away? One of the few things I knew about Sybil was that she was a stoop-sitter. She had sat on a stoop to pose for the one picture of her my mother has.

If Sybil shot herself in the heart while sitting on the stoop, the impact of the bullet and the blast would have propelled her backward and left onto the porch, not forward and right onto the pump.

In the unlikely event that she actually did sit on the pump and shoot herself, the thrust would have knocked her off of it. To attain the awkward position of angling a handgun so that the muzzle touches the chest and is aimed at the heart, a woman would have to hold the pistol below her breast in such a way that the barrel is tilted upward. The impact would have jolted Sybil's body upward, off the ground, and backward, off the pump. But her body must have been found in a position that gave the impression she shot herself sitting on the pump—lying on the ground, face up, with her buttocks across the pump.

The pump was not where Sybil shot herself, but where she ended up. That meant the gunshot took place in a perimeter of a body length or more around the pump to allow her to fall straight backward to land with her buttocks on the pump.

If that was what happened, that meant Sybil was dead before she hit the ground. If she were not, maternal instinct would have taken over: She would have turned over to look for her baby and died on her side or face down.

And what about the pistol? Since her death was immediately judged a suicide, a pistol must have been found near the pump, probably in or at her hand. If Sybil shot herself in a standing position, she had to be facing away from the pump to land on her back with her buttocks across it. But the backfire of the pistol and her death spasm would have thrown the gun to her front—away from the pump—as she fell backward onto it. Depending on where she was standing, the pistol could have ended up ten, fifteen, even twenty feet from the pump, landing in the grass or even the bushes against the house, but nowhere near the pump or Sybil's body.

If you discount suicide, that means somebody shot her in the vicinity of the pump. But why would Sybil allow a stranger to get close enough to her to shoot her in the chest, presumably point-blank to ensure a one-shot kill to make her death look like a suicide? Sybil had been so terrified of something—meaning, somebody—that she had called her father in Oklahoma City the day before and begged him to come to Pawhuska.

A stranger could have gotten within point-blank range in only two ways. Perhaps Sybil didn't see him coming: she was shot from the porch, perhaps as she was stepping onto it, and the blast propelled her backward onto the pump, three or four feet from the porch door. Or, the gunman grabbed little Kathleen in the back yard, and Sybil either froze in place, allowing him to approach her, or ran to her baby, approaching the gunman.

But someone else, besides a stranger, easily could have gotten near her in the back yard without arousing her suspicion or panic—a family member. Her stepfather. Her mother. Her—

Harry, I thought with an "Oh God." Just when I had him in the clear, there he was in the back yard, holding a gun—thanks to the detail that Sybil sat on the pump cover "when she did herself in," the clue that came not from Cara Mae, or Theil Annett, or Claribel Shaw, but from—Harry himself, via his "closest pal," Bat Nelson.

How did Harry know?

And what would it mean if he were the only person who knew that detail?

As the four of us walked around the house to the front yard to leave, a blond woman pulled up in the driveway next door. We walked over, introduced ourselves, told her that our great-grandmother had owned the house back in the twenties, and asked her what had happened to it.

The woman hadn't heard of the Woodwards. For the decades that she had lived next door, another family had lived there.

Fifteen years ago, she said, squinting up at the house, their teenage boy committed suicide in his bedroom upstairs, shot himself in the head. It was such a tragedy, she said. The family just . . . fled.

"I wish the city would tear it down," she said, suddenly wrapping her arms around herself, as if to fight off a chill in the searing heat. "That house gives me the creeps. It scares me so bad I don't even like to stay in my own house when my husband travels. You can hear things coming from there at night. It scares me to death. The house is haunted. It really is."

Carolyn, Jenny and April had joined the woman in grimacing up at the house in horror, to the point of showing teeth.

I looked at their faces, then up at the house, then off into the mental space of lost time and fading memory that we call history—and from its consigns came into focus the decomposing picture of my grandmother, the only one I had ever seen: Sybil sitting on a stoop.

"Is there any way I can get in there?" I asked.

They all suddenly looked at me as if I had just thrown up at the dinner table.

THE CHEROKEE WOMAN at the bar was right. I was back in no time—that afternoon, in fact. It was a Wednesday. I drank until Saturday night, leaving my room only to buy more beer or browse Bartlesville bars. One of those days, I moved to a four-cockroach-rated motel in Bartlesville. My room overlooked an auto repair shop. One night, watching two-steppers boot-scoot around the dance floor of a cowboy disco, I calculated that Kevin, now sixteen months old and due to visit with Fleur in a couple of weeks, would arrive in Pawhuska at the identical age, to the day, that my mother had been when she lost her mother.

Miraculously I woke up in time—and in good enough shape—to go to church on Sunday.

It was not my intention to be hypocritical. Before leaving Baltimore, I had arranged to meet my parents for mass at the Pawhuska Catholic church. They had planned to arrive in Pawhuska Saturday night, and my mother wanted to see the church. She had been told she was baptized there. That was where her parents were married. Her mother's funeral took place there. And the Immaculate Conception Catholic Church in Pawhuska was regionally famous for its stained-glass windows.

One of them—depicting the baptizing of Osages by a Jesuit priest—had required a special dispensation from the pope because, rather than imagined representations of religious figures, it portrayed actual living people: Osages had posed for the window's drawings. Artisans in Bavaria had crafted the stained glass, and carried the pieces of glass from Germany to Pawhuska and assembled them in the church.

Was it Sybil who killed that boy living in her house, drove him to it? I asked myself during mass. *Is she angry? Does she want revenge?*

All through this, I've thought Sybil was guiding me to get back into the family. What if she's guiding me to get back AT the family?

Am I being set up for some horrible disaster?

After mass, my mother took me to the window of the Osages and told me who the people in it were. A young girl depicted in the window had died, and the child's father, who also had posed for the window, was so aggrieved that he left the Catholic Church, returning to the peyote-based rituals of the Native American Church. My mother had read an article about the window years ago and, of course, remembered each word of it. I always wished I had inherited her photographic memory, her instant, word-for-word recall of things she had read or heard. I would have had a more successful time at college, which I approached as if I had a photographic memory.

In inimitable fashion, my mother, who had been in the church a whole hour, started leading a young couple on a tour of the church. The young woman, like my mother, had been baptized there.

I suddenly felt weak and sleepy, though I had had shakier mornings-after on less to drink. I wandered down the middle aisle toward the front door. *Make the best of it,* I decided. *Stop drinking. Stop feeling sorry for yourself. Start working. Do what you came here for. Finish your research. Play it out. You can't change what happened, or what is going to happen. Get to know some Osages.*

But first I had to find them. I hadn't seen many, including at mass that morning. Occasionally I passed an Indian, presumably an Osage, driving a pickup or a big American car. I had noticed that Indians drive slower than whites. Speeding tickets are costlier to Indians. The fines represent a higher proportion of their income, as do tanks of gas and car repairs. A lot of the cars there seemed to be fifteen to twenty years old, aging reminders of the last good oil years in Osage County, when headrights reflected Arab-propelled gas prices, rising to a sky-high of $26,680 in royalty payments per capita in 1980, although the amount's spending power was pocket change compared to that during the bonanza days of the twenties. In 1980, the Osages' principal chief, Sylvester J. Tinker, got into political hot water when he was quoted as saying, "We've been doing pretty good since them Arabs started causing problems. I bless 'em every morning." I was disappointed there were not more Osages around. Sometimes I got the feeling that coming to Pawhuska was like going to the National Zoo in Washington to see the giant pandas, precious but threatened creatures: Some days they just don't come out. Sometimes I wondered if I misread the map and drove to the wrong Pawhuska—a little like the time I bought a plane ticket in Berlin for Panama City and found out at the airport that the travel agent had routed me to Panama City, Florida. I had come all this way, spent so much time on research, gone to all this trouble—taking a leave of absence from work, disrupting our family—just to spend the summer in some broken-down town of poor whites. I could have gone to a coal-mining town in West Virginia or southern Pennsylvania—two hours' drive, max—or even to parts of Baltimore to find the same thing. I came to this place, the Osage Nation, to find my people, but now that I'm here, I can't find them.

As I neared the church front door, I pulled out a cigarette to light up the instant I hit fresh air. I fished around for my lighter but dropped it as

I pulled it out of my pocket. As I straightened out from picking it up, I saw the window.

It was the first one on the right as you walk into the church. It depicted a young woman with auburn hair in bangs and a short bobbed haircut standing at Christ's lap. In the foreground, crawling up a step toward them, was a baby.

"Suffer the Little Children to Come unto Me," the inscription read.

Then below it, in white letters on black glass, it said:

"In Memory of Sybil Bolton by Arthur and Kathleen Woodward and Nicholas and Angela Andretta."

Which I had trouble reading through the tears welling up and beginning their groundward fall—like Sybil Bolton in her life's last eye blink.

TRIBUTES TO A
VANISHING RACE

Chapter Nine

Traces of Sybil's life were as hard to find as her crypt.

If you stand on tiptoe on the back stoop of her mother's house, and look northwest, you can almost see the house that holds Sybil now. The mausoleum is just over the hill, a pistol shot from the spot where Sybil fell.

The twenty-five-acre Pawhuska cemetery stretches across a permanent camping ground that the Osages used for centuries when they were en route to, or going home from, their semiannual buffalo hunts farther west. They stashed tepee poles and other equipment at the site—as well as at other stopping places—to speed the women's work of setting up camp after a day's travel. Even when they were on their Kansas reservation, the Osages took the same routes west that they had during their millennium in Missouri, traveling south to their ancient, buffalo-hunting trails along a path that, paved, became Route 75 south to what is now Bartlesville. From there, they walked familiar ground, heading west over thickly forested and bouldered hills along a trail that became Route 60 west, the road to Pawhuska. The long-legged Osages typically could cover forty miles a day—no small feat—but the ruggedness of the terrain west of Bartlesville slowed them to twenty-five tough miles—to the western side of the two hills that now nestle Pawhuska on their eastern slopes. William Conner, as a boy and young adult taking part in the buffalo hunts from the Osages' Kansas reservation, used to stretch out under the stars on the same spot where first his granddaughter and then his only daughter would be stretched out in a place where starlight would never enter.

The mausoleum rises from the top of a slight hill that the cemetery climbs from its entrance. The structure is granite and Greek, about fifty by a hundred feet, and has a heavy steel door tall enough to let giants pass without stooping. The groundskeepers keep the door locked nowadays. Thieves were making off with the flowers placed at the crypts and reallocating them to the graves around the mausoleum—or so the guy told me who unlocked the door and let me in. The building had just been renovated; some of the white marble covering the crypts was replaced, and the foundation was regirded to correct a decided but disturbing lean that the mausoleum had acquired in recent years. Cemetery officials had feared the building might topple. Now, there's a headline for you: "Mausoleum Tumbles Down Hill; Heads Roll."

"Place looks pretty good now," the man said. "You're lucky you come now."

The mausoleum had no wasted space: There was no foyer in which to fret about the next room. The door groaned open, and daylight flooded in on wall-to-wall white marble, crypts stacked from floor to ceiling, six to eight bodies high, maybe more. I wasn't counting. I was reading. On the tombstones were Indian names and white names. On some crypts were both the Indian and white names of the deceased. Others also bore their Osage occupants' original allottee numbers. Studying the crypts lining the T-shaped aisle was like taking an Osage history class. I saw name after name I had seen before, but not the one I had come to see.

The Woodwards were about halfway down the left arm of the T, facing the front. One long marble slab covered three crypts. Centered and overlayed on the slab was an elongated nameplate, in marble, saying "Woodward." My great-grandmother was in the middle crypt.

"Kathleen S. Woodward, Dec. 10, 1878–Oct. 2, 1945" was engraved in the slab. She had cheated on her birthday, making herself a year younger so she would not be, for all posterity to see, a year older than her husband, entombed to the left of her. A small, rectangular marble plate overlaying that slab said, "Arthur T., Nov. 10, 1878–Oct. 26, 1950." The crypt on the right was empty, its nameplate blank. On a narrow ledge running the length of the three crypts were two bouquets of artificial flowers, one at each end, red carnations on the left, yellow roses on the right. Two marble flower vases were attached to the ledge, and the one nearest the empty crypt held a single plastic red rose. In the middle of the ledge, centered on Kate Woodward's name, was a small wreath of four artificial red roses.

Someone had remembered her. Someone also seemed to have had a preference for the empty, right side, at least in terms of flower placement. That's where Sybil was supposed to be—next to her mother.

Was she?

I took a lap of the mausoleum, then another, then another, then another, and couldn't find Sybil. I kept ending up at the empty crypt next to Mrs. Woodward and staring at the blank nameplate.

Sybil was not anywhere else. Was that where she was?

Those bastards, I thought suddenly. They didn't even put her name on her tombstone. I was so exasperated I thought I was going to gag, though that sensation could have been caused by the acrid, ammonia smell choking the stale air. I felt suddenly ill. All these years, and she didn't even rate a name.

I took another lap, and again came up empty.

I can't believe this, I kept saying to myself. This can't be right. Maybe old Mr. Johnson was wrong and Sybil had been buried outside, not interred here. I hoped so. I went outside, got in my car—which I had parked next to Mr. Johnson's tombstone in what looked like the choicest spot in the graveyard—and drove the five hundred yards to the groundskeepers' building at the cemetery entrance downhill.

"No, that crypt is empty," said the man who had unlocked the door. "Your grandmother"—he was studying a chart of the crypts—"is right here." He pointed to her name, penciled inside a square that appeared to be located underneath the Woodwards.

I drove back. Sybil wasn't underneath the Woodwards. The Leahys were. I looked below the Leahys, then above the Woodwards, then across the aisle from them, then made another lap, then drove back to the groundskeepers.

"You must think I'm stupid, but I can't find her," I said.

"No, no." He didn't sound very convincing. He showed me the chart again. "She's on the north side," he said. And then he must have noticed I was peering out toward the left side of the mausoleum, for he pointed to the right side of the building.

I found her there. I had been standing right in front of it, looking dead at it for a few moments, saying to myself, Where the hell is she? when the words came slowly into focus: in large capital letters centered across the top, BOLTON; then under it, in smaller caps, SYBIL; and under that, the dates of her short, sad life. She was in the second row from the end, near a solitary window. Her crypt faced the rear of the building, and was about chest-high. I must have looked at it a dozen times on my search. The faint lettering was embossed rather than engraved. The words appeared barely raised and were barely visible.

A tombstone written in invisible ink. It was as if they were trying to hide her.

There were no flowers on her ledge, and probably hadn't been any in my lifetime at least.

So they hadn't moved her next to her mother, as Mrs. Woodward had wanted. This thought was slow to build as other emotions subsided: my relief at finding Sybil's crypt, my exasperation at not having been able to find it, my disappointment at seeing the shoddy workmanship of the lettering of her name. Granted, Harry had been neither cooperative nor encouraging when Angela Andretta had called to ask for his permission to move her sister next to her mother. "Frankly, Angela, I don't give a damn what you do with her body," he had said, but he had not said no. They could have moved her. Harry would not have cared as long as it didn't cost him anything. That's what her mother had wanted. Mrs. Woodward obviously had bought the three crypts together so she and Sybil could be interred side by side.

But they would not move her fifty feet so they could be together. For forty-seven years now, the final resting places of mother and child had been like public rest rooms: just down the hall and to the right of each other, at opposite ends of the mausoleum.

That would have been A. T. Woodward's doing. Presumably he was his wife's benefactor, certainly her executor, charged with carrying out her wishes. Woodward must have decided he had better things to do with Mrs. Woodward's money than spend it on the dead.

He knew he would be interred next to his wife. Maybe Woodward didn't want to end up so near to Sybil, didn't want her anywhere around him. Maybe the thought made him nervous, made his conscience hurt. Woodward may not have killed her, but he surely helped cause her second death: the cover-up of her murder as a suicide. "As a favor to" Woodward, the mortician McCartney had speculated, the authorities had not performed an autopsy. Sybil would not have been written off as a suicide without Woodward's acquiescence.

Or maybe there was another reason. Maybe in life, as in death, Woodward didn't want Sybil around, either.

I HAD ABOUT AS MUCH luck at the library.

Sybil left few footprints in Osage County, and the ones I found were all in her mother's footsteps. With the exception of her marriage, Sybil never set out on her own, never split off from her mother's path to pave her own. She never really had the chance. She was, after all, only twenty-one when she died, a fact I sometimes failed to keep in mind. It's hard to think of your grandmother being no older than twenty-one.

Something else was suggested by the faint trace of Sybil in the public records: She was overshadowed by a prominent, powerful and driving mother, and was just outside the circle of spotlight shining down on her sister, Angela Gorman Andretta, four and a half years older.

In the summer of 1922, for example, the "Social News" column of the *Pawhuska Daily Capital* hardly let a day pass without some mention of Mrs. Woodward hosting a party, tea or club meeting, at which she invariably performed classical music on the piano. On June 1, 1922, though, Sybil made the news. Miss Sybil Woodward, the newspaper announced, hosted the Vanity Club, a group of young women belonging to Pawhuska high society, of which Sybil was a member. Nine days later, a "delightful dance" was held in Sybil's honor, celebrating her recent graduation from Notre Dame Academy in Philadelphia. On June 20, Sybil and her stepfather, A. T. Woodward, "motored to Bartlesville" to play golf. Two days later, she was off to New York City for three weeks with her mother and her half-cousin, Theil Conner.

But the purpose of the New York vacation, the article made clear, was to meet Angela Gorman and her husband—Mr. and Mrs. Nick Andretta. Upon Sybil's return to Pawhuska, on July 15, she and Theil hosted an "informal bridge," which the *Capital* judged a newsworthy event. But then, on the twentieth, Angela and Nick Andretta arrived from their home in Hartford, Connecticut, for a month's stay at the Woodwards'.

The "Social News" was relentless in recording Angela's every move: a "morning musical," a "delightful musical," a party "honoring Mr. and Mrs. Andretta," another party "honoring Mr. and Mrs. Andretta," one "honoring Mrs. Andretta" alone, another "complimentary to Mrs. Andretta." During this stretch, Sybil rated only one mention—as an also-ran at a bridge party put on for Angela. Sybil had the "low score."

I found an explanation for the to-do over Angela in a 1957 Osage Agency book commemorating the tribe's "semi-centennial celebration" of allotment. The book has a 1920s picture of Angela. By then in her twenties, she has the brooding look of an underweight teenager taking life too weightily. Angela's hair is dark, long, braided, parted down the middle and held by a colorful headband. She is pictured in an Indian buckskin dress, the "costume" she wore when "she appeared in one of Cadman's operas" at the . . . Metropolitan Opera House in New York. The ellipsis represents the double take that nearly wrenched my neck when I read it.

In another book, I found this: "Three Osage women have been performing artists in the 20th century. . . . The first was Angela Gorman, who studied in New York and became a noted opera singer in the 1920s. Her performing career was advanced enough that in 1919 the tribe honored her achievements. In a ceremony conducted by Chief Fred Lookout, Gorman was given the name Eagle Maiden, reflecting her membership in the Eagle clan. 'I must prove the qualities of my ancestry as well as be the pioneer blazing the trail for other girls in the tribe,' she said. Among those other Osage girls," the book said, "were the internationally renowned ballet dancers of the 1950s, Maria and Marjorie Tallchief.

After the news of Sybil's "low score" on August 5, 1922, her name appeared only three other times in the local papers—at least in stories I found. They reported the three most important events remaining in her life: her wedding on June 6, 1923 (the Pawhuska paper hyped it as "one of the most important social events of this spring"); the birth of her daughter, Kathleen Sybil Bolton, in Kansas City, Missouri, on June 24, 1924 (the newspaper reported it circuitously by announcing Mrs. Woodward's departure for Kansas City, where her daughter, etc., etc.); and her death (the *Bartlesville Daily Enterprise,* under the headline "Ends Own Life," said that Sybil committed "the rash act . . . by shooting herself through the heart").

It did not take long for me to grow frustrated over my inability to find anything more about Sybil's life in the public record. Since arriving in Pawhuska, I seemed to have lost a knack that I sensed I had acquired over the last year: I could open any book, magazine or newspaper to the exact spot of something pertinent to "my project." The trail that led me to Pawhuska had grown cold as soon as I got there. I had lost my touch. After all the weeks of day after day after day of poring over page after page after page in the Pawhuska library, I found evidence of Sybil's life—proof that she did more than just die in it—in only two other places: the Osage tribal roll book, where she is listed as Osage allottee number 933 and where her birthday is erroneously printed as December 26, 1905; and these confusing entries in the microfilmed "Register of Letters Received" at the Osage Agency in 1925:

4-23-25 #984 (Letter of April 18 1925). Refers for information action and file authority approved April 16 1925 to amend approved roll so as to show date of birth of Sybil F. Beekman as December 26 1903 instead of December 26 1905. Action: Roll books corrected and notices mailed purchasers 6-25-25.

Item #1596: 6-23-25 Indian Office [forwards] . . . letter from Mrs. Sybil Bolton and advises her application for certificate of competency is now before the Department. Reference or action: Wrote AT Woodward 6-25-25. Wrote Mrs. Sybil Bolton 6-25-25. Wrote Mrs. Sybil Bolton 8-3-25.

7-20-25 #1904. Encloses certificate of competency issued July 10 1925 in favor of Sybil F. Beekman Bolton. Action: Wired

AT Woodward 7-20-25. Wrote Sybil F. Beekman Bolton 7-21-
25. Wrote Sybil F. Beekman Bolton 8-3-25. Wrote Sybil F.
Beekman Bolton 8-26-25.

I stared at the microfilm screen—which showed the entries as a photographic negative, white letters on a black background—a long time before I understood what I was looking at: the explanation for what may
have ruined the marriage of my grandparents, and the reason for Sybil's
presence in Pawhuska that November of 1925.

The roll-book error in the year of her birth had prevented Sybil from
gaining prompt access to her Osage oil money after her twenty-first birthday—or in the jargon of the Indian Affairs bureaucracy, being issued her
certificate of competency. No longer a legal minor, she was finally entitled
to manage her own financial affairs and receive her headright money directly—as soon as she was issued her certificate of competency. In 1925,
for an Osage such as Sybil whose Indian blood quantum was less than one-
half, issuance of the document was routine so long as no one—the Osage
Agency, her parents, her guardian, her spouse, her creditors—claimed she
was incompetent. (Different, more complex rules applied to Osages whose
degree of Indian blood was one-half or more.)

But when Sybil wrote the Osage Agency after New Year's of
1925, saying she had just turned twenty-one and would like to be issued
her certificate of competency, a clerk checked the roll book, saw the
December 26, 1905, entry for her birth date, and wrote back saying, No,
you're not twenty-one, you're nineteen.

I can only imagine the dumbfounded looks on Sybil's and Harry's
faces when they read the Osage Agency reply. And I will leave it all to the
imagination, because no dramatic re-creation could probably ever do justice to Harry's reaction when he realized that he was being deprived of
Sybil's money because of a typographical error in 1907 that for eighteen
years no one had ever bothered to correct—not his wife, not his mother-
in-law, not even his wife's stepfather, the Osage tribal attorney.

Harry may not have married Sybil for her money, but he
sure went into debt for her. Harry was of the last generation of white
Americans to pay cash for everything. Even in the last decades of his long
life, he paid his bills in full and at once—cars, clothes, his house, all its

contents. To him, and others of his age, indebtedness was a disgrace, a measure of a man's failings, the social equivalent of imprisonment.

Indians, on the other hand, were America's first modern consumers. Like credit-card users of today, Indians charged everything, mostly because they rarely had cash on hand or in pocket, most of it having gone to the previous month's or quarter's accounts. That their debts were practically guaranteed by the U.S. government made Indians attractive customers to white merchants, who tended to complete all sales in their shops by going to the account books rather than the cash registers.

Sybil, I'm sure, thought nothing of piling up the bills. It was the Indian Way, the only way she knew—and she knew, as well, she was good for all of it, and much, much more, on Osage Payday, her twenty-first birthday. But the debts must have galled Harry, must have made him apoplectic in fact, especially as his bills—documents of his disgrace, affidavits to his failings—mounted with each passing month of bureaucratic delay.

Wheels of government turned just as slowly then as now, perhaps more so. Sybil's birth certificate had to be authenticated and submitted with sworn statements to its validity by her mother and father. Then the Osage Agency had to get around to the complicated task of crossing out the incorrect year and writing in the correct one, making Sybil officially twenty-one. That done, the known purchasers of the roll book had to be notified of the error and the correction. In a panic, Sybil—no doubt taking dictation from an exasperated Harry—wrote a complaint in June to the Bureau of Indian Affairs in Washington. Coincidentally, the process of correcting the typo was completed at the end of that month.

Now the agency was ready to *start* the process of approving Sybil's request for her certificate of competency, and issuing it. That took another month. It took one more month to get it to her.

Sybil was now up to the beginning of September 1925. She had only two months to live, although she didn't know that. She knew only that the strain caused by the crisis over her certificate of competency was killing her marriage to Harry Bolton. Now, finally, nine months into her twenty-second year, that crisis had passed.

But she still didn't have any of her Osage money. She only had the key to it. Sybil could use this key to open the door to the vault in which her money was contained and had been accumulating, with interest, since she was three—as soon as she found out where that vault was located.

But that information was known only by her guardian—officially her mother, Kate Woodward, but in reality her stepfather, A. T. Woodward. In 1925, however, he was no longer the Osage tribal attorney, having resigned the previous year to take a job at a bank in El Dorado, Arkansas—one hundred miles south of Little Rock, almost on the Louisiana state line. But the Woodwards hadn't entirely left Pawhuska. They kept their East 11th Street house open, and Mrs. Woodward lived in it much of the time, on extensive and extended visits.

A. T. Woodward couldn't get away from the bank to return to Pawhuska until October. He would meet Sybil there and turn the whole thing—savings accounts, state bonds, federal Liberty bonds, even stocks—over to her then. That would be a good time for her to go to Pawhuska anyway, because the last quarterly payment in 1925—the Osages' richest year to date—would take place some time in the first two weeks of October, whenever the Osage Agency had finished adding up all the oil-bonus money, royalties and interest of the previous quarter, had announced the per capita amount and had received the money transfer from a federal bank to Pawhuska.

Sybil would go to Pawhuska then, in early October, and for the first time in her life, would experience the thrill of going up to the Osage Agency pay window, certificate in hand, and of receiving the due that was her birthright as an Osage Indian, her headright money.

And while she was there, she would take a few weeks off from Harry, maybe even longer. Let the marriage cool down, and let Harry cool off.

Sybil was a bona fide adult now—and a competent one at that, with a certificate to prove it. She would take stock of her young life, decide what to do with the rest of it, decide if it was with Harry that she wanted to grow old.

She would stay at her mother's house, and take the baby, of course.

THE PAWHUSKA LIBRARY had a copy of Kate Conner Woodward's book, *Tributes to a Vanishing Race.*

It was privately printed in Chicago in 1916, and bound in a rich, red suede. Even seventy-six years of aging and of exposure to pollution and the public have not worn the thick, ivory-colored pages—or dulled the point of my great-grandmother's words. The 101-page book is a compilation of seventy poems and short essays about Indian customs, their lore and their loss. Most of the entries are locally written. There also are some unauthorized guest appearances by Whittier, Thackeray, Longfellow and other nationally known writers. Even operameister Charles Wakefield Cadman contributed, although he may not have been aware of it: a short tract on Indian influences on music.

Two of the book's essays were written by To-wam-pah, as Kate Woodward signed herself. One is a short article about war bonnets; the other, entitled "Nature's Children," follows:

> Our fund of strange lore has not been learned from the "Talking Leaves" that unfold a store of fairy tales to the Paleface children, but from "The Story Teller" who, wrapped in blankets as if enshrouding himself in mystery and solemnity, repeats for future generations these myths.
>
> Very early the Indian Child assumed the task of preserving the legends of his ancestors. Thus, they have reached us through many generations, and ere these Real Americans, like the buffalo, have passed into the shadows of forgetfulness, I gather these Nature thoughts of my people for a newer page in the great record of events. They are utterances of a once mighty and noble race, whose greatest crime was in owning this vast domain, America, in which remnants of all nations now unite and sing "My Country, 'tis of Thee," and, taking Poor Lo by the hand, bid him swear allegiance to the flag of the only country he has ever known.
>
> Children of Nature? Yes! and rightly so; for no greater privilege asked we than to roam these rolling, broad plains that reached from our wigwam door to the setting sun, . . . enjoying the luxury of nature, Happy! Free! Oblivious that the Wheels of Fate would grind, change and assimilate a human race.
>
> We do not challenge the poet who said "There is a Divinity that shapes our lives, Rough hew them as we may."

Lift we then the curtain of the past, for a brief recounting of our losses.

. . . Lands of the "Sun Symbols" have we ceded by treaties that bore good promise. True, they yielded towering cities—marvelous commercial centers—but their very foundation is the human mold of many of our ancestors.

. . . Though depleted by events that men call history, still our pride remains undaunted, and we stand till the last drop of Indian blood has become extinct, "The best and noblest of a ransomed land."

I wonder if she ever shook her head at the wonderment of it all.

It takes a leap of imagination to picture Kate Conner Woodward growing up in a wigwam—an Indian woman who published a book, who was a gifted pianist, and whose daughter had appeared at the Metropolitan Opera.

The Indian village of sparse lodges that had sheltered her in her childhood had metamorphosed, like some movie special effect, into an array of mansions by the time her children were growing up. Silk had replaced buckskin. Squaws had become mistresses to maids. Braves no longer used bows and arrows, but Pierce-Arrows. White chauffeurs tended to the Osages' herds of limousines, keeping them fit and fed, and speeding their passengers along the bumpy, dusty Indian trails of Osage County and the paved roads beyond—around the state of Oklahoma, throughout the country, to the ports that would transport them to other worlds.

She had been called Kate since birth and used Kathleen as her formal first name, although legally she was neither. She was born on December 10, 1877, as To-wam-pah, and baptized nine months later with the Christian name Sarah Catherina Conner. Over the years, as the name on her Osage Agency files grew to Kathleen Conner Gorman Beekman Woodward, she filled her life, and her daughters' lives, with the sound of music and the drumbeat of history, for she not only was a talented musician but also had an ear for the march of events, especially the continuing clash of white and Indian cultures.

Kate Conner had been a small victim of such a clash. As an infant, she had lost her mother, Angeline Penn. Osage men did not raise their children, so Kate's father, William Conner, gave her over to the care of

Maggie Bellieu, later Lawrence, an Osage woman who probably was a relative. Kate later would call her Aunt Maggie. Kate grew up in the village of Chief Strike Ax's band at Cana, in the far northwestern corner of the reservation. She was born and baptized in the village, and her years there were happy ones. "I remember as a child," Kate would write in her book, "our stock of calico ponies was increased one with every plucking of the tail feathers of [an] eagle." Osage men carried eagle feathers during ceremonial dances, and wore them in their headgear—"roaches" that resembled scalp locks. "As my aunt had a large cage containing a number of these valuable birds, swapping was rife, and the herd of Indian ponies added materially to our financial standing in the community."

Kate's world had changed, however, by 1882, when her half-brother Woodie Conner was born. Her father had remarried, and five-year-old Kate was now under the care, and thumb, of a white stepmother, the former Adeline Newman. The new Mrs. Conner was not impressed by Kate's familiarity with feathers or other things Indian, but rather by the child's lack of knowledge about white culture, which the white woman equated with ignorance.

Kate formally entered the world of whites in November 1887, when a Catholic boarding school for girls opened in Pawhuska, thirty miles from her village. Not quite ten, she was forced to live away from home during the eight-month school year. Any hope that her father would change his mind and bring her home to the Indian village she missed dissipated the next year, when the Osage tribal council, pushed by the U.S. Indian agent, decreed it mandatory for all children to attend school, under threat of withholding annuity payments to their parents.

The U.S. government was pushing education as the key with which "savages" could gain entry to the "civilized" world. "We hear no longer advocated among really civilized men the theory of extermination" of Indians, said the 1880 annual report of the Board of Indian Commissioners, with just a trace of disappointment. "The only alternative left is to fit him by education for civilized life." Education for girls, considered a luxury for whites, was being touted as a burdensome yet necessary expense if taxpayers were to get their money's worth out of the boys. "It is impossible to overestimate the importance of careful training for Indian girls," the commissioner of Indian affairs reported in 1881. "The labor and expense of educating Indian boys while the girls are left untaught is almost entirely thrown away. Of what avail is it that the man be hard-working and indus-trious, providing by his labor food and clothing for his household, if the wife, unskilled in cookery, unused to the needle, with no habits of order or neatness, makes what might be a cheerful, happy home only a wretched abode of filth and squalor? Is it to be wondered at that he succumbs under the burden and is dragged down to the common level? It is the women who cling most tenaciously to heathen rites and superstitions, and perpet-uate them by their instructions to the children."

The St. Louis School in Pawhuska was a fifteen-by-twenty-two-foot, two-story house in which Kate Conner lived with at least forty other girls. A new building soon was added to accommodate up to another forty boarders. The girls' schoolwork consisted mainly of housework, with time out for singing and piano lessons. Mending was their greatest challenge—an alien concept to them. The children continually protested that they shouldn't have to learn such a chore because Osages "don't wear patched clothes." Like schoolchildren everywhere, recess was their favorite hour. "Every day at recreation they will take a shawl or other clothing and make a tent; then they all crush themselves tightly into it and begin to pray or sing," one of their nuns wrote. "The only thing you can hear for an hour is 'Higha! Higha!' "

On the night of February 14, 1889, a white man decided the world would be a better place without the seventy little Indian girls sleeping in-side the St. Louis School, including eleven-year-old Kate. At 1 A.M., he threw an incendiary bomb into the building, and even all the tears of the nuns and children could not douse the flames. The school quickly burned down. Miraculously, the nuns managed to save all the children.

With the St. Louis School an ash heap—and the Quaker-run federal Indian Affairs commission in Washington refusing to approve a tribal council appropriation of $60,000 to rebuild a facility for Catholics—William Conner had few options for fulfilling the Osages' mandatory school law. He could enroll Kate in the overcrowded government-run school in Pawhuska and run the risk of having her transferred to one of the other Indian schools in Lawrence, Kansas; Houghton, Iowa; or Carlisle, Pennsylvania—all of which had the reputation for literally beating the In-dian out of their pupils. Or he could send her to the sister academy to the Catholic school that he had attended as a boy—at the Osage Mission on the former reservation in Kansas, now the town of St. Paul, Neosho County.

He chose the latter. Kate's new school, St. Ann's Academy, was situated on a hundred acres of former Osage land eighty-five miles northeast of Pawhuska. The schoolchildren were not all Osages or other Indians. Whites from other parts of Kansas and from other states boarded as well, and all the girls were required to wear full-length dresses or skirts. To the whites, the dress code was the familiar fashion of the day, but to the Indians, wearing such clothes each day was every bit as alien and arduous as their daily lessons in reading, writing, geography, needlework, embroidery and drawing.

St. Ann's was no little schoolhouse on the prairie. Its two main school buildings were large—each four stories high and forty feet wide, with four chimneys, and fifteen stairs leading to a massive wooden front door. Cut into the front of its ivy-draped stone facade were eighteen man-size windows and eight attic dormers. But it was in St. Ann's smallest building that Kate stood the tallest—the school music hall. There, at the piano, her musical talent budded.

Kate was so talented, in fact, that her teachers persuaded her father to send her to the nationally renowned Conservatory of Music at St. Mary's Academy (now St. Mary's College) in Notre Dame, Indiana, run by the Sisters of the Holy Cross, where she enrolled in the Senior Department (the equivalent of high school). In her first year there, the 1893–94 school year, she won a first premium, an honors prize, in advanced piano, and a similar award in mending, the dreaded subject at the St. Louis School. Kate learned sketching at the school of art and design, and received a second premium in that subject. The prize lists show her as "Conner, K., Indian Territory."

The next year, she excelled even more at the Conservatory of Music: a first premium in general theory of music, a first premium in piano. She also took a drawing course and won a third premium.

There is no record of her graduating from St. Mary's, but by the summer of 1895, when she left St. Mary's, she was nearly eighteen, and ready for the world.

She had husbands to marry.

Over the years, Kate would continue her musical education with private piano lessons while keeping attuned to the dissonance of history. As a housewife and mother of two girls in the oil-boom town of Pawhuska, neither her talent nor her hobby was of much use, but she found a place for them both, socially and personally. When she was not hosting lunchtime or evening musical recitals, often playing the piano to the delight of her guests, she was holding meetings of the Heeko Club, a women's historical society that she cofounded and that later evolved into the Osage County Historical Society Museum. Theil Annett would remember her Aunt Kathleen as "an encyclopedia" of the Osages—"all the time interested in [them], always talking to me about those things."

Kate pushed her two girls into music. Angela, the eldest, had a beautiful voice and soon was singing opera to her mother's piano accompaniment. Sybil, as she grew older, showed a talent for the harp. The duo soon was amplified to a trio, yet softened by the addition of the soothing, raindrop sounds of Sybil's Irish harp. At night, mixed with girls' giggles and a mother's praise, the classical, operatic, European music of these Osage "savages" emitted from the walls of their house on East 11th Street, and rose to the sky. There, it clashed with the competing noise of a culture alien to it, the crassness of "civilized" American life taking place below on the streets of Pawhuska.

SEWELL BEEKMAN RIGHTLY blamed himself for his daughter's death. He had not taken Sybil's panicky phone call seriously the day before she died. Perhaps she had cried to this wolf before.

But it was not by his refusal to visit his daughter in Pawhuska on November 7, 1925, that he killed her. He did that eighteen years before— by the typo he helped cause in Sybil's entry in the Osage tribal roll. Sybil's presence in Pawhuska the day of her death was the direct result of her father's misdeed. Sewell Beekman killed his daughter just as surely as the bullet that ended her life.

In the early 1900s, Beekman was an agent for the Kansas and Texas cattlemen renting Osage reservation land to graze their herds. The 1887 Dawes Act had broken up all the other reservations in Indian Territory, making the 1.5 million acres of Osage reserve the last open stretch of bluestem-tallgrass prairie—the most fattening grass for cattle—and producing a bonanza for the Osages. The rich Indians grew richer as they leased tens of thousands of acres of their prairie to cattlemen, who pastured hundreds of thousands of cattle there before transporting them by rail to markets in St. Louis, Kansas City and Chicago. By 1893, 57 percent of the reservation—more than 830,000 acres—had been rented out.

The Osages did not personally rent land to every cowboy passing through. Rather, the Indians became absentee landlords to about two dozen cattlemen, granting three-to-five-year leases to huge tracts of pasture, each typically ranging in size from 10,000 to 40,000 acres. The lessees paid the tribe an annual rent of three to ten cents an acre, and those who did not pasture their own cattle on the land subleased it to other white cattlemen, paying the contractual rent to the tribe and pocketing the profits.

Several Osages got in on the leasing action as well. One was William Conner, who leased 16,000 acres in 1893 for three years, paying the Osages an annual rent of $560. Maggie Lawrence, Kate's Aunt Maggie, leased 12,000 acres for $1,200 in 1898. Another lessee was William Conner's twenty-three-year-old divorced daughter, Kate Gorman, who signed a three-year lease in 1901 for 2,190 acres at $372.80 annually.

It was because of this lease that Kate Gorman met Sewell Beekman, who was shopping around the Osage reservation for pasture to sublet for his cattlemen clients.

The Gorman at the end of Kate's new name was John A., a high-powered government lawyer from Washington who first visited the Osage reservation in May 1894 (Kate was sixteen) as part of a three-man Indian Affairs commission to persuade the Osages to accept allotment under the Dawes Act. Perhaps Gorman was the reason Kate did not finish school at St. Mary's; perhaps Kate was the reason that Gorman spent seven months in Pawhuska without accomplishing anything.

He and his fellow commissioners did talk the tribe into taking a vote on allotment. On voting day, Gorman sent kegs of whiskey to the Indian villages, hoping the Osages would get drunk and vote yes. The ploy didn't work: Band chieftains posted armed guards around the kegs; sober, the Osages voted no, then they got drunk. Gorman and the rest of the commission returned to Washington just after Kate's seventeenth birthday in December, having secured only a vague nod from the Osages that they would accept allotment if, among other unlikely occurrences, they of-

ficially became the Sixth Civilized Tribe (they didn't) and their tribal roll
was purged of non-Osages who had finagled their way onto it to share in
the Osages' good and massive fortune (it wasn't).

Kate Conner and John Gorman waited four years to get married, doing so on September 8, 1898. They had a daughter, Mary Angeline Gorman (but called Angela), on June 12, 1899. Kate's Osage Agency
marriage card notes that she and Gorman were divorced at the District
Court in Pawnee County, Oklahoma, but does not provide the date. It was
at least before December 3, 1902, when Kate Gorman became Mrs.
Charles Sewell Beekman in Wichita, Kansas.

Two years after Sybil Frances Beekman was born on December 26,
1903, the Osages agreed to the inevitable—the Dawes Act dismantling of
their reservation, which destroyed their lucrative leasing deals with cattlemen. Under the Osage Allotment Act of 1906, each Osage received title
to 657 acres, while the tribe retained mineral rights in community—regardless of who owned the surface area—to all land encompassing the former reservation.

This concession on oil rights was made by a U.S. government anxious to remove the last roadblock to white Oklahomans—potential voters
and taxpayers—clamoring ever more loudly for statehood. But there was
small print appended to the Osages' exclusive mineral rights: They would
expire in twenty years—in 1926. After that date, Osage County would become like every other place in the United States—whoever owned the land
pocketed the wealth that was pumped from it.

The concession on mineral rights soon made the Osages the richest
people per capita in the world, as it was discovered that their land bridged
an ocean of oil. As the years passed, the approaching expiration of their
unique oil rights gave them another distinction: The Osages became the
most-murdered people per capita in the world.

When Oklahoma was admitted into the Union as the forty-sixth
state on November 16, 1907, the Osages' last reservation became Osage
County, Oklahoma, and the countdown started ticking on the 1920s
Reign of Terror. And Congress, ever sympathetic to white voters who
missed out on the earlier rape of other Indian reservations, set the stage for
the slaughter by instituting an allotment system for the Osages that guaranteed that the Indians would not be owners of their land for long.

Each Osage's 657-acre allotment was a total figure, not a contiguous area. An Osage's individual land possessions were spread out across the former reservation in four plots of roughly 160 acres each. Few of the tracts were adjoining, and all but one—a 160-acre parcel that the holder declared his homestead—could be rented or sold right away.

Cattlemen were the first to realize that Congress had sent them an engraved invitation to steal. With enough graft, they calculated, they could craft a permanent grazing home on the Osages' bluestem-tallgrass range. Riding point for the cattlemen's raiding party on Osage land was Sewell Beekman.

The complexity of the congressionally mandated method of dividing and distributing the allotted land would have defied comprehension even by the corporate tax lawyers of today. Just taking the total acreage of the reservation, dividing by 2,229, and assigning tracts equal to the result would have been much too simple for government to concoct—as well as making it much too difficult for whites to swindle the Indians out of their land.

First, land was set aside for incorporation into five Osage County towns—Pawhuska, Hominy, Fairfax, Foraker and Bigheart. Under the terms of the allotment act, whites could buy land in town, so the town limits were laid out large enough to accommodate New York City. Even today, one drives a couple of miles past Osage County city-limit signs before seeing any sign of a town. Three Indian villages—where mostly fullbloods still lived outside Pawhuska and Hominy and at Gray Horse, outside Fairfax—were excluded from allotment, and each accorded 160 acres. (These areas technically comprise the only Indian reservation in Oklahoma today.) The Osage Agency took eighty-eight acres for its "campus," and the Osages deeded land to two Catholic schools. A twenty-five-acre cemetery in Pawhuska also was mandated by the allotment act.

The rest of the land—1,465,380.56 acres, or 657.41 acres per capita—was disbursed in four stages between 1906 and 1909: Each Osage made three separate selections of 160-acre tracts, and a fourth pick equal to 160 acres generally in 40-acre plots, plus 17 more acres in parcels as small as 2.5 acres to equal the per capita share. To protect the allottees from any possibility of chicanery by whites during the land-selection process, the government had classified the tribal roll officially top secret.

It took Sewell Beekman all of fifteen dollars to breach government security, persuading an Osage Agency clerk to sell his country down the river by slipping the cattlemen's spy a copy of the classified document. Its secrets held merely the names of tribal members in alphabetical groupings by family—families headed by full-bloods first, comprising numbers 1 through 874. Each allottee's entry also listed birth date and family relation, whether the allottee was a head of household, spouse, son or daughter. (In 1921, the allottee's degree of Indian blood was added in roll books made available to the public.)

Beekman was not the only buyer of the classified roll. It was in such demand on the black market at the base of Agency Hill that the government clerks rushed through their work of transcribing the Indian names onto the roll to get the hot product into the hands of the highest bidders, and the kickback into theirs. Thanks in part to Sewell Beekman, the final tribal roll was full of mistakes, including Sybil Bolton's year of birth.

The Osage allottees were given time to make their first 160-acre selection at will, and these generally became their officially declared homesteads, which could not be sold or taxed for twenty-five years. For the remainder of the process, "to avoid any foundation for suspicion of collusion or favoritism shown to one [tribal] band or faction over another," the secretary of the interior decided that a lottery should be held to determine the order in which individual Osages would make their other land selections.

The drawing was held at the Constantine Opera House in Pawhuska on July 8–9, 1907. On stage were two blindfolded Indian children and two wheels—one containing 2,229 cards, each with an Osage's name; in the other, cards bearing the numbers 1 through 2,229. After a full-blood boy spun his wheel and drew a name card, a mixed-blood boy drew a card from the number wheel to match with the name, thus determining that Indian's place on the Round Two order of selection. Round Three was the same list but in reverse, and Round Four the same order as Round Two.

In the audience at the Constantine was Sewell Beekman, writing down the names and numbers. During a later conversation with agency officials that he may or may not have known was being recorded, Beekman criticized a competing cattlemen's agent, William M. Dial. "He got right up in front and was taking down the numbers," Beekman said. "I was more decent about it, and took the numbers from farther back."

Once the Round Two land picks began, Beekman went into action, armed with his illegal copy of the tribal roll and order of selection, both of which he had surreptitiously acquired. He used the roll to track down the full-bloods, who tended not to care about allotment, the land selections or—as far as the white government officials supervising the process could discern—much of anything. The head of the Osage Allotting Commission, Charles E. McChesney, complained that the full-bloods were "very indifferent to their second selections of land and will not even go with the Commission's surveyors to make selections, claiming the weather is too hot or that they have to attend a 'smoke' or some similar excuse. The simple fact of the case is that the Osage full-bloods are the laziest and most worthless tribe of Indians I have any knowledge of and the same remark will apply to a number of the mixed-bloods."

The full-bloods had lost interest in the agency's selection process because the Beekman selection process was providing them with something the government couldn't: cash. Beekman and the other cattlemen's agents were making the second-round (and later, third- and fourth-round) selections for the full-bloods in the northern part of the reservation, where the tallgrass prairie abounded. The full-bloods tended to live in the Hominy and Gray Horse Indian camps in the southern half of the county and had made their first-round land selections near there. They didn't care beyond their homesteads, probably having the innate sense to know that, regardless of where any of their land was, it wouldn't be theirs for long anyway.

Osage Agency officials cited Beekman as by far the most effective of the agents, and in the recorded conversation they had with him on December 30, 1907, Beekman boasted that his success stemmed from trying to make third-round picks adjacent to Round Two selections—and paying bigger bribes: usually $50 per land pick. As soon as one of Beekman's full-blood customers agreed to his land selection, the agent handed him a long-term lease—and more money as inducement to sign, this time with rent added in—allowing cattlemen to graze their herds.

The vast majority of Osages never gained possession or use of their land leased through Beekman and the other cattlemen's agents. The Indians soon were induced—with more cash—to sell the land that most probably they had never even seen, much less cared about. My great-grandfather thus swindled the Osages out of tens of thousands of their acres to carve out of their former reservation some of the largest white-owned ranches in Oklahoma.

Beekman's business dealings so horrified his wife that she divorced him. After their divorce (no date given), Kate Beekman took control of managing their daughter's 657 acres—not surprisingly some of the choicest picks of land in the county. Some of Sybil's land Kate leased to her Aunt Maggie, who, thanks to Beekman's shady dealings, now possessed one of the largest of the new ranches, the Maggie Lawrence Ranch, located on splendid tallgrass prairie just west of Grainola, formerly the Osage village of Cana.

Kate also kept Sybil away from her father. Over the years, Sybil became so estranged from Sewell Beekman that she willingly took the name of her mother's next husband.

EVEN IF SEWELL BEEKMAN had not conned himself into divorce, Arthur T. Woodward probably would have done it for him. The shaky earth that my great-grandparents' marriage was built upon probably began to move the instant Woodward rode into town in 1907. Kate Conner Gorman Beekman, soon-to-be Woodward, seemed to have a thing for powerful government lawyers from Washington.

While Sewell Beekman was defrauding the Osages out of much of their land, A. T. Woodward was taking part in an even larger and costlier swindle of the Osages—the compilation of their final tribal roll.

In the years following the passage of the Dawes Act of 1887, the Osages presented the U.S. government with a dilemma: Although the communal ownership of their reservation was exactly the economic condition the act intended to destroy, the Osages had become owners of their common property in the manner that the government was seeking to encourage—capitalistically, with their own money. This time, the Americans couldn't just send in the cavalry to get what they wanted. They had to wait out the Indians, allow them the time to come around to their way of thinking. But, of course, the Americans took it upon themselves to speed up the process.

The U.S. government began packing the Osages' membership roll with whites and non-Osage Indians who claimed to be mixed-blood Osages—and who favored allotment. The inflated number of allotment advocates would one day soon tip the scale in a tribal vote on whether to accept the inevitable. However, new names could be added to the roll only upon approval of a branch of the tribal government: an investigative committee of the National Council on Osage Citizenship comprised of two full-bloods and two mixed-bloods. (My great-great-grandfather William Conner sat on one such membership committee in 1874.) But after 1887, the Osage Agency started adding names to the roll, sometimes without even informing the tribal government. Records of Osage annuity payments showed about 800 mixed-bloods on the tribal roll in 1896, up from 163 in 1879. Tribal leaders complained in 1894 to John Gorman and his fellow commissioners that since 1881 hardly a person added to the roll was of Osage descent.

The Osages promised the commission that they would accept allotment if certain conditions were met, principally that their roll be purged of fraudulent members. True to their word, in 1896 they submitted a list of suspects to Washington for investigation. It was 446 names long, containing more than half the mixed-bloods in the tribe. But the government's immediate response was to set 1880 as an arbitrary cutoff date for the investigation; any name on the Osage roll before then would not be examined. That left 232 names. Of those, an investigative commission ruled that 92 had "no Osage blood whatever in their veins," and in 1897, the Indian Affairs commissioner recommended that the Osage Agency purge them from the tribal roll. At the same time, however, the BIA solicited a ruling from the Attorney General's Office that would restrict the agency in its task: No written evidence, such as birth certificates or government documents, could be used as grounds for removing names (a moot point because a tragic but convenient fire had destroyed most tribal genealogical records in 1893). That left mostly inconclusive oral evidence at their hearings as the sole cause for revoking Osage citizenship, and in the end only 38 names were purged. Only those people found to have bribed their way onto the tribal roll were removed. However, their children were allowed to remain on it.

Having done half a job, the commish sat back and waited for the Osages to show their full appreciation. But the ingrates, in the next tribal election, voted into office a government controlled by full-bloods who were solidly anti-allotment. Osage government had been a two-party democracy since 1881, set up under a constitution based on the U.S. and Cherokee charters and crafted by the Osages' last hereditary chief, James Bigheart, and his Kansas Jesuit mission school buddy, William Conner.

They created five electoral districts and the two political parties, the Mixed Bloods and the Full Bloods. After the Dawes Act, the Mixed Blood Party became the Progressives, or Civilization Party, and the Full Bloods the Non-Progressives. The Progressives favored allotment, for they had grown more American than Indian in outlook and were attracted to allotment's promise of U.S. citizenship, private land ownership and recognition as being "civilized." But not all the mixed-bloods favored allotment. The French Osages—descendants of the early traders who had married into and moved in with the tribe—were as hard-core as the full-bloods in their opposition to allotment or to any change of the Indian way of life. So even with the mixed-bloods' number growing, the pro-allotment faction still found itself in the minority.

It did not take long after the 1898 election for the Indian Affairs commissioner to perceive his miscalculation in recommending that any potentially pro-allotment voter be stripped of Osage membership. In fact, he realized that he had been duped by the Osages. They had demanded that their roll be purged of fraudulent members before they would vote to accept allotment; but purging the roll of pro-allotment voters, albeit frauds, would guarantee that the allotment opponents would keep the numerical edge for years to come. There was only one thing for the government of the greatest democracy on Earth to do—abolish democracy for the Osages.

Citing "the selection of ignorant men as officeholders" in the 1898 election, the Bureau of Indian Affairs suspended Osage government indefinitely. That year, the tribal roll grew by 29 mixed-bloods. By 1900, their number had increased to 917, and in 1906, the year the full-bloods begrudgingly gave up their battle against allotment, there were 1,369 mixed-bloods on the roll.

But there wouldn't be that many for long, the full-bloods decided. In the Osage Allotment Act of 1906, the tribe secured a promise from the government to finally purge the roll of frauds. Having accepted allotment, the enrollment issue had grown in importance for the Osages. They did not want any non-Osages owning their most important possession: their land. They resubmitted a list of suspected fraudulent members, but the BIA's insistence on honoring the arbitrary 1880 cutoff date limited the tribe to only 244 names—most of whom had been on the previous list of suspects.

To assist the three-man Osage Allotting Commission (two Americans, one Osage) on the enrollment cases, the BIA sent a twenty-nine-year-old lawyer, Special Agent Arthur T. Woodward, to Pawhuska. A Spanish-American War veteran, he had grown up in Monmouth County, New Jersey, and in Philadelphia, and had received his law degree in Richmond. Woodward's job was to represent the tribe at hearings before the allotting commission on the cases of each contested family. To aid the Osages' investigation, he organized the names into twelve family groupings: Appleby, Brown, Clem, Fronkier, Herridge, Holloway, Javine, Labadie, Lombard, Lyman, Omaha and Perrier. He also refused to follow an instruction from Washington that affidavits against the families be made available to them thirty days before their hearings. Such a requirement, he argued, would have exposed those making the affidavits to the risk of threats, bribery or violence.

But Woodward lost each case. The commission rejected every claim of fraudulent enrollment, authorizing the placement of all 244 suspected non-Osages on the final tribal roll, including the 54 left on the roll in 1897 despite having "no Osage blood whatever in their veins." By 1906, they and their children accounted for 74 members of three families. The roll also contained 56 non-Osages who had been adopted into the tribe and 21 known non-Osages not investigated because of the 1880 cutoff date.

Professor Garrick A. Bailey of the University of Tulsa calculated in 1971 that the Osage headrights of these 151 non-Osages had paid a total of $31.5 million in oil royalties; adding in the value of each of their 657-acre allotments of land at 1971 prices—99,358 acres at $100 per—the known fraudulent enrollments had cost the Osage tribe more than $42 million. Extrapolating from the group not investigated in 1897, Bailey estimated that the true cost to the Osages of the U.S. government's packing of their tribal roll probably was between $100 million and $200 million.

Woodward's role in the swindle appeared minimal. One could argue it was even admirable. He worked for the interest of the tribe—ostensibly. His track record said otherwise, however, and it would not be the last time that A. T. Woodward's appearance of defending the Osages in the midst of massive swindling stood in stark contrast to the end result.

BUT SOMETHING FAR more criminal was taking place during those years than the foisting of a few frauds on the Osage public. The number of full-bloods was being systematically reduced as diseases not seen in decades began cropping up in the three mostly full-blood camps.

The Osages had been spared the horrifying level of decimation that epidemics had wrought on other Indian tribes during the nineteenth century. As whites spread across Indian country, so, too, did their germs and diseases, to which Indians were not immune and which often roared through their communities with the intensity and speed of prairie fires. And like those fires, many of the epidemics, especially smallpox, were purposely set, carried to Indians in deliberately contaminated clothing and blankets—worn by, rubbed against or wrapped around prior sufferers of the disease, then transported by the wagonload to other tribes.

The Osages' good fortune in avoiding much of the destruction from disease was mainly luck, but stemmed in part from their practice of splitting up into small bands and heading out to the open plains at the outbreak of disease, which tended to spread and strengthen in the close quarters of communal Indian camps. Cholera, flu, measles, scrofula, scurvy, smallpox and typhoid epidemics that came close to wiping out whole other tribes killed only about 2,500 Osages from 1829 to 1856, half of whom died in the last four years of that span, the last period of severe—and recorded—Osage epidemics.

But the 1883–1906 register of "sick, births, and deaths" kept by the Osage Agency's Sanitation Department, which operated the medical clinics in the three mostly full-blood camps, showed a drastic decline in the Osages' health from 1894 to 1906—the years when the U.S. government tried to force allotment on the tribe.

In May 1895, measles broke out at the Pawhuska Indian camp, and four months later a malaria epidemic seized the Gray Horse camp, where the highest number of full-bloods were concentrated. These were followed by a massive outbreak of flu, measles and whooping cough at the Pawhuska camp from February to May 1897, and six deaths were recorded at the Gray Horse clinic among eighteen cases of "congestion" in March 1899.

The last page of the Gray Horse clinic log for February 1900 lists twenty-three cases of smallpox. There is no report on the duration or deadliness of this smallpox outbreak. The disease's previous appearance on the Osage reservation fifteen years earlier had killed between five hundred and a thousand Osages, nearly all of them full-bloods. The Osages no longer had wide-open plains to retreat to and recuperate in, and their ancient custom of burying their dead in aboveground cairns only fueled the disease. Worse, they could not get medicine to the reservation. A shipment finally arrived at one of the Kansas border towns, but it had spoiled by the time an Osage Agency official arrived to pick it up. Someone had taken it off the train and left it baking in the sun.

As if this were not bad enough, a close inspection of the medical logs reveals an even more odious attempt at population control. Unbeknownst to the Osages, they were being subjected to their first reign of terror, which was in many ways more insidious than its 1920s successor, for it was conducted by the federal government against those Osages least able to defend themselves.

Abortions began to appear on the Gray Horse doctor's register with revolting regularity after 1895.

There are few actual names on the Gray Horse log. Most of the patients are listed in the name column only as "Indian," and occasionally "Indian woman," "Indian baby," "Indian boy," "Indian child," or "half-breed." This suggests that the Osage Agency doctor at Gray Horse did not speak "Indian." It also suggests that the "Indian" patients of the Gray Horse clinic did not speak "American," for if they did, they most likely would have given the doctor a Christian or Anglicized name that he would have understood and written on the log.

In April 1895, the first recorded abortion took place at the Gray Horse clinic. The recipient was a no-name. In June, Ka-ah-wah-see, as the doctor wrote her name, had her pregnancy ended.

The next year, two abortions were performed in February, for the wives of Hun-a-pusy and Co-da-wah-ay. Also that month, the doctor made this notation for a patient named Grace: "abortion threatened."

In April 1896, the wife of Koo-se-wal-re was given an abortion.

Grace returned in May 1896 to have her baby. In the "Disease" column of the register, the doctor wrote "obstetrics," and added this: "child died."

The wife of Tall Chief was next, in May 1897.

An abortion was performed in November and another in December of that year, and both months the "name" of the patient was the same: "Virgin."

A "Mrs. Heridge," obviously an English-speaker, received an abortion in April 1898—the last such operation noted on the Gray Horse log.

While the number of recorded abortions is small, it is important to keep a number of things in mind. It is surprising, first of all, that any abortions took place in the medical facilities of a U.S. federal government agency still dominated by Quakers and other Protestant religious denominations. Most of the Osages were Catholic, and the Catholic Church's opposition to abortion needs no introduction here; neither is its stance new. Finally, the population at each full-blood Indian camp was very small— probably just a couple of hundred. Of those, only a small percentage were likely to go to a white doctor for any reason, and of those, a minuscule percent, if any, for pregnancy. Apart from being white, doctors were male, and a taboo existed among the Osages, as among all Indians, against men's involvement at all in the process of giving birth—post-conception, that is.

Abortion is such an inflamed issue among Americans today that it is difficult to comment on any aspect of it without offending. It is not my intention to add an off-key voice to the chorus of yea- or naysayers, but there is a difference, I think, between a woman who wants to have an abortion and one who does not know she is having one. Today, the battle lines over abortion are drawn between the rights to life and to choose; the Osage abortions of a century ago involved an unspoken "right" of Americans over Indians: the right to choose to deny us life, and get away with it.

The medical records also suggested one other thing: suicide, so prevalent as an official cause of death in the 1920s, seemed to be a disease that whites introduced to the Osages after allotment in 1906. On the doctors' logs for the twenty-three preceding years, not one suicide was recorded. And, discounting the abortions, there was only one recorded murder, that of Le-he-la-tah in September 1888.

In 1915, A. T. Woodward was working as an Osage Agency financial clerk, handling "probate and guardianship cases and matters pertaining to division of estates, appearing in court when necessary." He was making $1,500 a year.

But Woodward had other income.

Through his marriage in 1908 to the former Kate Conner Gorman Beekman, Woodward was able to supplement his meager government clerk's salary, controlling nearly 2,000 acres of his wife's and stepdaughters' land, the surface of which was rented out to cattlemen as pasture.

But it was what lay beneath the tallgrass prairie of their land that was enabling Woodward to live the good life. America's entry into World War I gushered oil production on what was now the Osages' "underground reservation," as historian Terry P. Wilson has aptly called it, and an Osage headright was suddenly worth some real money. The 1917 annuity was $2,719, a nearly ninefold jump from the payments of 1906 to 1916, when each allottee's oil-royalty annuity averaged $335 a year. After breaking the four-digit threshold in 1917, each year's per-capita payment rose steadily, and sometimes sharply: 1918, $3,672; 1919, $3,930. In 1920, the headright payment more than doubled, to $8,090. In 1921, it was $8,600. There was a dip to $7,700 in 1922, but the next year more than compensated. The 1923 annuity was the first to top the $10,000 mark: $12,400. Payments dropped slightly to $11,600 in 1924, and in 1925, a headright brought in $13,400, the peak payment of the 1920s.

Multiply these amounts by two—the shares of Sybil and her mother—and that was the headright income of the Woodward household in the 1920s. (Mrs. Woodward, I would discover, inherited fractional headrights from deceased relatives, including her Aunt Maggie, so the Woodwards made even more money.)

In today's dollars, factoring in extremely low prices and even lower taxes, these seemingly small sums had the spending power of roughly fifty to a hundred times the amounts. For example, in November 1925, the month Sybil died, *The Washington Post* advertised a townhouse in Georgetown for sale at a price just under the amount of the Osage allotment for that year—$13,400. The house today would sell for more than $1 million.

Other ads in the *Post* listed prices that a consumer would kill for today: A new Ford top-of-the-line Roadster—$995. A Packard sedan—$2,585. A four-piece bedroom suite "with chest and attractive toilet table"—$295. A ring of "3 sparkling blue-white diamonds, set in a distinctively engraved 18 kt. white gold mounting"—$85. Men's wing-tip oxford shoes in calf or Russian leather—$9. A men's Hamilton English overcoat—$50. Hand-tailored suits, including English worsteds and handmade Irish tweeds—$55 and $65. A velvet chiffon dance frock—$35. Wool coats "for little girls of 2 to 6 years"—$9.95.

And these were inflated East Coast prices.

In Osage County, it cost only $500 and a used car to hire someone to kill an Osage Indian.

By 1916, Woodward was moonlighting as an officer of the Mosier Oil Field Company, which was buying Osage oil leases. In 1918, his salary at the Osage Agency was raised to $2,000 a year. He was in charge now of legal matters involving the superintendent's office and representing the agency boss in county court. The next year brought a $1,000 raise, and in 1920, his job title was renamed to that of Osage tribal attorney. As such, he handled, among other legal matters, oil leases to companies such as his previous, on-the-side employer. Conflict of interest appeared to be a nonexistent concept in the 1920s. It also appeared as deeply entrenched as oil in Osage County. For any job dealing with the Osages, conflict of interest seemed to be not a disqualifying factor but a necessary requirement.

To the Osages, their tribal attorney was the most important U.S. government official—read "white"—working for their benefit. His was a permanent position, while the superintendent of the Osage Agency, the top man, was a rotating BIA appointment, and tended to deal more with Washington—the Bureau of Indian Affairs commissioner and his boss, the secretary of the interior—than with individual Osages. It was to the tribal attorney, their outside link to the white man's system of law and justice, that they came with their problems.

Which by the 1920s had grown considerable. Their rising oil wealth had brought a new invasion of mean, money-mad, mercenary, miscreant whites. Signaling to its readers what kind of news it thought fit to print, the white-run Osage County newspaper, the *Hominy News-Republican,* ran this motto in its masthead: "1,000 White People and 900 Osage Indians Drawing Thousands of Dollars Yearly." Car dealers and shop owners doubled and tripled their prices for Osages, and let them ring up unlimited credit at exorbitant interest rates. Local banks were notorious for making quick cash advances to illiterate full-bloods, who wound up signing, unawares, repayment papers for sums ten, twenty, thirty times the amount of the loans. Doctors, lawyers, even morticians had special rates for the Osages. Sybil's coffin, remember, cost $1,500. One mortician (not Mr. Johnson) was found to have sold the same coffin in fifty burials.

Single Osage women became objects of hot pursuit. The Osage Agency was swamped with letters such as this one from C. T. Plimer of Joplin, Missouri: "I . . . want a good indian girl for a wife. . . . For every Five Thousand Dollars she is worth I will give you Twenty Five Dollars. If she is worth 25,000 you would get $125 if I got her."

All of this was on the order of the to-be-expected: almost-innocent rip-offs of rich redskins by red-blooded American whites—good clean fun. After all, these were extremely wealthy people who had not exactly worked for their money and did not seem to hold it in the same currency as white people who did not have any. Besides, just a few years ago they were scalping whites, so what was the harm in returning the favor by fleecing a few of them?

The harm was that it gave many people who were unhappy with the state of affairs in Osage County—namely, the fact that Indians had all the money—the opportunity to complain, and eventually Congress heard them.

Newspaper and magazine reporters spread stories about Osages building huge mansions and sleeping in their garages or yards. One reporter wrote: "The whites sold them expensive sets of knives and forks, the latest and most expensive from Fifth Avenue—and the Indians put their food in a big yellow bowl and, squatting around it in the yard, reached in and ate with their fingers, while the knives tarnished in the kitchen. I have seen them use the big cut-glass bowls the merchants had sold them to wash their vegetables in, and cloisonné vases to hold their baseball bats. They [even] bought pianos."

The visiting journalists, shapers of white opinion back in Washington, could barely disguise the envy and disgust in their dispatches: "The [Osage] Indians took the 'easy money' like gluttons they were, gulped down everything that it would buy for them, and spread on their person and about them gaudy and costly trappings," wrote one. "Simple-minded folks, as are all Indians, the Osages have been ruined by too much money."

Another: "The demoralizing influence of riches is everywhere apparent [among the Osages]. Marriage is entered into recklessly, and divorce is appallingly frequent. Immorality is prevalent and venereal disease is said to affect 75 percent of the tribe."

One reporter may even have run into Sybil, or so I sometimes imagine from this description of a young Osage woman in 1922: "Fortunate

Daughters of Chance are these mixed-blood Osage girls. . . . They have known only luxury and ease. Their clothes are the best obtainable—a hat costing $90 is a mere trifle. They are modish, and very chic, and oftentimes surprisingly handsome. . . . A stranger chancing to observe one of these Daughters of Chance . . . would think *une tres jolie demoiselle* of the Paris boulevards had inadvertently strayed into this little reservation town. The resemblance in type is amazing. There is the same glossy black hair, the same alluring dark eyes, the same white, colorless skin. The gown is Parisian, the hat is Parisian, the high heels are trippingly French. French, too, is her air of insouciance, the little mannerism of a deep-rooted egotism. Fortunate Daughters of Chance!"

The chairman of the Board of Indian Commissioners visited the Osages in 1920 to investigate the veracity of various complaints and stories he had heard. He was stunned by what he found. He told Congress: "Their wealth literally has been thrust upon them, unwittingly on their part. They are almost, if not quite, dazed by it. I have been over many of their household accounts—bills for family expenses run up with local merchants. Many of the totals are appalling. For example, in a family of two, an average for months of over $400 per month for meats alone; while four or five pairs of blankets a month are being purchased by the same couple. Other expenditures are in proportion. . . . That the money is being largely squandered is evident."

Then he added, with discernible envy, "Of course, a great deal of it goes into automobiles; many Osages have several, and they are all high-priced cars. One rarely sees an Osage in a Ford."

And then with a degree of disgust: "These people do not know what they are doing; they have never been trained, nor have they the opportunity to learn what it all means."

Congress decided in 1921 to give the Osages that opportunity, deeming that it was their own fault that they were being swindled of the money the Great White Father had accidentally allowed them to acquire. Their indebtedness, the good, rich white men of Washington ruled, was but a sign of their incompetence.

Henceforth, Congress decreed, full allotment payments would be made only to "competent" Osages. Those Osages whose Indian blood quantum was one-half or higher would have to demonstrate Christian values of sobriety and fiscal responsibility before being issued a certificate of competency. All others in that group would be considered "restricted," and would have a guardian appointed by the courts who would put them on a strict allowance and budget, and otherwise keep them from being led astray. Those Osages whose blood quantum was less than one-half were not affected by this new law, unless (like Sybil Beekman) they were under the age of twenty-one.

Once again, acting with good intentions, Congress had paved a road to hell for the Osages.

The key word in the new law was "courts." These were not federal courts, striving to fulfill Congress's trust responsibility toward the Indians, but the courts of Oklahoma, striving to fulfill their trust responsibility toward the whites who ran the state. And what better way to make the great state of Oklahoma a better place for its citizens (read "whites") than to pass around some of the undeserved wealth of its undesired residents (read "Indians"). So the people who ran the courts for the people who ran the state (read "lawyers") saw to it that they would keep Oklahoma's best interests at heart by appointing themselves the Osages' guardians. The new law elevated petty swindling to the big leagues, and created a perfect circle of corruption: The Osages' money was now enriching the white men who ran the system of justice in Oklahoma and the Osages had no legal recourse besides the Oklahoma courts to fight the corruption against them.

The man who would determine whether each Indian got a certificate of competency or a guardian was Osage Tribal Attorney A. T. Woodward. And although the guardians were officially appointed by the county court, accounts suggest that it was Woodward who matched the lawyers with their wards, with the court merely approving a done deal. Woodward himself, conflict of interest be damned, even became the guardian of four full-blood Osages, all of whom managed to die before 1923.

The new law required that the quarterly cash payments of restricted Indians be disbursed to their court-appointed guardians, who were then permitted to pay their wards only $1,000 a quarter. However, in its rush to save the Osages from exploitation, Congress failed to place effective safeguards on the restricted Osages' "surplus" funds—the amount of the quarterly allotment left after the $1,000 was paid. The superintendent of the Osage Agency was authorized to buy federal or state bonds for the restricted Indians with their surplus funds, but the guardians were not required to turn over the money to the agency, or account for it in any way.

Of the $8,600 to $13,400 that individual headrights were drawing from 1921 to 1925, restricted Osages were receiving only $4,000 each year, in four quarterly payments of $1,000. The quarterly payments for 1925 averaged $3,350; restricted Osages got $1,000 of that, and their guardians pocketed the remaining $2,350.

The guardians would not perform this service for free, however. Their typical annual legal fees for carrying out the complicated task of paying allowances to restricted Osages and stealing the rest of the money was $1,200—subtracted, of course, from the $4,000 the restricted Indians received. A government study estimated that by December 1924, about 600 guardians had managed to make $8 million in surplus funds disappear.

Congress acted yet again, holding hearings on the Osage guardianship program in 1924. It heard tales such as these:

A guardian bought a used car from another guardian for $250 and then sold it to his ward for $1,250.

An Osage woman "stated that she was in debt $24,000 although she had received $20,000 during the year. In explaining her indebtedness, she said that she owed her former guardian $12,000 and that of this sum, $2,000 was represented by a note she signed when she was ill, and she didn't know what it was for. . . . [The guardian] loaned her $8,000 on her home on what she understood to be a 5-year mortgage, but now, 'I come to find out that it is not, and is due next year.' . . . She was unable to account for the balance of the $20,000 . . . and had no property to show for expenditures."

A full-blood Osage, under guardianship for three years, had received $86,142.31 in headright payments over a ten-year period and was $1,200 in debt. "His only property was a car valued at $350 on which he still owed $400."

In the case of an Osage man with a blood quantum of 11/16, all he had to show for his $100,200 in headright payments was a debt of $14,000 and a $19,630 house, on which he was still paying an annual mortgage of $1,200 at 10 percent interest, considered usury in those days. He had bought the house from his guardian, the recipient also of the Osage's mortgage payments.

Outraged, Congress ordered the Osage Agency to determine who were "good" guardians and "bad" guardians prior to a new law to take effect in February 1925 that would place the guardianship program under the federal Interior Department. Thereafter, guardians would be forced to submit to the agency annual statements of their wards' accounts, and seek written approval of any purchases for restricted Osages that would require withdrawals from their savings.

The man tasked with investigating and passing judgment on these lawyers, who would be expected to grow angry, dangerous and perhaps desperate enough to drag their accomplices down with them, was the Osage tribal attorney.

But it would not be A. T. Woodward. After the 1924 hearings in Washington, in which he took part, he returned to Pawhuska and abruptly quit, taking a job out of state, at the Exchange Bank in El Dorado, Arkansas.

IN THE MICROFILMED Osage County District Court records for 1924 and 1925, I found no petition to end the Bolton marriage, no filing for divorce by Sybil or Harry. Instead, I found this:

> Ruben Hilt, plaintiff, vs. Arthur T. Woodward, defendant.
>
> Now on this 24th day of September, A.D. 1925 . . . the defendant appearing not, neither in person nor by attorney . . . [the court finds] that the defendant, Arthur T. Woodward, is indebted to the plaintiff, Ruben Hilt, in the sum of $818.86 with interest thereon at the rate of six per cent (6%) per annum, payable annually, from July 30th, 1924, and in the total sum of $872.00, and that the plaintiff is entitled to judgment.

Five weeks before Sybil's death, someone was angry enough at her stepfather to take him to court.

Was someone angry enough at him to kill?

T here were days when I was sickened by the morbidness of it all. My whole life had become a sole death.

Before Fleur and Kevin arrived in late June, I rented a small apartment on the hillside above Pawhuska. I've lived in a lot of places, but never in one with porcelain electric outlets. The light switches were not up-and-down knobs, but push buttons. The building was at least as old as my grandmother's death, but the place had bucked the trend in Pawhuska by staying habitable. In fact, it was in great shape, a testament to the love, work and money that its owners, Ron and Judy Coday, had put into it. At one time, they had operated a bed-and-breakfast in it.

The building's dark, almost black, red bricks matched those that composed the steep street in front. Running the length of the building, the street curb bent inward, toward the sidewalk, in three or four places, forming long, shallow U's—about a foot deep and four feet long. They were for parking Model T's on the hill.

When I was not in the library, my days in the apartment were filled with the sound of hammering and of the crack and thud of falling wood. Next door, a man and his wife, as grimy, weary, weathered and red as their pickup truck, were dismantling a rotting house, plank by plank, which they stacked neatly next to a mound of long, rusty nails they had extracted and seemed to be saving.

The apartment building, named "The Virginia," sat halfway up the Pawhuska hill, at the corner of Kihekah and East 10th Street. I was living one block away and directly downhill from the house where Sybil died.

My apartment was on the top floor, the fourth—a long walk up ladderlike steps. If it were not for old, gigantic, thickly foliaged trees in the back yard, I would have been able to stare directly into the Woodward house from the screened porch off the kitchen.

I spent much of my time on the back porch. It was my smoking room. I was amused to discover that after so many years of not being allowed to smoke in the house, I no longer was comfortable doing so alone in my own place. So, as at home, I went outside to smoke—in this apartment, to the porch.

The view from there sometimes looked like an amateur's pastoral painting. A gnarly, gnomelike blackjack oak dwarfed the back yard. Mornings, the tree would hold about a half-dozen breeds of birds and three or four squirrels, all taking turns at a feeder filled to the overflowing point with sunflower seeds. An old, gray-haired groundhog, the size of a cocker spaniel, would munch on the spillings. One morning, cars on Kihekah screeched to a hurried halt to let pass a line of skunks—a momma and her five babies—crossing the road for a snack in the back yard.

I spotted animal droppings on my porch floor one morning. A door leading from the porch to the outside back stairs was slightly ajar. Some critter had been snooping around. I thought nothing more of it until that night. There was no light on the porch, so I was smoking in the dark. A flapping sound and streak of black suddenly shot past my head. I nearly knocked myself out ducking. Bats!

My first thought was, Oh God, I'm going to have to give up smoking. Of course, I didn't. I bought a flashlight instead.

Night after night, standing on the porch in the dark not a hundred yards from the Woodward house, facing it, straining my eyes to penetrate the blackness of night and of tree shapes—my puffs making my cigarette pulsate like a firefly, and my flashlight sweeping the ceiling like an airport spotlight searching the skies for incoming planes—I thought of Sybil and how she might have died.

It took my father only minutes in the Woodward back yard to map out possible death scenarios.

Generals look at landscape differently from you and me. He did a quick, hard squint at the back of the house, at the stoop, at the driveway, at the garage in the far corner of the yard, at the fence along the paved alley in the back. You could almost see grid lines of military topography forming at computer speed behind his eyes.

It was a two-man operation, he finally decided. They parked their car in the alley, behind the garage. It could have sat there for hours without anyone seeing it.

One of the men could have stood watch over the yard, shielding himself from view against the corner of the garage. When Sybil came outside with the baby, they jumped the fence.

Or they could have waited in the car for the sound of the garage door opening. That would have been Sybil going to her car.

Or—and my father preferred this scenario, on the assumption that every lie holds at least one tiny grain of truth—one of them walked around to the front of the house and knocked on the door. The Pawhuska paper had said that "a call at the door made the opportunity." That would have drawn the maid, Eleanor, to the front of the house, away from the scene of the crime.

The man in the alley then jumped the fence, probably at some pre-arranged signal—say, on the count of twenty-five after seeing the other man tip his hat as he walked past the driveway heading toward the front door.

Before Eleanor answered the door, the man could have run off, perhaps down the driveway to cut off a possible escape route for Sybil from the gunman approaching her from the alley.

Or the man at the door could have waited for Eleanor to answer, grabbed her when she did, stuck a gun to her head while Sybil was getting shot in the back yard and said something threatening, such as: "See this face, nigger. That's the last thing you'll ever see if you talk."

That would have been in keeping with the terror of the times, when Osages were killed with impunity and were so frightened that they strung the perimeter of their houses with bright lights. And Eleanor would have been the easy part of the plot. The accomplice at the door would not have had to worry much about a black woman volunteering to die for her domestic employers, who were Indians. He also could have stressed to the maid, making the point with the pistol pointed at her head, that Sybil's death was suicide and that if Eleanor said any differently, she, too, would shoot herself.

This scenario also presented a last possibility that made the most sense to me. The man at the door, after threatening Eleanor, forced his way into the house and chased Sybil into the back yard. She saw or heard him coming and grabbed the baby, whom she may have been feeding in the kitchen.

She ran out the kitchen door onto the stoop, and saw the other man jump the fence and run toward her. In a panic, she stopped, turned around to run back into the house, and ran right into the man who by this time had come through the house and kitchen door.

He shot her on the stoop, and she fell backward, landing on the pump cover. They dropped the pistol by her outstretched hand, and ran to the back fence, jumped it and drove away.

But what about the baby?

The scenario implies Sybil was holding my mother. The gunmen had to ensure that they did not shoot the baby. They didn't worry about it too much, though. If the baby got shot, Sybil's death would have been declared a murder-suicide.

But it would have been much better to spare the baby. The death of this Osage Indian woman in the midst of a widespread, and well-known, undercover FBI investigation would have attracted less attention if a baby were not killed. There was no mention of the baby anywhere in the Pawhuska newspaper article, for example.

Getting the baby away from Sybil meant that her killers did not shoot her suddenly on the stoop. They took their time.

They grabbed her on or at the stoop. One of the men held her, and the other yanked the baby away from her and, in the same motion, threw the infant off to the side, into the yard and onto the ground. With Sybil being held, probably with her arms behind her back, the gunman was able to press the pistol against her chest at the target he was shooting for—her heart.

These kinds of evenings on the porch—reliving Sybil's last moments of life, tracking her last steps in my imagination—always ended the same for me: by rubbing my neck, running my fingers along it from one side across the Adam's apple to the other, tracing the path of the red rash that always formed on my mother's neck whenever anyone touched it.

I'd shudder and go back to the light of my apartment, and invariably walk down the hill into Pawhuska and get a beer at Frosty's, the nearest bar.

And I'd catch myself rubbing my neck for the rest of the night.

The gunmen must have grabbed the baby by the neck to wrench her away from her terrified, screaming mother.

That baby was my mother.

That red rash on her neck was the bloodstain of the subconscious wound that Sybil's killers inflicted on the only witness to her murder.

WHEN CLARIBEL SHAW saw my mother, she clutched her and exclaimed with watering eyes behind slightly opaque glasses, "You look just like your grandmother!" When she saw me, she did and said the same thing, "You look just like *your* grandmother!"

Claribel Shaw was my link to a living Sybil. I had found Sybil's tomb. But I hadn't found her.

Claribel was as warm, welcoming and youthful-sounding in person as her voice was on the telephone. She carried the aura of a Grandmother Earth, the one you always wanted, the one you hope your children will have. My mother, father and I had arrived early. Claribel greeted us in her bathrobe at the front door of her ranch-style house. The Shaw Ranch was located just west of the former oil-boom town of Burbank, about a half-hour's drive west from Pawhuska.

While Claribel changed, we thumbed through the Osage tribal roll book, which she had left out on the coffee table for us. We checked out her birthday—sure enough, she was born Claribel Clewien on the same day of the year as my mother, eighty-eight years ago. She was six months younger than Sybil. The roll book, a burgundy-colored paperback entitled *Authentic Osage Indian Roll Book* had been updated to 1957 but still listed the incorrect 1905 as the year of Sybil's birth. Her name had been underlined in pencil.

"I didn't know Sybil was a whole year younger than I am," Claribel said with almost a giggle of delight when she returned to the living room and saw us studying the roll book. "She was born in nineteen-and-five."

I told her about the fateful mistake.

"There are several mistakes in there," she said, "and they just glare at you."

By the zest, vitality and cheerfulness radiating from this woman, I tried to guess the personality and temperament of Sybil, Claribel's best friend. Was their friendship a case of opposites attracting? Perhaps. Would a gloomy, despondent person pick Claribel for a friend? Absolutely. Claribel could cheer anyone up, lift anyone's spirits. But would someone so sunny, joyful and energetic stick with a friendship that did not bring out her best, easiest and most natural qualities? I doubted it—and perhaps only because I wanted her to be, I decided my grandmother must have been a happy and fun-loving person.

"She was, she was," Sybil's college roommate replied when I told her. "She was moody, though. I'll tell you that. Now, that's true. I hate to admit it, but she was moody. For instance, she had a peculiar thing that she did that just amazed me because I was a little country. She'd put makeup on at night. I'd say, 'Sybil, why in the world are you putting makeup on at night?' "

"Before she'd go to bed?" I asked.

"Yes. She says, 'There might be a fire.' That's what she says, 'Oh, you never know, there might be a fire.' She was that conceited, you know, that she wanted to look just so. She was always that way, about everything."

"Was she pretty?" I asked.

"Awful pretty."

"Did you all do much together?"

"We did everything together."

"Did she like to tell stories?" I was reaching for some sense of Sybil. "Was she a good talker? Was she the silent type?"

"No, she wasn't [the silent type], she was pretty talkative, but I can't remember what we talked about." Claribel chuckled.

"Was she a good student, a bad student, a lazy student?" I knew the answer. I had gotten a copy of her report card at the University of Kansas. But I wanted to test the reliability of Claribel's memory. She said the right thing by diplomatically not saying anything. Sybil was an awful student.

"Well, she was awfully good in Italian, I'll tell you that," Claribel said.

"Was she? Was she fluent in it?"

"She lived over there [in Italy] for a year, and she could just rattle it off."

Sybil couldn't rattle it off in the classroom, though. But I've known lots of people who did not do well studying the languages they were fluent in. I flunked freshman English, for example.

She enrolled as Sybil Frances Woodward at the School of Fine Arts of the University of Kansas in Lawrence on September 11, 1922. A. T. Woodward was listed as her "parent or guardian."

Sybil's report card:

> First Semester:
> Voice Culture C
> Musical Theory (Harmony) . . . . . . .D
> Sight Singing and Ear Training . . . .D
> Recitals . . . . .F
> Rhetoric .D
> Italian . . . . .F
> Harp C
>
> Second Semester:
> Exercise . . . . .F
> Hygiene .C
> Voice . . . . .D
> Harmony .F
> Sight Singing and Ear Training . . . .F
> Recitals . . . . .Withdrew
> Italian . . . . .Withdrew
> Harp . . . . .Withdrew

My grandmother and I have something in common. She didn't go to class, either.

"Did she speak Osage?" I asked.

"No."

"Did she know anything at all about the Osages?"

"Well, I doubt very much if she knew [much]," Claribel said. "You know, at that time, there was a time if you were an Indian, you were not too well thought of. My mother and Mrs. Woodward always resented that attitude by people. Tremendous resentment."

"Prejudice," I said. "Well, also, resentment of the Osages because of the money."

"Absolutely. Jealous."

Claribel sighed and said dreamily: "But I never will forget Sybil. Oh, I tell you, but I really, I just thought, 'That Sybil, she speaks Italian, and her mother's such a lovely person, plays the piano so well, her sister is an opera singer.' You know that kind of impressed me. And Sybil played the harp, and of course that was another thing. I thought, 'My word, any-body that plays the harp, oh, aren't they wonderful.' "

"Was Sybil impressed by that? Was she a snob?" I asked.

"I don't think so, I don't think she made any big deal out of it. I don't recall her . . ." Claribel thought for a moment. "She was very dom-inating."

"Oh, she was?" my mother asked with surprise.

"Uh-huh."

"Well, she and my father must have had terrible battles," my mother said.

"Oh, they had awful battles," Claribel said. "That was the thing that pushed me away from the whole . . . from Sybil and Harry was the fact that they would have terrific fights. I mean just . . . I didn't like the way he treated Sybil, no matter what she did. I just couldn't stand him. That's why we didn't ever get together. We lived together for a year at school, and lived five miles from each other [afterward in Kansas City]. We didn't even see each other. Now, what Sybil's reason was, I don't know, but my reason was I didn't like to get into the, be present at this . . . cussin'."

"Oh dear," my mother said.

"I knew that Sybil was awfully upset, and I hated to see her upset."

"When you lived together in school, was it in the dormitory?" I asked.

"No, we had a room in a little—in a woman's house, a little house."

"Do you know how they met, Sybil and Harry, were you around then?" I asked.

"Harry and Judge Kerr and Tubby Bolleen," Claribel said, pausing to think, "Tubby Bolleen had a Cadillac. They picked Sybil and I up walking home from school on the campus. And that's how they met."

"It just goes to show you," I quipped, "you should never get in the car with strangers."

"Oh mercy," Claribel laughed.

"It changed her life," said the daughter of Harry and Sybil.

"Didn't it, though," Claribel said.

"I understand Mr. Beekman bought her a car at K.U.," my mother said.

"Yes. A Ford coupe. It was a little Ford coupe. We had it in school sometime after Christmas, I think. Oh yes! We were hip," she said with verve, then added with a burst of laughter, "We didn't have to depend on those pickups."

"Did she drink?" I asked.

"Yes, but very moderately. Very moderately."

My mother told Claribel what Theil Annett had said. Sybil was an alcoholic. She drank herself to death—or would have. Theil also had said that Mrs. Woodward "would threaten Sybil. 'You straighten yourself out, 'cause Harry's going to take that baby away from you. He can do it, you know. He's a lawyer. He's going to take that baby away from you.' "

"And Sybil would just sit there holding me on her lap," my mother said, "rocking back and forth, almost clutching me to her. Theil said she practically never let go of me, carried me around everywhere."

"Well, you never know," Claribel said. "I can't follow an alcoholic's thinking, but . . ."

"But she was not an alcoholic?" I asked.

"As far as I ever knew her, she, well maybe she had a few drinks, but she wasn't an alcoholic. When we were going to school, there wasn't any such problem. There absolutely wasn't. But this is something that transpired after I was pregnant with my first baby, when Sybil was killed."

"Oh, you didn't go back to school either then, did you?" my mother asked. "You didn't finish at K.U.?"

"No, I was too damn smart," Claribel said with a laugh. "I was just much too smart for that school. Instead, I married. I lived in Kansas City, and I made many trips down here. But at the time when Sybil died, I didn't get to come down for the funeral because I was not in any condition to travel."

Mom told Claribel something she had learned from Cara Mae: One of the few things about Sybil that "Harry did tell her [was that] at the funeral, he came and stayed with you and that he asked you if she was murdered, was it murder or suicide? He said you told him, 'I'm sorry, Harry, but it was suicide. Sybil killed herself.' "

"I wasn't even here."

"So he lied about that."

"It didn't bother him too much to lie," Claribel said.

"Why did they get married?" my mother asked abruptly.

"Well, I don't know. I just do remember that they had terrific battles."

"Even before they married?" Kathleen asked. "Well, why did they get married if they battled?"

"I don't know."

Maybe they loved each other, I thought. Love seems to be the one word that never gets said in a conversation about Harry and Sybil. But there must have been love. Time just has a way of rewriting our scripts, editing out the words that are off-key in the chorus of our explanations. On June 6, 1923, love must have been there.

But curiosity certainly was in order. Harry did not apply for the marriage license. A. T. Woodward did that, the day before the wedding. Harry was twenty-three, Sybil nineteen.

Harry arrived the afternoon of the fifth, in time to attend a dance in honor of the bride and groom at the Pawhuska Country Club. The next morning, the newspaper heralded their "wedding today [as] one of the most important social events of this spring." It may have been, but no one was invited. Just family members witnessed the couple exchanging vows in the Catholic priest's rectory. Harry apparently did not want to test his oft-stated vow never to be caught dead in a Catholic church.

Sybil wore "a frock of dark blue with accessories to match," also described as "a traveling costume of dark blue crepe." Angela Gorman Andretta, Sybil's sister, was matron of honor; best man was Frank McCain, a K.U. fraternity brother of Harry's. Harry did not invite his father to the wedding.

After the private ceremony, a reception and buffet luncheon were held at the Woodward house, attended by members of the Vanity Club and by other friends "who had entertained her," as the newspaper put it. The dining table was clothed in "venetian lace centered with a large wedding cake and adorned with candlesticks of Italian pottery holding green candles intermingled with garlands of southern smilax and baskets of white roses. The bride cut the cake which was served with the iced course. Punch was served" by two Vanity Club members. Angela Gorman Andretta provided the music, singing "At Dawning" by Cadman.

The new Mrs. Bolton was described as "the charming daughter of Mr. and Mrs. A. T. Woodward. She was born and reared in this city and was educated in several Eastern schools. . . . Mr. Bolton is a young man of splendid character and holds a position in one of the banking institutions in Kansas City, where they will reside after a wedding trip of several weeks in the East."

I said to Claribel, "I think one of the most important questions we all want to know is, did Sybil love the baby?" I don't know if "we all" wanted to know this—referring to my mother, of course—but I did.

"Oh yes, I'm sure she did," Claribel said, her eyes suddenly saddening. "I feel sure she did. But why would anybody want to leave their baby? Now, that's the big question there, too. That preyed on my mind for years and years: for this poor baby"—looking at my mother—"to lose her mother and not even know that she lost her and not know why she lost her, how she lost her." Claribel paused, thinking, maybe remembering. "I don't think it was lack of love. I think it was just, just so despondent, so down with her family life that she just couldn't, she just couldn't handle it. Sybil just couldn't handle it."

"But you do believe it was suicide. You don't believe that somebody murdered her?"

Almost a whisper: "No, I think it was a suicide. I mean, just from everything I have heard"—whispering even lower—"I believe it must have been suicide. She would get awfully, awfully despondent. But she was a . . . she was a conceited person, so she . . . you know you would think a conceited person wouldn't . . ."

"Shoot herself," I said.

"Wouldn't shoot herself," Claribel said.

"Wouldn't mess herself up," I said.

"Wouldn't give in to her feelings," Claribel said.

"That's why she shot herself in the heart," my mother said, still on the idea that a conceited person like Sybil, always worried about her appearance, would not have messed up her face by blowing her head off.

"Well, still, that's pretty messy," shooting oneself in the chest, I said.

"Well, any suicide is messy," Claribel said.

I told her the murder theory I had formed since reading in the FBI reports on the Reign of Terror murders that A. T. Woodward had been subpoenaed, along with two brothers named Bolton. "And days later Sybil dies of a gunshot in the back yard," I said. "We think somebody who was afraid of what Woodward would say to the grand jury decided to kill two birds with one stone and scare the Woodwards and scare the two Boltons, thinking that [Sybil] may have been related to these people—by then she was going under the name Bolton."

I could tell by looking at her that Claribel wasn't buying, and I felt disappointment and impatience taking hold of me. If I could convince Claribel, I had thought, then I'm right. Sybil didn't kill herself. But what if I couldn't convince her? Claribel knew Sybil in life. I didn't. But I knew more about Sybil in death, and I realized I was afraid of Claribel's knowledge. I didn't want what Claribel knew about Sybil ruining what I knew about her.

"I don't think there was any connection," Claribel said with no hesitation. "I really don't. Now, I didn't know those Boltons, but . . . now, they may have been connected with the murders, but I don't think it has any connection with Sybil—even with the similarity of the name and Mr. Woodward's connection. Now, I . . . ."

She paused and squinted, struggling to summon up a memory that probably was in the same shape as our photograph of Sybil.

Claribel said slowly, hesitantly: "There was some little question, I remember, recall. My father was in the sheriff's office, and I can recall his . . . he didn't talk much about the case, but I can remember him saying things that weren't too flattering about Mr. Woodward."

"Do you remember what?"

"No, just a general thought about Mr. Woodward. Well, he was at the [Osage] agency, he was the [tribal] attorney and what he would, you know, just flashes of [her father saying], 'He would have known such-and-such and such-and-such.' Facts that he would have known."

"About the murders."

"Uh-huh."

WHAT WOODWARD KNEW was enough to get Sybil Bolton killed, along with a couple of hundred other Osage Indians.

By 1924, Woodward's office of the Osage tribal attorney had become every bit as much a mortuary as Mr. Johnson's funeral parlor. Old Mr. Johnson got the bodies of dead Osages; young Mr. Woodward got their paperwork.

And there was a lot more paperwork than there used to be, for a whole lot of dying was going on among the dwindling Osage population. It seemed that the more money the Osages made, the less chance they had to spend it.

The FBI counted 24 recently murdered Osages when it began investigating the deaths in 1923. Other counts went as high as 45 to 60 by that time. Granted, the number is minuscule by today's staggering standards of mayhem. In the city where I work, Washington, D.C., 453 murders were recorded in 1992; 24 murders were only about two and a half weeks' worth of shootings and stabbings; victim number 60 was laid to rest by about the third week of February.

But statistically, the Osage murders take on a more abhorrent appearance. The numbers represent 1 to 3 percent of the Osage Nation, murdered over a short period. That translates to the equivalent today of the murders of 2.5 million to 7.5 million Americans—the entire population of Chicago, Los Angeles, or New York City. Television and newspapers may give the impression that Americans are being murdered in those numbers today, but in 1992, homicide accounted for only 22,540 of the 2.2 million deaths recorded in the United States, or one-hundreth of 1 percent of the population.

Washington's 453 murders in 1992 gave the nation's capital the distinction of having the highest per capita homicide rate among major U.S. cities—76 per 100,000. The 24 to 60 murders of Osages translate to a staggering rate of 1,500 to 3,000 per 100,000, giving the world's richest people per capita another superlative: the most-murdered people per capita in the world.

However, the numbers of Osage murders—even the high of 60—were conservative guesses. Because the killers were working in cahoots with Osage County doctors, who routinely falsified death certificates, the real number will never be known. But two documents I found gave me a fleeting glimpse of the magnitude and horror of the Reign of Terror.

One document, buried amid 3,274 pages of the FBI's Osage murder file, is an interview that records a senior FBI official's exasperation over the bureau's Osage investigation: "There are so many of these murder cases. There are hundreds and hundreds. One murder case is quite a big thing to handle ordinarily, but [here] you have scores of murders, bringing in scores of people and scores of facts."

The other murder record is the *Authentic Osage Indian Roll Book,* which notes the dates of death of many of the original allottees. By July 1, 1923, only 1,624 original allottees were still alive. There had been 2,229. Over the sixteen-year period from 1907 to 1923, 605 Osages died, averaging about 38 per year, an annual death rate of about 19 per 1,000. The national death rate now is about 8.5 per 1,000; in the 1920s, when counting methods were not so precise and the statistics were segregated into white and black racial categories, it averaged almost 12 per 1,000 for whites.

By all rights, their higher standard of living should have brought the Osages a *lower* death rate than America's whites. Yet Osages were dying at more than one-and-a-half times the national rate—and these numbers do not include Osages born after 1907 and not listed on the roll. Of this group, only 476 had survived. Total Osage population had fallen to 2,100, as of July 1, 1923—a 6 percent decline, while the U.S. population, even that of "Negro and other," was multiplying.

There is no record, in any of the files, that Woodward ever questioned any of this: the mounting death certificates, probate proceedings and estate settlements in his morgue of files—and there could have been only one reason he did not: He already knew the answer. The guardians were killing off the Osages to line their own pockets. The Osage Agency tolled no alarm bells until March 1923, but by then, the damage had been done to the Osage Nation, its destruction sealed.

THE ONLY GOOD INDIAN was not just a dead Indian anymore, but a dead-drunk Indian, one who died from alcohol poisoning. It was easier to write them off that way, fewer questions asked. Everyone knew about whiskey and Indians.

"In connection with the mysterious deaths of a large number of Indians," one FBI report said, "the perpetrators of the crime would get an Indian drunk, have a doctor examine him and pronounce him drunk, following which a morphine hypodermic would be injected into the Indian and after the doctor departed, the [killers] would inject an enormous amount of morphine under the armpit of the drunken Indian, which would result in his death. The doctor's certificate would subsequently read 'Death from alcoholic poison.' "

The guardians' scheme was to allow their Osage wards to accumulate as many headrights as possible. Regardless of the number, the restricted Osages would still only get $1,000 a quarter and the lawyers the rest. And so the guardians killed off their wards' family members who were holding headrights—whole generations above and below, from grandparents to grandchildren, and any aunts, uncles, nieces, nephews, cousins and in-laws along the way. And if an Osage made the fatal mistake of trying to extricate himself from the grip of his guardian, or if he discovered just how much money his guardian had stolen and demanded it back, then he, too, would die dead drunk.

These killings were clean, coldly clinical. There was no in-your-face, look-you-dead-in-the-eye, blood-sweat-and-tears type of terror, or fear, or passion, or any kind of discernible feeling at all, except maybe a shrug of regret at payday—which made these murders all the more chilling. Nothing so crass, so uncivilized, as shooting was allowed. Guns attracted too much attention, and were too messy. The lawyers wouldn't want to splatter their clothes, or certainly redden their hands for risk of smearing their suits.

So it sickened their sensibilities greatly when a couple of local cowboys committed copycat killings of Osages with—how gauche—guns.

William K. Hale and his nephew, Ernest Burkhart, were, in the vernacular of the place, "bumping" or "getting shut of" all the members of the full-blood Osage family that Burkhart had married into—and doing it loudly.

Hale was a cowboy-turned-rancher who had gotten rich leasing the Osages' pastureland. He leased so much of it—45,000 acres (he also owned an additional 5,000 acres)—that he earned the nickname "King of the Osage Hills," King also being his middle name. His ranch had made him so rich that he bought the bank in the Osage County town of Fairfax and a general store there. A portion of his fortune allegedly came from insuring his pasture for $1 an acre and having his cowboys torch 30,000 acres one night.

A 1926 *New York Times* article described Hale, fifty-one years old, as "a picturesque figure, one of the old plainsmen, even though he wears excellent clothing and makes a neat figure in an ordinary business suit." The FBI called him "an uneducated, more or less uncouth cow puncher and cattle thief, but possessed of a domineering personality. . . . [a man] who affected a military air with shoulders back and chest out, self-confident, the owner of many fine horses. . . . He has a very high opinion of himself and is money mad, as well as woman crazy."

Others portrayed Hale as a sort of Will Rogers of Indian-killers. Hale was likable and popular, he told jokes, he did rope tricks, he had Indians murdered. He had the reputation around Fairfax for "giving presents, suits of clothes, as well as [freely co-signing loan] notes for different people . . . and being kind to those who are afflicted, as well as to old people," according to one account. John Shaw, Claribel's eighty-six-year-old husband, grew up in Fairfax and, as a boy, remembered seeing Hale often. "He was a nice guy, 'cept he killed Osages," John said. "But kids loved him." Hale would see a youngster looking despondent and say to a ranch hand, "Buy that boy a pony."

" 'Course they only cost five dollars back then," John Shaw quickly noted.

Hale first came to Osage County when it was still the Indian reservation. He was a Texas cowboy and had passed through these parts on a cattle drive. Something about the Osage landscape moved him to veer his horse away from the herd. He summoned his wife from Texas to join him, and for a while they lived in a tent, pitched on the Gray Horse Indian camp.

Hale, having become a respected and rich rancher, banker and businessman, encouraged his nephew, Ernest Burkhart, to move to Osage County and get in on the headright action by trying to marry an Osage. Burkhart did. The lucky woman was Mollie Kyle Burkhart, a full-blood, allottee number 285. The FBI later described Burkhart, an Army cook during World War I, as a "squaw man, in his early thirties . . . completely dominated [by Hale and] a weak-willed individual who did his uncle's bidding."

Mollie Burkhart had three full-blood sisters, two of whom had married the same man, W. E. (Bill) Smith. Minnie Kyle Smith—or Wah-shah-she, allottee number 283—and Rita Kyle Smith—or Me-se-moie, allottee number 284—had continued the ancient Osage tradition that a woman married her older sister's husband if the sister died. Minnie Smith had drawn the short straw, dying of "a peculiar wasting illness" in 1918. At the insistence of the girls' mother, Lizzie Kyle—known by all as Lizzie Q, allottee number 282—Rita had stepped in to fill the sad void in the life of Minnie's poor husband—or rather, poor Minnie's husband, since Bill Smith had grown suddenly rich by inheriting half of his late wife's headright. The other half was probated to Lizzie Q. Marrying Rita gave Smith the added comfort of controlling one-and-a-half headrights.

In 1920, Lizzie Q, then seventy-one years old, "developed a malady which very evidently would result in her death," according to one account, and moved in with Mollie and Ernest Burkhart. It was a bad move. Hale and Burkhart started plotting for ways to add to Lizzie Q's large estate—she possessed several other headrights from deceased relatives—which would be equally divided by her daughters at her imminent death.

The obvious candidate for enlarging Lizzie's largesse was the third sister: Anna Kyle Brown—or Wah-hrah-lum-pah, allottee number 258, twenty-five years old. Hale and Burkhart knew her well, in the biblical sense. She had been married twice and was looking for Number Three but doing it all wrong. She had been doing Hale and Burkhart, among others, and had gotten pregnant. Hale was the father, she had announced in very public places. That was her fatal mistake. Anna Brown hadn't learned the one thing that everyone else in Osage County knew.

You didn't screw with William K. Hale.

Just like the Pawhuska lawyers, whose scheme to ax an Osage's family tree he borrowed, Hale did not want to bloody his hands, so he hired a pair: Bryan Burkhart, Ernest's younger brother, and Kelsey Morrison. Bryan Burkhart had not been as lucky as his brother, for he had not yet found an Osage woman to marry and support him. He had to work for a living, such as doing this job for Uncle Billie, as he called Hale. Bryan also was working hard on his marital status. He, too, was an occasional lover of Anna Brown, and he was also dating twenty-year-old Katherine Cole Morrison, or Gra-to-me-tsa-he, full-blood Osage, allottee number 157. To complicate this web further, Katherine was the estranged wife of Kelsey Morrison, who was yet another of Anna Brown's lovers. Morrison, thirty-five, was another "squaw man," whom the FBI later described as "a neat appearing man of very bad reputation." For killing Anna Brown, Hale provided Morrison with a .32 automatic and promised him $1,000, a used car and cancellation of a $600 debt.

One night in mid-May 1921, Bryan and Kelsey and Katherine and Anna went on a "drinking spree." After boozing it up all over Fairfax, the two couples "stopped under a tree near a ravine" to do some real drinking, according to Katherine's account. They were a few hundred yards off the Pawhuska–Fairfax road, near the turnoff to the Gray Horse Indian camp. The two men got out, opened the back door, "both reached in and helped [Anna] out of the car, Bryan being on the right side and Kelsey on the left side. They walked her away from the car, going towards the ravine. . . . I stayed in the car alone about 25 or 30 minutes, until they returned. Anna Brown was not with them, and I never saw her alive again."

But Anna was still alive when Kelsey and Bryan got back in the car. They had merely ditched her in the ravine when she passed out. They told Katherine that there were other people partying in the ravine and that Anna had decided to stay with them. They took Katherine home, but the men decided they needed re-fortifying for the task that awaited them, so they called a bootlegger friend, Matt Williams, and ordered two quarts of whiskey for fifteen dollars. They gave him directions to the spot where they would be murdering Anna, and told him to meet them there with the bottles.

Bryan and Kelsey drove back to the ravine. Anna hadn't moved. Bryan figured, well, what the hell, this would be his last shot at Anna Brown, why waste the opportunity? The sexual act revived Anna somewhat, and was still *in medias res* when Williams walked up with the whiskey. "While Bryan Burkhart was loving Anna Brown," Williams later said, Kelsey hit her hard on the head with Hale's pistol, hoping to knock her out. Instead, it brought her to. Kelsey hit her several more times with the pistol butt, but Anna fought back. The struggling trio rolled down the slope toward a creek. Williams heard cursing. Bryan managed to grab Anna, pinning her arms behind her, and the last thing Williams heard before Kelsey's gunshot was Anna's scream. Kelsey later told Williams it was the nastiest murder he had ever committed, and never wanted to do another one.

But the boys had been good killers: They had done what they were told by leaving behind the whiskey bottle they had been passing around before Anna passed out, and passed on. And despite the struggle, Kelsey had shot her at the crown of her skull so as to conceal the bullet hole. The entry wound was covered by Anna's thick black hair, and decomposition, spring rain and bugs would erase most of the blood. What little remained could be attributed to falling and hitting her head. There was no exit wound. The bullet had gone down into her body.

Hunters found her about a week later, on May 21. They reported the death to a Fairfax undertaker, F. S. Turten, who went to the scene with two Fairfax physicians. The doctors conducted what the FBI later described as "a very hurried examination . . . a rude autopsy. . . . For some reason, they began their search for the bullet by opening the skull by sawing it in half vertically, rather than removing a cap horizontally." Then they chopped Anna Brown's body into pieces, even cleaving the flesh from her bones with a meat ax. The FBI suspected that the doctors did not want to find a bullet, so that Anna Brown could be declared another victim of whiskey poisoning.

But later, as undertaker Turten was preparing the body for burial, "the scalp slipped from the skull and he discovered a bullet hole," according to an FBI report. An agent later examined the skull and "ascertained that the bullet was of a .32 caliber, traveling in a direction slightly downward from the plane of the head."

Clearly, Anna Brown had not drunk herself to death.

Anna Brown's mother, Lizzie Q—still living with Mollie and Ernest Burkhart—inherited all of her daughter's headright and estate, said to have been worth $100,000. That was the last good thing that ever happened to Lizzie Q. Two months later, she too died. According to one story, Lizzie Q became violently ill while eating dinner and may even have been dead before she fell out of her chair and hit the floor of the Burkhart house. No autopsy was performed on Lizzie Q, for it was obvious what had killed her—indigestion. Now Mollie Burkhart and her sister, Rita Smith, were worth an estimated $2 million in Osage headrights. Two more deaths—those of Rita and Bill Smith—would put all of that money under the roof of Ernest Burkhart, who was under the control of William K. Hale.

The fear of Mollie's divorcing Burkhart and marrying again seems to have driven Hale to commit the second killing later attributed to him. In 1922, Hale set his sights on Henry Roan Horse, also known as Henry Roan, Osage allottee number 721, a cousin of Mollie Burkhart. Hale wanted Roan out of the way because of his increasingly close relationship with his apparently more than kissing cousin. Mollie Burkhart was beginning to make noises about leaving Ernie and marrying Henry—which of course would ruin Hale's cushy, and cashy, deal in Osage County. Hale wasn't about to let that happen.

Although Roan and Mollie Burkhart were related, there was no chance of her getting his headright upon his death. Every Osage is every Osage's cousin, or so it seems. Hale, however, apparently couldn't stand the thought of wasting a perfectly good Osage without making some money, so he took out a $25,000 insurance policy with the Capitol Life Insurance Company of Denver on Roan—against an alleged, and spurious, IOU from Roan for the same amount.

Roan apparently had developed into a despondent, suicidal drunk and had tried to end it all on some recent occasions. Hale saw some easy money in the making. Roan was going to kill himself one day anyway, so why not profit on his death? This was a sure thing, for life insurance policies apparently did not have suicide exclusions in those days—or at least those policies sold in Osage County. Roan was running a one-horse race, and Hale was going to place a little wager, that was all. Hale wouldn't even have to fix it. The only ones to get hurt would be some insurance fat cats in Denver.

Taking out a life insurance policy on a soon-to-die Osage was a long-established practice in the county. So common was the practice that during Henry Roan's insurance physical in Tulsa, the examining doctor and Hale casually joked about the Indian's life expectancy now that he was insured for $25,000.

"You going to bump him?" the doctor quipped. The doctor later said Hale laughed and replied, "Sure!"

But a year after taking out the policy, Roan was still alive and drinking, and Hale was drumming his fingers on the table. He had lost his patience. Perhaps the annual premium was due, and so Hale hatched a plan for Kelsey Morrison to take the Indian out and get him drunk on a jug of corn whiskey saturated with strychnine. But Kelsey had a slight problem with alcohol. Before he got out of Hale's driveway, Kelsey had started sipping, strychnine and all, and before long had drunk the whole jug. After he came to, a gratefully living alcoholic, Morrison began boasting he had discovered that "corn whiskey kills the effect of strychnine!" His friends, however, noticed that Kelsey started acting peculiar. Some even guessed he was losing his mind. In later years, Morrison would do time in the Oklahoma pen, where he would walk around the prison yard and say openly, "I wish I could get out of this damn place. If I could, I'd [kill] me some more red asses if they wasn't all broke."

Hale then changed tactics and decided that Roan would shoot himself. For this job, he turned to someone with whom Roan had something in common—a boozer named John Ramsey, whom Hale had met through Henry Grammer, a former world champion rodeo-star-turned-bootlegger-turned-murderer. Grammer put Hale and Ramsey together because Ramsey had once taken the rap for Grammer for rustling cattle and had even served a prison sentence rather than betray him.

Burkhart would later recount Hale's plan: "He would put Ramsey on Henry Roan's trail [and] Ramsey would . . . shoot him and lay a gun beside him, and everybody would think he committed suicide. . . . Hale told me he had given Ramsey the money to buy a Ford Roadster, as Ramsey had no way to get around and kill Roan and get away, that it would be necessary for Ramsey to steer Roan around and . . . get him to a place where he could bump him."

One day, George Bolton and Henry Ward, "both reputable citizens of Fairfax"—presumably meaning they did not sleep with "squaws"—saw Hale riding with Ramsey in his new car. Ward quipped to Bolton, "I wonder who will be the next one."

Ramsey was wondering the same thing, and he was driving around with Hale that day, because Hale was going to point out to him "the Indian that he wanted killed," as Ramsey later put it. "I don't remember Hale ever telling me the Indian's name," Ramsey said.

Several days later, Ramsey met Roan in a restaurant in Fairfax. "He sat down beside me," Ramsey recalled, "and I smelled whiskey on his breath and we got into conversation about whiskey and I told him I could get him some. . . . I told him to meet me out on the road running through Sol Smith's pasture," which Hale had recommended as a good killing field. "I left him and went to Grammer's and got some whiskey and drove back on the road leading through Sol Smith's pasture, and found this Indian sitting in his car waiting at a point near Salt Creek. I drove up and got out of my car, and we took several drinks from a bottle I had. I then got in my car and went to Fairfax. Several times after that, I met this Indian and gave him drinks. This went on for several days, and I was trying to rib up a little more courage. Finally, one day, I decided to pull the job, everything being favorable." It was January 26, 1923.

"I told this Indian to meet me," Ramsey continued. "We sat on the running board of his car and drank what whiskey we had. The Indian then got in his car to leave, and I shot him in the back of the head. I suppose I was within a foot or two of him when I shot him."

Ten days later, Roan's body was discovered in a half-sitting position behind the wheel of his Buick. The gunshot had knocked him over toward the passenger seat, and his shattered head was resting in his hat, which he had taken off for his last swigs of whiskey. He was frozen stiff in that position.

The hat was all that lay beside Roan in the car—Ramsey had forgotten to drop his .45 by the body to make the death look like suicide.

Something else did not go as Hale had planned: He did not get the $25,000 insurance payoff. The insurance company discovered that Roan had been rejected for a previous policy with another company, because he had a venereal disease and incipient tuberculosis. Capitol Life claimed that Roan had committed fraud, which voided the policy. Hale, furious, sued the insurance company in federal court to recover the money. The Capitol Life Insurance Company of Denver, he vowed, would learn what everyone in Osage County knew:

You didn't screw with William K. Hale.

HALE'S NEXT TRICK spectacularly demonstrated the breadth of his power: He made Bill and Rita Smith disappear.

The explosion of their house in Fairfax on the night of March 10, 1923, a month and a half after Henry Roan's "suicide," was heard ten miles away. The blast knocked John Shaw, Claribel's husband, out of bed. Neighboring houses were damaged, and clothes and bedding from the Smith house were found dangling in trees, on telephone poles and from electric wires for a three-block radius. Bill Smith was found out in the yard, entwined in the mattress that he had been sleeping upon moments before. Rita had landed on top of him. She was dead. He was alive, but just barely. There was no immediate trace of their white housekeeper, Nellie Brookshire, also sleeping in the house. Ernest Burkhart, their neighbor and brother-in-law, helped man the fire-bucket brigade.

Bill Smith was rushed to the Fairfax hospital, where he was attended by the night-duty nurse, Margaret Mitchell. He talked unintelligibly and "muttered several times various names" that she could not understand, Mitchell later said. At one point, however, Smith said plainly, "They got Rita and now it looks like they have got me." He came to every now and then, and would ask Mitchell "if he had mentioned any names during his sleep, and on being told he had not, would seem relieved."

Even dying, Smith was afraid of William K. Hale. Smith had figured out what Hale was doing, and had even been telling people that he had hired a detective to investigate the shootings of Anna Brown and Henry Roan. Perhaps talking was what got Bill Smith killed. There was one thing, though, that Smith had not told anyone; if he had, it might have saved him and Rita. The two had secretly changed their wills. If they both died, their new wills said, Rita's headrights would go to a daughter of Bill Smith by a previous marriage who lived in Arkansas. When Bill Smith died that morning in Fairfax hospital, his last thoughts may have been imagining the look on Hale's face when he heard the news that he had just made some young Arkansan a very rich woman.

Twelve nights after the explosion, in the most bizarre act of the Reign of Terror, someone blew up Ruth Tall Chief's grave in the Fairfax cemetery.

Blowing up the grave may have been someone's idea of a joke, or even an attempted robbery "with intent of securing diamonds and other valuables supposed to have been entombed with the body," as an FBI report surmised. Or perhaps there was a more subtle reason behind it. Perhaps the chain reaction of this explosion was intentional, for it raised the terror level, drew further attention to Hale's and Burkhart's mayhem in Fairfax, and made them appear more fearsome.

They were out of control. They were now killing *dead* Osages. Something had to be done about them.

The Pawhuska lawyer-guardians must have despised Hale and Burkhart. These cowboys had gotten too obvious. Their murders were attracting too much attention, and if they were not stopped, they could bring the whole house down on everyone. The Interior Department might even get Congress to launch a thorough investigation of the conditions of Osage Indians. One such investigation had ushered in the guardianship program. Another such investigation might usher it out, as the gruesome truth became known in Washington.

The county and state authorities were letting Hale and Burkhart get away with murder. The only way to stop them, before they ruined everything for everyone, was to bring in the feds. Until now, the FBI had stayed out of the Osage murder cases. It lacked jurisdiction. All had taken place in Osage County, and no bodies had turned up on the Osage Agency campus in Pawhuska or in the three Indian camps, the only federal property in the county.

The feds had poked around Osage County a lot, though. The FBI had been a feature of the western landscape since 1908, when the bureau was formed in response to President Theodore Roosevelt's demands to do something about federal "land thieves" out West. World War I gave it another focus: draft dodgers and spies. The FBI got into the car-chasing business in 1919 with the National Motor Vehicle Theft Act. By 1923,

Indian-killers were not yet on the FBI's list of eligible bad guys to chase, but gangsters were. Just as in the outlaw days of old, the hills around the Osage town of Okesa were still the hiding place of choice for gangsters and other bad guys who committed crimes against whites. An FBI report had cautioned that any agent venturing into the area have "a great deal of experience in handling desperate situations, as there is no question but that Osage County, Oklahoma, has more criminals in it than perhaps any other county in the state or any state in the Union."

But blowing up the Smiths changed the nature of the murders. It no longer was a case of killing sixty Indians in isolated spots around the Osage countryside—out of sight and earshot of its white residents—but of one white man in the middle of a crowded white town.

Even before Bill Smith died, the telephones in the state capital sprang to life. From the governor on down, Oklahoma's elected officials got an earful from their white constituents in Fairfax, both the horrified and the outraged: *They broke my windows! There's underwear in my tree! There's an arm in my yard!* The state attorney general, George F. Short, wrote a worried letter to Charles H. Burke, the commissioner of the Bureau of Indian Affairs in Washington.

Smith's "death is expected momentarily," Short wrote, the latest of "a series of deaths, under the most unusual circumstances [that] have occurred among a family of Osage Indians." Short went on to say that the state was "prepared to spend several thousand dollars investigating this series of murders . . . [and] I write to inquire if I may have the cooperation and assistance of your office and the Department of Justice." (Short later told the FBI that he lacked confidence in the ability, will or honesty of state and local authorities to solve the murders.)

Upon receiving Short's letter, Burke queried Superintendent J. George Wright of the Osage Agency about "what action should be taken to cooperate with the state authorities in making a thorough investigation." Wright responded immediately. With his assistance, the Osage Tribal Council passed a resolution offering a $5,000 reward "for information leading to the arrest and conviction" of the killer of any Osage. The council also requested that the secretary of the interior "obtain the services of the Department of Justice in capturing and prosecuting" Osage killers and offered to pay for the FBI investigation. Finally, the council authorized the secretary of the interior "to ask for an appropriation from Congress of Osage tribal funds to cover the provisions of this resolution." Wright also got L. R. Heflin, president of the Fairfax Chamber of Commerce, to circulate a petition among the town's leading businessmen, calling for a federal investigation of the murders. Thirty signed.

On March 24, 1923, a package from the BIA commissioner containing Short's letter, the Osage Tribal Council resolution, and the Fairfax petition landed on the desk of FBI Director William J. Burns. He ordered his Oklahoma City office to give the Osage murders "specific attention."

Agent Frank V. Wright (no relation to George) arrived in Pawhuska on April 2, and his first stop was the Osage Agency. George Wright walked Frank Wright down the hall to the office of the man who could tell him everything he needed to know—Osage tribal attorney A. T. Woodward.

Over the course of two hours, Woodward laid it all out for Agent Wright: Anna Brown, Henry Roan, the $25,000 life insurance policy, the Smiths—and their killers. Agent Wright ended his report with the conclusion that "strong suspicion is warranted: First, of WM. HALE as being the master mind. . . . Second, of the BURKHART brothers as being accomplices and possibly guilty of the actual commission of some of the crimes. Third, of KELSEY MORRISON being one man who had direct connection with . . . one or more of the murders." Woodward also told Agent Wright that the Osage Agency possessed no files or reports of its own on the murders.

Agent Wright snooped around Pawhuska and Fairfax for four days, following leads furnished by Woodward and others. Wright returned again on April 10 and 11, and made a quick stop on April 14—and never came back.

As the weeks passed, it became clear that the Department of Justice was in no hurry to keep Osages alive, or to mete out justice for those who weren't. On May 25, Deputy Director J. Edgar Hoover reminded Director Burns that "there is a serious situation on the Osage Indian Reservation in Oklahoma," and suggested that another agent be assigned the Osage case. But it was not until July 17, more than three months after Agent Wright's last visit, that the new FBI agent on the case, Calvin S. Weakley, retraced his predecessor's stroll down the hallway of the Osage Agency and into the office of the tribal attorney.

Woodward repeated to Weakley what he had told Wright: "that the Indian Agency had at no time especially detailed any man to make investigation of any of these offenses, and therefore had no investigative reports on file in [his] office which showed any evidence secured in this matter."

But then Weakley talked to Sam Tulk, the agency's Indian enforcement agent at Fairfax, who contradicted Woodward's assertion. Tulk said that he had investigated the Anna Brown murder and had gathered "considerable information as he had worked on the case in assisting the local authorities," turning over all his information to Woodward. He also reported that he and Woodward had personally questioned two early suspects in the Anna Brown murder and had recorded the interrogation on a Dictograph machine.

For some reason, Woodward didn't want the FBI to see his case files containing the evidence secured by Tulk and other Osage Agency investigators. Apparently Woodward wanted agents Wright and Weakley to know only what he wanted to tell them.

The real story was that the agency had unleashed on Osage County an army of detectives. After the murders of Anna Brown and another Osage, Charles Whitehorn (their bodies had been discovered on the same day), the Osage tribal council had offered a $2,500 reward for their killers' capture, and the county probate court had authorized the administrators of those Osages' estates to hire private detectives to investigate the cases. The Osage Agency was clearly lurking in the shadows, especially since Woodward himself was directly responsible for all Osage probate matters. After the Smith killings, the tribal council doubled the reward and, as Superintendent Wright reported to the BIA, "with the assistance of this office . . . arrangements [were] made for employing [new] detectives." Indeed, one of the FBI's first observations about the murder case was that Osage County was "overrun with private detectives and others seeking to share in the rewards."

The man most closely identified with the Osage Agency's proxy investigation was William W. Vaughn, a Pawhuska lawyer and former Tulsa judge "well-acquainted with the Indians." Records are unclear about his formal role or motive in the investigation, but many surviving accounts portray him as a sort of high priest to the investigation, the earthly representative of the Man on the Hill, A. T. Woodward of the Osage Agency. Judge Vaughn apparently was spotted so often on Agency Hill, with Woodward and in and around his office, that Vaughn was referred to as an Osage tribal attorney.

By June, Vaughn was able to tell one of his lawyer colleagues, E. J. McCurdy, that he had gathered "sufficient evidence to put Bill Hale in the electric chair." But at the same time, someone else had figured out a sure-fire way to rekindle the FBI's interest in the case and bring the feds back to Osage County in a hurry to get rid of Hale and Burkhart.

The plan: Murder the Osage Agency's murder investigator—and make it look like Hale and Burkhart did it.

Vaughn apparently knew that something was afoot. In late June, he told his wife, Rosa, that he had stashed away some crucial evidence, "along with a whole bunch of money." Apparently he no longer trusted Woodward, and had ceased relaying information to him about the case. Vaughn told Rosa where the hiding place was. "If something should happen to me," he said, "you get that [evidence], and you turn that in, and that's where the money is."

Vaughn's fears unfolded with deadly precision on June 29, 1923.

That day, an Indian known to all Osages and holding a special distinction among them was carried into a hospital in Oklahoma City with an unknown but life-threatening ailment. He was George Bigheart, the only son of the Osage's last hereditary chief, James Bigheart.

George Bigheart had fallen ill at his home in Fairfax, and had been taken by train to Oklahoma City by William Hale and Ernest Burkhart. Hale was a friend and neighbor of Bigheart's, and recently had taken over the Osage's financial affairs as his guardian. Bigheart was a big drinker, and his sudden illness had coincided with a binge of several days.

Poison was suspected (but never diagnosed) in Bigheart's ailment, and his condition—still alive—was considered lucky for him, but luckier still for the Osage Agency. Woodward immediately dispatched Vaughn to Oklahoma City.

Vaughn talked to Bigheart before the Indian died, but the substance of their conversation was never known. That night, Vaughn boarded the Midland Valley Railroad train back to Pawhuska. The last to see him alive—or rather, the last to admit he saw Vaughn alive—was the Pullman porter. Vaughn, in his pajamas, asked him to wake him up at Pershing, in

Osage County. The next morning, Vaughn's naked body was found on a railroad right-of-way not far from Fairfax.

The body was so badly messed up that a coroner's jury could not decide whether he fell off the train and the fall tore him up and killed him, or whether he was beaten to death and pushed off the train. The coroner ruled Vaughn's death suspicious—but not a murder.

When Rosa was told her husband was dead, she went to the hiding place, as he had instructed her. But all the evidence he had hidden there was gone, along with the money. Rosa, a music teacher, "was left with absolutely not a dime" and ten children.

Hale and Burkhart obviously poisoned Bigheart, took him to the hospital in Oklahoma City, saw Vaughn interviewing him, followed the lawyer to the train, boarded it, then killed him, either by beating him to death or pushing him off the train. It was obvious who did it.

It was too obvious.

It wasn't their style. They were killers, but they killed like lawyers—not with their own hands. They would have hired someone to poison Vaughn, shoot him or blow him up.

It also was not in Hale's interests to kill Bigheart. Hale had just become his guardian, and probably had not had the chance to steal his money. Hale would have benefited from his business relationship with Bigheart only over the long term, with the Osage alive. Dead, Bigheart was of no value to Hale. Neither he nor Burkhart would inherit Bigheart's headright.

It was probably not Woodward's idea, but he played a crucial role in the plot to kill his investigator, who had hidden evidence from him. Vaughn must have been afraid of Woodward and his links with the Indian-killers—not the amateurs such as Hale and Burkhart, but the big-league, bloodless murderers of "hundreds and hundreds" of Osages.

It was Woodward who was running the guardianship program for the Osage Agency. Woodward was a guardian himself, and all of his wards—four of them—had managed to die by 1923, while Vaughn was actively investigating.

Three other whites previously had been killed because of evidence they were harboring. In 1921, Barney McBride took a train to Washington from Osage County to turn over information to the FBI about the Osage murders. He nearly got there. His mutilated body was found in

Meadows, Maryland, just outside Washington. Henry Bennet was shot to death in 1923 two blocks from the state capitol in Oklahoma City. He was on his way to meet with the governor to give him information about the Osage murders—or so Bennet had said before he left Osage County. When Bennet was killed, his buddy, Hugh Gibson, went to Oklahoma City with the same information—Bennet had given it to him just in case. Gibson met with the same fate.

Could a couple of cowboys from Osage County have been so powerful as to pull off those killings? Could their reach have extended so far?

That Bennet, Gibson and McBride were killed suggests that each of them had told someone what they planned to do. But if they knew anything about the murders, they would have known that the killers, as the FBI later put it, were "reliably reputed to dominate completely" the county attorney's and sheriff's offices. That left only one other point of official contact—the trusted Osage Agency.

All Woodward had to do was make sure he sent Vaughn to Oklahoma City. Not only would Hale and Burkhart be pinned with obvious murders, but the evidence that Vaughn had been hiding could be found out. Woodward must have known Vaughn was keeping something from him. Perhaps E. J. McCurdy, the man Vaughn had confided in, had confided in Woodward.

The plan probably went like this: They poisoned Bigheart, and kept watch on him. Then they had someone follow Hale and Burkhart to the Oklahoma City hospital. Then the phone rang in Woodward's office.

Woodward called Vaughn and told him to take the next train to Oklahoma City.

There's one more story about the train from which Vaughn disappeared. Someone reported seeing a passed-out drunk being helped onto the train by two men, each supporting one of the drunk's arms and dragging him.

That would make more sense that beating Vaughn to death on the train. Wouldn't someone have heard him scream? If Vaughn's hidden evidence and money were stolen before his widow got to them, that meant Vaughn was tortured into telling his killers where the hiding place was. Torture is not something that takes place in silence.

Vaughn probably was killed in Oklahoma City by whomever called Woodward. Then Vaughn was dragged onto the train. One too many, his "helpers" probably said to passersby, or the conductor. Dead-drunk, sure hate to be him in the morning. One of his killers then posed as Vaughn, even dressing in pajamas and asking the porter to wake him up in Osage County. That was a nice touch. One of the things that E. J. McCurdy later said was that he "examined the berth assigned to Vaughn, and which Vaughn was supposed to have occupied, and that it showed that no one had disturbed it in any manner."

It was a testament to Hale's pull that he probably swayed members of the coroner's jury to split on the cause of Vaughn's death. If it had been ruled a murder and Hale and Burkhart charged with it in 1923, the Reign of Terror might have had a different outcome.

Sybil Bolton might have lived through it.

VAUGHN'S KILLING WAS MURDER MOST WHITE, and it brought the feds back to Osage County. To show its good faith, the FBI accepted the Osages' kind offer to pay for the investigation and generously started the meter running as of July 1, 1923. (The amount the FBI could charge the Osages later was limited, either by the BIA or Congress, to $20,000.) The FBI's commitment to the Osages was sealed—at least for one more year. J. Edgar Hoover, who was now the bureau's acting director, "discontinued" the investigation in August 1924 because of lack of progress, but kept his decision secret, perhaps hoping that neither the BIA nor the Osage Agency would notice the absence of FBI agents or reports on the case. But they did. On December 13, 1924, three days after he was named permanent FBI director, Hoover responded to a "what-gives" query from BIA Commissioner Burke by issuing "special instructions today to our Oklahoma City office to take up the matter de novo." To make sure the new director would not kill the murder case again, Pawhuska lawyers launched a letter-writing campaign to Senator Charles Curtis of Kansas, an Osage and reputedly a direct descendant of old Chief White Hair, asking him to put some heat on Hoover.

At some point—it is not clear when, or who devised the idea—the FBI decided it had jurisdiction in the Hale murders after all. Its legal argument went like this: Any land owned by "restricted" Osages (those under guardians) could be construed as being federal property, since the restrictions placed on the Indians were the result of an act of Congress. Rita Smith was a restricted Osage and owned the house in which she, her husband and their servant were blown up. Therefore, the house was federal property. Anna Brown and Henry Roan also were restricted Osages, but they were not murdered on their own property. However, according to the cartographic records of the Osage Agency, their bodies were found on land owned by restricted Osages—federal property, in other words. Therefore, the FBI had jurisdiction in those cases, too.

For two years, FBI agents compiled about 1,500 pages of hearsay, unsubstantiated rumor and circumstantial evidence about Hale and Burkhart from about 150 witnesses. No single piece of evidence—nor any or all of it together—probably would have resulted in their indictments, and certainly not in convictions—in a perfect world, that is. But this was Oklahoma. In the summer of 1925, the FBI decided that, with a little luck and a whole lot of dumb jurors, a federal grand jury might indict Hale and Burkhart. In early August, Hoover authorized four agents ("men carefully selected because of their knowledge of Indian and frontier life, their indomitable courage and persistence over seemingly insurmountable obstacles") to go undercover "among the natives in Osage County." The G-men posed as an insurance agent, a Texas cattle buyer, a real estate agent and, hoping to gain the confidence and loosen the tongues of reticent Osages, an Indian "medicine man." A federal grand jury was scheduled to convene a month later in Guthrie, Oklahoma. The government's case against Hale and Burkhart would be presented then. No sooner had the undercover investigation begun than T. B. White, agent-in-charge, pleaded for more time, and the convening of the grand jury was delayed to November 1, 1925.

Hale was following all this with great interest. He had been reading many of the FBI reports—who was saying what about him. Throughout their investigation, FBI agents complained continually that their case files and field reports were ending up in the hands of Pawhuska lawyers, who were showing them to "prospective defendants"—Hale and company. One Pawhuska lawyer kept copies on his desk, a report said. Their source remained a mystery, but the U.S. attorney's office in Oklahoma City and the Osage Agency in Pawhuska were regular recipients of copies of the reports, and the leak obviously came from senior officials in one of those places, or maybe both. One FBI official even demanded "an immediate and general investigation" of Oklahoma's U.S. attorney, a request Hoover denied.

Hale knew, for example, that the Fairfax Catholic parish priest, Father Achtergael, was an FBI informant, and had given the agents details of Ernest and Mollie Burkhart's home life that the priest had learned in, well, private conversations with Mollie Burkhart in church. (The FBI reports do not use the word "confession.") During the undercover investigation, Father Achtergael apologized that he had nothing new to report, because Ernest Burkhart was forbidding his wife to go to church, locking her in the house on Sundays.

Hale even befriended one of the undercover agents, F. S. Smith, opening their conversation at the Smith-Williams Hotel in Fairfax on August 16, 1925, by saying, So you're one of the FBI men. Alluding to FBI efforts to put him in the cooler, Hale boasted that he was "too slick . . . to catch cold."

Maybe he was *too* slick, or all that Osage blood on him made him stickier than he thought. So sure was Hale of his ability to outsmart the FBI and get away with murder that he decided to speed things up, to burn rubber on the wheels of justice.

The only way out, he decided, was through the courts. He would get himself arrested, get tried, get acquitted. Oklahoma Governor Martin E. Trapp had circulated among the jails and prisons in the state the offer of a $10,000 reward—and the promise of immunity—for a confession that would implicate accomplices and crack the Reign of Terror cases.

Hale persuaded Bert Lawson, another of his "squaw man" buddies (who had once worked on Bill Smith's ranch), to confess that Hale had paid him to blow up the Smiths. By confessing, Lawson would get immunity for the killings, plus $10,000, plus more cash from Hale. The deal was too sweet for Lawson, who was doing seven years at the state penitentiary at McAlester for second-degree burglary, to pass up.

On October 23, 1925, Lawson gave a great confession, the most dramatic and detailed in the FBI file, implicating Hale as the mastermind behind the bombing. Not only did Hale give him the explosives, Lawson stated, but arranged to have Lawson let out of the Pawhuska jail for the night, and drove him back to jail after he blew up the house. The FBI—no fan of the Osage County Sheriff's Department—believed every word of it.

In a flurry of telegrams, Hoover and his agents congratulated themselves for finally cracking the case.

But Hale had made up the whole story, every word of it. Hale's plan was to get arrested based on the bogus confession, then prove in court that the government's case against him was built on lies. Among other things, he had an airtight alibi: He had been in Fort Worth at the time of the explosion, attending the Texas Fat Stock Show, and not in Osage County, as Lawson had testified. If all else failed, Hale's trump card was Lawson himself. He could be persuaded to testify in court that his confession had been coerced and he was merely saying what the FBI wanted to hear.

Hale's ploy probably would have worked, except for what the FBI described as "the weak link in William K. Hale's organization"—his nephew Ernest Burkhart. The instant FBI agents stuck a gun to Burkhart's head during his interrogation, out it all came. He confessed—in a statement as dull as he probably was in life—to plotting with and helping his Uncle Billie to arrange the murders of Henry Roan and the Smiths. (Anna Brown was not mentioned.) Hale, Burkhart said, had suggested two methods to kill the Smiths: set their house on fire and shoot them when they came running out, or blow it up. Henry Grammer had arranged for a man named Asa (Ace) Kirby to place the "soup" under the house, and John Ramsey, Henry Roan's killer, took part by pointing out the Smith house to Kirby.

Ramsey? The FBI men looked at one another dumbstruck. After two years of investigating the Osage murders, they had never heard of John Ramsey. Hale had vastly overestimated the vaunted and feared FBI.

Ramsey was arrested the day after Burkhart's confession, but the FBI did not have to pull a pistol to persuade him to talk. All the agents had to do was to bring Burkhart into the interrogation room. Ramsey "slumped in his chair and said, 'Ernest, have you told everything?' Burkhart answered, 'Yes, I have told it all.' John Ramsey then asked permission to speak privately with Burkhart, which request was granted him. After he had talked with Burkhart a few minutes, he turned to the Government agent and said, 'Well, I guess it's all off my neck. Get you a pencil.' "

Ace Kirby was not able to talk. Three months after blowing up the Smith house, Kirby had been blown away by a storekeeper in a town east of Osage County near the Kansas-Oklahoma border. The shop owner, Fay

Beard, had gotten a telephone tip that Kirby was on his way, intending to rob him. Beard blasted him with a shotgun through the front door before Kirby even opened it.

Neither was Henry Grammer available for questioning. The month after the Smith killings, his body was found in a crashed and burned car. Rumors ran rampant through Osage County that the brakes had been tampered with, but an autopsy found that Grammer had been shot under the armpit.

Hale also did not confess. He was arrested the same day as Burkhart, but held out through his interrogation—even when the FBI men put a black hood over his head and strapped him in an electric chair. He dug in his heels and waited for his trial.

THE BERT LAWSON CONFESSION took place on October 23, 1925—fifteen days before the death of Sybil Bolton. But the FBI did nothing for two and a half months. To give the FBI more time to prepare its list of witnesses to be subpoenaed, the federal grand jury was postponed from November 1 to January 7, 1926.

Hale and Burkhart were not arrested until January 4, three days before the federal grand jury was to convene, but their arrest came solely on the basis of the Lawson confession. No new evidence had been found after October 23, 1925.

Burkhart confessed on January 6; Ramsey on January 7. In other words, after the Lawson confession, phony or not, it took the FBI only a matter of hours to wrap up the Reign of Terror.

To someone who lost a family member during the FBI's delay, this is galling. I don't recall ever seeing an FBI movie or television show in which agents screech their Fords to a stop in front of a house containing the suspect and Efrem Zimbalist, Jr., announces boldly into a bullhorn, "This is the FBI. We're not ready yet." If a movie is ever made of the Reign of Terror, it should be called *The Unmovables.* Eliot Ness never waited two and a half months after finding a warehouse full of bootleg booze to smash it up. I must have forgotten the part about the FBI agent slipping a note to John Dillinger asking if he wouldn't mind sitting through *Manhattan Transfer* a few more times until the feds got the movie theater surrounded.

But Dillinger wasn't killing the Just Indians of America. He was upsetting white people.

What was the rush anyway? These were years-old cases.

FBI Director Hoover had not yet spent all the money offered by the Osage tribal council. The Osages would pay $20,000 of the FBI investigation, and that was nearly exactly what Hoover gave them: a $21,509.19 investigation, from inception to end result: the grand jury indictments of Hale, Burkhart and Ramsey in January 1926.

According to a budget memo to Hoover, dated November 13, 1925, "the cost of the Osage Murder case, chargeable" to the Osages, was $18,897.93 for the period from July 1, 1923, when the FBI started its investigation, to October 31, 1925, a week after the Lawson confession.

A thousand bucks to go.

Prolonging the FBI investigation for two and a half more months added another $2,611.26 to the Osage bill—$1,295 for "salary," $600 for "per diems," $65.95 in "incidentals, including carfares, porterage, taxi, telephone, telegrams, etc. etc.," and $650.31 in "Railroad, Pullman and Steamship fares" for the eight agents who variously worked the case.

Even the FBI appeared to be fleecing the Osages.

The Reign of Terror was not the FBI's finest hour. It took the bureau two and a half years to put behind bars a couple of cowboys whose murders of Osages had been common knowledge in Osage County for years.

The FBI's work fell far short of the results that its agent in charge of the investigation had expected even as late as August 1925. In a letter to Hoover, Agent T. B. White wrote: "I think we already have sufficient evidence in order to get an indictment against 24 different individuals, if not more, and I am sure after we get these arrested that the case will open up to the fullest extent."

Hoover failed to take seriously the frequent complaints of his agents that their reports were being distributed around Osage County. The FBI made no attempt to trace the source of the leaks, especially the possibility that they were emanating from the Osage Agency, or to tighten the security—and thus confidentiality—surrounding the reports. That breach may have gotten Sybil Bolton killed.

The Osage murders did not appear to have been a high priority for Hoover. The files show that he took little active interest or role in the cases, and suggest he lost interest in the investigation as it dragged on.

Memos from him, for example, were more frequent early in the file than later. On September 12, 1925, at the height of the undercover investigation, Hoover made his agents come in out of the cold to rewrite a report. "The synopsis of the attached report is not in accordance with Bureau instructions," he quibbled. "It is descriptive or administrative rather than an actual synopsis of the facts as obtained. Please advise the Agent who prepared the report. Signed, Director." White was forced to spend valuable time away from the Osages to write a slavering apology: "I feel that I, myself, am altogether to blame for I looked over this report and gave it my approval, and forwarded it to you. I will endeavor to not let this occur again on my part. I am doing everything I possibly can to see that the reports of the agents from this office are forwarded to you in correct form, and will make a double effort to see that they are forwarded in such form that they will meet with your approval."

Six days later, Hoover sent a stern letter to White, disallowing lunch and dinner expenses with potential witnesses and chastising him for allowing an agent to rent a car and hire a confidential informant. "Please give this matter prompt attention," Hoover fumed, "and also inform [the agent] that the hiring of this Confidential Informant or the travel by automobile must not be made a regular practice."

The prosecutions of Hale, Burkhart and Ramsey accounted, technically, for only three dead Osages and two dead whites. But besides the Brown, Roan and Smith killings, the FBI made no serious attempt to investigate any other Osage murder case. By focusing exclusively on Hale and Burkhart, the FBI ignored the other, more odious side of the Reign of Terror—the "hundreds and hundreds" of murders committed by the Osages' lawyer-guardians.

FBI agents even ignored the murder that had gotten them back into the Osage cases—that of William W. Vaughn, the Osage Agency murder investigator thrown off the train.

Woodward, no doubt, was relieved.

The coroner's jury ruling that Vaughn's death had been merely suspicious meant that Woodward escaped being accused of complicity in murder. That may have eased his conscience, but probably did not do much for his fears. If the other Osage County lawyers involved had so easily killed Vaughn, whom they had known and worked with for years, what would keep them from sparing Woodward?

I think Woodward finally panicked in 1924, the year after Vaughn's murder, when he attended congressional hearings in Washington on the Osage guardianship program. Woodward knew it was all over. Perhaps the deaths of his four Osage wards would be examined. In any case, he knew his role in the program would be under scrutiny and that there would be tough investigations of the guardians. Some of them would be looking for someone to blame.

I think that's why he quit as Osage tribal attorney after the hearings, and left the state. Woodward must have feared two things terribly—getting caught, and getting killed.

I think that whoever blew up Ruth Tall Chief's grave also killed Vaughn, and that whoever killed Vaughn also killed my grandmother.

In late October or early November 1925, when the FBI's abstract of grand-jury witnesses got into the hands of Pawhuska's lawyers, just as the other FBI reports had, someone was shocked to see that A. T. Woodward would testify.

At about the same time, on October 27, the *Pawhuska Daily Journal-Capital* reported that Mr. and Mrs. A. T. Woodward had arrived in Pawhuska from their home in El Dorado, Arkansas. Mr. Woodward, it said, was in town to conduct business at the Osage Agency, where he used to be employed as the Osage tribal attorney.

They must have thought he was talking, had turned state's evidence, had cut a deal.

The Woodwards left Pawhuska on November 1. Six days later, the last murder of the Reign of Terror took place.

I know my grandmother didn't kill herself, because I didn't.

I went to Pawhuska to solve the mystery of Sybil's death. Instead, I solved the mystery of my life. Fleur estimates that over that summer and fall, I spent $5,000 in bars. And I drank only beer.

At the time, I excused my bar habit as loneliness. I missed my family. It was something to do in a do-nothing place. I was passing the time in a town that time had passed by, holding the blues at bay in a place that, from its looks, had never recovered from the Depression. Sitting in a bar was better than staying in my apartment alone, where I could barely get a TV signal. I could watch TV and people in bars, and talk to someone—if only the bartender—after a day of sitting in solitude and silence at the library. It was part of my research. I read at the barstool. I even took notes. I was studying Indian drinking habits.

But now I've exhausted my excuses. I'm left with only the reason.

Often I was the only customer. The few others I saw while I was making and drinking my rounds were mostly whites—old cowboys and car-pokes, a few young ones, but no drunken Indians.

Well, one.

Times were either very good and Pawhuskans had no troubles to take to bars, or very bad and they couldn't afford to. I suspect the latter, from the looks of the town and the appearance of the small clientele at Betty's Lounge and the Kihekah Lounge, or Frosty's, after the owner. I preferred Betty's, because it had a window, but Frosty's was within walking distance, a block away from my apartment.

The beer of choice at Frosty's was Old Milwaukee. It cost only a dollar. I drank the expensive stuff—$1.50 Bud in long-neck bottles. Invariably, the pull of green bottles of German and Canadian imported beer, my drink of choice—three dollars and change for a Heineken—drew me to drive to Bartlesville and the Hotel Phillips, where you can use your Phillips gas card at the bar.

The first time I went to Frosty's, a sign in the pool-table area in the windowless, front end of the bar caught my eye. "We Never Sleep" it said, "Smith Ringgold—Bail Bonds."

One afternoon in June, I noticed another sign against a wall so shadowed in dim bar light that the writing was nearly illegible. Live music from "9 Till ??," it said. It was that day's date. Oh good, I thought, I can watch some country-music dancing tonight.

After nine, I asked Frosty what had happened to the band. He gave me a puzzled look. I motioned toward the sign.

"Well, goddamn," he said with an embarrassed chuckle, "that was last year. I just never got 'round to taking it down." Frosty tended to inject "well, goddamn" into his speech with the same frequency that teenagers say "you know."

It was a scary place, and a scary lot. Often I could see the outlines of knives in the back jeans' pockets of pool players. Other customers sat apart from everyone, casting the glare of a caged look about the room like a spotlight sweeping a prison yard, looking as if they were waiting for a glance to pounce on.

But none was scarier than I, putting fifty to seventy-five miles on my car during my nightly barhops between Pawhuska and Bartlesville, especially during the "back again" drive. Often I had to cover one eye to correct a recurring problem with double vision.

One night, I got lost on my way back to Pawhuska—a neat trick, since there's only one road. I have no idea where I was or how I got there, and I was unable to retrace the route later in daytime. It was so dark at the spot where I finally stopped and turned around that the black sky paled gray against a blacker outline of the tops of steep hills far above me. In a flash, all the fear and horror still lurking in those same hills and ravines from the murders that took place in them suddenly roared down the hillside slopes, crashed through my car window and grabbed me by the throat—or at least, that's how I remember it.

I was so shook up that I resolved that never, ever would I do this again—drive home after a twenty-beer night, that is. Instead, I would check into a hotel in Bartlesville.

My last calendar week there, I checked into the Bartlesville Holiday Inn twice—and I left on a Wednesday.

My last night there, July 22, I again wound up in Bartlesville and kept saying to myself that I didn't belong, I didn't fit in, I'd never be an Osage, *who are you kidding?,* I had to get out of here—which I did after witnessing an especially bloody barroom brawl. I'd have left during it, but some guy was blocking the front door, kicking another guy who was on the floor yelping as he tried to crawl under the cigarette machine.

As it did every morning, the sun blazing through my windows woke me up. As I lay with my eyes closed, I heard a loud sound that puzzled me. A truck was gearing past, and it sounded just a few feet away. Odd for a truck to be driving past my fourth-floor window, I thought. I opened my eyes.

The ceiling of my car came into focus, then the steering wheel, then other cars parked around me.

I was at an interstate rest stop.

I won't detail my litany of "Oh my Gods." I got out of the car and headed for the men's room. I walked past one of those oversize road maps posted at rest stops. It was a map of Missouri.

I have no recollection of how I got there. I even had to drive through a couple of toll booths.

Standing there looking at a spot circled on the map in Magic Marker with "You Are Here" written under it, I decided I needed to go home.

Home.

But where? East or west of where I stood?

The family I had, in the place I didn't want to be, east of Eden? Or the home I wanted, the home of my ancestors, the home of my people who wouldn't have anything to do with me?

I drove west, back to Pawhuska, packed the car, and drove east. I would stay with my family a couple of weeks, I decided, then have another go at it. I knew what was wrong with me. I was bored, and I missed them. I needed them. I was homesick.

I never went back to Pawhuska.

I would like to have been able to salvage some self-esteem, and say that that horrifying episode forced me to realize the obvious, but I can't. I still had a family, a house and a job to lose, and I set to the task in short order.

While I was away, Fleur had started recycling our trash—newspapers, plastic bottles, aluminum, tin cans, glass. I can close my eyes now, anytime, day or night, and still sharply hear the clank of another empty green bottle landing in the tall, yellow rubber bin reserved for glass. I grew embarrassed at how quickly I filled it up, but most of all I was mortified to have to take the bottles to the recycling center—Fleur wouldn't. The recycling center wouldn't let me just pour the contents of our bin into a dumpster for glass. There were workers to do that, to ensure that some environmental neophyte didn't screw up the system and thus the ecology by mixing recyclables. Glass had to be divided into clear, green and brown bottles, and a long work table was erected in front of the dumpster for that purpose. So I was forced to place each empty on the table—admission, evidence of how much I drank.

Soon I started to hide the empties in the back of my car, or sometimes under the sink or in the basement.

One day finally, fed up, I saw the light. Look at me, I thought. This is crazy. I resolved never to drink again . . .

At home.

So I resumed my love affair with bars. I went out every afternoon, some mornings, most of the nights. I did not wake up in another state again—just in a couple of hotels and at a truck stop on I-95 outside Baltimore.

Not surprisingly, we ran out of money in September. But rather than cut short my leave of absence and return to work, I quit my job. I knew that when I left the *Post,* I would receive the balance of my retirement savings plan. I often shudder over the what-might-have-beens had my boss, Foreign Editor David Ignatius, not talked me into reconsidering.

I resumed work the first of October, but had trouble on workdays coping with the fourteen-beer-a-day minimum habit I had developed. Intense cravings for alcohol were starting around 10 A.M. Most weeks, I called in sick at least one day—not because of hangovers—but because I couldn't fight the craving any longer and started drinking. I couldn't have one beer, I had to have fourteen, and if I drank before work, I wouldn't go in. I would not mix drinking and work. (I always feel the need to throw in that qualifier—my way of saying, "Well, I wasn't *that* bad. I didn't drink on the job.") One reason I did not drink and work was because I did not want to give myself away there. Most people I knew at work were not even aware that I drank. I stayed away from social events, and I tended not to drink at the few I attended. I would drink en route, and going home, but rarely in front of people I knew.

On December 9, I gave in to my cravings again. I started drinking in the morning. I was scheduled to work that afternoon, so I called in sick. But in the course of the phone call, I abruptly quit my job again.

That night, I hit bottom. For a person who woke up in Missouri with no idea of how he got there, my bottom was pretty tame. I stole a pack of cigarettes. The cigarette machine was all of twenty feet from the bar, and I had money, but I just didn't feel like walking over there. So I pocketed an open pack of Marlboros (not even my brand) next to me on the bar.

The next morning, I saw the cigarettes and remembered what I had done. I said to myself, "My God, what has happened to me?"

Smoking my stolen cigarettes, I figured it out, and admitted it. Later that morning, I called my immediate supervisor, Deputy Foreign Editor Virginia Hamill, and told her I was an alcoholic and needed help. She helped get me into the drug- and alcohol-abuse treatment center at Sheppard-Pratt psychiatric hospital in Baltimore.

That day was December 10, my great-grandmother's birthday, my Independence Day.

On December 15, filling out the admission forms, for the first time in my life on a document, I identified my ethnic background as Native American.

I WORRY THAT OSAGES who read this will be offended by an implicit affiliation of my alcoholism with them. It is not my intention to give the impression that now that I've acknowledged I'm an alcoholic, I have something in common with them. I do, but it's the common history of our ancestors and not my alcoholism.

Every Osage I met in Oklahoma, I wished I could be like. They were remarkable people—warm, open, kind, generous, loyal, committed, upfront, focused, forgiving, understanding, moral, religious, sober—all the things I haven't been but strive to be now.

They may not like to hear this coming from a drunk, but I now feel more like them than ever before—not because I learned I was an alcoholic, but because of what happened to me afterward.

I learned what it was like to suffer.

At first it was the sometimes knuckle-baring, fingernail-digging riding out of the cravings when I first stopped drinking at the start of treatment. I relapsed twice within a month. Because I had become so impulsive, I agreed to take Antabuse, the drug that makes you violently ill if you drink with it in your system.

I had a one-in-a-billion reaction to the drug. It affected me neurologically. I'd fall asleep at the wheel. By then, I had resumed work at the *Post*. One night on the way home, I dozed and ran off I-95. Another night, I misjudged the curve of the exit ramp on my turnoff from the Baltimore Beltway and ran over the traffic island. I had trouble concentrating. In speaking, I'd forget what I was saying by the time I got to the end of a sentence.

Finally, one night at work I forgot how to do my job. I couldn't remember even the rote aspects of it. When I got home, I had to ask Fleur how to turn off the light. I had forgotten how.

I stopped the Antabuse, and those problems vanished. But then, being for the first time in my life without any kind of crutch—the green bottle or the little white pill—the brave, new, nonalcoholic world I found myself in became a very scary place. I started having anxiety attacks. One mushroomed into a panic attack that imitated both a heart attack and a stroke. I thought I was dying. I couldn't move. I had to be lifted out of the car and wheeled into the hospital. I spent three days in one of the psychiatric wards of Sheppard-Pratt.

One of the main things that got me through all this was the knowledge I had acquired about the Osages, about my Indian heritage, about the suffering of my people and of my Osage family. Their pain was far greater than mine, and they endured and survived with dignity. I drew strength from that, and tried to do the same. I drew strength from my history.

And I drew strength from a craving that with time had replaced the one for alcohol—to go back and try again, fully aware of my very great limitations. I would not try to prove anything this time. I would only try to be accepted by them. Maybe that can happen, now that I've accepted myself.

I know all I'll ever want to know about how to be murdered as an Osage, about how to die as one. Now I'd like to learn how to live as one.

I want to dance in the In'-lon-ska. The dances are held yearly over separate weekends, usually in June, at the three Indian camps in Osage County. Osages come from all over America to take part in them. No pictures are permitted—the dances are sacred to the people. To quote something said in awe that I overheard while watching the dancers in Pawhuska: "Look at them, they're beautiful. They're absolutely transformed."

The dancers wear elaborate and richly colored Osage traditional clothing. The feature that stands out most prominently is the "roach" headgear of porcupine quills surrounding an eagle feather mounted on a spreader of elk horn. The men wear a breechcloth and wool broadcloth leggings, usually dark blue. A loose-fitting cotton shirt, variously colored and patterned, is tied at the waist with a heavy, beaded belt, as well as one of yarn. Attached at the neck and hanging down the back to the ground is a long strip of otter hide. The rest of the ensemble includes armbands, various ribbon and bead decorations, garters with streamers, a bandolier, a neckerchief secured with a slide, deerskin moccasins and bands of bells that hold the leggings below the knee.

Most of these items have been handed down to the dancers in their families. My family history has deprived me of that gift. I will have to buy them, or pay someone to make them. The complete Osage tribal uniform costs about $5,000. It takes a lot of money to be a poor Indian these days.

Anyone watching the television news on October 18, 1993, was fortunate to see some of the Osages, as well as glimpse their dignity and cleverness. That morning, 300 bison were released into the Tallgrass Prairie Preserve, 36,600 acres of ranchland swindled out of the Osages by my great-grandfather, Sewell Beekman. The land is now owned by the Nature Conservancy. The environmental group plans to allow the original prairie ecosystem to return to the preserve by reintroducing buffalo to it and periodically burning off the grass. The land has never been plowed, and hundreds of original plant species still grow on it. Five hundred different grasses and wildflowers so far have been identified on the preserve. The controlled burning—imitating lightning- or Indian-set fires that used to burn across the prairies in the dry season—frees new grasses and plants to grow, often springing up within days of a burn. Twenty-six thousand acres of the land were torched in the spring of 1993. Eventually, 1,800 buffalo will be set loose on the preserve.

The place is an ecologist's dream, but the Osages hated it—many even boycotted local merchants who supported the Nature Conservancy's purchase of a portion of the Chapman-Barnard Ranch in 1989. To the Osages, the preserve effectively took 36,600 acres of their land out of oil production. (The tribe still holds the rights to the oil underneath. In February 1925, Congress extended for another twenty years the soon-to-expire limit on the Osages' mineral rights, and eventually granted the Osages the rights in perpetuity.) Dozens of oil wells dot the preserve. Some of the tract covers the old Burbank oil field.

The Nature Conservancy, which used major contributions from oil companies to buy the land, has given a nod that it will allow the tribe to continue to drill on the preserve. So far, it has been "a good neighbor," as Osage Principal Chief Charles O. Tillman, Jr., put it. However, he and other tribal leaders doubt that good relations will last long if there is ever a major oil strike "out there in the middle of that pristine prairie," Tillman said.

On Opening Day—October 18—the Osages stole the Nature Conservancy's show by conducting a sunrise ceremony at the preserve's headquarters, about twenty miles north of Pawhuska. There, with an Indian blanket wrapped distinctively around his shoulders, was retired General H. Norman Schwarzkopf, bowing his head solemnly as Ed Red Eagle, Sr., head of the Eagle clan, made the Persian Gulf War hero an honorary member of the tribe and gave him the Osage name Tso-zho-ki-he-kah, Eagle Chief. "I shall carry my name with pride, not only in this life, but in lives to come," Schwarzkopf told gathered newspaper and television reporters.

The journalists almost forgot for the moment that they had gone there to cover buffalo, distracted as they were by the Osages' reminder of their presence. An indication of the Conservancy's sensitivity toward the original owners of its land came in remarks by project director Harvey Payne after the release of the buffalo: "No one ever dreamed we'd be able to . . . see what the settlers saw."

Why Schwarzkopf? The general sits on the Nature Conservancy's board of governors. General Eagle Chief's membership in the Osage tribe might come in handy one day.

I must confess that when I first heard about Schwarzkopf's naming, a bolt of jealousy shot through me. I greeted the news with a "Hrumpf." Schwarzkopf may be the most successful and best-known general since Eisenhower, but *I* was an Osage. I was not welcomed by the Osages with open arms. I was not welcomed at all, in fact.

But now that we are honorary blood brothers, I am obliged to say only nice things about Tso-zho-ki-he-kah. Claribel Shaw told us that Osages have to be careful what they say about anyone in the tribe because that person might be a relative. In explaining to my mother why Mrs. Woodward had been so standoffish during their two visits, Claribel also described how Osages initially treated me: "That's the Indian. Now, that's what we call the Indian Way. It's just characteristic. They push you off, and they leave you out there, and they check you out. That's what they do."

But gradually—through just plain persistence, I guess—I got a toe-hold in the tribe, and began to believe I was making progress in being accepted. That was what I found most puzzling about my unexpected trip to Missouri. That day had been my best yet with the Osages, and gave me cause for hope.

I had made friends with Billie Ponca, site attendant of the White Hair Memorial, and her assistant, Jake Waller, both Osages. The White Hair Memorial, named for Chief Pawhuska, is an Oklahoma Historical Society cultural center, and also has the added distinction of being the house where Ernest Burkhart lived when he got out of prison in the 1950s. An exquisite, small, white villa, it sits surrounded only by thick trees and a thicker stillness in an isolated corner of southern Osage County. The hours of conversations with Billie and Jake were the most enjoyable I spent during the whole time I was in Osage County, and I always looked forward to driving out there, ostensibly to look through microfilmed Osage Agency records, to continue our talks.

Billie had insisted that I attend Ed Red Eagle, Sr., Day on July 22. The day was declared to honor his years of service to the tribe, and the event took place on the Osage Agency campus. After speeches, there was an outdoor buffet lunch under the trees of a picnic area, then Indian dances. Beforehand, Billie had asked me if I had my powwow kit in the car. After a "Huh?" she gently explained that one should always be prepared for an Osage social event by keeping a lawn chair and spoons in your trunk. The lawn chairs are for the hours of sitting during these events; the spoons for eating. Osages do not eat with forks, at least at Indian events—only spoons. Billie promised that if I went to Ed Red Eagle, Sr., Day, she would bring for me an extra set of the required Osage gear.

I cannot describe the thrill and the warm sense of belonging I felt sitting in Billie Ponca's lawn chair and eating with a spoon. But those feelings were nothing compared to the pride that soared inside me whenever Billie introduced me to other Osages as an Osage. The key, she told me there, was to keep attending tribal events, being seen at them, and eventually—maybe a year or so—they'd accept me and warm up to me.

I felt there was finally hope that I might overcome the Osages' suspicion of my white appearance. There is still tremendous resentment over the tribal enrollment fraud. The first thing that at least a dozen Osages told me—quite nicely, of course—was that a lot of whites who call themselves Osages were placed on the tribal roll fraudulently. One said, "There are three kinds of Osages. Real Osages, Wannabe Osages and Ought-Not-to-Be Osages."

I worried sometimes what kind of Osage I was. Maybe their suspicions were correct. Maybe I was an Ought-Not-to-Be Osage. After all, A. T. Woodward was helping put together the roll, and my great-grandmother married him, and her father had the distinctly un-Osage name of William Conner. Maybe I was a fraud, too.

It took me a while to actually find the Osages. I was nearly correct in my mental quip that I'd come all the way out there and they had gone someplace else. Most have. Only about 3,000 Osages still live in Osage County, out of a total tribal population of about 15,000. That is why the In'-lon-ska has become so important for the cultural cohesion of the tribe. The "underground reservation" that has been the Osages' glue has been pumping out headrights worth only about $5,000 a year of late. Only one-third of the oil in Osage County has been produced; the rest is waiting for higher gas prices and cheaper technology to make it economically feasible to punch through a layer of granite to get at it. In the meantime, the oil is only trickling out of Osage wells.

But in the midst of these lean times, the Osages have discovered that blood is thicker than oil. Each year, the yearly dances attract more Osages. I met an older Osage from Montana or Wyoming who said he was dancing in his first In'-lon-ska in fifty years. Why did he come back? He didn't know, he couldn't enunciate it, but being there brought him happiness, a state I was not in when I talked to him. The Osage Tribal Museum and the White Hair Memorial have started Osage language classes. The White Hair Memorial has modernized the Indian tradition of elders orally passing along their knowledge of customs, language and traditions by videotaping just about everything that transpires in the tribe—the language classes, interviews with the elderly, tribal ceremonies and dances other than the In'-lon-ska. Jake Waller filmed the speeches, dances and audience at Ed Red Eagle, Sr., Day.

There's even hope for poor Pawhuska, whose economy may perk up from tourism brought by the prairie preserve. The tumbledown Triangle Building, I've heard, is being renovated and turned into an art school. It now has windows.

And things are not nearly as vicious or deadly in Osage County these days. Maybe there are fewer people; maybe there is some sort of genetic exhaustion that has been passed down to a new generation of Osage Countians. On the Richter scale of present-day Osage County crime—whose baseline is alcohol-related offenses—only occasionally is there a quake, such as the reported arrest of a Pawhuska man on charges of "attacking a Pawnee woman and attempting to choke her with battery jumper cables and breaking the windows out of her car." Not to anyone's surprise, he was also charged with public intoxication. While I was there, two issues of the *Journal-Capital* reported eight other arrests for public intoxication, as well as one for "transporting open container," presumably of alcohol, and one for fishing without a license.

In separate incidents that make me now shudder over driving those deserted, winding, hilly two-lane roads at night in the state I was in, two women were charged with nearly identical offenses: "transporting open container . . . failure to secure insurance verification . . . DUI . . . driving under suspension . . . driving left of center . . . operating defective vehicle . . . resisting arrest."

Their arrests make me think that perhaps Pawhuska gas stations should consider stopping their practice of selling beer.

Sometimes I wonder why I never got caught.

I REALIZE NOW THAT for all my desire to be an Indian and for all my belief that I really was one, what I actually did was ride into Pawhuska like the cavalry, ready to strike a blow for justice, to defend my grandmother's name, vindicate her death, prove she was murdered, find out who did it.

It was from that starting point that I began to grow into an Indian—and it was that feeling that I drank on, that I tried to drink away, because I *hated* it. And it's the same feeling—the Indian Feeling—I get today, sober, whenever I think back on Pawhuska and Sybil.

It is the frustration, disappointment, hurt, shame and anger of not being able to achieve what you want to, because the world constructed around you is alien to your instincts, runs contrary to your composition, has made you dysfunctional.

My own dysfunctionality—alcoholism—originates in the particular Indian gene I carry. It cannot tolerate alcohol. It triggers a disease that will kill me if I drink it. We did not have this disease before whites came.

Those of us who inherited the gene from our ancestors still are dying the way many of them did—at the hands of whites. The white world we live in now—so much of which revolves socially and personally around alcohol—is still killing Indians. It is a deadly place for those of us suffering from the disease of chemical addiction. Indian death rates from alcohol-related diseases are four times higher than the national average and three times higher from alcohol-related accidents. Fetal alcohol syndrome—the cause of birth defects, including physical and mental retardation, and the result of women's drinking during pregnancy—is thirty-three times higher in Indians than in whites.

The reason I first got the Indian Feeling of failure in Pawhuska was because I was unable to accomplish what I set out to do.

I failed.

I did not prove who killed my grandmother. I failed her, and my mother, and myself.

But it was not only because of my alcoholism. It was because they ripped out too many pages of our history. The white system devised to swindle and kill Indians was too efficiently constructed. They were just too good at killing us and burying the evidence. There were just too many lies, too many documents destroyed, too little done at the time to document how my grandmother died.

She did not get an autopsy because she did not have that right. It wasn't included in the Osage Allotment Act of 1906. She could become rich, if she dared. She could vote. She could be buried in a congressionally legislated cemetery. But she did not have the right to be dealt with decently in death.

She was just an Indian. There was no police or coroner's investigation, because to do so might implicate a white in her murder. Indians were not the people whom the authorities served.

American justice was not intended for Native Americans like Sybil Bolton.

And understanding that fact is how I finally knew that I really was an Indian, a "real" Indian. By depriving Sybil of the right to an autopsy because she was an Indian, the white authorities deprived her grandson of the right to know for the same reason—because I am an Indian.

A murdered Indian's survivors don't have the right to the satisfaction of justice for past crimes, or of even knowing who killed their children, their mothers or fathers, brothers or sisters, their grandparents.

They can only guess—like I was forced to.

Because I am an Indian.

My mother did not fail, however. She had nothing to prove except the truth of what she saw that day, November 7, 1925.

Kathleen McAuliffe was not entirely convinced about Sybil Bolton's murder. She wanted to believe that her mother had not shot herself in front of her, and ostensibly she did, talking often about Sybil's "murder," or "when she was killed." But every few weeks or so, "killed" was downgraded to "died," and soon "suicide" would slip back into her lexicon.

She was not entirely persuaded by my murder theory, either. Even I had my doubts at times. There were a few holes in it. For example, if Sybil was so frightened the day before her death that she called her father, from whom she was estranged, why didn't she just get in her car and leave?

I couldn't go to the Southwest regional archives at Fort Worth, where Sybil's guardian and probate files were stored. I couldn't go anywhere, or didn't want to. I did not trust myself to travel alone overnight. Hotels had bars, and as they say at AA, "an alcoholic alone is in bad company."

So my mother and father went for their own reasons. My father suspected Woodward, and had since the beginning, and wanted to see what was in his personnel file, also archived in Fort Worth. My mother wanted to find one clue, any clue, that would point firmly toward a cause of death.

What she found finally freed her of her fear.

Luckily for us, Sybil's bills in Pawhuska were not paid at the time of her death because she had monthly charge accounts with stores. As a result, her probate file contains numerous itemized bills that eventually were charged against her estate.

"Eleanor the maid," as she was identified by the Pawhuska newspaper and Theil Annett, was Elliner Williamson, who billed Sybil's estate $25 for "packing up household goods K.C."—Kansas City—in October 1925. Elliner also charged the estate $120 for "2 months cooking, washing and domestic work."

In October, when Sybil arrived in Pawhuska, she went to the Stork Nest clothing store and bought two handmade silk gowns, two handmade "teddies," two "boudoir caps," two pair of hose, three dresses—the most expensive being $17.50—and curiously, two "gents" handkerchiefs.

In seven days of November before she died, Sybil returned to the store and bought a hat, a fan, six pair of half socks, three "gertrudes," two pair of "Storkpants," one box of children's handkerchiefs, one doll, a purse, "garters—ostrich trim," perfume, a stuffed toy and a bonnet with lace trim.

On the day before she died, Sybil bought hose and teddies at Pickens Ladies Wear. From October 12 to the end of that month, she also purchased a coat, two hoods, four dresses, a hat, four pair of hose, six handkerchiefs and a purse. Of the dresses, the two most expensive—$74.50 and $69.50—she bought on October 29. The next day, eight days from her death, she bought another hat and a French dresser ornament.

Other outstanding debts were caused by bounced checks, written in the last days of her life. They were returned by her bank: a check for $22.25 for pressing and cleaning; $33.40 for drugstore purchases; $14.40 for the Cinderella Boot Shop.

Dr. Roscoe Walker charged her $8.60 for declaring her dead of suicide.

In addition to Mr. Johnson's bill of $1,742.25 for mortuary services, the Pawhuska Mausoleum Company charged $450 for her crypt, and $10 for the barely visible "lettering on marble shutter."

One bill answered a question I had: $93.05 to F. G. Button & Sons. It was a garage. Her car was in the shop when she died.

The absence of another bill also answered a question. There was no record for the pistol Theil said Sybil had purchased in Pawhuska. If she had bought a gun, the sale undoubtedly would have shown up in her probate records, since she appeared to be buying everything on credit, and since she obviously had no cash on hand, having written bad checks at the drugstore, laundry and shoe shop.

In the last week of her life, Sybil ordered Christmas cards.

She appears to have left Kansas City for Pawhuska on, or just after, October 10, 1925. On that day, she bought—on credit—pearls for $18 and a robe for $32.50 at Harzfeld's, a department store on Petticoat Lane in Kansas City. The day before, she charged a hat, a $177 coat, three bottles of perfume, a bag, a cigarette case, six handkerchiefs and a $65 dress. She also ordered a $1,200 mink coat that she never got to wear. It wasn't sent to her until November 28. The coat was returned by the administrator of her estate on January 28, 1926.

On October 22, Sybil talked to A. S. Sands, a Pawhuska lawyer, about divorcing Harry Bolton. It was a first visit, in which Sands gave Sybil "advice in property matters" should a "suit of Bolton vs. Bolton" be initiated. Sands charged Sybil a $250 retainer. He also traveled to Kansas City on her behalf to retain attorney John S. Bates to represent her there. Sands charged Sybil's account $22 for a round-trip train ticket, and $60 for Bates's retainer fee.

The County Court in Pawhuska, in its final order on April 7, 1927, decreed that Sybil's four-carat, platinum-mounted diamond ring—valued at $2,000—would be "the sole property of the minor child, Kathleen Sybil Bolton," that Harry would be sole owner of Sybil's Nash Roadster, valued at $300, and that Harry and Kathleen would share "in equal one-half parts each" Sybil's 657 acres of Osage County land and her Osage headright, number 933.

At Harry's request, the court appointed the Citizens Trust Company, which was the administrator of Sybil's estate, to be Kathleen's guardian.

The administrator disallowed—in a decision supported by the Osage Agency and the court—a $7,620 claim against Sybil's estate by Mr. and Mrs. A. T. Woodward because "the administrator is doubtful of the authenticity of the claim."

On April 5, 1926, Sybil's estate received a lease check for 280 acres of her land. It was from William K. Hale.

At the time of her death, there was about $24,000 in Sybil's Osage Agency account, "No. B-128," also referred to in the court papers as "her original trust fund held by the Secretary of the Interior." (Sybil's headright payments had been deposited in this account until Woodward became her guardian in August 1916.)

On November 14, 1925, two days after Sybil's funeral, Mrs. Woodward went to the Osage Agency and made out her first will. She left $100 to her granddaughter, Kathleen. Mrs. Woodward possessed one and nine-twentieths headrights: her own, one-quarter that she inherited from Nah-hah-sah-me, a full-blood woman, allottee number 436, and one-fifth inherited from her Aunt Maggie Lawrence. Mrs. Woodward left one-half of her estate to her daughter, Angela Gorman Andretta, and one-half to Mr. Woodward, on the condition that upon his death, he bequeath the headrights to Angela.

He did not. Kathleen Conner Woodward died on October 2, 1945, in Pawhuska of a heart attack brought on by shock at hearing that Woodward had overturned his car on the way home from work. A few months before Woodward's death in 1950, he remarried, and left his half of Mrs. Woodward's headrights to his white wife, Nora Ferguson.

I DIDN'T SEE IT AT FIRST.

What I saw was the picture of my grandmother I had been looking for all along.

In this one, she was smiling. She was finally happy. She was busy, shopping and buying dresses, frilly underwear, hats, a mink coat, lots of perfume.

In my picture, she was smiling at herself standing in front of a full-dress mirror, looking at herself wearing an ostrich-trim garter—one of those Roaring Twenties feather hats that hung down the side of a woman's face. You can't look at yourself in something like that and not smile.

A person so despondent that she shoots herself in front of her baby a few days later does not go out and buy Christmas cards. Sybil was looking to the future. She was making plans for it. And it was a happy time.

I also filled my brain with trying to read significance and suspicion into the leasing of Sybil's land by William K. Hale, and into Mrs. Woodward's first will, made two days after she buried her daughter.

Was she afraid of something?

And Elliner's two-month bill for $145—probably a year's salary for her—what did that mean?

But early one morning, at about three, I woke up with the answer.

I swung my legs over the side of the bed and, sitting there in the dark, simply asked myself, So what happened to the other $75,000 Sybil was supposed to have?

There was no roll of drums, no flash of recognition. I uttered no breathy "Oh my God." The clouds did not part, the sun did not come out. There was no sudden crescendo of music. The only soundtrack was the snoring of our Clumber spaniel, Nick.

Woodward stole it, I said to myself, feeling around with my feet for my slippers.

Nobody else could have.

And how did he get away with it?

He killed her. It was that simple. It was no more complicated than that.

Sybil found out that her money had vanished.

She found out, somehow, the day before. That's what she became so terrified about. She knew what happened to Osages when they discovered that their guardians had stolen all their money.

Did Woodward go to Pawhuska and do it himself?

No. He just called someone.

He called someone in Osage County and said he needed to "get shut of" Sybil. He needed to "bump" her, and make it look like suicide.

He had the perfect alibi.

He was in Arkansas.

And if Sybil were not declared a suicide, if her death were ruled a murder, Woodward could say exactly what I had been saying for more than two years now: Her killer—be it Hale or someone else—saw Woodward's name on the FBI subpoena list, and killed Sybil as a warning to Woodward to keep his mouth shut. And Hale and the others were still at large, thanks to the FBI's two-month delay in convening the federal grand jury.

Woodward knew he was going to get subpoenaed. The business he was attending to the week before at the Osage Agency was probably to discuss his testimony.

The FBI's investigation of the Reign of Terror, and its meticulous preparation for the federal grand jury, had enabled A. T. Woodward to commit the perfect murder.

THE OTHER THING we didn't see for several weeks after getting Sybil's probate papers. My sister Kathie was the one to figure it out.

Kathie has a ninety-year-old friend named Grace Henslee Massie. Kathie visits with her often, reads to her, talks about Sybil with her. Grace has become our 1920s fashion expert. Kathie called her for a translation of "garters—ostrich trim," for example.

A few weeks later, Kathie went over all of Sybil's bills with Grace, who was shocked at the prices, two or three times what they should have been.

Especially for the maternity clothes.

The "Storkpants" were the giveaway. They were stretch pants for pregnant women, like girdles, to keep from showing too much in those days of the straight, no-curve, no-breast, no-bulge, slim fashion look.

By the last week of her life, when she bought two pair of Storkpants, Sybil was beginning to show.

The Stork Nest, where Sybil did most of her shopping in Pawhuska, was a maternity clothing store.

My grandmother was pregnant.

No wonder my mother was told that in the last months of Sybil's life she was swollen and often ill.

No wonder Harry hated her so much.

To him, Sybil did more than kill herself. She killed his next child.

WE KNOW THE STORY but not when it happened. My mother had been told she arrived at the Beekmans in Oklahoma City when she was eighteen months old. That would have made it January 1926. But in Mrs. Woodward's will of November 14, 1925, Kathleen had been excluded, getting only $100, ten times less than Mrs. Woodward bequeathed to her maid, Elliner Williamson.

So maybe the baby was gone by then.

When Harry arrived in Pawhuska after Sybil's death, Elliner wouldn't let him in the house. He was locked out. The story my mother heard from her grandfather, J. N. Bolton, was that Harry jumped in the car and drove to Pawhuska as soon as he got the phone call about Sybil's suicide. But he couldn't get in the house. Elliner, under instructions from Woodward no doubt, had locked all the doors, and left Harry pacing on the lawn. That's probably why he knew the death took place on the pump cover. He saw the blood.

Woodward was trying to keep something from Harry: Sybil's body, and Sybil's baby.

Harry's sudden appearance at the house obviously presented a problem for Woodward. Harry was notified of the death immediately, but it was apparent he was not expected to have jumped in his car and arrived in Pawhuska that afternoon. Why should Harry care? He and Sybil were separated, and Sybil had even inquired about a divorce.

That Harry was locked out of the house, and left standing on the lawn near where his wife was gunned down, suggests that Sybil's body was inside. Pawhuska was a small town, and there was only one mortician. Perhaps Mr. Johnson had gone fishin', taken the day off—it was Saturday. Or maybe he was rendering his professional services elsewhere.

Until Mr. Johnson got to her, Woodward did not want Harry Bolton to see Sybil's body. Perhaps he had something to hide. Perhaps the bullet hole was in the wrong place for a suicide. Perhaps there was more than one wound.

Harry was Woodward's only worry.

Woodward did not worry about Mr. Johnson. Let him charge $1,742.25 for his services, silence included.

Sybil would pay for it.

Woodward did not worry about Elliner. Let her charge Sybil a year's salary.

Sybil had been known for her generosity.

And Woodward did not worry about his wife. Let Kate believe the truth: Sybil was murdered. The Reign of Terror had caught up with them. My God, Kate, he would tell her, it could have been you instead of Sybil—and you could be next. She would be convinced that her only hope to live would be to leave Sybil's death a suicide, to communicate to the killers that Woodward would cause them no trouble.

The killers could deny Sybil a place on earth, he would tell her, but not in heaven. Tell the priest the truth. Get Sybil a Catholic requiem mass.

No, Kate Woodward was not the problem. She would be too busy, in fact, to dwell on her loss; the new baby would see to that. The baby's father, though—he could be the problem.

After Harry had left, Mr. Johnson came to the house and moved the body to his funeral home. There, he prepared Sybil's remains for burial— rendering the outward appearance of her "body in perfect condition," making her "face perfect," as her funeral report states. He placed Sybil in a Pershing bronze casket.

Harry did not see Sybil's body until it lay, dressed in her ermine coat, in an open coffin during the requiem mass at the Pawhuska Catholic church.

Not allowing Harry into the house also prevented him from taking his daughter. The Woodwards did not want Harry near her. They kept her hidden from him—"kidnapping" is the term we use now.

The instant Sybil landed on the pump cover, her baby had her head-right, or so Woodward assumed. She was sixteen months old. That gave Woodward nineteen years and eight months to "manage" Kathleen's head-right, just as he had "managed" Sybil's.

And when Kathleen turned twenty-one, Woodward would worry then how to "manage" things when she found out he had stolen all her money—just as he "managed" things with Sybil.

He would cross that pump cover when he came to it.

JUST AFTER SYBIL'S DEATH, Harry Bolton called the one person he knew in Osage County outside of the Woodwards.

Harry needed help. He needed a lawyer, not only to attend to the probating of Sybil's estate but to help him get his daughter back.

For help, Harry Bolton called William K. Hale.

Part of Hale's 45,000-acre ranch was 280 acres that belonged to Sybil Bolton. Hale had been leasing the land from her—probably since she had acquired it at allotment in 1907. Unlike the Osages' oil money, which was disbursed by the Osage Agency, lease income was paid directly to the Osage landowners by the lessee.

Hale was a name Harry knew well. It was on the rent checks Sybil had received from Hale for as long as Harry had known her. Harry may even have met Hale and gotten to know him personally. Perhaps Hale had stopped by and said hello and chatted with the Boltons on trips to Kansas City. After all, Hale was a friendly, likable guy.

Sure, Hale told Harry, use my lawyers. They're good, and they're tough. Hale gave Harry their names: Grinstead, Scott, Hamilton and Gross.

E. E. Grinstead had already gained notoriety in Osage County and at FBI headquarters for being the lawyer Hale had used to sue the Denver insurance company to pay up on the Henry Roan policy. The other lawyers in the firm—especially Hale's personal attorney, W. S. Hamilton—would become notorious in the same places for representing Hale and, at times, Ernest Burkhart and John Ramsey through four trials lasting to 1929. They even took Hale's challenge to federal jurisdiction to the U.S. Supreme Court, and lost. For a while, the FBI considered slapping Hamilton with charges of harassing witnesses and conspiring to commit perjury and obstruct justice. Witnesses had said Hamilton had threatened them with his pistol. One of the lawyers was even said to have stuck a gun to a man's head and threatened to blow it off if he didn't change his testimony. Hale, Burkhart and Ramsey eventually got life sentences—and the Justice Department got the bill for the $160,000 that trying the Osage murder cases had cost.

There was some justice after all for the Osages.

While Grinstead, Hamilton, Scott and Gross were trying to spare William K. Hale, Ernest Burkhart and John Ramsey from the justice they deserved, they also were administering Sybil Bolton's estate.

On November 13, 1925, the day after Sybil's funeral, Harry walked into Osage County Court, accompanied by the lawyers. Harry asked that the Citizens Trust Company, headed by Grinstead, be appointed administrator of Sybil's estate, and stated for the record that Hamilton was his personal attorney. County Judge L. A. Justus, Jr., set a hearing for 9 A.M. on November 24.

But Harry was not about to wait that long to get justice for his daughter. As he would later recount to his father and to Kathleen, that afternoon he returned to his room at the Duncan Hotel—the only one in Pawhuska—where Sewell Beekman was waiting for him. They stayed in the room so they couldn't be spotted by anyone who knew them, while Tom Ward, a giant of a man who was Beekman's business partner, went to the hardware store on Kihekah. He bought some tools, which he stuck in his coat pocket, then a ladder, which he hoisted over his shoulders for the hike five blocks, straight uphill, to the Woodward house. He hid the ladder alongside the back of the garage in the alley behind the house.

As midnight approached, the three men left the hotel. The hour was upon them.

They took a taxi up the hill, and told the driver to park in the alley. Beekman stayed in the cab with the driver. Harry and Tom Ward strode grimly and quietly to the ladder, hoisted it and themselves over the back fence and crept across the back yard. They went around the side of the Woodward house and gently propped the ladder under a darkened window. A tree and bush blocked the view from the street and the neighboring house.

While Ward held the ladder, Harry climbed the rungs. The window was up, so he didn't need the tools Ward had bought to jar it open. Harry cut the screen, and disappeared into the room. He kept saying to himself, Please don't cry, please don't cry.

The baby was awake, standing in her crib, and greeted the sudden sight of her father with a smile and a squeal, burbling at him in delight.

Harry clapped his hand over her mouth swiftly and gently, swept her into his arms and dropped a note in her place in the crib.

"Now try and get her back," it said.

He wrapped Kathleen in a pink angora shawl. He turned toward the window and saw on the dresser her silver knife, fork and spoon set— engraved with her initials, K.S.B. He scooped them up, stuck them in his pocket and went out the window.

They left the ladder against the house. Across the back yard they ran. Ward jumped the fence first, then Harry handed the baby to him, and he ran to the taxi and gave her to her grandfather. They then raced to the train station, having timed her kidnapping to the arrival of the midnight train to Oklahoma City.

On the train, Kathleen laughed, chatted and played the whole trip, despite the late hour. Not an eyelid closed among the three exhausted men. Arthur, Beekman's chauffeur, was waiting at the train station, and drove them home, where Harry met Leila Beekman for the first time, and then presented her with her new step-granddaughter.

Sybil Bolton was dead, and her baby had begun her new life.

I've decided we're like those turtles crossing the road to Pawhuska.
We carry our homes with us. All these years I've been looking for a home, and it's been inside me. God knows, my home is not where my heart is, not that beat-up thing.

Rather, my home is my history, and now all of my history is in my son.

We're like those turtles. Some of us make it—sadly, only a few—the rest don't. Those of us who do are just the lucky survivors, nothing more. Just dumb luck.

I survived. God knows how, but I did. And we survivors get to cross the road, and we get to give our lives to someone else who will come upon that road again. Sadly we also pass along all the wounds and scars that we incurred getting there.

I pray that when that time comes for my son, he is not weighed down by the wounds that I carried, and I pray that he makes it across.

I pray that I haven't given him the wound that came closest to killing me.

But if I have, at least he will know about it—and long before his father learned. One of the biggest crimes of Sybil Bolton's death—her last one, the killing of her memory and the trace of her—is that by not knowing about her and her family, we did not know the dangers that lurked in their bloodlines. My son at least will know he should be more concerned about what he puts into his kidneys than what comes out of them.

He also will have the privilege of growing up in the splendid mansion his father has constructed since returning from Pawhuska. Indians are luckier than whites in one regard, at least. Indians live in larger houses.

Most white Americans live in only a one- or two-room house, one room for their parents, one for their grandparents, the limit of their knowledge about the generations of their family histories. The exceptional ones have a third room for their great-grandparents.

Indians, on the other hand, have a much longer reach into history. They have a firmer grasp of who they are and who they were. They are aware of the tragedy and suffering that went into making the life in them, and the lives they will pass on. They preserve that history inside them by honoring the memory of the people who gave it to them, by knowing who they were. And the more generations they know, the more rooms their houses hold.

That is why Kevin now lives in a mansion of rooms filled with his ancestors. It will never be empty. Surrounded by his ancestors, he will never be alone, never be in want of company or companions. And in the times of his crises, they will give him the strength that they now give his father.

There is a room for Chief Pawhuska, White Hair, my great-great-great-great-great-grandfather.

His eldest daughter, Marie Pa-hu-shan, married the tribe's interpreter, the French-Osage Noel Mongrain. They lived on the Kansas reservation. I found Mongrain's signature on the United States' peace treaty with the Osages after they sided with Britain in the War of 1812. The last trace of Noel Mongrain and Marie Pa-hu-shan I found was their baptismal record. In 1820, they became the first Osages to convert to Catholicism, having themselves and their nine children baptized. There is a room for them in my house.

One of their sons, Jean Baptiste Mongrain, became a principal chief of the Osages. A daughter, my great-great-great-grandmother Pelagie Mongrain, married a French Canadian, Antoine Penn, in 1842, and they share one of my rooms. Antoine Penn escorted the Jesuit priests of the Osage Mission in Kansas as they went about the Indian villages, baptizing thousands of Osages into Catholicism. Antoine Penn was the godfather in more than a hundred Osage baptisms. He died in 1853 after a measles epidemic broke out at the Osage Mission, where he was buried on April 19. He was about thirty. Their daughter, Angeline Penn, was seventeen months old at the time of her father's death.

She married William H. Conner, and my great-great-grandparents live in a very large room of my house. To me, he was the most special of my ancestors, the son of William Conner, probably a white Kansas trader, and Metier-hon, an Osage woman. Born on the Osage reservation in Kansas in January 1846, the Conner child became a student at the Jesuits' Osage Mission school; a founding father of the Osage Nation who coauthored its U.S.-style constitution in 1881; and a rich rancher. He also committed the last known scalping associated with a religious rite known as the Osage Mourning Dance. The practice stemmed from the belief that a deceased had to be ransomed into the Happy Hunting Ground with the scalp of an enemy. In 1873, Conner and another Osage scalped the chief of the Wichitas, an act that nearly sparked a Plains Indian war against the Osages. The U.S. government intervened, forcing the Osages to compensate the Wichitas for the scalping with $1,500 in ponies, cash, blankets and guns. An Osage Agency family register listed William Conner as deceased by 1901, but no date was given. I have seen three pictures of him, and in each he looks entirely different. In the first, he is a longhaired, wild-looking Indian; in the second, a cowboy with a mustache; in the last, he is fat and swollen. As anyone who has seen me at least three times can attest, I seem to have inherited William Conner's tendency to change my appearance often. I also carry his disease. Based on what seemed to be his erratic, unpredictable and extreme behavior, William Conner was an alcoholic, like his great-great-grandson. His wife, Angeline Penn, died during her daughter's infancy.

There are rooms in my house for their daughter, Kathleen Woodward, who lost her mother when she was just a baby, and for her daughter, Sybil Bolton, whose daughter lost her when she was just a baby. One day, sadly, there will be a room for her, Kathleen Sybil Bolton McAuliffe.

And one day I will pass into a room of what will become Kevin's house.

And that is why I've written this book. I'm sober today. But, as I've learned from AA, I know I have one more drunk left in me, but I'm not sure I have another recovery. I've relapsed twice writing this book. I want to make sure my son hears these stories. I want to make sure he knows who he is, and what he might become.

It was all for him anyway.

I was right about one thing I kept telling Fleur. It really didn't have anything to do with me.

On the day Fleur and Kevin arrived in Pawhuska, he was sixteen months old, the same age to the day that my mother was when Sybil died. The coincidence spooked me. We were staying in the apartment directly downhill from the house where Sybil was killed. The day they arrived also was the last day of my parents' visit.

During Kevin's afternoon nap, I went to buy milk. When I got in the car, I noticed a foot-long white streak down my dashboard, running over the glove compartment door. It was still wet. My windows were open about three inches. I figured that a bird had gotten into the car.

I drove to the Homeland supermarket. I was probably in there for twenty minutes before driving back. About an hour later, Kevin woke up, and we all headed out to go sightseeing. My mother started to climb into the back seat of the car when she shrieked.

There, sitting in Kevin's infant car seat, was a light gray baby bird.

It had been in the car the whole time, during my drive to the store and back, and for the hour afterward.

The bird hopped off the baby seat and hopped around the car seats until I was able to cup it in my hands. Gingerly I held it until I was outside the car. Then I opened my hands with a little push.

I see it now in slow motion, how it spread its wings and flapped away flying west. I watched it till it disappeared into the corner tree.

The streak is still on my dashboard. It won't wash off. Only a few months ago, I figured out what it meant.

She had wanted to see Kevin. My mother had come. I had.

Suffer the little children to come unto me.

My being there sealed what would follow—and how it would follow—because I was finally away from the controls of work that I had put on my drinking. I was now free to begin my rapid descent into alcoholism.

It was coming anyway. I did not become an alcoholic because I went to Pawhuska. I was born with the disease. In Pawhuska, it merely shifted into a higher gear.

And it was bound to happen eventually. If it had not happened the way it did—if the sudden rush of clues beginning July 2, 1991, had not lured me to Pawhuska—who knows how it might have turned out?

I was very lucky, and I'm very grateful. I did not kill anyone with my car. I did not kill myself with it. I did not end up in jail. I never got a DWI. I still have a wonderful, loving wife. I still have the same family and the same job.

If my fall to the bottom had happened any differently, I was a good risk to carry on my Osage family tradition of a child losing a parent in its infancy.

And that's why I've decided it was all for Kevin. She wanted him to grow up with a father, with both of his parents.

That bird was my grandmother. She's gone now. She's finally free.

SEPTEMBER 25, 1993. Yom Kippur, the Jewish Day of Atonement. Kevin and his Catholic father were going for a walk while his Jewish mother and brother were attending services at their synagogue.

Kevin, then two years and seven months old, was learning to talk, and was at that wonderful stage where he repeats the last word you say.

"Do you want to play with your toys?" I asked.

"Toys," he said.

And we played until he wanted to do something else.

"Do you want to watch a video?"

"Video," he said.

"Do you want to go for a walk?"

"Walk," he said.

At the corner, where the Indian mill is, he stopped and pointed in its direction.

"You want to go there?"

"There," he said.

I carried him down the hill to the lower ledge and held him as we looked down into the mill's mossy boulders set into the hillside. He squirmed and made a noise, pointing down.

"You want to throw rocks?"

"Rocks," he said.

I wouldn't let go of him, but backed up and grabbed a handful of red clay. He took about half the handful and threw the dirt over the edge. We watched it fall upon the rock floor of the Indian mill.

Ashes to ashes.

Kevin started taking the rest of the dirt from my hand, but stopped and said:

"Try."

A chill went up my spine.

I threw only some of the dirt into the mill. As it fell, I said something I had memorized in Osage:

"Osh-kun-pe-she-o-lah-hah-wah-she-a-be-ne-gon."

Forgive us our trespasses.

And I threw the rest of the dirt.

"Osh-kun-pe-she-lo-tse-don; wah-ge-gla-sha-be."

As we forgive those who trespassed against us.

I backed away from the ledge and put Kevin down.

"Let's go home," I said.

And this precious great-grandson of Sybil Bolton took my outstretched finger and said:

"Home."

I was home. I'd come home.

T his book was written in spite of myself. If my will had had its way, this never would have made the transition from future to past tense. You are holding tangible proof that miracles really do happen.

I take no credit for this book, and I am very uncomfortable attempting to do so. This is no boast of humility—I say it honestly. You have to believe in something; what I believe is that I merely provided the time and fingers on the keyboard, and others did the rest. Some of those others include people—my family, my friends and my colleagues whose encouragement, enthusiasm, example and an unreal faith in me would not let me fail. I hope I haven't let them down.

These acknowledgments—an extended thank-you note—are a small and imperfect measure of my appreciation.

To my family: Fleur, Adam and Kevin; my mother and father; my sisters Carolyn and Kathie. My wife is probably the only person in the history of the world to become jealous of her deceased grandmother-in-law, but I could not have made any part of this trip—the physical and especially the mental—without Fleur. I used to boast that at one time in the 1970s, my parents, sisters and I all lived on different continents; now I'm just happy we're so close. One last word about my mother: I hope that all the future generations of her children will inherit and live by her joy and her incredible strength.

To Paul Golob, my editor at Times Books. He has been right up there with family these past two years. If I had to choose only one reason this book exists, it is Paul Golob. His name, as much as mine, belongs on the cover; some of the best lines in the book I shamelessly stole from him (I'll acknowledge that but won't say which ones); and his editing services included pushing this vehicle across the finish line when its driver ran out of gas. To every happiness (finishing this book) there is a sadness. Fleur and I were talking about what I would do with the rest of my life now that the book was finished. She suddenly looked at me with the shock of realization, and a mix of disappointment and alarm, and said, "You mean, Paul isn't going to call anymore?" I hope that's not so.

To my friends: Charles and Laura Johnson of Smith Mills, Kentucky; Marc and Debbie Attman of Pikesville, Maryland; Jake Waller and Billie Ponca of Osage County, Oklahoma. Charles has always opened his heart and his home to me. (I'd return the favor, but he hates coming to Washington.) He provided sanctuary for me several times during my "project," and it was at Charles and Laura's wedding in March 1993 that I decided to have another go at this. (My first attempt ended up, deservedly, in the trash can.) Debbie and Marc kindly offered me the use of their basement when my home housed too many distractions from writing, and some of the early material in the book was written there. As was the case when I was in Pawhuska, I still enjoy what has amounted to hours of conversation with Jake and Billie, as my telephone bill attests. They read the manuscript and offered suggestions, which I hope I heeded to their satisfaction. I look forward to the day when I can see them again.

To Michael Getler, Jackson Diehl, David Ignatius and Virginia Hamill, my various current or former bosses at *The Washington Post,* whose compassion saved my job—and all the other things, such as my life, that go with it. To my colleagues, current and former—friends all—on *The Washington Post* Foreign Desk: fellow editors Edward Cody, Gene

Bachinski, Lew Diuguid, Emily Gold, Richard Homan, Al Horne, Andy Mosher, Don Podesta, Tod Robberson, James Rupert, John Sharkey, Dita Smith and Valerie Strauss, as well as Peter Harris, Yasmine Bahrani, Jana Long and Alice Crites. All helped me in some way, whether by working for me when I was racing, with all the speed of evolution, to finish the book (only a year late), or by providing an elusive word or phrase and sometimes something even more elusive: understanding, distance when I needed it or the nearness of hearing range when I needed that.

And to others: In Pawhuska, librarians Edna C. Conley, Alison Yvonne Rose and JoAnn C. Hunt; Carol Maupin of the Inn at Woodyard Farms for her kindness and generosity to my parents during their stay there; Ron and Judy Coday, who went out of their way to make sure my family and I were comfortable in the apartment I rented from them; Crayton and Harry Bolton, who introduced me to the agonies and ecstasies (though I experienced none of the latter) of Indian bingo; Ed Red Eagle, Sr., for his consideration and example; and Louis F. Burns, whose genealogical research made it possible for me to discover my ancestors, a finding that has changed my life. In New York, to my agent Rollene W. Saal, whose early efforts made the rest of the story possible; and, finally, to Times Books's patient staff (writers such as me being their patients), who did a lot of finger-drumming on their desks waiting for this book and actually made me believe it was worth the wait: especially to publisher Peter Osnos, publicist Malka Margolies and copy chief Nancy Inglis and her copyediting staff, who saved me from a few gushers of embarrassment. I know what a thankless job they had, since I worked once as a copy editor at the *Post,* where, in a men's room in a corner of the newsroom, there are three urinals in a row, successively labeled "Chiefs," "Indians" and "Copy Editors." I now proudly use the middle one.

To all of you, those named and many unnamed, either by necessity or negligence, thank you.

All interviews were conducted by the author, unless otherwise noted.

PAGE

Epigraph   **"They plucked our fruit"**: Quoted by Don Podesta and Douglas Farah, "Latin American Indians Survive Their 'Discovery,' " *The Washington Post,* October 10, 1992.

CHAPTER ONE

10   **playing savage:** This depiction of Osage-French relations, I discovered, was news to the Osages; other accounts of an ill-fated Osage visit to France in 1827 involve more swindling than sex. John Joseph Mathews offers a more conventional description of the journey in *The Osages, Children of the Middle Waters* (Norman, Okla: University of Oklahoma Press, 1961), 539–547: The trip was arranged and led by a con man, David Delauney, who visited the Osages' Kansas reservation wearing a U.S. Army uniform and persuaded a dozen Osages to join an "official" delegation to France. Six wised up and dropped out before getting on the boat in New Orleans; the other six—four men and two women—arrived in Le Havre, France, on July 27, 1827, to great fanfare. Crowds mobbed them in Paris. The Osages were introduced at the court and met King Charles X. They were entertained nightly at the theater and opera, and toured French cities, as well as Amsterdam, Dresden, Frankfurt and Berlin. One of the Osages, Big Soldier, later boasted that he had gotten "married" many times on these visits (page 545)—apparently the basis for the version I read. Unbeknownst to the Osages, Delauney was charging their admirers for the opportunity to see these "Missourian Majesties" (page 541), as they were billed. Eventually interest in them disappeared, as did Delauney. In January 1829, a French newspaper reported from Munich that "these unfortunates who are without

friends, without a country, abandoned in a land they do not know, isolated by the language and their habits . . . find themselves in the greatest destitution, suffering from hunger . . . in civilized Europe" (page 546). The bishop of the French city of Montauban, M. Du Bourg, led a charity drive to save the Osages, and even Lafayette raised money for their return home. They were finally put on a boat for Norfolk, Virginia, in April 1830. Two died of smallpox en route. Today, the Osage tribe and the city of Montauban host biannual cultural exchanges to commemorate the Osages' rescue from one of the first major swindles of them.

13 **Harry Ben Bolton:** I note here that my grandfather, Harry Bolton, is not related to Crayton Bolton or her son, Harry Bolton, two Osages well known among the tribe and in Osage County.

17 **"centennial book on Alta Vista":** *Centennial, Alta Vista: 1887–1987, 100 Years* (published by the Centennial Book Committee, Alta Vista, Kan., 1987).
"YOUR STORE": Ibid., 48.
Topeka, Kansas, newspaper: *The Topeka Capital Journal.* Date of article not available.

CHAPTER TWO

37 **book on the Osages:** Mathews, *The Osages, Children of the Middle Waters.*
"blue highways": William Least Heat-Moon, *Blue Highways: A Journey Into America* (Boston: Houghton Mifflin, 1982).

CHAPTER THREE

38 **Over a seventeen-year period:** Figures from *1907–1957: Osage Indians Semi-Centennial Celebration* program (published by Osage Tribal Council, Pawhuska, Okla., 1957), no page numbers in book.

39 **"finest looking Indians":** Washington Irving, *A Tour on the Prairies,* quoted in Mathews, *The Osages, Children of the Middle Waters,* 585.
"most gigantic men": Thomas Jefferson, quoted in Louis F. Burns, *A History of the Osage People* (Fallbrook, Calif.: Ciga Press, 1989), 208.
"tallest race of men": George Catlin, quoted in Alice Marriott, *Osage Indi-*

ans II: Osage Research Report and Bibliography of Basic Research Reference (New York: Garland Publishing, 1974), 79, 81.

Osage names: Mathews, *The Osages, Children of the Middle Waters,* 138–140; "Kansas" translated on 87; "Padoucas" on 126; "Neosho" and "Verdigris" on 181.

40   **They got their name:** Ibid., 106–108.

40 percent of Indian trade: Gilbert C. Din and Abraham P. Nasatir, *The Imperial Osages: Spanish-Indian Diplomacy in the Mississippi Valley* (Norman, Okla.: University of Oklahoma Press, 1983), 96, 298. Trade goods listed in Marriott, *Osage Indians II,* 157–158; St. Louis founding, Ibid., 154–155; see also Burns, *A History of the Osage People,* 168–169, on the role of St. Louis and Osage trade percentages.

41   **Heads on stakes:** Ibid., 66.

"Those barbarians": Din and Nasatir, *The Imperial Osages,* 78.

"put on a spit": account of boy being forced to travel with his father's head, and **"those abominable dances":** Ibid., 102.

"pernicious . . . perverse": All quoted in Din and Nasatir, *The Imperial Osages,* 83, 82, 76, respectively.

"It is a treacherous": Marriott, *Osage Indians II,* 149.

"There remains for us": Din and Nasatir, *The Imperial Osages,* 77.

Osages gained territory: Marriott, *Osage Indians II,* 227–235.

Chickasaw chief quotes: Din and Nasatir, *The Imperial Osages,* 235–236.

du Tisné encounter: Ibid., 35–36; Mathews, *The Osages, Children of the Middle Waters,* 178–183.

42   shooting at George Washington: Ibid., 222–227.

Pierce-Arrows: Terry P. Wilson, *The Underground Reservation: Osage Oil* (Lincoln, Neb.: University of Nebraska Press, 1985), 129.

limousines often bore: Estelle Aubrey Brown, "Our Plutocratic Osage Indians," *Travel,* October 1922, 22.

Description of clothes: William G. Shepherd, "Lo, the Rich Indian!," *Harper's Monthly Magazine,* November 1920, 726.

"It has been stated": Brown, *Travel,* 34.

43   Whizbang: Photo in Kenny A. Franks, *The Osage Oil Boom* (Oklahoma City: Oklahoma Heritage Association, 1989), 61; **"whizzed all day":** quoted in Michael Wallis, *Oil Man: The Story of Frank Phillips and the Birth of Phillips Petroleum* (New York: Doubleday, 1988), 186.

twenty-eight boomtowns: Listed in Franks, *The Osage Oil Boom,* 87.

45,000 roustabouts: Wallis, *Oil Man,* 186.

Shidler: Ibid.

Million-dollar bids: From plaque titled "Oil in the Osage Indian Nation and the 'Million Dollar Elm,' " by the Oklahoma Historical Society with the Oklahoma Petroleum Council, 1970, located at Osage Agency campus, Pawhuska, Okla.

Frank Phillips, other names: From Wallis, *Oil Man.*

"Olympian indifference": Phrase from *Sundown,* a 1934 novel by John Joseph Mathews, quoted in Wilson, *The Underground Reservation,* 132; grocery bills: Brown, *Travel,* 22; price of steak: Wallis, *Oil Man,* 150.

$100 a week to feed his dogs: C. B. Glasscock, *Then Came Oil: The Story of the Last Frontier* (Indianapolis: Bobbs-Merrill, 1938), 275.

lunch money: Brown, *Travel,* 22.

Shopping spree: W. David Baird, *The Osage People* (Phoenix, Ariz.: Indian Tribal Series, 1972), 74; also in Wallis, *Oil Man,* 150.

44   **"small, dreary one-horse town":** "The 'Black Curse' of the Osages," *The Literary Digest,* April 3, 1926, 44.

"this joke": Shepherd, *Harper's,* 726; **"queer turn of fate":** Elmer T. Peterson, "The Miracle of Oil: Chapters on the Human Consequences of the 'Gusher'—I. The Indian," *Independent,* April 26, 1924, 234; **"the richest nation":** Ibid.

Osage population figures: Burns, *A History of the Osage People,* 325. Population for **"last days in Kansas"** from Bureau of Indian Affairs, *Annual Report of the Commissioner of Indian Affairs for the Year 1871* (Washington, D.C.: Government Printing Office, 1871), 483.

"all them other Indians": Principal Chief Sylvester J. Tinker, quoted in William J. Broad, "Despite Feds, a Tribe Keeps Its Oil Flowing," *The Washington Post,* June 8, 1980.

45   Cherokees' generosity: Francis Paul Prucha, *The Great Father: The United States Government and the American Indians (Abridged Edition)* (Lincoln, Neb.: University of Nebraska Press, 1984, 1986), 140–143.

"communism": Quoted in D. S. Otis, *The Dawes Act and the Allotment of Indian Lands* (Norman, Okla.: University of Oklahoma Press, 1973), 11; **"savagism":** Quoted in Ibid., x.

"Common property": Commissioner of Indian Affairs T. Hartley Crawford, quoted in Ibid.

"What shall be": Unidentified member of Congress, quoted in Ibid., 17.

46   **"Indian Emancipation Act":** Quoted in Ibid., x.

More than 50,000: Glenn Shirley, *West of Hell's Fringe: Crime, Criminals, and the Federal Peace Officer in Oklahoma Territory, 1889–1907* (Norman,

Okla.: University of Oklahoma Press, 1978), 6–10. Estimates of the number of settlers who made the "run" go as high as 60,000.

Oklahoma statehood: Wallis, *Oil Man*, 97. "The stage had been set to create the forty-sixth state when the work of the Dawes Commission was completed and the small tribes in the northeastern part of the territory divided their land and accepted the white man's system of land tenure. The federal government was finally convinced that Indian Territory was ready for statehood." See also Prucha, *The Great Father*, 256–262, for details about the creation and expansion of Oklahoma Territory; the forcing of allotment on the Five Civilized Tribes; the Five Civilized Tribes' unsuccessful movement—blocked by Congress—for separate statehood for Indian Territory, to have been called the state of Sequoyah; and the union of the two territories and proclamation of statehood for Oklahoma.

"horrible": Charles Joseph Latrobe quoted in Din and Nasatir, *The Imperial Osages*, 7.

48   **payment window:** Mathews, *The Osages, Children of the Middle Waters*, 777.

CHAPTER FOUR

64   **a favorite vacation spot:** Wilson, *The Underground Reservation*, 130: "Colorado Springs, Colorado, drew the Osages in the summer, and San Antonio, Texas, was a preferred winter retreat."

CHAPTER FIVE

82   **Mathews had been too pained:** Wilson, *The Underground Reservation*, x.
another book: Terry P. Wilson, *The Osage* (New York: Chelsea House, 1988). According to *Books in Print 1993–94*, *The Osage* is written for "5th graders and up."
"local lawyers": Wilson, *The Osage*, 77.
"Osage Reign of Terror": Ibid., 77; other information and quotes in paragraph appear on 78.

84   **His other book:** Wilson, *The Underground Reservation.*

85   **1990 census** and rise in Indian population: Figures, percentages and quotes from Ben Winton, *Phoenix Gazette*, reprinted in "Indian tribes watch out for Princess Wanna-bes," *The Baltimore Sun*, November 22, 1992.

"If you let": Wilson, *The Osage,* 91.

86   "FBI agents began": Wilson, *The Underground Reservation,* 146.

Oklahoma's seventy-seven counties: Figures, including population, from *The World Almanac and Book of Facts 1993* (New York: World Almanac, 1992), 441.

87   burned the letter: Burns, *A History of the Osage People,* 207.

"an inhuman practice": Thomas Jefferson, *Notes on the State of Virginia,* William Peden, ed. (New York: W. W. Norton, 1982), 61. First published in 1787.

"equal to the white man": Jefferson, quoted in *The Jeffersonian Cyclopedia: A Comprehensive Collection of the Views of Thomas Jefferson,* John P. Foley, ed. (New York: Funk & Wagnalls, 1900), 422.

88   small penises: Jefferson, *Notes on the State of Virginia.* De Buffon's theory is quoted on pages 58–59, including his assertion that "the savage . . . has small organs of generation"; Jefferson's refutation is on pages 59–65; "seen some thousands myself" and "masculine": Quoted in *The Jeffersonian Cyclopedia,* 422; "neither more defective": *Notes on the State of Virginia,* 59.

"multiply less than": Ibid., 61.

"Indian women": Ibid.

"a useless, expensive": *The Jeffersonian Cyclopedia,* 420.

"for us to procure": Ibid., 421.

"will perceive how useless": Ibid., 423.

"we shall push": Ibid.

89   owned black slaves: Prucha, *The Great Father,* 141. After the Civil War, the United States forced the tribes that had sided with the Confederacy to sign treaties committing them to abolish the practice of slavery, free their black slaves and incorporate them into their nations "on an equal footing with the original members." The tribes were especially "hesitant" on this last point, Prucha said.

the men had learned: *The Jeffersonian Cyclopedia,* 421; "the women to spin": Ibid.

"To read *Aesop's Fables*": Ibid.

resettle them west: Din and Nasatir, *The Imperial Osages,* 358; Burns, *A History of the Osage People,* 203, 245–246; quoting Marriott, *Osage Indians II,* 192: When Jefferson looked at a map west of the Mississippi, he saw "a dumping ground for eastern Indians."

"It is essential": *The Jeffersonian Cyclopedia,* 420. Jefferson also hoped to remove Indians on the cheap; quoting Marriott, *Osage Indians II,* 193: The voluntary removal policy required "the Indians . . . to take the initiative, bear the expense, and make the effort of transferring their own people."

"The truth is": Jefferson, quoted in Burns, *A History of the Osage People,* 208–209.

"our country and towns": Jefferson's speech to White Hair and the Osage delegation, quoted in *The Complete Jefferson,* Saul K. Padover, ed. (New York: Duell, Sloan & Pearce, 1943), 466–468. **Show of force:** Interpretation from Din and Nasatir, *The Imperial Osages,* 369.

90   **St. Clair's Defeat:** Details from *The Encyclopedia Americana, International Edition* (Danbury, Conn.: Grolier, 1990), Vol. 24, 104; *The New Encyclopaedia Britannica, 15th Edition* (Chicago: Encyclopaedia Britannica, 1993), Vol. 10, Micropaedia, 313; and Burns, *A History of the Osage People,* 257.

One of the casualties: W. W. Graves, *History of Neosho County* (St. Paul, Kan.: Journal Press, 1949; reprint, Osage Mission Historical Society, St. Paul, Kansas, 1986), 5, citing Timothy Flint, *Recollections of the Last Ten Years in the Mississippi Valley,* Boston, 1826. A popular variation of the scalping story can be found in Burns, *A History of the Osage People,* 110, and others: White Hair killed the soldier and merely lifted his wig. But this version lacks the detail of the soldier resuscitating and running away, and thus ignores the special powers that White Hair attached to the wig. Burns also cites one Osage authority, Francis La Flesche (in *Dictionary of the Osage Language,* Bureau of American Ethnology, Bulletin No. 109, Washington, D.C., 1932), dismissing the wig story altogether and insisting that White Hair's name was merely a traditional appellation alluding to the sacred white buffalo. Burns says he believes "both stories are true because it suited White Hair's purposes to take a valor name that was also a traditional name."

91   White Hair's burial with Bible: Mathews, *The Osages, Children of the Middle Waters,* 539. The New York Missionary Society presented White Hair the Bible, which, like his wig, "he cherished . . . as a fetish" (page 582); Jefferson's gifts to White Hair: Ibid., 357.

"I felt a fire": Graves, *History of Neosho County,* 5 (White Hair quoted by Flint, *Recollections of the Last Ten Years in the Mississippi Valley*).

survivors repatriated east: Burns, *A History of the Osage People,* 203, 245–246.

Jefferson realized: Din and Nasatir, *The Imperial Osages,* 372–373; Marriott, *Osage Indians II,* 192, quotes historian Grant Foreman: "The presence of the eastern Indians drove the game farther to the west. . . . Holding that the Cherokee had driven away the game which was their staff of life, it is small wonder that the Osage ravaged the herds of the civilized Indians with a feeling of honest reprisal. The Osage became a scourge to all the tribes in the southwest [and] a serious menace to the plans of the Government to remove the civilized and other eastern Indians to the west of the Mississippi."

"Nation of Bad Indians": U.S. Indian agent Dr. John Sibley, quoted by Mathews, *The Osages, Children of the Middle Waters,* 343.

"grass grows and the waters flow": Burns, *A History of the Osage People,* 235, 222. This was a standard clause in many of the more than four hundred treaties that Americans subjected on Indian Nations between 1778 and 1871.

The U.S.-Osage treaty of 1808: Details from Din and Nasatir, *The Imperial Osages,* 375–382; details on Mongrain and Chouteau as interpreters: Burns, *A History of the Osage People,* 225–228.

92   **"Having briefly explained":** George C. Sibley, quoted by Laurence F. Schmeckebier, *The Office of Indian Affairs: Its History, Activities and Organization* (New York: AMS Press, 1972; reprint, Baltimore: Johns Hopkins Press, 1927), 60. A Brookings Institution study.

They thumb-marked: Treaty compensation and Osages' rejection from Din and Nasatir, *The Imperial Osages,* 378.

93   **In this treaty:** Details from *1907–1957: Osage Indians Semi-Centennial Celebration* program.

British flags: Baird, *The Osage People,* 30.

Battle of Claremore's Mound, and treaty terms: Ibid., 32–33, and from *1907–1957: Osage Indians Semi-Centennial Celebration* program. Treaty signing was in September 1818.

94   **The government immediately sold:** Ibid.

refused to return: Baird, *The Osage People,* 34.

1825 treaty terms: *1907–1957: Osage Indians Semi-Centennial Celebration* program.

95   **"This tribe of Indians":** *Annual Report of the Commissioner of Indian Affairs for the Year 1971,* 487–488. Isaac T. Gibson's report, dated "Tenthmonth" 1, 1870.

"It is almost without precedent": Emphasis added.

97   **"First witnesses heard":** *The New York Times Index, January–February–March 1926,* Vol. XIV, No. 1, 306.

"the Osage murder mystery": Associated Press, "Arrests Awaited in Osage Deaths," *Evening Star* (Washington, D.C.), January 4, 1926.

"the United States Government's": Associated Press, "Murder of Osages Startles Probers," *Evening Star* (Washington, D.C.), January 9, 1926.

"a definite effort": Associated Press, "140 Subpoenaed in Osage Murders," *Evening Star* (Washington, D.C.), January 2, 1926.
"months": Wilson, *The Underground Reservation,* 146.

CHAPTER SIX

101 "It took Father Schoenmakers": Quoted by Wilson, *The Osage,* 52.
my favorite gory detail: Evan S. Connell, *Son of the Morning Star* (San Francisco: North Point Press, 1984), 4.
Dates of Custer's and Sheridan's residence in the Old Sutler's House are from the Fort Leavenworth Public Affairs Office.

102 **Mrs. Sheridan was supposed to have died, and the rumor of her ghostly presence:** I hate it when facts get in the way of a good story. Irene Rucker Sheridan did not die in the house; in fact, according to Roy Morris, Jr., in *Sheridan: The Life and Wars of General Phil Sheridan* (New York: Vintage Civil War Library, 1992), 391, Mrs. Sheridan was at General Sheridan's bedside when he died in Chicago of a heart attack on August 5, 1888. Sheridan was still a bachelor when he lived at Fort Leavenworth—which accounts for a much-publicized photograph of him and his horse in the living room of the Old Sutler's House. He married only once, and late in life—on June 3, 1875. I decided to tell the Mrs. Sheridan "ghost story," despite its obvious flaws, because one, I like it, and two, that's the way I heard it from my mother, who heard it from the previous occupant of the house and told it to the new residents who moved in when my parents left the house and Fort Leavenworth in 1974. For all I know, the current occupant still thinks it's Mrs. Sheridan who's slamming the doors, rocking the chairs and petrifying the pets in the house. Someone, or something, is—it's just not Mrs. Sheridan. According to the Fort Leavenworth Public Affairs Office, the Old Sutler's House is included on an Army list of several suspected haunted houses on the base.
"the Indians' commissary": General Sheridan, quoted by Ian Frazier, *Great Plains* (New York: Penguin Books, 1989), 112; "Let them kill": Ibid.
"the last really good time": Ibid., 180.
My Life on the Plains: General George A. Custer, *My Life on the Plains,* ed. Milo Milton Quaife (Lincoln, Neb.: University of Nebraska Press, 1966; reprint, Chicago: Lakeside Press, 1952). According to Quaife's introduction, the book was published in 1874—an 1891 edition came out under the

title *Wild Life on the Plains and the Horrors of Indian Warfare*—and was a compilation of twenty articles that Custer wrote for *Galaxy* magazine.

103 **"reduced in power":** All quotes in this paragraph are from Ibid., 271–272.

"seemed to glide": All quotes in the remainder of the Custer section are from Ibid., 313–368.

108 Cheyennes' death toll: Burns, *A History of the Osage People,* 368; **a "few" children:** quoted in Ibid; **875 Cheyenne horses:** Custer watched this carnage—and the carcasses mount—without batting an eye, which would later fill with tears when he came across the remains of his dead dog, Blucher. Custer had brought Blucher along for the fun, but the disloyal dog "dashed from the village and joined the Indians, who no sooner saw him than they shot him through with an arrow" (Custer, *My Life on the Plains,* 367).

"some of these Osages": Quoted in Burns, *A History of the Osage People,* 368, from what he calls a "citation" in the "Kansas Historical Collections." The quoted document says these Osage scouts "were killed" at the Little Big Horn battle, but Burns, also in Ibid., cites what he calls a tribal "rumor" that an Osage and a Delaware Indian, sensing the danger they were in, slipped away from Custer's ranks just before the Sioux attacked and eluded the hostile Indians by keeping their blankets over their heads. The November 1993 issue of *Inside Osage,* a monthly newspaper, featured a photograph of Toby Mongrain, a full-blood Osage, identifying him as one of Custer's scouts. Mongrain probably was the English-speaking Osage quoted in *My Life on the Plains*—his ancestor was Noel Mongrain, the Osages' tribal interpreter.

The battle that saved Custer's career: Initially it nearly ruined his career. Custer began writing the twenty magazine articles that became his autobiography to put his spin on a major scandal—"the most serious blot upon Custer's entire career" (quoting editor Quaife's introduction, xxxiii)—that erupted from the Battle of the Washita. After the initial attack, Indians from other villages surrounded Custer. In his rush to retreat, Custer abandoned twenty missing members of one of his four detachments, including its commander, Major Joel Elliot. Custer had "given [them] up as killed" (Custer, 370), but he made "no effort," in the words of General Sheridan, to determine their fate (Quaife, xxxiv, quoting Sheridan's *Personal Memoirs*).

"The only good Indians": The story is probably more legend than fact, and General Sheridan vehemently denied ever saying it, or anything resembling it. His biographer, Morris, said the phrasing of the sentence sounded like something Sheridan might say, however. Information for my version of the story comes from the footnotes accompanying the quote in Bartlett's *Familiar Quotations, 16th Edition* (Boston: Little, Brown, 1992), 516. The reporter was identified as Edward Sylvester Ellis. Another version appears in Connell, *Son of the Morning Star,* 179–180; in this one, Tosawi, or Silver Brooch, a Penateka-Comanche chief, was the "good Indian" who triggered Sheridan's retort.

110 **Mrs. Wilder's unwitting association:** Facts about Laura Ingalls Wilder's life and books are from William Anderson, *Laura Ingalls Wilder: Pioneer and Author* (New York: Kipling Press, 1987).

111 **"positive representations":** Ibid., 45.
Railroads passed the good news: Frazier, *Great Plains,* 71–72.
Oh, come to this country: Lyrics from Anderson, *Laura Ingalls Wilder,* 2.
"dirty-faced children": Mathews, *Wah'Kon-Tah: The Osage and the White Man's Road* (Norman, Okla.: University of Oklahoma Press, 1932), 288.

112 Encounter with the Osage: Laura Ingalls Wilder, *Little House on the Prairie* (New York: Harper Trophy, 1935; revised edition, 1953), 227–229.
General Sheridan's racist remark: Ibid., 211. Mrs. Wilder doesn't even bother to put the offending sentence in quotes.

113 **Descriptive adjectives** and other offensive remarks: For examples, see Ibid., 134, 137–140, 142–143, 211–212, 226–227, 229, 233–234. HarperCollins, the corporate parent of Harper Trophy, denied permission to quote directly from the book.
Four days: Ibid., 208.
He unabashedly told little Laura: Ibid., 237.
"kind and generous": From report of Isaac T. Gibson dated "'Tenthmonth" 1, 1870, *Annual Report of the Commissioner of Indian Affairs for the Year 1871,* 486.
More than 500 hundred families, and **"built their cabins":** Report dated "Sixthmonth" 1869 of U.S. agent G. C. Snow, quoted by Gibson in his "Tenthmonth" 1, 1870, report, *Annual Report of the Commissioner of Indian Affairs for the Year 1871,* 484–485.

114 **1870 U.S. census,** and **"a claim was not filed":** From a plaque at the Little House "historical site" outside Independence, Kansas. The log cabin at the site is a replica, filled with Laura Ingalls Wilder memorabilia and photos—but, curiously, no pictures of her pa. The directors may have feared scaring the visitors away. If Pa had stayed put on the property, the Ingallses—or at least their children—would have struck it rich: The Little House is surrounded by oil wells. The property also was the site of the Sun-

nyside School from 1872 to 1946, and the Wayside Post Office from 1874 to 1876. The post office building now houses the Little House Gift Shop, which sells, among other things with a Laura Ingalls Wilder motif, a complete set of her Little House books for $33, a Little House tote bag for $9, and a Little House coffee mug for $6. I didn't catch the price on the Little House engagement calendar and the Little House cookbook. The shop also offers a photocopy of Laura Ingalls Wilder's allegedly handwritten Bible references—for a quarter.

"taken possession," and other quotes: G. C. Snow, quoted by Gibson, *Annual Report of the Commissioner of Indian Affairs for the Year 1871,* 484–485.

"Shoot the half-breed": Quoted by Velma Nieberding, "Catholic Education Among the Osages," *The Chronicles of Oklahoma,* Autumn 1954, 294.

"pledged to defend each other": This and subsequent Gibson quotes from *Annual Report of the Commissioner of Indian Affairs for the Year 1871,* 485.

115 "one of their head-men": Ibid., 488.

"true friends of the Indians": *Second Annual Report of the Board of Indian Commissioners for the Year 1870* (Washington, D.C.: Government Printing Office, 1871), 3–4.

"peace policy": Prucha, *The Great Father,* 160. Grant said in his inaugural address, "The proper treatment of the original occupants of this land—the Indians—is one deserving of careful study. I will favor any course toward them which tends to their civilization and ultimate citizenship" (Ibid., 158).

"so just that in itself": *Second Annual Report of the Board of Indian Commissioners for the Year 1870,* 3–4; "of the overruling goodness": Ibid., 11.

116 "the air was filled": Quoted by Wilson, *The Underground Reservation,* 1.

Osages left Kansas in late fall: Ibid.

a traffic jam of Indians: Wilder, *Little House on the Prairie,* 303–311.

Joseph Mosher: Account in letters from Isaac T. Gibson to Vincent Colyer, secretary of the Indian Peace Commission, dated "12th Month" 24, 1870, and January 12, 1871, included in *Second Annual Report of the Board of Indian Commissioners for the Year 1870,* 83–84.

123 up to sixty: This number was derived from interviews in Osage County, where Reign of Terror experts—both officially and casually—abound. The FBI, without offering any proof, deemed that "two dozen Osage Indians died under suspicious circumstances . . . just prior to the investigation of the Osage Indian Murder Cases by the United States Bureau of Investigation" (FBI, "Osage Indian Murders," File No. 62-5033, Serial 787, Novem-

ber 9, 1932, 6). (Hereafter, FBI reports will be identified by serial number, date and page where possible.) FBI, 294, January 18, 1926, mentions "the twenty-five murdered committed in [Osage] county." Technically what is today known as the FBI was in the 1920s called the Bureau of Investigation, but I decided to use "FBI" throughout the book to avoid confusion. The FBI has had nearly as many name changes as directors. According to *The World Almanac and Book of Facts 1994,* 98, it was created as the Office of Chief Examiner in 1908, and was renamed the Bureau of Investigation in 1909, the U.S. Bureau of Investigation in 1932, the Division of Investigation in 1933 and, finally, the Federal Bureau of Investigation in 1935.

enter the case: FBI, 1, March 24, 1923; 2, March 26, 1923; 4, April 12, 1923, 1–5.

Osages had to pay: Wilson, *The Underground Reservation,* 146.

woman is chopped: FBI, 381, May 5, 1926, 5; 787, November 9, 1932, 8; 370, February 12, 1926.

woman's grave: FBI, 3, April 13, 1923, 1–2; 138, March 12, 1925.

family's house: FBI, 787, November 9, 1932, 9.

white lawyer: *The New York Times,* January 10 and 17, 1926; *Tulsa World,* January 5, 1926; Franks, *The Osage Oil Boom,* 115–116; Arthur H. Lamb, *Tragedies of the Osage Hills,* (Pawhuska, Okla.: Raymond Red Corn Press, 1936), 152.

$25,000 insurance policy: FBI, 787, November 9, 1932, 9; 113, November 18, 1924, 2; 246, November 12, 1925, Abstract of "Henry Roan Murder Case," 15–24.

124 **Catholic priest:** FBI, 224, October 8, 1925, 5; 225, October 10, 1925, 5–6.

going rate: FBI, 338, February 25, 1926, Statement of John Ramsey on January 6, 1926.

"one after another": From a feature article in *The New York Times,* January 17, 1926, Section IX, 3, 7.

bright lights: FBI, 225, October 10, 1925, 6.

headright-holding Osage relatives: FBI, 787, November 9, 1932, 6.

125 **grand jury dates:** FBI, 188, July 30, 1925, 2; expected November 1 date in FBI, 218, September 28, 1925, 1.

"abstract": FBI, 246, November 12, 1925.

"yellow": FBI, 4, April 12, 1923, 8.

Witness number 97: Ibid., Abstract of "Osage Indian Murders: W. E. 'Bill' Smith Case," 9.

"this witness was": Ibid.

126 **"a great mistake,"** and following quote: FBI, 714, November 5, 1928, 3.

CHAPTER SEVEN

135   the Monongahela unleashed: Travel routes from Frazier, *Great Plains,* 4.

147   eighty lawyers, and Pawhuska's population: Wilson, The Underground
       Reservation, 140.

       almost as many lawyers: From feature article in *The New York Times,* Janu-
       ary 17, 1926, Section IX, 3, 7. The article went on to say: "Estimates of lit-
       igation brought on by the meddling of the whites keep the court dockets so
       tangled that a session of the District Court is necessary every month. There
       is much crime, and criminal sessions of court are as frequent as civil ses-
       sions. Ten large buildings are necessary to handle the legal business of the
       county, while one building is ample in the average county in the state. Fees
       of 25 percent of each estate are charged by the lawyers for handling the
       cases. As the average Osage estate is valued at $100,000, it can be seen that
       any reign of terror that may center upon Pawhuska will not be caused by
       wolves howling around the doors of the attorneys who handle the estates of
       'Poor Lo.' "

149   a newspaper report: *The New York Times,* July 12, 1926; September 4,
       1926

151   old Osage foot trail: Burns, *A History of the Osage People,* 144. On pages
       128–145, Burns charts the numerous Osage trails in Missouri, Kansas and
       Oklahoma that became the foundation of the modern U.S. road network in
       those states.

152   Branson: Quotes from billboard signs and tourist brochures.

153   Osage Beach: Quotes from tourist brochures.

155   Figures on poverty levels of South Dakota reservations: Reported by Avis
       Little, "Ten Years Later: Shannon Still Poorest County in the Nation," *In-
       dian Country Today,* February 11, 1993.

       "White man cannot": Wah-ti-an-kah, quoted by Mathews, *Wah'Kon-Tah,*
       33–34.

156   William Conner: My mother kept records related to a 1972 settlement of a
       longstanding claim against the U.S. government by the Osage tribe, in
       which she inherited from the estates of—and thus is related to—the follow-
       ing full-blood Osages, all original allottees: Embrey Gibson and his wife,
       Helen Gibson (Tsa-me-tsa); their son, Edward G. Gibson (Hun-kah-hop-
       py), and his wife, Ethel Bryant; and Ah-hu-shin-kah and his wife, Nah-
       hah-sah-me. Embrey Gibson was further identified as Pressing-Him-Down
       by Mathews in *The Osage, Children of the Middle Waters,* 759–766. According
       to Mathews, Embrey and Edward Gibson danced on the side of the Tsi-sho,

or Sky People—one of the two Grand Divisions of the tribe—in the last mourning dance of the Thorny Valley People, one of the five physical divisions of the tribe. In a memoir of the early history of the Osage County town of Fairfax (in *Osage County Profiles,* 465), Carmen D. Metts wrote, "One of our earliest memories was of an Indian named Hun-kah-hop-py [Edward Gibson], who walked to the top of the hill by our house every morning to mourn. He was chief mourner for the tribe." Unfortunately, I was unable to trace how we are related to any of these Osages, whether on my great-great-grandfather William Conner's side, or that of my great-great-grandmother, Angeline Penn (Hum-pa-to-kah). I include this information only in the hope that it will flag unknown Osage relatives and encourage them to contact us. As for Osage names, many of their original Indian names are lost, such as William Conner's, because the only existing records of that time were all written by Americans—whether official or not—and they tended not to write down an Indian's original name if he had an alternative "American" name. As part of their forced "civilizing," Indians were given Anglicized, Christian names much the way blacks were: by authority figures, indiscriminately. In the Osages' case, they received their American names from their teachers or priests—often the same—or from Osage Agency officials, who tended to be Quaker and to name Osages from the Quaker membership roll—thus we have relatives named Penn and Gibson. The Conner name also is common among Quakers.

"It'll be a long time": William Conner quoted by Laban S. Records, whose "recollections" were reported by Ralph H. Records, "Recollections of the Osages in the Seventies," *The Chronicles of Oklahoma,* Spring 1944, 75–76.

157 Conner's **tall tales of hunting adventures:** In Ibid., 76, Laban S. Records recalled how he trumpeted "Conner's exploits" during a story-swapping session one day, when Augustus Captain—the Osage who prompted Kansas Governor Crawford's encouragement to a constituent to "shoot the half-breed"—"whirled around and remarked with a tone of scorn and contempt, 'Bill Conner, who is he? He's nothing but a renegade white man!' " As Ralph Records phrased it, "That silenced Conner's Boswell." Conner and Captain were members of the Osage governmental Business Committee, and obviously did not get along.

"It was necessary for them": Isaac T. Gibson, letter of "Ninthmonth" 19, 1874, to Special Commissioner J. W. Smith, *Sixth Annual Report of the Board of Indian Commissioners for the Year 1874* (Washington, D.C.: Government Printing Office, 1875), 96.

"Finding but few": From testimony of Ah-kah-ka-he-kah, Che-hah-ka-she and Ne-hah, through Osage interpreter Paul Aiken, ibid., 91; subsequent details and quotes, ibid., 91–92.

158 **"and all their other"**: Isaac T. Gibson, report dated "Ninthmonth" 1, 1874, in *Annual Report of the Commissioner of Indian Affairs for the Year 1874* (Washington, D.C.: Government Printing Office, 1874), 227.

"War-parties never take": From testimony of Ah-kah-ka-he-kah, Che-hah-ka-she and Ne-hah, through Osage interpreter Paul Aiken, *Sixth Annual Report of the Board of Indian Commissioners for the Year 1874,* 92.

"act of murder": From report dated September 28, 1874, of Special Commissioners F. H. Smith, J. W. Smith and Wilson Shannon, ibid., 91.

159 **Congress authorized**: Isaac T. Gibson, in *Annual Report of the Commissioner of Indian Affairs for the Year 1874,* 225.

"odious. . . . They insisted": Isaac T. Gibson, report dated "Ninthmonth" 1, 1875, *Annual Report of the Commissioner of Indian Affairs for the Year 1875* (Washington, D.C.: Government Printing Office, 1875), 276; Osages' interest and disbursement figures.

From Mathews, *The Osages, Children of the Middle Waters,* 706; and Wilson, *The Underground Reservation,* 24. The 1878 annuity roll was published and analyzed by Louis F. Burns, *The Osage Annuity Roll of 1878* (Fallbrook, Calif.: Louis F. Burns, 1980). According to the roll, William Conner's household also included an eight-year-old cousin, George Conner, whom William Conner adopted and named in 1875, after his Osage parents were killed in a buffalo-hunting accident; and a twenty-six-year-old handicapped Osage named Larry No Legs.

"fed like dogs": quoted by Mathews, *Wah'Kon-Tah,* 28.

Wah-ti-an-kah played a decisive role: The account of Wah-ti-an-kah's encounter with the Indian affairs commissioner and their quoted conversation are from Mathews, *Wah'Kon-Tah,* 35–39.

161 **"riff-raff," "rowdies" et al**: From many of the above sources, mostly Mathews, *The Osages, Children of the Middle Waters,* as well as "The Black Curse of the Osages," *Literary Digest,* April 3, 1926; Frank F. Finney, "The Osage Indians and the Liquor Problem Before Oklahoma Statehood," *The Chronicles of Oklahoma,* Winter 1956; William R. Draper, "Depression in the Osage: Lo, the Poor Redskin—He Spent It, Too," *Outlook and Independent,* January 27, 1932; and Bill Burchardt, "Osage Oil," *The Chronicles of Oklahoma,* Autumn 1963; and Jean Hager, "On the Banks of the Arkansas: Blackburn, an Oklahoma Town, *The Chronicles of Oklahoma,* Winter, 1980–1981.

"cut a baby's throat," and "the vile and the wicked": Wallis, *Oil Man,* 55, 56.

white marshal: Details on Osage police force and the Daltons derived from

Wilson, *The Underground Reservation,* 54–58; recollections of Littleton Dalton (another brother), in Frank F. Lata, *Dalton Gang Days* (Santa Cruz, Calif.: Bear State Books, 1976), 47–49; Harold Preece, *The Dalton Gang, End of an Outlaw Era* (New York: Hastings House, 1963), 19–54; Bill O'Neal, *Encyclopedia of Western Gunfighters* (Norman, Okla.: University of Oklahoma Press, 1979), 80–86; and Frank F. Finney, Sr., "Progress in the Civilization of the Osage, and Their Government," *The Chronicles of Oklahoma,* Spring 1962, 11–12.

162 **"most-efficient":** Preece, *The Dalton Gang, End of an Outlaw Era,* 54.
List of outlaws: From Wallis, *Oil Man,* 55.
Okesa translation: Burns, *A History of the Osage People,* 59.

163 Elmer McCurdy story: Wallis, *Oil Man,* 198. Detail on Mr. Johnson standing McCurdy's body against wall from photo in Osage County Historical Society Museum.
compilation of Osage County crimes: Burchardt, "Osage Oil," *The Chronicles of Oklahoma,* 258–260.

164 Lee and May Worthington: Details from *Pawhuska Daily Journal-Capital,* November 6–7, 1924; and Lamb, *Tragedies of the Osage Hills,* 143–145.

165 Dodge City: Frazier, *Great Plains,* 150–151, 265.

167 Song lyrics from "One": Bono and U2, copyright 1991 U2 Admin. by Chappell & Co. (ASCAP).

CHAPTER EIGHT

170 **strongest and deadliest bows:** Burns, *A History of the Osage People,* 152.
descent from your grandmother: Discussed in Vine Deloria, Jr., *Custer Died for Your Sins: An Indian Manifesto* (New York: Avon, 1969), 11.

172 **Firewater:** Origin of name in Burchardt, "Osage Oil," *The Chronicles of Oklahoma,* 257.

173 **"There's still a danger":** U.S. diplomat, quoted by Ruth Marcus and John Lancaster, "U.S. Pulls Rangers Out of Somalia," *The Washington Post,* October 20, 1993.

175 assimilation: Discussion of BIA policy derived from Prucha, *The Great Father;* Deloria, *Custer Died for Your Sins;* Schmeckebier, *The Office of Indian Affairs;* Robert M. Kvasnicka and Herman J. Viola, *The Commissioners of Indian Affairs, 1824–1977* (Lincoln, Neb.: University of Nebraska Press, 1979); Vine Deloria, Jr., and Clifford M. Lytle, *The Nations Within: The Past and*

2

Future of American Indian Sovereignty (New York: Pantheon, 1984); and interviews.

176 List of terminated tribes: Prucha, *The Great Father,* 348.

177 "anti-Indian activities": Quoted by Kvasnicka and Viola, *The Commissioners of Indian Affairs, 1824–1977,* 307.

"cold-bloodedly": Deloria, *Custer Died for Your Sins,* 76.

"immense moral": Richard M. Nixon, quoted by Prucha, *The Great Father,* 364.

Ben Nighthorse Campbell: Details and spokeswoman's quote from "Fine-Feathered Friend," Washington Whispers column, *U.S. News & World Report,* November 16, 1992, 28.

178 Number of tribes: From BIA.

"fairly stringent": BIA spokesman, quoted by *The Baltimore Sun,* November 22, 1992.

BIA's new role: Figures from BIA and *Almanac and Book of Facts 1993,* 459. Scholarship blood-quantum requirement, from BIA; Indian Health Service requirement, from that agency; employment figures, from BIA.

179 Navajo Indians: Jason DeParle, "Tribal Dispute Keeps Some Navajos in Squalor," *The New York Times,* August 16, 1992.

180 number of living "original allottees": From minutes of Osage Tribal Council meeting on March 16, 1994, "Council News," *Inside Osage,* March 1994, 4.

182 Gregory Kidder: Details and quotes from minutes of Osage Tribal Council meeting on August 18, 1993, "Council News," *Inside Osage,* August 1993, 4.

184 casino and bingo figures: William Claiborne, "Rhode Island Stakes a Bet Against the Narragansetts," *The Washington Post,* May 16, 1993.

"to a very limited": From Donald Trump's lawsuit, quoted in "Issue of Indian Sovereignty Behind Gambling Case," *The New York Times,* June 11, 1993.

"so offensive": Colorado governor Romer, quoted by Claiborne, *The Washington Post.*

The tribes also receive very little: U.S. Department of the Interior, Office of Inspector General, "Audit Report: Issues Impacting Implementation of the Indian Gaming Regulatory Act," Report No. 94-I-113, November 1993.

188 ecosystem of tallgrass: Details and figures from William K. Stevens, "Home on the Range (Or What's Left of It)," *The New York Times,* October 19, 1993.

190 **"marble office buildings"**: "The 'Black Curse' of the Osages," *The Literary Digest*, 44.

191 Triangle Building: Details from "All Roads Lead to Pawhuska," special issue of *The Pawhuska Daily Journal-Capital*, April 8, 1992, 9.

198 History of stained-glass windows in Immaculate Conception Catholic Church: In part, from brochure titled "Cathedral of the Osage."

199 1980 headright payment: Broad, "Despite Feds, a Tribe Keeps Its Oil Flowing," *The Washington Post*.
"We've been doing": Sylvester Tinker, quoted in Ibid.

CHAPTER NINE

203 **permanent camping ground**: Burns, *A History of the Osage People*, 138. Details on trails and camps from Ibid.,128–145.

204 **forty miles a day**: Ibid., 282; Burns quotes another historian saying up to eighty—skeptical, I cut the figure in half.

208 **"morning musical"**: This and subsequent quotes about Angela Andretta's visit in "'Social News," *The Pawhuska Daily Capital*, August 2–19, 1922. Sybil's **"low score"**: August 5, 1922.
Angela Andretta photo and quote: *1907–1957: Osage Indians Semi-Centennial Celebration* program.
"Three Osage women": Wilson, *The Osage*, 96.

209 **"one of the most"**: *The Pawhuska Daily Capital*, June 6, 1923; the circuitous birth announcement: Ibid., June 24, 1924; **"Ends Own Life"**: Associated Press, *The Bartlesville Daily Enterprise*, November 7, 1925 (the story was the same AP report mentioned earlier, but unedited for taste; it appeared in the Bartlesville afternoon paper the day of Sybil's death).
Osage tribal roll book: *Authentic Osage Indian Roll Book* (Pawhuska, Okla.: Sam McClain Press, 1957), 24.
"Register of Letters Received": National Archives—Fort Worth Branch, Record Group 75, Record of Bureau of Indian Affairs; Osage Agency, 7r1-160; Register of Letters Received (Indian Office), 1880–1957, Entry 2, on microfilm at White Hair Memorial, Ralston, Oklahoma.

210 Rules regarding issuance of certificate of competency: Osage Agency, *The Osage People and Their Trust Property, A Field Report of the Bureau of Indian Affairs*, Anadarko Area Office, 1953, 17–19; Prucha, *The Great Father*, 308–309; Wilson, *The Underground Reservation*, 138.

212 **resigned the previous year**: From obituary of Kathleen Conner Wood-

ward, "Mrs. A. T. Woodward Was Leader in Culture Among Osage Indians," *The Pawhuska Daily Journal-Capital,* October 4, 1945.

Kate Conner Woodward's book: Mrs. Irene C. Beaulieu and Mrs. Kathleen Woodward, compilers, *Tributes to a Vanishing Race* (Chicago: privately printed, 1916); essay of Kathleen Woodward: 79–80.

214 Section on Kate Conner Woodward's early life: Derived from her obituary in *The Pawhuska Daily Journal-Capital,* October 4, 1945; Louis F. Burns, *Osage Mission Baptisms, Marriages, and Interments, 1820–1886* (Fallbrook, Calif.: Ciga Press, 1986), 439; Burns, *The Osage Annuity Roll of 1878;* Nieberding, "Catholic Education Among the Osages," *The Chronicles of Oklahoma,* 301–303; Graves, *History of Neosho County,* 227–230; Finney, "Progress in the Civilization of the Osage, and Their Government," *The Chronicles of Oklahoma,* 9; archives, St. Mary's College, Notre Dame, Indiana; conversations with Theil Annett, Claribel Shaw and Betty Smith, curator of the Osage County Historical Society Museum.

215 **"I remember as a child":** Toh-wam-pah, "'The War Bonnet," *Tributes to a Vanishing Race,* 68.

"We hear no longer": *Twelfth Annual Report of the Board of Indian Commissioners for the Year 1880* (Washington, D.C.: Government Printing Office, 1881), 7–8.

Education for girls: *Annual Report of the Commissioner of Indian Affairs for the Year 1881* (Washington, D.C.: Government Printing Office, 1881), 188–189.

216 **"don't wear patched clothes":** Quoted by Nieberding, "Catholic Education Among the Osages," 303.

"Every day at recreation": Ibid., 302.

William Conner's attendance at Osage Mission school: Orpha B. Russell, "Chief James Bigheart of the Osages," *The Chronicles of Oklahoma,* Winter 1954–1955, 386, 388.

218 Section on Sewell Beekman as cattlemen's agent: Derived from Berlin B. Chapman, "Dissolution of the Osage Reservation, Part Three," *The Chronicles of Oklahoma,* March 1943, 78–88; Robert M. Burrill, "The Establishment of Ranching on the Osage Indian Reservation," *The Geographical Review,* October 1972, 533–543; Robert M. Burrill, "The Osage Pasture Map," *The Chronicles of Oklahoma,* Summer 1975, 204–211; Burns, *A History of the Osage People,* 478–501, especially lists of lessees of 1893, 1898 and 1901, 485, 486, 489 and "Appendix A—Ranchers," 649; Berlin B. Chapman, "Dissolution of the Osage Reservation, Part One," *The Chronicles of Oklahoma,* September 1942, 244–254; Wilson, *The Underground Reservation,* 39, 89–90, 94; Mathews, *Wah'Kon-Tah,* 282–283; Berlin B. Chapman, "Disso-

lution of the Osage Reservation, Part Four," *The Chronicles of Oklahoma,* September 1942, 171–182; Daniel Swan, "Spatial Patterns in Osage Homestead Selections: A Preliminary Analysis of the Relationship Between Band and Village in Osage Socio-Political History," *Papers in Anthropology,* Fall 1980, 77–104.

222 **"to avoid any foundation"**: Commissioner Leupp, urging Interior Secretary Hitchcock to approve lottery, quoted by Chapman, "Dissolution of the Osage Reservation, Part Three," *The Chronicles of Oklahoma,* 88.
"He got right up": Sewell Beekman, quoted in Ibid., 82.

223 **"very indifferent"**: McChesney, quoted by Chapman, "Dissolution of the Osage Reservation, Part Two," *The Chronicles of Oklahoma,* December 1942, 386–387.

224 Section on A. T. Woodward and tribal roll derived from his obituary in *The Pawhuska Daily Journal-Capital,* October 27, 1950; Garrick A. Bailey, "The Osage Roll: An Analysis," *The Indian Historian,* Spring 1972, 26–29; Wilson, *The Underground Reservation,* 30–32, 40–42; Chapman, "Dissolution of the Osage Reservation, Part Two," *The Chronicles of Oklahoma,* 381–383; Russell, "Chief James Bigheart of the Osages," *The Chronicles of Oklahoma,* 388; Burns, *A History of the Osage People,* 516.

226 **"the selection of ignorant men"**: quoted by Bailey, "The Osage Roll," *The Indian Historian,* 27.

227 **"no Osage blood"**: Ibid., 28.

228 **The Osages' good fortune,** and disease fatality figures: Burns, *A History of the Osage People,* 125, 320.
Records and registers of the Sanitation Department of the Osage Agency from 1883–1906 are on microfilm at the White Hair Memorial, Ralston, Oklahoma. The original records are located at National Archives—Fort Worth Branch; Record Group 75, Record of Bureau of Indian Affairs, Osage Agency.

230 A. T. Woodward's job titles, quoted job descriptions and salaries: From efficiency reports in his personnel file at National Archives—Fort Worth Branch, Record Group 75, Record of Bureau of Indian Affairs, Osage Agency. Osage annuity figures: From Osage Agency, *The Osage People and Their Trust Property,* 16, and from "Per Capita Payments," a section of the *Annual Report, Osage Indian Agency, Oklahoma, for Fiscal Year 1931,* which lists all per-capita payments to Osages from 1880 to 1931. (Copy of report section contained in FBI, "Osage Indian Murders," File No. 62-5033. Serial number, date and page not listed.)

231 **ads in the *Post:*** Selected at random from early November 1925 issues of *The Washington Post.*

232 "1,000 White People": Wilson, *The Underground Reservation,* 135.
Swindling details derived from Ibid., 127–144; Shepherd, "Lo, the Rich Indian!" *Harper's,* 723–734; Brown, "Our Plutocratic Osage Indians," *Travel,* 20–22; Baird, *The Osage People,* 74–78; "The 'Black Curse' of the Osages," *The Literary Digest,* 42, 44; Osage Agency, *The Osage People and Their Trust Property,* 50–55, 64–66.
fifty burials: Russell, *The Chronicles of Oklahoma,* 387.

233 **"I . . . want a good":** Quoted in Wilson, *The Underground Reservation,* 142–143.
"The whites sold them": "The 'Black Curse' of the Osages," *The Literary Digest,* 44.
"The Indians took": Draper, "Depression in the Osage," *Outlook and Independent,* 113.
"The demoralizing influence": G. E. E. Lindquist, *The Red Man in the United States* (New York: George H. Doran, 1923; reprint, Clifton, N.J.: Augustus M. Kelley, 1973), 175.

234 **"Fortunate Daughters of Chance":** Brown, *Travel,* 20.
"Their wealth literally": George Vaux, Jr., quoted in Schmeckebier, *The Office of Indian Affairs,* 113–114.
Details on act of March 3, 1921, and certificates of competency: Osage Agency, *The Osage People and Their Trust Property,* 17–19; Prucha, *The Great Father,* 308–309; Wilson, *The Underground Reservation,* 138.

235 Woodward as guardian: Detail from his guardian file at National Archives —Fort Worth Branch, Record Group 75, Record of Bureau of Indian Affairs, Osage Agency.
Details on quarterly cash payments and "surplus" funds: Osage Agency, *The Osage People and Their Trust Property,* 17–19, 50–72; Wilson, *The Underground Reservation,* 138.

236 Lawyer's fees: Ibid., 139.
Study of missing funds: Ibid., 138.
tales such as these: Examples and quotes in following four paragraphs are from Osage Agency, *The Osage People and Their Trust Property,* 50, 55–56, 56, 57.

237 On Woodward taking part in the 1924 hearings and quitting afterward: Woodward's personnel file at National Archives—Fort Worth Branch contains an official letter written by J. George Wright, the Osage Agency superintendent, to Woodward, in his capacity as tribal attorney. The letter, dated March 6, 1924, was addressed to Woodward "c/o Commissioner of Indian Affairs, Washington D.C."

CHAPTER TEN

244 **Sybil's report card:** Archives, University of Kansas, Lawrence, Kansas.

247 **marriage license:** From microfilmed records of Osage County Court, Marriage Record No. 7, 1923–24, 8; located at Pawhuska Public Library.
country club dance and quote: *The Pawhuska Daily Capital,* June 6, 1923; details on exchanging vows: Ibid., June 7, 1923.

248 **"frock of dark blue":** *Pawhuska Osage Journal,* June 6, 1923; **"a traveling costume":** *Pawhuska Daily Capital,* June 7, 1923; subsequent details from *Pawhuska Osage Journal* article.

250 Reign of Terror death count: The figure 24 runs throughout the FBI reports, but there is no document in the case file listing who the victims are or might be. There is a document in the National Archives—Fort Worth Branch listing all Osages who died before January 1, 1926; presumably it was prepared for the federal grand jury that month. The figures 45 to 60 were developed by a number of Reign of Terror authorities with whom I talked. They are historians, writers or just interested local people who grew up hearing Reign of Terror stories. Discussing the murders—or planning to write a book about them one day—is a cottage industry in Osage County. The White Hair Memorial in Ralston has the heavily used microfilm of the FBI records.

251 Washington murders in 1992: Keith A. Harriston and Avis Thomas-Lester, " 'Murder Capital' Reputation Derided by New D.C. Chief," *The Washington Post,* January 9, 1993; U.S. homicides in 1992: *The World Almanac and Book of Facts 1994,* 967; Washington's ranking as highest per capita homicide rate: Harriston and Thomas-Lester, *The Washington Post.*

251 **"There are so many":** FBI, "Osage Indian Murders," File No. 62-5033, Serial 187, July 24, 1925, 31–32. (Where legibility permits, the FBI reports hereafter will be identified by serial number, date and page.)
Osage population figures: *The Pawhuska Daily Capital,* March 17, 1924; national death rates: *The World Almanac and Book of Facts 1994,* and *Historical Statistics of the United States, Colonial Times to 1970, Part 1,* 59.

252 **"In connection with":** FBI, 787, November 9, 1932, 6.

253 **vernacular:** "Bump" from FBI, 338, February 25, 1926, Statement of Ernest Burkhart on January 6, 1926; "get shut of": Ibid., Statement of Dewey Selph, no date.
Details on Hale's ranching and businesses: 787, November 9, 1932, 4.
torch 30,000 acres: FBI, 211, September 14, 1925, 3.

"a picturesque figure": *The New York Times,* January 17, 1926.

"an uneducated": FBI, 787, November 9, 1932, 4.

"He has a very": FBI, 247, November 13, 1925, 11.

"giving presents": Ibid., 12.

"He was a nice guy": Interview with John Shaw.

Details on Hale's and Burkhart's origins in Osage County: Wilson, *The Underground Reservation,* 145; Burchardt, "Osage Oil," *The Chronicles of Oklahoma,* 261.

254 Burkhart's Army service: FBI, 415, July 14, 1926.

"squaw man": FBI, 787, November 9, 1932, 5.

had married the same man: FBI, illegible serial no., September 8, 1953.

"peculiar wasting illness": Quoted by Franks, *The Osage Oil Boom,* 117.

probated to Lizzie Q: FBI, illegible serial no., September 8, 1953.

"developed a malady": FBI, 381, May 5, 1926, 4.

Hale and Burkhart started: Ibid.

knew her well: Ibid.

gotten pregnant: FBI, 784, November 4, 1932.

255 Details on Bryan Burkhart, Kelsie Morrison and Katherine Cole Morrison: FBI, 787, November 9, 1932, 5–8; 342, February 26, 1926, 6; Lamb, *Tragedies of the Osage Hills,* 162–163 (trial testimony).

"squaw man" and following quote: FBI, 787, November 9, 1932, 5.

Hale provided Morrison: Ibid., 8; 387, May 27, 1926, 2–6; Lamb, *Tragedies of the Osage Hills,* 162–163 (trial testimony).

"drinking spree": Quoted in FBI, 220, October 3, 1925, details in FBI, Report of Agent F. S. Smith, "7/17 to 8/31" 1925, 2–3.

"stopped under a tree," and following quote: FBI, 338, February 25, 1926, Statement of Katherine Cole on January 30, 1926.

they called a bootlegger, and subsequent details: FBI, 342, February 26, 1926, 5–6; undated, unrecorded draft of case summary that became Serial 787, November 9, 1932, 8–9 (hereafter called Draft Summary 1932).

256 "Burkhart was loving," and subsequent details on killing: FBI, 342, February 26, 1926, 5–6; 387, May 27, 1926, 2–6; Summary 1932, 8–9; 787, November 9, 1932, 8; Lamb, *Tragedies of the Osage Hills,* 162–163 (trial testimony).

Kelsey had shot her: FBI, 101, August 18, 1924, "RE: Anna Brown Murder," 5.

Hunters found her, details on Anna Brown's autopsy and quote: Ibid., 4–5; 381, May 5, 1926, 5; 787, November 9, 1932, 8.

The FBI suspected: FBI, 787, November 9, 1932, 8.

"the scalp slipped": FBI, 101, August 18, 1924, Report of Agent J. R. Burger, "RE: Anna Brown Murder," 4–5.

257   Anna Brown's mother: FBI, illegible serial no., September 8, 1953; 381, May 5, 1926, 6; Franks, *The Osage Oil Boom,* 117.

$2 million: Associated Press, "2 Oklahoma Men Held in Indian Deaths," *The New York Times,* January 5, 1926.

The fear of Mollie: Lamb, *Tragedies of the Osage Hills,* 203 (trial testimony).

$25,000 insurance policy: FBI, 787, November 9, 1932, 8; 246, November 12, 1925, Abstract of "Henry Roan Murder Case," 15–24.

had tried to end it all: Ibid., 13–14; 338, February 25, 1926, Statement of Ernest Burkhart on January 6, 1926; 785, October 27, 1932, 1.

258   long-established practice: *The New York Times,* January 17, 1926.

the examining doctor: Lamb, *Tragedies of the Osage Hills,* 178: The quote is a paraphrase of following trial testimony from Hale: "The doctor who testified that he asked me if I intended to kill and the Indian and I said yes, is mistaken."

Details on Kelsey Morrison drinking poisoned whiskey: FBI, 242, November 5, 1925, 5, 7; "corn whiskey": Ibid.

losing his mind: Ibid., 7.

"I wish I could get out": Ibid., 21.

Details on John Ramsey: FBI, 787, November 9, 1932, 4–5, 8; FBI, 338, February 25, 1926, Statement of Ernest Burkhart on January 6, 1926.

"He would put": Ibid.

259   George Bolton and Henry Ward quotes: FBI, 341, February 26, 1926, 1–2.

"the Indian that he," and subsequent quotes: FBI, 338, February 25, 1926, statement of John Ramsey on January 7, 1926.

000   Roan's body: FBI, 787, November 9, 1932, 9.

260   Ramsey had forgotten: 785, October 27, 1932, 3.

venereal disease: FBI, 113, November 18, 1924, 2; 246, November 12, 1925, Abstract of "Henry Roan Murder Case," 13–14.

sued the insurance company: Ibid., 15–24.

Details on Smith house explosion: FBI, 101, August 18, 1924, Report of Agent J. R. Burger, "W. E. Smith et al," Lamb, *Tragedies of the Osage Hills,* 120–122, and interview with John Shaw.

"muttered several times": FBI, Report of Agent F. S. Smith, "7/17 to 8/31," 1925, 4–5.

Smith had figured out: FBI, 101, August 18, 1924, "Digest of Facts," 31.

secretly changed their wills: FBI, illegible serial no., September 8, 1953.

261 **Ruth Tall Chief's grave:** FBI, 3, April 13, 1923, 1–2; 138, March 12, 1925.

"**with intent of securing**": FBI, 3, April 13, 1923, 1.

Background on FBI: *The Encyclopedia Americana, International Edition* (Danbury, Conn.: Grolier, 1990), Vol. 11, 68.

262 "**a great deal of experience**": FBI, 9, May 1, 1923, 1–2.

elected officials got an earful: FBI, 4, April 12, 1923, 1.

"**death is expected**": Ibid., as are other quotes from Short's letter.

Short later told: FBI, 26, July 27, 1923, 1–2.

"**what action should be taken**": FBI, 2, March 26, 1923, Wright letter, 1.

With his assistance: Ibid.

"**for information leading to**": Ibid., Tribal Council Resolution No. 22, as are other quotes and details.

263 **Fairfax Chamber of Commerce petition:** Dated March 13, 1923, included in FBI, 4, April 12, 1923, 2.

"**specific attention**": FBI, 1, March 24, 1923.

his first stop: FBI, 4, April 12, 1923, 5.

"**strong suspicion**": FBI, 3, April 13, 1923, 6.

April 14: Wright's report from Osage County is FBI, 6, April 20, 1923. He wrote it April 16, 1923.

"**there is a serious situation**": FBI, 14, May 29, 1923.

264 **Woodward repeated to Weakley,** and quote: FBI, 26, July 27, 1923, 3.

Indian enforcement agent: Ibid., 9; "**considerable information**": Ibid., 3; **turning over all:** Ibid., 11.

recorded the interrogation: Ibid., 11.

$2,500 reward, and other details: FBI, 2, March 26, 1923, Wright letter, 1.

"**with the assistance**": Ibid.

"**overrun with private detectives**": FBI, 9, May 1, 1923, 1.

"**well-acquainted with**": FBI, 25, July 17, 1923, quoting notes of John Moran, a private detective who had investigated the Anna Brown murder.

265 **Osage tribal attorney:** *The New York Times,* January 10, 1926.

"**sufficient evidence**": FBI, 220, October 3, 1925, 4.

stashed away: details and quotes from interview in Pawhuska with Kelly Vaughn, W. W. Vaughn's granddaughter.

Details on deaths of George Bigheart and W. W. Vaughn: *The New York Times,* January 10 and 17, 1926; *Tulsa World,* January 5, 1926; Franks, *The Osage Oil Boom,* 115–116; Lamb, *Tragedies of the Osage Hills,* 152.

coroner's ruling: *The New York Times,* January 17, 1926.

266 **When Rosa was told,** and quote: interview with Kelly Vaughn.

Detail on Hale's guardianship of Bigheart: Franks, *The Osage Oil Boom,* 115; Don Whitehead, *The FBI Story: A Report to the People* (New York: Random House, 1956), 115.

Three other whites: Deaths of Bennet and Gibson from Franks, *The Osage Oil Boom,* 118; of McBride, from Whitehead, *The FBI Story,* 115, and FBI, 188, July 30, 1925, 2.

267 **"reliably reputed":** FBI, 101, August 18, 1924, Report of Agent J. R. Burger, "W. E. Smith et al," 10.

Detail on Vaughn's body being carried onto train: Lamb, *Tragedies of the Osage Hills,* 152.

268 **"examined the berth":** FBI, 220, October 3, 1925.

as of July 1, 1923: FBI, 254, November 27, 1925.

$20,000: Wilson, *The Underground Reservation,* 146.

"discontinued": FBI, 112, August 28, 1924; 114, letter of November 17, 1924, and letter of December 13, 1924.

Hoover was named acting director of the Bureau of Investigation on May 10, 1924, and director on December 10, 1924 (*The World Almanac and Book of Facts 1994,* 98).

"special instructions today": FBI, 114, letter of December 13, 1924; Burke's letter: Ibid., letter of November 17, 1924.

letter-writing campaign: Letters to Curtis can be found in FBI, 122, February 6, 1925.

direct descendant: Graves, *History of Neosho County,* 5–6.

jurisdiction: Draft Summary 1932, 4–5. FBI's claim of federal jurisdiction in the Smith and Brown cases was rejected when they went to trial, but the cases were later tried in state court on the basis of confessions obtained by the FBI.

269 **"men carefully selected":** FBI, 381, May 5, 1926, 10.

"among the natives": FBI, 198, August 8, 1925; initial request via telegram: FBI, 191, August 5, 1925.

The G-men posed: FBI, 787, November 9, 1932, 11–12; 784, November 4, 1932.

A federal grand jury: Initial September 7, 1925, date cited by Hoover in FBI, 188, July 30, 1925, 2. Expected November 1 date in FBI, 218, September 28, 1925.

FBI agents complained, and quote: FBI, 204, August 19, 1925; FBI, Report of Agent F. S. Smith, "7/17 to 8/31," 1925, 5; 231, October 23, 1926,

4, states that Pawhuska lawyer A. W. Comstock had "conveyed" to "William K. Hale and others" information that Comstock had received about the case.

"an immediate and general": FBI, 204, August 19, 1925.

270 Father Achtergael as FBI informant: FBI, 224, October 8, 1925, 5; 225, October 10, 1925, 5–6.

Hale even befriended, and quote: FBI, 247, November 13, 1925, 11–12.

$10,000 reward: FBI, 242, November 5, 1925, 10–11.

a great confession: Ibid., 17–21.

271 **flurry of telegrams**: FBI, 232, October 26, 1925.

Hale had made up: FBI, 787, November 9, 1932, 7.

agents stuck a gun: FBI, 367, March 25, 1926, page 2 of Burkhart's lawsuit against FBI. (FBI, of course, denied any rough stuff.)

He confessed: FBI, 338, February 25, 1926, Statement of Ernest Burkhart on January 6, 1926.

"slumped in his chair": Draft Summary 1932, 7.

Ace Kirby: FBI, 787, November 9, 1932, 10; Lamb, *Tragedies of the Osage Hills,* 125–126.

272 Henry Grammer: FBI, 787, November 9, 1932, 4.

Details on Hale in electric chair: FBI, 409, June 28, 1926, 2–3; Lamb, *Tragedies of the Osage Hills,* 157–158, trial testimony.

their arrest came solely: FBI, 787, November 9, 1932, 5.

273 **$18,897.93**: FBI, 254, November 27, 1925 (actual date of memo was November 13, 1925).

$2,611.26, other figures: FBI, 290, January 18, 1926.

"I think we already": FBI, 198, letter dated August 5, 1925, 2.

274 **"The synopsis"**: FBI, no serial number, September 12, 1925.

"I feel that I": FBI, 219, September 28, 1925.

"Please give this matter": FBI, 209, September 18, 1925.

275 Woodwards' visit reported in "Pawhuska News" column of *Pawhuska Daily Journal-Capital,* October 28 and 30, 1925.

CHAPTER ELEVEN

283 **Tallgrass Prairie Preserve**: Figures and details from Stevens, *The New York Times.*

Schwarzkopf: Details from Stevens, *The New York Times;* Lianne Hart, "Where the Buffalo Roam Again," *Los Angeles Times,* October 19, 1993; and interview with Jake Waller, who took part in the naming ceremony.

284 **"I shall carry my name"**: Schwarzkopf quoted in *Inside Osage,* October 1993, 4.

"No one ever dreamed": Payne, quoted by Hart, *Los Angeles Times.*

board of governors: Ibid.

286 **one-third of the oil:** Teresa Lamsam, "Oil, Gas Experts Address 'State of Industry,' " *The Osage Nation News,* August 1993.

reported arrest, and following quote: "County Court Actions," *Pawhuska Journal-Capital,* June 24, 1992.

Arrests reported: Ibid. and *Pawhuska Journal-Capital,* June 20, 1992.

287 **nearly identical offenses:** Quotes from Ibid.

288 Indian death and fetal alcohol syndrome rates: Melanie Haiken, "Liquor Ads Targeted at Indians Dismay Some Tribal Leaders," *The Washington Post,* September 22, 1992.

296 Details on E. E. Grinstead: FBI, 246, November 12, 1925, Abstract of " 'Henry Roan Murder Case," 24.

297 Details on Hamilton and other lawyers: FBI, 407, June 21, 1926; 433, August 27, 1926; 443, October 6, 1926; 445, October 25, 1926.

trials and sentences: FBI, 787, November 9, 1932, 14; Lamb, *Tragedies of the Osage Hills,* 180–181; on Supreme Court ruling: *The New York Times,* June 2, 1926; bill for trying cases from Wilson; *The Underground Reservation,* 146.

EPILOGUE

300 Details on Pawhuska's daughter, Marie Pa-hu-shan, marrying Noel Mongrain: Burns, *A History of the Osage People,* 110, 228.

Baptisms of the Mongrain family: Burns, *Osage Mission Baptisms, Marriages, and Interments, 1820–1886,* 137.

301 Marriage of Pelagie Mongrain and Antoine Penn: Ibid., 135; Penn as godfather: Ibid., from a count of entries listing him as godfather; birth of Angeline Penn: Ibid., 239; death of Antoine Penn: Ibid., 379.

Birth of William Conner: Ibid., 149. Identified by Louis F. Burns, in conversation, as having scalped the Wichita chief; details on the scalping and controversy: Mathews, *Wah'Kon-Tah,* 189–206; death of Angeline Penn in her daughter's infancy: From interviews with Claribel Shaw and Theil Annett.

304 Osage words of "The Lord's Prayer": *1872–1972 Osage Indians Centennial Celebration* program (published by Osage Tribal Council, Pawhuska, Oklahoma, 1972).

About the Author

DENNIS MCAULIFFE, JR., is an assistant foreign editor at *The Washington Post*. Before joining the *Post* in 1983, he worked as an editor at the European *Stars and Stripes* in Germany, as a freelance reporter in Panama and as a sportswriter for the now-deceased *Washington Daily News*. He is the winner of two consecutive Front Page Awards for his work on the *Post*'s National Weekly Edition and of Vanderbilt University's 1968 Grantland Rice Scholarship for Sportswriting. He lives in Baltimore with his family.

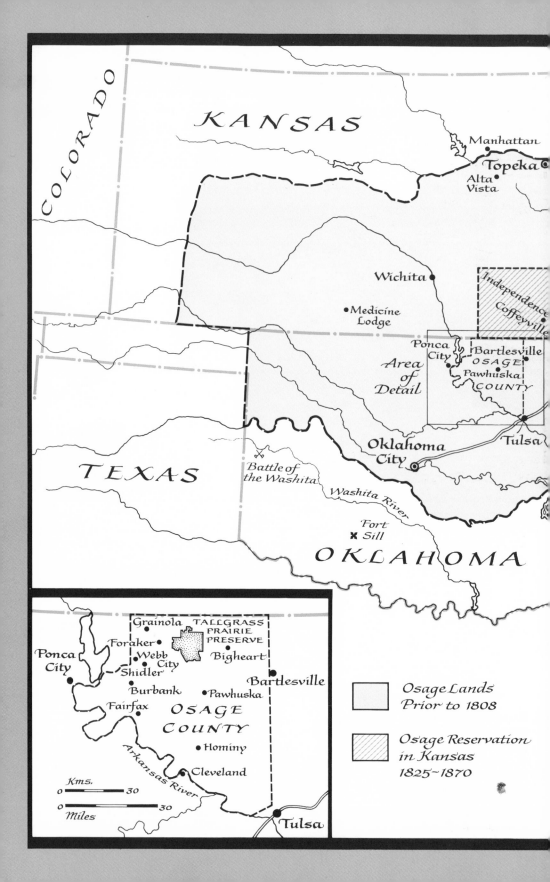

COLORADO

KANSAS

Manhattan
•Topeka
Alta •
Vista

Wichita •

• Medicine
Lodge

Independence •
Coffeyville

Ponca
City •
Bartlesville
OSAGE
Pawhuska •
COUNTY

Area
of
Detail

Oklahoma
City ◎

Tulsa

TEXAS

✗ Battle of
the Washita

Washita River

Fort
✗ Sill

OKLAHOMA

Grainola TALLGRASS
PRAIRIE
Foraker • PRESERVE
• Webb • Bigheart
City
Shidler •

Ponca
City

• Burbank • Pawhuska

Fairfax • OSAGE
COUNTY

Bartlesville

• Hominy

Arkansas River

• Cleveland

Kms.
0   30
0   30
Miles

Tulsa

Osage Lands
Prior to 1808

Osage Reservation
in Kansas
1825~1870